# Returning to Interpersonal Dialogue and Understanding Human Communication in the Digital Age

Michael A. Brown Sr.
*Florida International University, USA*

Leigh Hersey
*University of Louisiana at Monroe, USA*

A volume in the Advances in Human
and Social Aspects of Technology
(AHSAT) Book Series

Published in the United States of America by
IGI Global
Information Science Reference (an imprint of IGI Global)
701 E. Chocolate Avenue
Hershey PA, USA 17033
Tel: 717-533-8845
Fax: 717-533-8661
E-mail: cust@igi-global.com
Web site: http://www.igi-global.com

Library of Congress Cataloging-in-Publication Data

Names: Brown, Michael A., Sr., 1956- editor. | Hersey, Leigh Nanney, 1971-
    editor.
Title: Returning to interpersonal dialogue and understanding human
    communication in the digital age / Michael A. Brown, Sr. and Leigh Hersey,
    editors.
Description: Hershey, PA : Information Science Reference, [2018]
Identifiers: LCCN 2017029257| ISBN 9781522541684 (hardcover) | ISBN
    9781522541691 (ebook)
Subjects: LCSH: Information technology--Social aspects. |
    Communication--Social aspects. | Human-computer interaction.
Classification: LCC HM851 .R475 2018 | DDC 303.48/33--dc23 LC record available at https://lccn.
loc.gov/2017029257


This book is published in the IGI Global book series Advances in Human and Social Aspects of Technology (AHSAT) (ISSN: 2328-1316; eISSN: 2328-1324)


British Cataloguing in Publication Data
A Cataloguing in Publication record for this book is available from the British Library.

All work contributed to this book is new, previously-unpublished material.
The views expressed in this book are those of the authors, but not necessarily of the publisher.


For electronic access to this publication, please contact: eresources@igi-global.com.

# Advances in Human and Social Aspects of Technology (AHSAT) Book Series

ISSN:2328-1316
EISSN:2328-1324

Editor-in-Chief: Ashish Dwivedi, The University of Hull, UK

## MISSION

In recent years, the societal impact of technology has been noted as we become increasingly more connected and are presented with more digital tools and devices. With the popularity of digital devices such as cell phones and tablets, it is crucial to consider the implications of our digital dependence and the presence of technology in our everyday lives.

The **Advances in Human and Social Aspects of Technology (AHSAT) Book Series** seeks to explore the ways in which society and human beings have been affected by technology and how the technological revolution has changed the way we conduct our lives as well as our behavior. The AHSAT book series aims to publish the most cutting-edge research on human behavior and interaction with technology and the ways in which the digital age is changing society.

## COVERAGE

- Information ethics
- Technology Adoption
- Technoself
- Philosophy of technology
- Public Access to ICTs
- Human-Computer Interaction
- ICTs and human empowerment
- Computer-Mediated Communication
- Cyber Bullying
- Human Rights and Digitization

IGI Global is currently accepting manuscripts for publication within this series. To submit a proposal for a volume in this series, please contact our Acquisition Editors at Acquisitions@igi-global.com or visit: http://www.igi-global.com/publish/.

# Titles in this Series

*For a list of additional titles in this series, please visit:*
*https://www.igi-global.com/book-series/advances-human-social-aspects-technology/37145*

*Information Visualization Techniques in the Social Sciences and umanities*
Veslava Osinska (Nicolaus Copernicus University, Poland) and Grzegorz Osinski (College of Social and Media Culture, Poland)
Information Science Reference • ©2018 • 356pp • H/C (ISBN: 9781522549901) • US $195.00

*Handbook of Research on Civic Engagement and Social Change in Contemporary Society*
Susheel Chhabra (Periyar Management and Computer College, India)
Information Science Reference • ©2018 • 445pp • H/C (ISBN: 9781522541974) • US $245.00

*Corporate and Global Standardization Initiatives in Contemporary Society*
Kai Jakobs (RWTH Aachen University, Germany)
Information Science Reference • ©2018 • 394pp • H/C (ISBN: 9781522553205) • US $205.00

*Computational Psychoanalysis and Formal Bi-Logic Frameworks*
Giuseppe Iurato (Independent Researcher, Italy)
Information Science Reference • ©2018 • 332pp • H/C (ISBN: 9781522541288) • US $215.00

*Psychological, Social, and Cultural Aspects of Internet Addiction*
Bahadir Bozoglan (IF Weinheim Institute, Germany)
Information Science Reference • ©2018 • 390pp • H/C (ISBN: 9781522534778) • US $200.00

*Experience-Based Human-Computer Interactions Emerging Research and Opportunities*
Petr Sosnin (Ulyanovsk State Technical University, Russia)
Information Science Reference • ©2018 • 294pp • H/C (ISBN: 9781522529873) • US $165.00

*For an entire list of titles in this series, please visit:*
*https://www.igi-global.com/book-series/advances-human-social-aspects-technology/37145*

701 East Chocolate Avenue, Hershey, PA 17033, USA
Tel: 717-533-8845 x100 • Fax: 717-533-8661
E-Mail: cust@igi-global.com • www.igi-global.com

# Editorial Advisory Board

# Table of Contents

# Section 2

# Detailed Table of Contents

## Section 1

**Chapter 1**

The Rise of Darknet Markets in the Digital Age: Building Trust and
Reputation ................................................................................................................... 1

*Yulia Krylova, George Mason University, USA*

The last decade saw the rapid development and growth of online markets of illegal goods, known as darknet markets or cryptomarkets. This chapter explores recent trends in the development and evolution of these markets. In particular, the chapter analyzes specific mechanisms used by participants of darknet commerce to establish trust, build reputation, provide quality assurance, minimize fraud risks, and overcome potential violations of contracts. These mechanisms include a wide variety of different tools, such as clients' ratings of purchases, comments on transactions, vendors' track records, anonymous user forums, and online chat rooms that facilitate sharing and distribution of information about marketplaces. As this chapter shows, a distinctive feature of trust building in cryptomarkets is the widespread use of third parties, such as administrators of marketplaces and operators of forums. By providing escrow services and conflict-resolution mechanisms, they serve as "centers of trust" and guarantors against fraudulent activities.

In different regions of the world, the growth in home broadband adoption and development of e-services depends on a number of factors which can decrease digital divide in size or can result in widened "gaps" between developed and developing economies as well as between rich and poor regions or social groups. These factors comprise both drivers of, and barriers to, development of broadband access and growth of e-services as well as human communication and digital interactions in terms of comprehension and relationship building (i.e., the successful collaboration in contemporary society). Using a human communication point of view, this chapter provides insight into a concept of information divide, specifies the distinction between digital and information divide, examines each of the factors that condition the mass-market broadband adoption, and considers the impact of techno economic stratification for the development of web-based e-services.

This chapter examines the path of human interaction by using modern technologies. There are two sides: those in favor of using modern technologies and those who argue that modern technologies have unwanted, detrimental effects on people's lives and health. This chapter explores virtual communication's properties. It focuses on the impact that using social media instead of face-to-face interaction has on the users' health, specifically mental health. In this viewpoint, social media is not an alternative to face-to-face interaction but a complementary device that reminds us the vitality of interaction even with those who are physically unavailable to us.

# Chapter 4

Many thinkers conceptualize authentic communication in terms of an interpersonal encounter, for example between an "I" and a "you," a living subject and a living subject, unmediated by objects, electronic gadgets, or ICTs (informatics and communication technologies), or through an authentic human dialogue involving openness, choice, freedom, courage, and almost always, some risk and uncertainty. In the elevated language of Buber and Maritain one might say an existentially charged encounter between two (or more) beings involves opening up to each other, calling each to the other, face to face, thus allowing living truth to emerge.

**Chapter 5**
*Michelle F. Wright, Pennsylvania State University, USA*
*Bridgette D. Harper, Auburn University – Montgomery, USA*

The purpose of this literature review is to describe youths' involvement in cyberbullying. The term "youths" refers to individuals in elementary school, middle school, and high school. The chapter begins by providing a description of cyberbullying and the definition of cyberbullying. The next section describes the characteristics and risk factors associated with youths' involvement in cyberbullying. The third section focuses on the psychological, social, behavioral, and academic difficulties associated with youths' involvement in cyberbullying. The chapter concludes with recommendations for schools and parents as well as recommendations for future research. The chapter draws on research utilizing quantitative, qualitative, mixed-methods, cross-sectional, longitudinal, and cross-sequential designs, and those from various disciplines, including psychology, communication, media studies, sociology, social work, and computer science.

**Section 2**

**Chapter 6**
*James M. Goodwin, Georgetown University, USA*

Interpersonal deception, issue acceptance, privacy and control of information, and relationship building are key challenges people face each day in their quests to communicate effectively. Conquering these challenges is important in achieving shared understanding and making interactions flow smoothly and contain feedback and communication adjustments. Uncertainty is a risk to effective communication, so this chapter offers methods to adjust behaviors, solve problems, and build trust to create and nurture communicative relationships. The literature addresses the various ways that communicators have attempted to achieve success over the years. This is followed by an explanation of the key challenges and how to address them. A flexible, full-cycle examination indicates ways to energize effective communication in both face-to-face and online interactions.

# Chapter 7

This chapter examines characteristics of information and communication technology (ICT) and face-to-face communication and their associations with subjective wellbeing among students. The participants were N=500 students who reported average time they spent in face-to-face (FtF) and ICT communications. They also reported dominant communication in two types of communication contexts (communication purpose and persons involved in communication) and estimated their happiness and life satisfaction. Students spent more time in FtF communication than in ICT. Those who spent more time in FtF communication with friends were happier and more satisfied with their lives. FtF communication was dominant when meeting new people, for personal talk, and for flirting, while ICT communication was dominant for casual and informative chat. Students most frequently communicated with close persons FtF. Students who use dominantly FtF communication for personal talk and with people from their private lives (i.e., parents, friends, partners) were happier and more satisfied with their lives.

A lack of face-to-face interactions affects society while digital influences on the world create and sustain communications characterized by limited feedback, incomplete information, tentative connections, and misunderstandings. Thousands of digital messages lack the full communication components—sender-receiver-feedback—creating barriers to communication completion. The ability to adapt to the receiver and the medium is enhanced in face-to-face communication, as defined within communication accommodation theory (CAT). CAT allows all parties to emphasize or minimize differences in verbal and non-verbal conversations.

Communication is key in the public sector as governments aim to interact with and respond to their residents. Citizens often participated in government through face-to-face communication like town meetings. Today, digital communication has become increasingly important to improving government-citizen relations. The authors explore how governments are using Web 2.0 and mobile government (m-government) to spread information quickly. As governments implement these new communication tools, they must also consider ethical implications associated with technology. The research identifies the elements that lead to successful integration and the biggest barriers that government employees are facing during the transition.

**Chapter 10**
*Michael A. Brown Sr., Florida International University, USA*

The rise of emotional intelligence (EI) and the continuing growth of online interactions work together to demonstrate the importance of participatory decision making as a motivational technique. However, participation in decisions requires that the leader act in a prosocial manner, focusing on outcomes that are beneficial to more than just the leader. A prosocial attitude leads to creation of buy-in through shared value and good management of emotions, requiring skill in both EI and empathetic approaches. EI is about connecting with one's own emotions and those of others to enable effective leadership communication. Empathy is the ability to understand someone else's emotions, feel them as if they were yours, and even to take some action in support or mitigation of those feelings. The lack of feedback or agreements on shared value in online interactions are highlighted when people are forced into face-to-face interactions and are subsequently unable to find these important communication tools. This chapter offers a new approach to leadership communication.

# Preface

Human communication is in trouble in today's society. Face-to-face interactions do not happen often enough and, when they do, they feature limited feedback, erroneous information, incomplete exchanges, and confrontation. Digital collaborations are abundant, but they can be inundated with connection problems. The lack of full-process messages – from sender to receiver to feedback – are made even more problematic due to missing information, gaps in communication, and language barriers, among other issues.

Human communication's struggle is a global crisis. Society no longer fosters face-to-face interactions. Compounded by the influence of the digital world, digitally-driven interactions in a multi-generation society have resulted in personal interactions

*Figure 1. Illustration of a new communication environment*

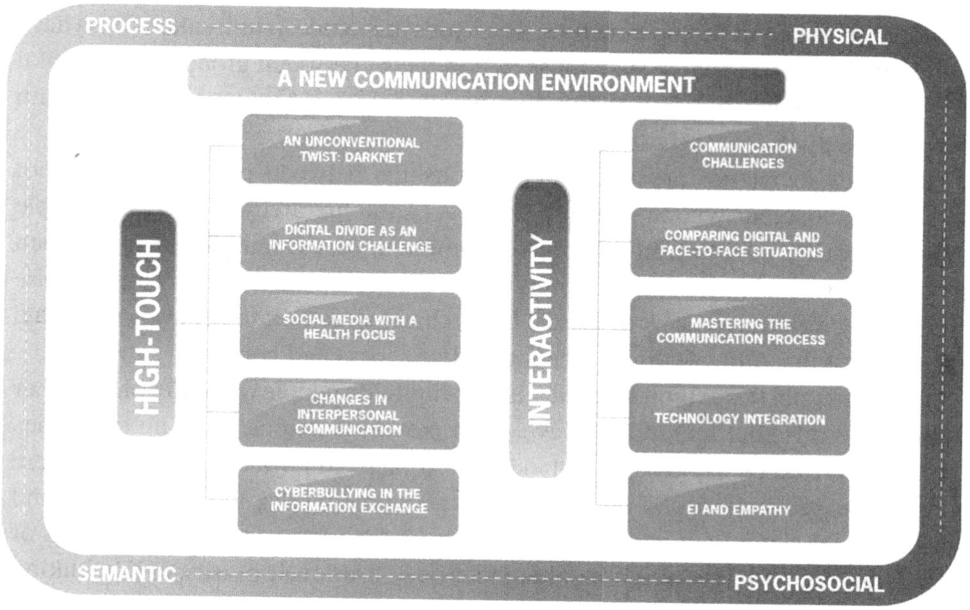

that are fraught with limited feedback and erroneous and incomplete information, leading to misunderstandings and even confrontations. Digital collaborations are abundant, but can be problematic because they are an incomplete solution to the human need for comprehensive communication. The 5,000 digital messages the average American receives daily lack full-process interactions from sender to receiver to feedback. This creates communication based on missing information, gaps in communication, misinterpretation of language, and other barriers.

Dr. Michael A. Brown Sr. (2017) examined these issues in the book *Solutions for High-Touch Communications in a High-Tech World*, exploring the strengths of face-to-face communication and outlining several ways to promote or strengthen those interactions. Strengths of face-to-face communication include taking advantage of the basics of the communication process, exchanging messages that are equally relevant to all parties involved, and communicating in high-touch, powerful, complementary, interactive, timely, compelling, and committed exchanges. *Solutions* also provides ways to achieve some of the richness of full-process communication in digital interactions. In this work, Dr. Brown is joined by Dr. Leigh Hersey to search for a deeper understanding of interpersonal communication in today's world.

High-touch, effective communication is about using social capital to build relationships and make information-sharing connections. It is important to improve internal and external digital communications and to demonstrate ways to positively affect productivity, levels of trust, and the ability to conduct bonding, bridging, and linking activities. Bonding is about establishing strong ties with people, while bridging fosters informal ties, and linking pertains to voluntary ties (Borgatti & Feld, 1994).

Bonding social ties are the ties people have between family and friends, or at least within a specific group structure. These ties are between individuals who have a high degree of connection, like those within the same social group, or horizontal ties. By developing bonding social ties, people improve their relationships with people already in their network.

Bridging social ties are informal relationships between people who are not personally close but who are in similar parts of the hierarchy. This helps people connect with like people in other groups or communities. Bridging social ties happen between individuals who are in different social groups, or vertical ties. These ties are often characterized by a lack of formal hierarchical structure; they have a moderate level of trust that allows communication and/or access and benefits.

Linking social ties exhibit vertical relationships with people who offer one another exposure to different hierarchical levels and power structures. Linking social ties are characterized by explicit, formal, or institutionalized power or authority, where norms of respect and trust allow interactions across networks. In fact, bridging and linking social capital are very similar, primarily differing in terms of the level of trust. Bridging social ties require only moderate or low levels of trust, while linking social ties lead to a higher level of trust. In this way, people may be able to obtain resources that will help in bringing about broader change. By paying attention to social ties, people can take advantage of high-touch activities that can lead to engagingly effective communication relationships with valuable feedback.

Interactivity is about dealing with emotions, discovering meanings in social contexts, and managing personal and social identity. A focus on the many types of digital interactions and on levels and types of comprehension over the last four decades sets the stage for this work. Evaluating ongoing changes in the way people communicate digitally can lead to solutions to alleviate the current misperceptions and conflicts in personal (face-to-face) communication. Due to an apparent lack of research targeted in this area of concentration, this work represents a necessary resource in academic and work environments.

Next, barriers to communication are very important. This book's communication approach emphasizes an analysis of four types of barriers to communication: process, physical, semantic, and psychosocial. Process barriers exist when there are issues with the sender or the receiver in terms of encoding, decoding, or feedback. There can also be process issues when the chosen medium is not appropriate for the interaction. For instance, it is unfortunate when a person sends an emotionally charged thread posts on social media instead of trying to make the communication connection face-to-face (Lunenburg, 2010).

Physical barriers refer to difficulties in communication caused by distances between people or objects such as walls or pieces of furniture that interrupt sound or eye contact. Any number of physical distractions can interfere with the effectiveness of communication, including a telephone call, drop-in visitors, distances between people, walls, and static on the radio. All of these can hinder communication.

Semantic barriers are words, phrases, or even language that are not commonly understood. Words that can have dual meanings are especially troubling when working toward effective communication. Words like "date," "engaged," "point," "right," or "type" can have more than one meaning, so senders and receivers should ensure the context conveys the intended meaning.

Finally, psychosocial barriers are characterized by the words sincerity, empathy, self-perception, role perception, images, culture, tradition, listening, noise, and feedback. Other considerations for effective adjustments to avoid distorting the message include good listening skills and choosing the right delivery method.

This work is the start of a new conversation that shines light on communication in all forms. What follows is an overview of this learning adventure. We will start with a grouping of authors who promote high-touch approaches, followed by those who seek interactivity as their basis for writing.

The first set of chapters offers various keys to high-touch interpersonal dialogue. These keys include building social ties, improving productivity and trust, creating strong or weak ties, and promoting feedback.

## HIGH-TOUCH FOCUS

### Non-Traditional Communication Approaches

The first set of chapters is about high-touch interactions, covering a very different communication approach than we're used to. After that, the section covers the digital divide, social media and health, changes in interpersonal communication, and cyberbullying.

*Figure 2. High-touch, effective communication is about using social capital to build relationships and make information-sharing connections*

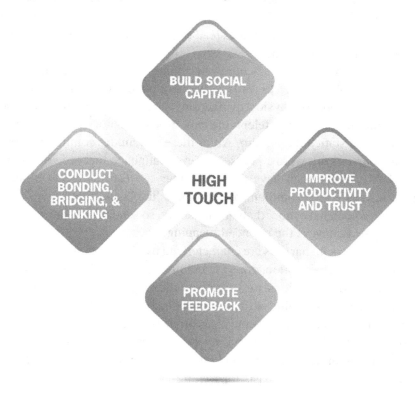

The section begins with an unconventional twist that looks at the Darknet. "The Rise of Darknet Markets in the Digital Age: Building Trust and Reputation" focuses on the last decade. This examination demonstrates a rapid development and growth of online markets of illegal goods, or cryptomarkets. It explores recent trends in their development and evolution, analyzing specific mechanisms used by participants of darknet commerce to establish trust, build reputation, provide quality assurance, minimize fraud risks, and overcome potential violations of contracts. These mechanisms include a wide variety of different tools, such as clients' ratings of purchases, comments on transactions, vendors' track records, anonymous user forums, and online chat rooms that facilitate sharing and distribution of information about marketplaces.

The next chapter moves to the digital divide as an information challenge. "Digital or Information Divide: A New Dimension of Social Stratification" focuses on different regions of the world where the growth in home broadband adoption and development of e-services depends on various factors which may decrease the digital divide in size or may result in widened "gaps" between developed and developing economies as well as between rich and poor regions or social groups. These factors comprise both drivers of, and barriers to, development of broadband access and growth of e-services. This chapter uses a human communication point of view to provide insight into a concept of information divide. The chapter also specifies the distinction between digital and information divide, examining each of the factors that condition the mass–market broadband adoption, and considering the impact of techno-economic stratification for the development of Web-based e-services.

A social media examination with a mental health focus is featured in the next chapter. "Social Media: A Threat to Mental Health or an Opportunity to Communicate?" examines the path of human interaction by using modern technologies. There are two sides: those in favor of using modern technologies and those who argue that modern technologies have unwanted, detrimental effects on people's lives and health. This chapter explores virtual communication's properties. It focuses on the impact that using social media instead of face-to-face interaction has on the users' health, specifically mental health. In this viewpoint, social media is not an alternative to face-to-face interaction but a complementary device that reminds us the vitality of interaction even with those who are physically unavailable to us.

Next, "Ghostly (Re-)Semblances and Specular (Con-)Figurations: The Age of Informatics and the End of Communication?" examines changes in interpersonal communication. The chapter poses new questions addressing the changes to and effects of information and communication technology on communicative relations in the twenty-first century. Is it still possible to speak of authentic interpersonal encounters in the light of the emergence of informatics and communication technologies and their proliferation in the digital age, in the paths opened up by thinkers like Buber and Heidegger? This chapter presents a different, questioning look at interpersonal communication, demonstrating yet another unconventional approach to human interactions.

The section finishes with cyberbullying, which has become a common problem in the information age. "Cyberbullying: A Negative Online Experience" describes youth involvement in cyberbullying. The term "youth" refers to individuals in elementary school, middle school, and high school. After defining cyberbullying, the authors describe the characteristics and risk factors associated with it, then focus on the negative psychological, social, behavioral, and academic difficulties it presents. The chapter concludes with recommendations for schools and parents as well as recommendations for future research.

*Figure 3. Interactivity is about dealing with emotions, discovering meanings in social contexts, and managing personal and social identity*

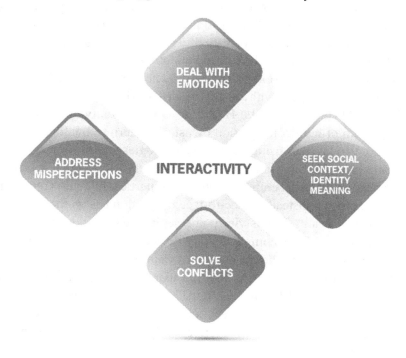

# INTERACTIVITY

## Addressing New Communication Challenges

The second set of chapters offers keys to creating interactivity in interpersonal dialogue focusing on dealing with new challenges, digital versus face-to-face interactions, mastering the communication process, technology integration, and leader focus on prosocial interactions.

The section on interactivity begins with a focus on the day-to-day communication challenges relating to interpersonal deception, issue acceptance, privacy and control of information, and relationship building. People strive to conquer these challenges as they search for shared understanding and a smooth flow of communication from sender to receiver and back. Because uncertainty is a key barrier to communication, this chapter offers methods to adjust behaviors, solve problems, and build trust to create and nurture communicative relationships. A review of relevant literature is followed by an explanation of the key challenges and how to address them. The intent is to identify a flexible, full-cycle examination to energize effective communication in both face-to-face and online sessions.

The next chapter moves to comparisons of digital and face-to-face interactions. "Virtual Happiness: ICT and Face-to-Face Communication and Wellbeing" examines characteristics of information and communication technology (ICT) and face-to-face communication and their associations with subjective well-being among students. Five hundred participants reported average time spent in face-to-face (FtF) and ICT communications, indicating whether communication purpose or the persons involved in communication was the dominant factor in the interaction. Happiness and life satisfaction were evaluated, and some of the findings demonstrated that students who spent more time in FtF communication with friends were happier and more satisfied with their quality of life. Also, FtF communication was dominant for meeting new people, personal talk, and flirting, while ICT communication was dominant for casual and informative chat. This kind of examination is vital to the interpersonal examinations in this book.

Equally important is mastering the communication process, as analyzed in "Communication Accommodation Theory: Adjusting to Today's Challenges." The lack of face-to-face interactions is affecting society. The digital influence on the world is characterized by limited feedback, incomplete information, tentative connections, and misunderstandings. Thousands of digital messages lack the full-process flavor provided by sender-receiver-feedback, creating barriers to communication. This chapter recommends Communication Accommodation Theory (CAT), which allows all parties to emphasize or minimize differences in verbal and non-verbal conversations.

Communication is key in the public sector as governments aim to interact with and respond to their residents. Citizens often participated in government through face-to-face communication like town meetings. Today, digital communication has become increasingly important to improving government-citizen relations. In "New Communication Technology Integration," the authors explore how governments are using Web 2.0 and mobile government (m-government) to spread information quickly. As governments implement these new communication tools, they must also consider ethical implications associated with technology. The research identifies the elements that lead to successful integration and the biggest barriers that government employees are facing during the transition.

Finally, the book moves to a chapter on EI, empathy and emotion leading to a prosocial approach to leadership. The widespread focus on EI and the continuing emphasis on emotion-based interactions work together to demonstrate the importance of participatory decision making as a motivational technique. Leaders must act in a prosocial manner, focusing on outcomes that are equally beneficial to team members. EI is about connecting with one's own emotions and those of others to enable effective leadership communication. Empathy is the ability to understand someone else's emotions, feel them as if they were yours, and even to take some action in support or mitigation of those feelings. Shared value in this participatory environment depends on feedback when people are forced into face-to-face interactions. This article offers a different view of participatory leadership communication.

All the authors contributing to this work hope that readers now have a deeper understanding of interpersonal communication in today's world. The intent of this book is to spark discovery, further research, and fresh discussions on the nature and intent of interpersonal communication. Happy reading!

## REFERENCES

Borgatti, S. P., & Feld, S. L. (1994). How to test the strength of weak ties theory. *Connections*, *17*(1), 45–46.

Brown, M. A. Sr. (2017). *Solutions for High-Touch Communications in a High-Tech World*. Hershey, PA: IGI Global. doi:10.4018/978-1-5225-1897-6

Lunenburg, F. C. (2010). Communication: The process, barriers, and improving effectiveness. *Schooling*, *1*(1), 1–11.

# Acknowledgment

*Many thanks to Dr. Michael A. Brown Sr. for inviting me to join him on this journey.*

*Dr. Leigh Hersey*

*I want to thank my family for all their love and support. I want to thank Dr. Leigh Hersey for the great partnership to produce this important work. I want to welcome and congratulate my good friend Jim Goodwin for advancing his educational pursuits to publishing with two chapters.*

*Dr. Michael A. Brown Sr.*

xxii

# Introduction

Interpersonal communication is vital to a strong civil society. Without the ability to communicate with those in our community, we would not have the connectivity that bonds us together. Through advances in technology, our sense of community has shifted and our ability to communicate has been enhanced in some ways. However, while some see technology as driving new communication methods, others see technology as something that impedes more traditional personal communications. Dr. Michael Brown and I came together for this book to share our interests in technology, communications, and civil society.

This book explores both the attributes and the concerns about modern communication methods. Today, messaging may travel to a broader audience quicker,

*Figure 1. The interpersonal communication environment*

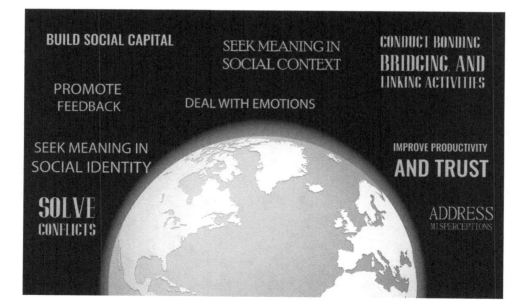

an important factor when informing the public of problems or concerns. However, this speed and spread may escalate troublesome messages, like those associated with cyber-bullying. Through this collection of chapters, we hope that the reader can gain a deeper understanding not only of the role of communication technology today, but also how these advances can be used in a productive way to enhance civil society.

Dr. Brown explains his journey that allowed this work to take shape.

## A NEW COMMUNICATION JOURNEY

Welcome to a new communication journey. This book represents both a destination and a new journey. This is the destination of my educational and professional search for improved ways to communicate and lead in the digital age. As a new journey, it is an attempt to engage in the discovery of the ways in which communication has changed.

Let me explain how I arrived at this destination. In 1998 and 1999, I was finishing a 24-year career in the U.S. Air Force and giving a lot of speeches on leadership and motivation in the Northern Virginia area. I took those two years to write a leadership and management manuscript called *The Leadership Toolbox*. I thought I had a great product with lots of good tips, but my mentors at the time informed me that I did not have the necessary credentials to be considered an expert in the field. So, I put the work aside and enrolled in a public administration and urban policy doctorate course at Old Dominion University (ODU) in Norfolk, Virginia.

My educational pursuit led me to study emotional intelligence (EI). Eventually, though, I got sidetracked from my EI inquiry because I could not convince my department at ODU to allow me to use it as my dissertation basis. My dissertation chair suggested I focus instead on social media. I finally had a topic area! That same day, I created all of my social media accounts – LinkedIn, Facebook, Twitter, etc. I successfully defended my dissertation on social networking and individual performance in 2011 and was asked to create a social media course for ODU. I taught my first course later that year. I expanded my discovery and development by creating social media and communication online courses for Florida International University (FIU).

The FIU social media courses needed a textbook, so I partnered with Tracy Schario, APR, to self-publish *Social Media 4EVR: Identifying, Achieving, & Nurturing Social Capital* (Brown & Schario, 2014). This book focuses on networking activities that use social media tools or platforms to share experiences, get advice, make decisions, develop trust, and reduce risk. The book also compares social networking and social media. Social networking refers to our actions and social media refers to the tools we use to energize those actions. *Social Media 4EVR* represented a significant change to the way people experience digital interactions, focusing on the "why" of social media participation. It is important to allow the destination, not the path or platform, to be the focus of your communication activities and I intended for *Social Media 4EVR* to be a helpful tool for those navigating this issue. The approach allows people and organizations to leverage time and efforts to promote positive social and environmental change. The real challenge is moving your frame of reference from solely which platform to use – Facebook, LinkedIn, Twitter, etc. – to a view of goal achievement and audience targeting.

EVR stands for Expectation, Value, and Return. You can achieve and/or sustain social networking success by delivering on an EXPECTATION of shared VALUE and a worthy RETURN on each participant's investment of time and attention. EVR is about using three keys to develop a winning social media plan that focuses your participation and encourages others to join your network. Keeping your profile alive as part of the digital conversation may prove helpful in ways you might not anticipate. EVR is the key to social networking participation and it offers three things. First, it offers the ability to get useful help in a two-way arrangement, which in turn provides the opportunity for a valued information exchange. Second is the opportunity for a valued information exchange. The third benefit to EVR is getting and giving recognition that matters to others.

My publishing interests continued to develop as I focused not just on social media but on individual performance and communication. As I pursued these interests, my research and writing eventually took me back to EI. I sensed I was arriving at the destination I mentioned earlier, creating a valuable body of knowledge.

I published two books in 2017: *Social Media Performance and Success Measurements* (Brown, 2017a) and *Solutions for High-Touch Communications in a High-Tech World* (Brown, 2017b).

I edited *Social Media Performance Evaluation and Success Measurements* with the intent to help organizations create social media policies that create return on investment of time or resources and analyze performance implications. This book argues for the identification of measurement tools that allow organizations to impact online interactions as they happen. The authors provide various helpful methods for affecting behaviors in support of the organization's goals and objectives. Digital interactions are examined based on participation, technology acceptance, trust, and social networking development.

According to Dr. Mohamad Alkadry, head of the Department of Public Policy, University of Connecticut, currently at the University of Connecticut, the book provides "tools and illustrations of the use of social media in different sectors." He writes, "It is our hope that we have created a rich sampling of information that will spark conversations and progress for years to come" (Brown, 2017a, 2017b).

My work on *Social Media Performance Evaluation and Success Measurements* was also important because it was how I met Dr. Hersey. She contributed an informative chapter about how a nonprofit organization can measure the return of its investment in social media to meet the organizational mission. She was instrumental, as were the other authors, in shaping the two major objectives in *Social Media Performance Evaluation and Success Measurements.* The first objective was to help organizations identify social networking participation expectations, value, and return on investment of time. The second objective was to highlight the true value of social networking, examining individual performance in digital communication activities with a focus on differences in participation, behavior, technology acceptance, and trust. We felt that the dynamic, evolving nature of the digital environment suggested a need for an edited collection of original thought and research.

I was now inspired for my second book of 2017, *Solutions for High-Touch Communications in a High-Tech World.* What I call the high-touch approach seeks to improve the reader's communication efforts through three important abilities:

1. A deeper understanding of face-to-face and online communication.
2. A focus on the gap in the communication process between the two methods.
3. Knowledge leading to resources to "bridge the gap" and create the best messaging interactions possible regardless of the method.

These abilities are important in finding value between sender and receiver. In the interest of feedback in interactions, resources to bridge the communication gap are high-tech considerations leading to a plan for changing and improving the way we exchange information.

*Solutions* offers a hybrid approach to communication that, while emphasizing the power and necessity of face-to-face communication, also provides a way to combine the best of digital interactions in any activity. This is an evaluation, dissection, and understanding of the gap that exists between the two approaches. It is an examination of theory, a dispelling of myths, an addressing of barriers, an introduction of new concepts, and an attempt to turn each method upside down to get the best of both worlds. The intention is for the reader to finish the book with a thorough understanding of the benefits and dangers, the pros and cons, of each method.

My next step was to bring a focus on EI to my published works. My discovery brought me back to my military roots, where I examined leadership and communication in terms of EI. The book, published in 2018, is called *Motivationally Intelligent Leadership: Emerging Research and Opportunities. Motivationally Intelligent Leadership* (Brown, 2018) provides methods to improve communications and to help each leader understand their own strengths and weaknesses and so that they can build a quality work life for the team. The "smartest" leaders can benefit from EI by finding the best way to create a bond with their team. The "street smart" leader can use EI to create working relationships that allow the best and brightest on the team to share their technical expertise with solid recommendations for action. In either instance, this is a way to build a collaborative culture, emphasize everyone's strengths, and work to improve weaknesses.

The edited book you are now reading represents the new journey I spoke about at the outset. We are compiling different views on digital and face-to-face interactions to start a broader examination of today's communication environment. We want to know how and why people communicate today, and we want to start the discussion about what tomorrow has in store. This analysis of online and interpersonal dialogue fosters comprehension and relationship-building. The integration of techniques for all human communication gives people resources to be successful collaborators in contemporary society, so we want that discussion to start here in these pages.

## REFERENCES

Brown, M., & Sr, A. (2018). *Motivationally Intelligent Leadership: Emerging Research and Opportunities*. Hershey, PA: IGI Global. doi:10.4018/978-1-5225-3746-5

Brown, M. A. Sr., (Ed.). (2017a). *Social Media Performance Evaluation and Success Measurements*. Hershey, PA: IGI Global. doi:10.4018/978-1-5225-1963-8

Brown, M. A. Sr. (2017b). *Solutions for High-Touch Communications in a High-Tech World*. Hershey, PA: IGI Global. doi:10.4018/978-1-5225-1897-6

Brown, M. A. Sr, & Schario, T. A. (2014). *Social Media 4EVR: Identifying, Achieving, & Nurturing Social Capital*. Yorktown, VA: CreateSpace Independent Publishing Platform.

# Section 1

# Chapter 1
# The Rise of Darknet Markets in the Digital Age:
## Building Trust and Reputation

**Yulia Krylova**
*George Mason University, USA*

## ABSTRACT

*The last decade saw the rapid development and growth of online markets of illegal goods, known as darknet markets or cryptomarkets. This chapter explores recent trends in the development and evolution of these markets. In particular, the chapter analyzes specific mechanisms used by participants of darknet commerce to establish trust, build reputation, provide quality assurance, minimize fraud risks, and overcome potential violations of contracts. These mechanisms include a wide variety of different tools, such as clients' ratings of purchases, comments on transactions, vendors' track records, anonymous user forums, and online chat rooms that facilitate sharing and distribution of information about marketplaces. As this chapter shows, a distinctive feature of trust building in cryptomarkets is the widespread use of third parties, such as administrators of marketplaces and operators of forums. By providing escrow services and conflict-resolution mechanisms, they serve as "centers of trust" and guarantors against fraudulent activities.*

DOI: 10.4018/978-1-5225-4168-4.ch001

# INTRODUCTION

The global development of electronic commerce gave rise to a new phenomenon of darknet markets, also known as cryptomarkets. They represent commercial websites on the dark web, which is not accessible through popular search engines, such as Google, Yahoo, or Microsoft's (MSFT) Bing. Darknet markets sell primarily illicit goods, such as drugs, counterfeit currency, stolen credit card information, and unlicensed pharmaceuticals. The most recent trend, however, includes an increasing share of legal goods sold by darknet vendors. Internet users might want to buy legitimate goods through darknet markets for various reasons, for example, personal preferences, concerns about privacy, or governments' bans on the use of open Internet websites in authoritarian countries with repressive regimes. Darknet markets offer new opportunities for individuals to protect their online activities from monitoring and surveillance by third parties, such as Internet service providers, e-commerce businesses, and governments. For example, in 2014, Facebook unveiled a new address specifically for those dark web users who would like to ensure anonymity of their communications and transactions (Paul, 2014). Within darknet markets, the use of internally developed technology platforms allows individuals to anonymize and customize their communications in ways that support their specific needs.

Similar to traditional online markets, one of the key advantages of digital communication within darknet markets is the ability of users to create connections all across the globe and to speed their transactions. Furthermore, the use of encryption in darknet markets allows users to protect the integrity, security, and confidentiality of their communications. Yet, anonymity poses new challenges to the process of building trust essential for any effective communication between actors. In addition to encryption software, almost all transactions in darknet markets use cryptocurrencies, such as Bitcoin, to ensure their anonymity. The related impersonality of transactions leads to the reduced ability of all parties to detect potential fraud and cheating. Due to their hidden nature, darknet markets are inherently characterized by imperfect and asymmetric information for their participants. In such circumstances, trust and reputation become essential assets for all market actors. However, the research into trust building mechanisms in darknet markets remains scattered and unfocused, largely because the dark web is a relatively new phenomenon.

To fill this gap, this chapter intends to look at the foundations for trust building in anonymous digital communications. Specifically, the chapter addresses the following questions: What analytical framework can be used to analyze trust relations among actors involved in darknet trade and what specific mechanisms help these actors overcome challenges related to anonymous communications in cryptomarkets? Although the notion of trust is critical for analyzing the interactions between actors in all environments, it is particularly important in the context of digital communications on the dark web. Cryptomarkets represent complex systems that include multiple actors who need to build trust to have confidence that their anonymous interactions will generate desirable outcomes. The importance of the research into trust building within darknet markets relates to the fact that they are currently understudied in comparison with traditional markets. In this respect, this chapter shows how the insights and findings of the study of traditional markets can be integrated with darknet commerce through developing a common framework for understanding their similar and unique characteristics.

Based on the data collected from the Dark Web News site dedicated to hidden online services, the chapter analyzes how the evolution of cryptomarkets impacts the development of trust building mechanisms and reputation in transactions that exclude face-to-face interactions among agents. In particular, this analysis focuses on specific mechanisms used by participants in darknet commerce to provide quality assurance, minimize fraud risks, and overcome potential violations of contracts. These mechanisms include a wide variety of different tools, such as clients' ratings of purchases, online comments on transactions, vendors' track records, anonymized user forums, online chat rooms, and darknet news sites that facilitate sharing and distribution of information about marketplaces. The chapter analyzes the role of administrators of darknet markets and moderators of hidden forums in creating an environment of trust and support and providing assistance in solving disputes that arise between sellers and customers. This research into trust building mechanisms in cryptomarkets has multiple practical implications for various users of the dark web. According to a recent study of the dark web, its legal content comprises 53.4 percent of all domains and 54.5% of all URLs, meaning that "anonymity does not equate criminality," but "merely a desire for privacy" (Gollnick & Wilson, 2016, p. 7-8). In the case of illegal goods, the research into trust in darknet markets has a great potential for law enforcement operations aimed at disrupting illicit trade. For example, several studies argue that destroying vendors' reputation and trust among market actors could be one of the most effective ways to disrupt illicit trade on the dark web (Caulkins & Reuter, 2010; Duxbury & Haynie, 2017). Overall, the results of this research shed light on the internal dynamics of darknet markets that highlight the importance of examining how new anonymizing technologies shape effective communications between actors in the digital age.

## BACKGROUND

Despite the rapid development of darknet markets and exponential growth in their sales volumes, there are still a limited number of studies of online trade in illicit goods. A few recent studies focus on the structure of darknet markets and their business models (Aldridge & Décary-Hétu, 2014; Christin, 2013; Dolliver, 2015; Dolliver & Kenney, 2016; Soska & Christin, 2015). The most common method used in this research consists of crawling darknet marketplaces to collect information about their operations and participants. This method allows researchers to identify major characteristics of hidden markets, including sales volumes, product listings, and vendor profiles. One of the most systematic studies in this area was conducted by Soska and Christin (2015) who scraped 35 different marketplaces a total of 1,908 times. Their study demonstrates the stability of product portfolios represented on darknet markets, with about 70 percent of all sales being related to cannabis, ecstasy, and cocaine (Soska & Christin, 2015, p. 34). It also identifies a mixture of highly specialized vendors selling one product and sellers with differentiated product portfolios. As for business models, Soska and Christin (2015) argue that darknet marketplaces are more like street dealers competing in the retail space than to large criminal organizations. Interestingly, Aldridge and Décary-Hétu (2014) find that a significant share of buyers in cryptomarkets represents low-level retailers who purchase drugs in "business-to-business" transactions.

Another common method to study business models of darknet markets and the relationship between their participants is an analysis of threads posted on anonymous forums. Darknet forums are platforms for market actors to discuss and exchange ideas about online hidden services. In the same vein as conventional online forums, they are comprised of threads started by an individual post with a question, concern, or idea. Some of them are related to darknet markets, while others are universal. A good example of research based on an analysis of threads posted on anonymous forums is the work by Holt and Lampke (2010). They analyze 300 threads from six forums devoted to the sale and exchange of bank records, personal information, and other electronic files obtained through hacks and computer attacks. According to their research, online markets of stolen data are like their real-world counterparts in several ways. For example, stolen data is distributed in these markets at a fraction of their true value. Also, the speed of communications between participants in these markets is critical to their ability to set up deals and sell goods. These findings are consistent with Holt (2013) who analyzes 10 publicly accessible Russian forums specializing in the distribution of malicious software. Based on his qualitative investigation of threads posted on these forums, Holt (2013) identifies three critical elements that shape the relationship between actors in darknet markets: price, customer service, and trust.

Another stream of the research into darknet markets analyzes the motivations of their participants (Barratt et al., 2014; Rhumorbarbe et al., 2016; Van Hout & Bingham, 2013, 2014). It often relies on surveys and interviews with vendors, sellers, and administrators of marketplaces. For example, the study by Barratt et al. (2014) is based on an anonymous online survey distributed among 9,470 participants from the United Kingdom, Australia and the United States. They find that the most common reasons for purchasing goods from darknet markets include wider range of products (75–89 percent of respondents), better quality of merchandise (72–77 percent), greater convenience (67–69 percent), and vendor rating systems (60–65 percent) (2014: 774). Van Hout and Bingham (2014) conduct similar research into motivations of darknet vendors. Based on a series of interviews with darknet sellers completed via the Tor mail and direct message facility, Van Hout and Bingham find that their decision to enter a market is "centered on simplicity in setting up vendor accounts, and opportunity to operate within a low risk, high traffic, high mark-up, secure and anonymous Deep Web infrastructure" (2014, p. 183). Furthermore, based on interviews with buyers, Van Hout and Bingham (2013) find that trust is one of the most important criteria for the selection of vendors in hidden markets.

An increasing number of studies are specifically devoted to an analysis of mechanisms that help build trust and reputation in darknet markets (Wehinger, 2011; Hardy & Norgaard, 2016; Tzanetakis et al., 2016; Janetos & Tilly, 2017). This body of darknet scholarship relies heavily on the trust literature that was developed for conventional markets of goods and services. This chapter applies the conceptual framework of building trust developed by Zucker (1986) to darknet markets. She defines trust as "a set of expectations shared by all those involved in an exchange" (1986, p. 54). Zucker (1986) distinguishes between three types of trust building: characteristic-based, process-based, and institution-based trust building. Characteristic-based trust building relies on social, ethnic, and any other similarities between individuals that affect their perceptions about each other. Process-based trust can be created through repeated interactions that help reduce uncertainty and specific procedures that help build reputation, such as gift giving. Institution-based trust building relies on the involvement of third parties as guarantors against violations of expectations shared by the community. These expectations can include standards, institutional procedures, codes of conduct, and other rules.

The problem of trust violations is very closely related to the concept of "adverse selection" in economics. In a broad sense, adverse selection means a situation where the asymmetric distribution of information between different parties in a transaction leads to inefficient decisions made by market actors. In his seminal paper "The Market for Lemons" (1970), Akerlof examines the problem of adverse selection that arises in the sales of used cars. The quality of a used car (informally called a "lemon") is known only to its seller, and the buyer can detect it only after the transaction takes place. As Akerlof (1970) shows, due to asymmetric information, high-quality cars are driven out by bad-quality cars, leading to market inefficiencies. Since darknet markets are also characterized by imperfect and asymmetric information, it seems fair to expect the existence of adverse selection similar to the market of used cars. However, several empirical studies of hidden markets show that they manage to mitigate this problem. Importantly, a number of studies confirm that the quality of drugs traded online is often higher than of those traded offline (Mounteney et al., 2016; Redman, 2016; Rhumorbarbe et al., 2017). This chapter shows that this paradox can be explained by the widespread use of vendor rating systems based on customer satisfaction and other trust-building mechanisms within darknet markets.

Relying on Zucker's (1986) conceptual framework, this chapter explores various mechanisms of producing trust and building reputation within darknet markets. The chapter demonstrates that sets of expectations shared by participants in exchanges that take place in cyberspace are very similar to those existing in traditional markets. Following Zucker (1986), they can be divided into three groups: characteristic-based, process-based, and institution-based modes. To better understand the nature of darknet markets, it is imperative to take a comprehensive look at all three modes of trust building used by participants in online trade.

## DARKNET MARKETS AND THEIR BUSINESS MODELS

### The Emergence of Darknet Markets

Since the invention of the Internet, illegal goods have been sold and bought online. The first online transaction related to drugs dates to 1971. It involved an exchange of marijuana between students of the Massachusetts Institute of Technology and Stanford University who used the Arpanet accounts in the Artificial Intelligence Laboratory (Martin, 2014). The expansion of the Internet further facilitated the growth of online illicit trade. At the same time, technological advances made it easier for law enforcement to trace market participants through their digital trails. In the early 2000s, the introduction of anonymizing software, such as Tor (abbreviated after the original project "The Onion Router") and I2P ("The Invisible Internet Project"), led to the rapid development of online markets in illegal goods hidden from law enforcement.

Tor software connects Internet users and websites' traffic through a series of virtual "tunnels" run by thousands of volunteers around the globe. The official site (www. torproject.org) defines the Tor network as "a group of volunteer-operated servers that allows people to improve their privacy and security on the Internet." This feature explains the popularity of Tor among participants in illicit trade who exploit the ability of this software to conceal their location, identity, and usage of the network, including visits to sites, online posts, instant messages, and other communication forms. In addition, darknet markets rely heavily on encryption programs to increase security of emails and other communications between their participants. The PGP (Pretty Good Privacy) encryption program is often applied by darknet markets for signing, encrypting, and decrypting e-mails, files, and directories. Finally, to provide security of financial operations, most darknet markets use cryptocurrencies, such as Bitcoin, Ethereum, Monero, Zcash, and Dash. The characteristic feature of cryptocurrencies is related to the fact that they do not rely on any standard financial institution to guarantee transactions. Instead, transactions in cryptocurrencies are verified by a voluntary network of Internet users who receive small rewards for their services. This rewarding process is called "mining" because it represents the key way to produce digital money in the payment system based on cryptocurrencies.

In recent years, Tor hosted several dozen hidden marketplaces trading in illegal goods. The pioneering illegal drug market "Drugstore" that operated on the Tor network opened in 2009 (Buxton and Bingham, 2015). It was followed by several other hidden marketplaces. In 2011, a significant share of the online market of illegal drugs was acquired by the Tor operated platform called Silk Road. Very quickly, Silk Road became popular among Internet users. In his interview with *Forbes*, its founder Ross Ulbricht, known by his pseudonym Dread Pirate Roberts, explained Silk Road as "an original idea to combine Bitcoin and Tor to create an anonymous market" (Greenberg, 2013). Bitcoin is the original cryptocurrency that was introduced in 2009 by Satoshi Nakamoto. The Bitcoin system is based on peer-to-peer transactions that are verified by network nodes and recorded in the public database called "blockchain." The use of Bitcoin helped Silk Road provide anonymity that significantly exceeded security properties of alternative online markets that were based mostly on traditional payment systems, such as PayPal and Western Union.

As a result, the Silk Road marketplace achieved impressive growth rates in terms of sales and revenues. According to Aldridge and Décary-Hétu (2014), sales on Silk Road increased from $14.4 million in 2012 to $89.7 million in 2013, which constitutes a more than 600 percent increase over the course of one year. Christin (2013) indicates that in 2012, Silk Road offered over 24,400 items representing 22 categories of goods, including illegal drugs, stolen digital data, pornography, clothing, art, books, music, and computer software. According to his estimates, the total revenues of the Silk Road sellers exceeded $1.2 million per month, while operators received $92,000 per month as commissions (ibid.).

In 2013, Silk Road was shut down by the FBI and its administrator Dread Pirate Roberts was arrested. In 2015, he was sentenced to life imprisonment without the possibility of parole. However, the void from the demise of Silk Road was quickly filled by other darknet markets, including the Sheep Marketplace, Agora, Evolution, Darknet Heroes League (DHL), and Silk Road 2.0. In 2014, law enforcement conducted another intervention in the dark web called Operation Onymous. It resulted in seizures of hundreds of domains associated with black markets functioning on the Tor network, including Silk Road 2, Cloud 9, and Hydra (Greenberg, 2014). However, an analysis of darknet markets shows that they are very resistant to takedowns by law enforcement, as well as closures by administrators in so-called "exit scams." The latter term refers to the situation in which administrators disrupt market operations by seizing all participants' money held in a common pool. In such cases, most buyers and sellers migrate to other hidden marketplaces. For example, in his interview, the administrator of AlphaBay admitted that "in the 3 days following the closure [of the Evolution marketplace], we had 18,000 new registrations, 7,000 new forum posts, and around $300,000 in trading volume" (Joshua, 2015). This raises a question about the effectiveness of law enforcement operations aimed at taking down darknet markets.

Despite regular law enforcement interventions, darknet markets show an exponential growth in sales of illicit goods. Over the three-year period from 2012 to 2015, their turnovers only from sales of illegal drugs increased from $15-17 million in 2012 to $150 million in 2015 ("Buying Drugs Online," 2016; Redman, 2016). In 2015, more than 20 anonymous markets were active in the dark web (Celestini et al., 2016, p. 218). Two years later, their number increased to forty. In 2017, AlphaBay was the largest darknet market, hosting more than 324,068 listings, including 220,578 drug related products (Dark Web News, 2017). In July 2017, its creator and administrator Alexandre Cazes, a Canadian citizen residing in Thailand, was arrested by Thai authorities on behalf of the United States (Department of Justice, 2017). After the FBI took down AlphaBay, its users migrated to other websites, including Dream Market, Silk Road 3, and Hansa. Although many darknet markets are periodically closed as the result of law enforcement takedowns or administrators' scam exits, new hidden marketplaces arise with increasing regularity. Based on their study of 35 darknet markets, Soska and Christin suggest that "anonymous marketplaces are extremely resilient to takedowns and scams – highlighting the simple fact that economics (demand) plays a dominant role" (2015, p. 46). Economics also has a significant impact on their business models.

## The Development of Darknet Business Models

The basis of darknet markets is the e-commerce retail business model. In many ways, the pioneering darknet market Silk Road was designed similarly to Amazon and eBay. As Christin notes, "When people accessed the site they found a professionally designed webpage where various categories of products were listed along with photographs" (2013, p. 7). However, Silk Road's imitations were not limited to web design. In its structure, Silk Road was very close to conventional online marketplaces where sellers can set up a virtual shop and post listings of their products. In terms of trust and reputation building mechanisms, one of the most valuable features of Silk Road was the ability of buyers to rank vendors on a 5-point scale based on their satisfaction and to write positive or negative comments about transactions. This rating system was very close to that of Amazon. Following the initial success of Silk Road, many other cryptomarkets that emerged after its closure adopted similar reputation-based ranking systems.

Van Hout and Bingham (2014) list other imitations derived from conventional e-commerce business models. Their list includes "professional advertising of quality products, professional communication and visibility on forum pages, speedy dispatch of slightly overweight products, competitive pricing, good stealth techniques and efforts to avoid customer disputes" (2014, p. 183). Not surprisingly, in interviews, buyers systematically pointed to a professional approach used by the Silk Road administrator to run his business, as well as his commitment to provide quality services (ibid.). Silk Road's innovation strategies resemble those used by global technology corporations specializing in Internet-related services and products. For example, like the Google Corporation, the Silk Road administrator encouraged users to provide their feedback and innovative ideas on how to improve market operations. In his interview, Dread Pirate Roberts admitted that "more often than not, the best ideas came from the community itself" (Greenberg, 2013). A good illustration is an upgrade of Silk Road that allowed customers to view prices on the website in their home currency. For vendors, this upgrade was also very useful since they were able to set prices in different currencies. Silk Road also imitated many marketing strategies of legal online retailers, such as special discounts and promotion campaigns. For example, on April 20, 2013, Silk Road launched the advertising campaign for cannabis known as "The Pot Day" (Christin, 2012, p. 2).

Due to the illicit nature of most products listed on darknet markets, they share many common features with street markets of illegal goods. For example, Holt and Lampke indicate that "the direct sales process, pricing structure, and influence of buyers suggest that stolen data markets operate in a similar fashion to real-world hawking markets for stolen goods" (2010, p. 47). Due to the time-sensitivity of products sold in both real-world and virtual markets of stolen data, sellers receive only a small portion of the true value of the data that they offer. Another mechanism that online markets of stolen data borrow from their real-world counterparts is bulk discounts that increase the likelihood that time-sensitive products will be sold before they become inactive. A similar phenomenon can be observed in darknet markets of illegal drugs that imitate certain sales mechanisms existing in street markets.

At the same time, cryptomarkets differ from their real-world counterparts in several important ways. Specific characteristics of transactions that take place within darknet markets have a significant impact on building trust and reputations among their participants. First, interactions in darknet markets are anonymous, which excludes an opportunity to build trust through direct personal encounters. Second, the fact that transactions in darknet markets do not involve face-to-face interactions between participants significantly reduces their ability to detect cheating and fraud through verbal communication, such as the enunciation, stress, and tone of voice, and non-verbal communication, such as body movements, gestures, eye contact, facial expressions, and other related signals. Third, most transactions in darknet markets are self-enforced since violence or intimidation do not have the same deterrent effect as in street markets of illegal goods. In conventional markets of illegal goods, violence is often used as a contract enforcement mechanism, conflict resolution method, or punishment for cooperation with law enforcement. For the most part, threats of violence are not effective in the context of anonymous and impersonal transactions on the dark web. Fourth, investigations of fraud committed in cryptomarkets present many challenges to law enforcements officials. Finally, darknet transactions take place in cyberspace, meaning that vendors and customers are not tied to each other in terms of geographical boundaries. Such transactions are completed in digital form independently of regional and social contexts. These distinctions dictate the need to take a comprehensive look at specific mechanisms of building trust and reputation between participants in darknet commerce.

## MECHANISMS TO BUILD TRUST AND REPUTATION IN DARKNET MARKETS

Following Zucker (1986), modes of trust building in darknet markets can be divided into three categories: characteristic-based mode focusing on personal features of participants, process-based mode focusing on actors' reputation, and institution-based mode focusing on third parties' services. Table 1 shows different modes of trust building in darknet markets.

*Table 1. Modes of trust building and their mechanism in darknet markets*

| Mode of Trust Building | Focus | Mechanisms of Trust Building in Darknet Markets |
|---|---|---|
| Characteristic-based | Personal features of market actors | • Communication in a foreign language.<br>• The level of education of market actors.<br>• The use of a unique argot or slang. |
| Process-based | Reputation | • Vendor rating systems.<br>• Customer feedback.<br>• Durability of virtual shops.<br>• The number and volume of transactions committed by sellers.<br>• Branding of goods as "fair trade". |
| Institution-based | The use of third parties as guarantor against fraud and cheating | • Vendors' bonds.<br>• Testing of merchandize samples.<br>• Escrow services provided by administrators of marketplaces.<br>• Verified status of sellers.<br>• Enforcement of digital contracts.<br>• Responses to customers' complaints.<br>• Closed markets. |

Due to the impersonal nature of darknet operations, the first mode is the least common in hidden online markets. However, communication in a foreign language, the ability to write in a grammatically correct way, and the use of slang or argot can influence perceptions of market actors about credibility of their partners. The second mode of trust building is based on reputation and relies heavily on vendor rating systems, customer feedback, branding, the durability of virtual shops, and the volume of sales completed by sellers. Finally, the third mode of trust building is provided by administrators of darknet markets and operators of anonymous forums. They have a wide range of different instruments to increase trust among market actors and decrease the risk of fraud, including charging vendors' bonds, testing product samples, offering escrow services, enforcing digital contracts, awarding a verified status to sellers, responding to customers' complaints, and providing invitation-based access to forums. The next sections analyze and discuss these mechanisms in more detail.

## The Use of Personal Features of Market Participants in Trust Building

In darknet commerce, the ethnic background and social status of participants can play a certain role in creating perceptions about the trustworthiness of market actors. For example, Wehinger (2011) indicates that in non-English language marketplaces, "the risk of fraud when buying in a German, French or Vietnamese forum may be perceived as being smaller than in an English language environment with its dubious offers from all over the world" (2011, p. 211). Also, despite the fact that darknet actors conceal their social status, their profiles can provide some indirect signals. One example is the participants' level of education. Thus Wehinger (2011) notes that "those [who are] able to write correctly may receive more trust because their higher educational level indicates that they do not need to fraud since other sources of income are available to them" (ibid.). Finally, some perceptions about the social background of participants can be derived from their use of slang related to a specific social or ethnic group. For example, exploring darknet markets of stolen data, Holt and Lampke find that "actors use a unique argot, including the term ripper, to internally police and regulate the market" (2010, p. 48).

## Building Reputation in Darknet Markets

To create reputation, vendors in darknet markets use mechanisms very similar to online markets of legal commodities that rely heavily on vendor rating systems and customer feedback. In the same vein, buyers in darknet markets can see the ratings of different vendors and comments by their customers about previous transactions. The importance of these mechanisms for building reputation in hidden markets was confirmed in several studies (Markopoulos et al., 2015; Hardy & Norgaard, 2016). These studies demonstrate that darknet communities are very active in providing feedback for transactions. Customers' positive feedback helps vendors create invaluable reputation for repeated transactions with their customers. To build a reputation, some vendors send higher amounts of purchased goods to new customers in the hope that they will return to them in the future (Tzanetakis, 2016, p. 62). Another strategy to attract customers includes innovative ways to hide the illegal content of packages. Darknet forums present an additional opportunity for vendors to introduce themselves and advertise their stealth methods. Some vendors brand their goods as "fair trade" and "sourced from conflict-free zones" (Martin, 2014). Vendors can also use forums to deal with customers' concerns in the case they post negative reviews in a chat or thread. An analysis of darknet markets shows that such forums often serve as "public shaming" platforms where customers can complain about negative experiences and share information about fraudsters.

A strong reputation based on high ratings and positive comments posted on anonymous forums allow vendors to charge premium prices for their goods. For example, several studies find a positive correlation between prices and ratings of sellers in online markets for both legal and illegal goods (Dellarocas, 2002; Cabral, 2012; Hardy & Norgaard, 2016, Janetos & Tilly, 2017). However, in comparison with conventional markets, a bad reputation is less important for sellers who operate in darknet markets since their identities can easily be changed. To mitigate this problem, administrators of darknet marketplaces often ask vendors to provide a record of their transactions completed in other marketplaces.

The disadvantage of darknet ratings systems, however, is that they are related mostly to vendors' reputation, while buyers' profiles contain much less information to judge their credibility and trustworthiness. Another disadvantage is the ability of market participants to manipulate their ratings by submitting fake reviews. For example, vendors often submit fake positive reviews to repair or improve their reputation. Also, vendors sometimes write fake negative reviews for their competitors. Markopoulos et al. (2015) suggest that law enforcement agencies may also interfere in operations in darknet markets, by manipulating buyers' reviews. Their study provides evidence that if completed on a large scale, such law enforcement operations can potentially provoke market failures, disrupting online trade in illicit goods.

Taking fake reviews into account, buyers often rely on other characteristics of vendors to form perceptions about their credibility and trustworthiness. They include the amount of time a vendor is listed on the market and the number of transactions that he has completed online. This is why most darknet markets display information about sellers' registration dates and transactions in their profiles. The durability of virtual shops is positively related to vendor ratings. Since it takes a lot of time to build credibility and trust, darknet sellers with high ratings are less likely to cheat their buyers. Sellers with low ratings are highly unlikely to stay in the market for a long time. For example, Janetos and Tilly find that "the lower a seller's ratings, the more likely he is to exit" (2017, p. 12). The number of transactions and their volumes might also serve as an indirect signal about the trustworthiness of a vendor. Some administrators of cryptomarkets also include these indicators, together with customer feedback, as criteria to assess vendors in their ranking systems.

## Trust-Building Services From Darknet Market Administrators and Forum Operators

The widespread use of third parties to provide trust and security of transactions is a distinctive feature of darknet markets. Third parties include administrators of marketplaces, operators of anonymous forums, and their teams. In his interview with *Forbes*, the former Silk Road owner, Dread Pirate Roberts, defined his administrative role as "a center of trust." He said, "The vendors trust me, and the customers trust me and by extension they trust those on my team that decide who is right and wrong in disputes, and they trust me to be responsible for their funds in escrow" (Greenberg, 2013). Administrators of darknet markets serve as protectors against fraud and cheating by providing escrow services and establishing conflict resolution mechanisms. For these services, they usually charge a commission from other market participants. This commission varies from one marketplace to another. For example, the administrators of the small marketplace for drugs called Tochka charge up to 10 percent of the transaction amount, while the commission in Valhalla ranges from 2-5 percent (Dark Web News, 2017). Commissions charged for every transaction incentivize administrators to identify and ban fraudsters from their marketplaces. In such a way, they can increase sales volumes and attract new trade participants by improving the marketplace's position in various ratings available on the Internet.

To secure the anonymity of participants, many administrators of darknet markets use two factor authentication, also known as 2FA. It represents an extra layer of security that requires not only a password and username, but also some private information known only to that user. Table 2 shows the estimates of the use of 2FA by administrators. These estimates are based on the data related to 20 darknet markets that was derived from the Dark Web News (2017). As Table 2 demonstrates, 90 percent of the analyzed cryptomarkets use 2FA. Further, to ensure the security of transactions, some administrators enforce the use of encryption programs, such as PGP. As Table 2 below indicates, 55 percent of cryptomarkets adopted this mechanism. Yet, periodic leaks of private messages from darknet markets show that "many users still send private data, like real names and addresses, unencrypted" (O'Neill, 2017).

To provide security for buyers, most administrators of darknet forums require vendors to buy a bond to access the market. Bonds serve as insurance against any trust violation or rule breaking by the vendors. The amount of vendor bonds varies significantly from market to market. For example, in 2017, the administrators of AlphaBay asked vendors to buy a $200 insurance bond, while to enter the Hansa marketplace, vendors were asked to pay 0.3 bitcoins, which was worth $1,334 based on the exchange rate of May 1, 2017 (Dark Web News, 2017). In Table 2, the percentage of administrators who asked vendors to buy a bond is estimated at 70 percent.

*Table 2. Mechanisms of security and trust building used by administrators of 20 darknet markets – Source: Calculated based on the data derived from Dark Web News (2017)*

| Mechanisms of Security and Trust Building | Number of Darknet Markets | Percentage of Darknet Markets |
|---|---|---|
| Two factor authentication (2FA) | 18 | 90% |
| Enforced vendor encryption via PGP | 11 | 55% |
| Vendor bonds | 14 | 70% |
| Invitation only forums | 3 | 15% |
| Multisignature escrow services | 12 | 60% |

In addition to bonds, many administrators require vendors to submit a sample of their product for testing before they can get a verified status. In their study of darknet markets of stolen data, Holt and Lamke (2010) find that 50 percent of administrators of the related forums require sellers to submit a sample of their merchandise (2010, p. 43). For example, to enter the market, a seller of malicious software might be asked to send its copy to the administrator or an appointed tester, who would then write and post a review with his recommendations for buyers. As Holt and Lamke (2010) note, "the review process acts as a sort of vetting process for the seller and gives potential buyers some knowledge of the person and their products" (2010, p. 43). Administrators award a verified status to those sellers who meet all standards set in the marketplace and successfully conclude the review process.

A verified status serves as a signal for buyers about the quality of the product and the trustworthiness of its seller. To keep their verified status, sellers need to be able to allay any concerns on the part of buyers. A seller can lose his verified status if his customers register complaints about the quality of his product or post negative comments about customer service, delivery, or communication. Sellers' responsiveness to complaints is a major factor for their success in darknet markets. If buyers identify a seller as someone violating the rules on darknet forums, administrators can permanently ban him from the marketplace.

Another mechanism to establish trust in darknet markets imitates conventional markets of illegal goods that are characterized by restricted access. They represent so called "closed" markets comprised of participants who personally know each other or who are introduced by common friends. Transactions completed in closed markets are less risky in terms of fraud and law enforcement intervention than open street markets accessible to everyone. For example, Hough and Natarajan (2000) indicate that an increased risk of law enforcement intervention often leads to the transformation of open markets into closed ones. They define closed markets as "those in which sellers will only do business with buyers whom they know, or for whom another trusted person will vouch" (2000, p. 4). In the case of offline trade in illegal drugs, the degree of "openness" of markets depends largely on the seriousness of threats posed by law enforcement. In the case of online trade in illegal drugs, this degree is mostly influenced by the risk of fraud and cheating by market actors. For example, Wehinger (2011) points to the existence of closed forums for illegal trade in stolen data that are accessible only by invitation. However, closed markets are less common in the dark web than in the real world. As Table 2 indicates, in 2017, access to only 3 percent of 20 darknet markets was limited by invitation.

A recent trend includes the introduction of the "digital contract" system by administrators of cryptomarkets. For example, in 2015, AlphaBay launched a new feature that allows buyers and sellers to sign "digital contracts" that help them establish long-term relations (Mounteney et al., 2016, p. 53). These contracts are also signed by administrators with a PGP key. Since the illicit nature of most goods sold on the dark web precludes victims of contract violations from filing legal complaints, administrators of cryptomarkets also perform enforcement services in exchange for a certain commission. For example, if one contract party files a complaint about contract violations, administrators launch dispute-resolving procedures which are very similar to those found in conventional online markets, such as eBay and PayPal. If another party is found guilty of contract violations, administrators can post a negative review on his profile or even ban him from the marketplace.

Finally, most cryptomarkets offer escrow services, meaning that administrators receive payments from buyers and hold them until confirmation of receipt of goods. In most cases, administrators also offer arbitration services in the case of disputes between market actors. Escrow services become particularly important when a deal is set up with new or unverified sellers whose reputation is unknown to buyers. In such cases, market administrators usually recommend buyers to use escrow services to mitigate the risk of fraud on the part of vendors. Sellers also face specific risks related to market takedowns and fluctuations in cryptocurrencies. To mitigate these types of risks, administrators offer sellers the opportunity to use the "finalize early" mechanism (FE). Generally, FE means that administrators transfer escrow payments to sellers before buyers receive their purchases. Yet, an early release of escrow payments can stimulate vendors not to deliver on their promises. Taking this into account, administrators introduce various insurance payments for vendors who use FE. For example, according to the AlphaBay rule, "Vendors must put a $300 guarantee deposit, and 0.5 percent per order is taken and put in a guarantee fund in case the vendor decides to exit scam" (Joshua, 2015). Also, vendors are often required to have good records of previous transactions before they can ask for FE.

Escrow services are also associated with a common risk shared by both buyers and sellers in cryptomarkets. The more a particular darknet market grows, the higher the amount of payments held in escrow. Potentially, a huge amount of escrow payments can stimulate administrators or external hackers to seize all the money held in a common pool. This happened in such markets as Atlantis, Cannabis Road 2, Pandora, Silk Road 2, and the Evolution Marketplace, among many others. The Evolution exit scam was one of the biggest in the history of the dark web. The administrators known by their aliases as Verto and Kimble stole over $12 million worth of the cryptocurrency Bitcoin (Woolf, 2017). Another large exit scam occurred in the Sheep Marketplace that was opened in 2013 and functioned only for several months. It was closed when one of the vendors stole around $40 million worth of bitcoins from other market participants (Redman, 2017). Two years later, the perpetrators, Jiřikovský and his wife, who apparently worked as Sheep's programmer, were arrested in the Czech Republic where they tried to launder the stolen money in the real estate market (Woolf, 2017).

Exit scams shake participants' confidence in the integrity of administrators and cryptomarkets. To mitigate this risk, many darknet markets introduce a special protection mechanism against this type of fraud called the multisignature (multisig) escrow system. According to the multisignature procedure, in multilateral relations between vendors, buyers, and administrators, no market actor can receive the payment without the approval of the other two participants. As Table 2 shows, about 60 percent of the analyzed hidden markets offer this mechanism to their participants. Multisignature transactions are considered the most secure guarantees against cheating, yet, they are also the most technologically challenging mechanisms.

Despite various anti-fraud mechanisms, cheating is a common phenomenon in darknet markets. In the real-world markets of illegal goods, violence is commonly used as a retaliation procedure in such cases. In darknet markets, there are alternative mechanisms of retaliation. For example, digital violence might take the form of distributed denial-of-service attacks (DDoS attacks). These attacks aim to make a marketplace unavailable to its participants by temporarily or indefinitely disrupting its services. For example, in 2015, the Middle Earth and Agora marketplaces were "the focus of the most serious attack Tor has ever seen" (Fox-Brewster, 2015). As a result, they were temporally shut down. Another retaliation mechanism in cyberspace is called "doxing." It involves the disclosure of private information related to fraudsters. In 2015, users of the Evolution Marketplace launched a crowdfunding campaign to dox their administrators Verto and Kimble (Pearson & Franceschi-Bicchierai, 2015). Doxing practices are not successful in darknet markets. The use of anonymizing software and encryption programs makes it extremely difficult to determine the identity of fraudsters. As a result, violence does not have a strong deterrent effect in darknet markets. Importantly, this specific feature makes online trade in illicit goods a much safer environment in comparison with conventional street markets of illegal goods.

## CONCLUSION

The precondition of darknet markets is anonymity, which helps minimize the risk of law enforcement intervention in the case of illicit goods and of monitoring and surveillance by third parties, such as Internet service providers and online businesses in the case of legitimate goods. At the same time, this precondition increases the risk related to fraud and cheating by market participants. As a result, trust becomes a central issue for the selection of trade partners in exchanges that take place in darknet markets. For example, a recent study found that "Vendors' trustworthiness is a better predictor of vendor selection than product diversity or affordability" on the dark web (Duxbury & Haynie, 2017). This suggests that trust is even more important for effective communications in darknet markets than in conventional e-commerce.

Not only do new technologies help anonymize trade in illicit goods, but they also offer opportunities for legitimate users to protect their privacy in online transactions. This explains the most recent trend observed in the dark web, which manifests itself in an increasing share of legal goods sold by darknet vendors. Yet, anonymity of transactions in the dark web poses new challenges to market actors who confront one of the most difficult questions in the digital age related to the relationship between privacy and security. Encryption software utilized in darknet markets offers privacy protection, allowing users to communicate and exchange information in a highly secure manner. At the same time, privacy protection often comes at a price in apprehending fraudsters. To tackle this issue, it is imperative to look at various mechanisms that could be used by actors to minimize fraud risks through building trust and reputation in digital environments.

An analysis of mechanisms of building trust and reputation in hidden markets is a relatively new stream of the research into online trade. As this chapter shows, this analysis is very useful for explaining the darknet paradox, according to which despite imperfect and asymmetric information, cryptomarkets manage to mitigate the adverse selection problem that leads to the prevalence of low-quality products in unregulated markets. According to the European Monitoring Centre for Drugs and Drug Addiction (EMCDDA), "thanks to reputation systems, the cryptomarkets have developed an organic method of self-regulation: vendors who sell low-quality products or who provide poor customer service will simply not receive good ratings, feedback, or reviews, so arguably only those providing high-quality products will survive" (Mounteney et al., 2016, p. 52). As the chapter demonstrates, darknet markets borrowed these reputation-based ranking systems from conventional online markets.

For example, Silk Road, one of the first darknet markets, imitated the customer feedback and five-star vendor rating systems adopted by Amazon. As Chen (2011) notes, this combination of anonymity technology and a sophisticated user-feedback system makes darknet trade easy and safe from third-party interventions. These features explain the increasing popularity of cryptomarkets among users.

However, given anonymity of transactions in darknet markets, it is more difficult for actors to have confidence in their partners. Unlike conventional e-commerce websites, darknet markets have a very limited number of characteristic-based mechanisms of building trust, which is explained by the impersonal nature of their operations. Therefore, trust building within darknet markets relies heavily on the process-based mechanisms that focus on actors' reputation and on the institution-based mechanisms that focus on third-party services. This study provides evidence that darknet vendors and sellers often use administrators of darknet marketplaces and operators of hidden forums to resolve conflicts and protect themselves against fraud. This constitutes a distinctive feature of trust building in cryptomarkets. On the one hand, this feature can be emulated by their legitimate users to enhance their privacy. On the other hand, it can be exploited by law enforcement agencies to dismantle illicit trade in darknet markets.

In this respect, further research is needed to assess the effectiveness of specific law-enforcement responses, including submitting fake reviews for vendors of illicit goods and decreasing confidence in darknet operations. The importance of such research is explained by the fact that darknet markets of illicit goods are remarkably resilient to takedowns by law enforcement. In recent years, the number of darknet markets has been continuously growing despite periodic closures. The void from arrests of darknet administrators or closures of particular marketplaces is quickly filled by their competitors. Both darknet vendors and buyers are very mobile and migrate very quickly to other marketplaces. In addition, darknet markets are not synonymous with other illegal markets since there is an increasing share of legal goods traded on the dark web. Another argument against takedowns of darknet markets was raised in the 2016 report of the EMCDDA, which shows that online markets provide a safer environment for users of illicit drugs in comparison with street markets (Mounteney et al., 2016). These considerations suggest the importance of the study of innovative mechanisms and tools used by darknet market actors in anonymous digital communications, especially taking into account their ever-evolving nature.

**NOTE:** This research received no specific grant from any funding agency in the public, commercial, or not-for-profit sectors.

## REFERENCES

Akerlof, G. A. (1970). The Market for "Lemons": Quality Uncertainty and the Market Mechanism. *The Quarterly Journal of Economics, 84*(3), 488–500. doi:10.2307/1879431

Aldridge, J., & Décary-Hétu, D. (2014). Not an "EBay for Drugs": The Cryptomarket "Silk Road" as a Paradigm Shifting Criminal Innovation. *SSRN Electronic Journal.* Retrieved May 12, 2017, from https://papers.ssrn.com/sol3/papers.cfm?abstract_id=2436643

Barratt, M. J., Ferris, J. A., & Winstock, A. R. (2014). Use of Silk Road, the Online Drug Marketplace, in the United Kingdom, Australia and the United States: Silk Road Global Survey. *Addiction (Abingdon, England), 109*(5), 774–783. doi:10.1111/add.12470 PMID:24372954

Buxton, J., & Bingham, T. (2015). The Rise and Challenge of Dark Net Drug Markets. *Policy Brief, 7.* Retrieved from http://www.drugsandalcohol.ie/23274/1/Darknet%20Markets.pdf

Cabral, L. (2012). Reputation on the Internet. In M. Peitz & J. Waldfogel (Eds.), *The Oxford Handbook of the Digital Economy* (pp. 344–354). Oxford, UK: Oxford University Press.

Caulkins, J., & Reuter, P. (2010). How Drug Enforcement Affects Drug Prices. *Crime and Justice, 39*(1), 213–271. doi:10.1086/652386

Celestini, A., Me, G., & Mignone, M. (2016). Tor Marketplaces Exploratory Data Analysis: The Drugs Case. In H. Jahankhani, A. Carlile, D. Emm, A. Hosseinian-Far, G. Brown, G. Sexton, & A. Jamal (Eds.), *Global Security, Safety and Sustainability - The Security Challenges of the Connected World* (Vol. 630, pp. 218–229). Cham: Springer International Publishing. doi:10.1007/978-3-319-51064-4_18

Chen, A. (2011). The Underground Website Where You Can Buy Any Drug Imaginable. *Gawker.* Retrieved May 8, 2017, from http://gawker.com/the-underground-website-where-you-can-buy-any-drug-imag-30818160

Christin, N. (2013). Traveling the Silk Road: A Measurement Analysis of a Large Anonymous Online Marketplace. In *Proceedings of the 22nd International Conference on World Wide Web* (pp. 213–224). ACM. Retrieved May 8, 2017, from http://dl.acm.org/citation.cfm?id=2488408

Dark Web News. (2017). *Darknet Markets*. Retrieved May 7, 2017, from https://darkwebnews.com/market-comparison-chart/

Dellarocas, C. (2002). Goodwill Hunting: An Economically Efficient Online Feedback Mechanism for Environments with Variable Product Quality. In J. Padget, O. Shehory, D. Parkes, N. Sadeh, & W. E. Walsh (Eds.), *Agent-Mediated Electronic Commerce IV. Designing Mechanisms and Systems* (pp. 238–252). Berlin: Springer Berlin Heidelberg. doi:10.1007/3-540-36378-5_15

Department of Justice. (2017). *AlphaBay, the Largest Online "Dark Market," Shut Down*. Retrieved November 8, 2017, from https://www.justice.gov/opa/pr/alphabay-largest-online-dark-market-shut-down

Dolliver, D. S. (2015). Evaluating Drug Trafficking on the Tor Network: Silk Road 2, the Sequel. *The International Journal on Drug Policy*, *26*(11), 1113–1123. doi:10.1016/j.drugpo.2015.01.008 PMID:25681266

Dolliver, D. S., & Kenney, J. L. (2016). Characteristics of Drug Vendors on the Tor Network: A Cryptomarket Comparison. *Victims & Offenders*, *11*(4), 600–620. doi:10.1080/15564886.2016.1173158

Duxbury, S. W., & Haynie, D. L. (2017). The Network Structure of Opioid Distribution on a Darknet Cryptomarket. *Journal of Quantitative Criminology*. doi:10.100710940-017-9359-4

Fox-Brewster, T. (2015, April 1). Tor Hidden Services and Drug Markets Are Under Attack, But Help Is on The Way. *Forbes*. Retrieved May 7, 2017, from https://www.forbes.com/sites/thomasbrewster/2015/04/01/tor-hidden-services-under-dos-attack/#758e66fb758e

Gollnick, C., & Wilson, E. (2016). *Separating Fact from Fiction: The Truth About the Dark Web*. Baltimore, MD: Terbium Labs.

Greenberg, A. (2013, August 13). An Interview with A Digital Drug Lord: The Silk Road's Dread Pirate Roberts. *Forbes*.

Greenberg, A. (2014, November 7). Global Web Crackdown Arrests 17, Seizes Hundreds of Dark Net Domains. *Wired*. Retrieved May 7, 2017, from https://www. wired.com/2014/11/operation-onymous-dark-web-arrests/

Hardy, R. A., & Norgaard, J. R. (2016). Reputation in the Internet Black Market: An Empirical and Theoretical Analysis of the Deep Web. *Journal of Institutional Economics*, *12*(03), 515–539. doi:10.1017/S1744137415000454

Holt, T. J., & Lampke, E. (2010). Exploring Stolen Data Markets Online: Products and Market Forces. *Criminal Justice Studies*, *23*(1), 33–50. doi:10.1080/14786011003634415

Janetos, N., & Tilly, J. (2017). *Reputation Dynamics in a Market for Illicit Drugs*. Retrieved May 7, 2017, from https://arxiv.org/abs/1703.01937

Joshua, G. (2015, April 20). *Interview with AlphaBay Market Admin*. Retrieved May 8, 2017, from https://www.deepdotweb.com/2015/04/20/interview-with-alphabay-admin/

Markopoulos, P., Xefteris, D., & Dellarocas, C. (2015). *Manipulating Reviews in Dark Net Markets to Reduce Crime*. Retrieved May 7, 2017, from http://www.teis-workshop.org/papers/2016/TEIS_2016_1_Dellarocas.pdf

Martin, J. (2014). *Drugs on the Dark Net: How Cryptomarkets are Transforming the Global Trade in Illicit Drugs*. London: Palgrave Macmillan UK. doi:10.1057/9781137399052

Mounteney, J., Bo, A., & Oteo, A. (2016). *The Internet and Drug Markets*. Luxembourg: European Monitoring Centre for Drugs and Drug Addiction.

O'Neill, P. H. (2017, February 3). *Dark Net Markets Moving to Adopt Bug Bounty Programs*. Retrieved May 11, 2017, from https://www.cyberscoop.com/dark-net-markets-bug-bounty-programs/

Online, B. D. (2016, June 16). Shedding Light on the Dark Web. *The Economist*. Retrieved May 8, 2017, from http://www.economist.com/news/international/21702176-drug-trade-moving-street-online-cryptomarkets-forced-compete

Paul, I. (2014, October 31). Facebook Says You Can Be Social and Secure, Acquires. Onion Address for Tor Users. *PCWorld*. Retrieved November 11, 2017, from https://www.pcworld.com/article/2841822/facebook-says-you-can-be-social-and-secure-acquires-onion-address-for-tor-users.html

Pearson, J., & Franceschi-Bicchierai, L. (2015, March 19). There's a Bitcoin Bounty Out on Those Alleged "Evolution" Drug Market Scammers. *Motherboard*. Retrieved May 11, 2017, from https://motherboard.vice.com/en_us/article/theres-a-bitcoin-bounty-out-on-those-alleged-evolution-drug-market-scammers

Redman, J. (2016, July 16). *Dark Net Markets Are Booming from Better Quality and Safety*. Retrieved May 8, 2017, from https://news.bitcoin.com/dark-net-market-quality-safety/

Redman, J. (2017, April 5). *Darknet Market Operators Who Stole 40 Thousand BTC Face Prison Time*. Retrieved May 4, 2017, from https://news.bitcoin.com/darknet-market-operators-who-stole-40-thousand-btc-face-prison-time/

Rhumorbarbe, D., Staehli, L., Broséus, J., Rossy, Q., & Esseiva, P. (2016). Buying Drugs on a Darknet Market: A Better Deal? Studying the Online Illicit Drug Market Through the Analysis of Digital, Physical and Chemical Data. *Forensic Science International*, *267*, 173–182. doi:10.1016/j.forsciint.2016.08.032 PMID:27611957

Soska, K., & Christin, N. (2015). *Measuring the Longitudinal Evolution of the Online Anonymous Marketplace Ecosystem*. Washington, DC: USENIX Association.

Van Hout, M. C., & Bingham, T. (2013). "Surfing the Silk Road": A Study of Users' Experiences. *The International Journal on Drug Policy*, *24*(6), 524–529. doi:10.1016/j.drugpo.2013.08.011 PMID:24075939

Van Hout, M. C., & Bingham, T. (2014). Responsible Vendors, Intelligent Consumers: Silk Road, the Online Revolution in Drug Trading. *The International Journal on Drug Policy*, *25*(2), 183–189. doi:10.1016/j.drugpo.2013.10.009 PMID:24268875

Wehinger, F. (2011). The Dark Net: Self-Regulation Dynamics of Illegal Online Markets for Identities and Related Services. IEEE Computer Society.

Woolf, N. (2015, March 18). Bitcoin 'Exit Scam": Deep-web Market Operators Disappear with $12m. *The Guardian*.

Zucker, L. G. (1986). Production of Trust: Institutional Sources of Economic Structure, 1840–1920. *Research in Organizational Behavior*, *8*, 53–111.

## KEY TERMS AND DEFINITIONS

**Adverse Selection:** A situation where due to imperfect and asymmetric information, market actors make inefficient decisions related to their choice of goods.

**Cryptocurrency:** A digital payment system that instead of a conventional financial institution relies on a voluntary network of Internet users who verify transactions in exchange for small rewards for their services.

**Dark Web:** A part of the World Wide Web that is not accessible through popular search engines, such as Google or Yahoo, and relies on the use of anonymizing software and encryption programs.

**Doxing:** A deliberate and malicious disclosure of private information about Internet users.

**Exit Scam:** A situation where market actors violate trust by stealing assets from other participants or from a common pool.

**Finalize Early Mechanism:** A payment mechanism, according to which escrow agents transfer money from buyers to vendors before confirmation of receipt of goods.

**Multisignature Escrow Services:** A payment procedure, according to which in multilateral relations between vendors, buyers, and administrators of online marketplaces, no actor can receive the payment without the approval of other two participants.

**Tor:** Anonymizing software that connects Internet users and websites' traffic through a series of virtual tunnels run by thousands of volunteers around the globe.

# Chapter 2
# Digital or Information Divide:
## A New Dimension of Social Stratification

**Zbigniew Hulicki**
*AGH University of Science and Technology, Poland*

## ABSTRACT

*In different regions of the world, the growth in home broadband adoption and development of e-services depends on a number of factors which can decrease digital divide in size or can result in widened "gaps" between developed and developing economies as well as between rich and poor regions or social groups. These factors comprise both drivers of, and barriers to, development of broadband access and growth of e-services as well as human communication and digital interactions in terms of comprehension and relationship building (i.e., the successful collaboration in contemporary society). Using a human communication point of view, this chapter provides insight into a concept of information divide, specifies the distinction between digital and information divide, examines each of the factors that condition the mass-market broadband adoption, and considers the impact of techno economic stratification for the development of web-based e-services.*

DOI: 10.4018/978-1-5225-4168-4.ch002

## INTRODUCTION

In the last decade, the rapid development and explosive growth of digital ICTs (Information and Communication Technologies) has changed the traditional boundaries between media and communications (Corazza, 2008). Simultaneously, the public increasingly use different devices (e.g. mobile phones and PDAs, desktops, notebooks, and tablet PCs, connected via diverse access network technologies) to access the Internet. In this scenario, the ability to deal with new challenging applications and multimedia services becomes a necessity (Ginesi, 2008). This brings about new and complex challenges for modern society, i.e. it assumes a world in which people are surrounded by mobile or fixed devices in a computing environment that supports them in almost everything they do (Horrigan, 2008). Fast and rapid communication remains a hot issue for the entire global world. In acknowledging this global application, there exists even more challenge of a for people in some regions (e.g. remote and rural areas), because tremendous development and revolutionary change in communication have not yet provided optimistic solutions for such areas (Hulicki, 2008a). Wireless communication and portable computing devices have become inseparable parts of our lives, moderating communication needs. However, the gap of communication abilities remains a challenge for telecom network operators and service providers in many regions and communities. Besides the technological constraints and forces, there are a number of barriers and factors which constrain development of broadband access and proliferation of Web-based e-services, and result in the slower development of national, regional, or local economies (Marine & Blanchard, 2004), (A Digital Agenda for Europe, 2010). Such barriers can lead to and increase the abovementioned gap that is often called the "digital divide" (Luise, 2008). Such a gap (or gaps) can be observed across the various countries of the European Union, within one country, or within one region, shown in Figure 1.

However, there is a strong illusion behind the definition of this term as a single gap in access to and usage of ICTs (Hulicki, 2008b). In fact, most people initially perceive this terminology deficit and refer to connectivity problems (Gupta, 2006), (Skowroński, 2006). Later, the concept of digital or technological divide evolved from the economic stratification in the availability of ICTs, to the inequality or differences in QoE (Quality of the user Experience) (Hulicki, 2008b), (EE Report, 2010). Hence, the concept of digital divide is more of a new label and less of a unique concept or gap. Unlike the traditional notion, it can serve as an indicator of the new techno-economic stratification of households, communities, businesses, and geographic areas.

*Figure 1. Usage of broadband access to the Internet (acc. to Eurostat)*

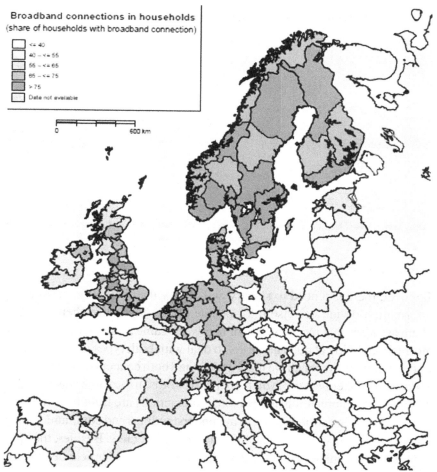

It should also be noted that there is a considerable literature on digital inequality that predates the digital divide concept. Some papers (World Information Society Report, 2007) discuss essentially a geographical division, i.e. the "global digital divide" between developed and developing countries, shown in Figure 2.

In many others (Barbera, 2006), (Gupta, 2006), (Hulicki, 2008a), the debate is moving away from "quantity" of basic connectivity to measures of "quality," "usability," and "empowerment." The authors debate the methods and tools to overcome the divide and reduce inequalities. Nevertheless, a number of question still need to be resolved because the digital divide is a result of the techno-economic stratification produced by a number of complicated socio-economic processes which affect also the information divide and finally lead to digital exclusion.

*Figure 2. Households with Internet access by level of development (acc. to ITU)*

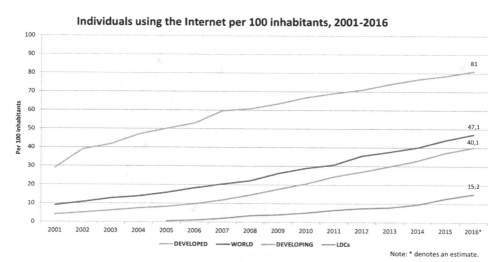

Moreover, there is a need to specify and clarify the distinction between digital and information divide because most people do not recognize them as different, treat them as words that mean exactly or nearly the same as thing, or do not perceive the information divide at all. Therefore, to deal with both types of gaps resulting in social stratification, first of all we must understand both concepts, i.e. problems arise when people mistakenly assume that others use words in the same way they do. As a result, human communication and personal interactions are fraught with erroneous and incomplete information leading to misunderstandings and communication gaps, precluding successful collaboration in contemporary society. Besides, the "people" aspect of the above-mentioned problems (Hulicki, 2008b)) Hulicki deals with user activity and appropriate information-processing capabilities (understanding), i.e. the infrastructure creates a base for capacity-building and usage of the resources, but the user should prove himself or herself ready for the corresponding activity. The challenge is how to stimulate activity that develops skills and improves the use of knowledge resources, supporting interpersonal communication in the digital era. This aspect is also linked up to the awareness of difference between digital and information divide what seems to be important for both educators and public administrators (and businesses as well) because they would like to improve levels of trust (or even reinforce productivity).

In this article, techno-economic stratification and its impact on the development of broadband access and *e*-services will be investigated using a diversified perspective. The phenomenon causing a new dimension of social inequalities will be discussed first, followed by a definition of the process – digital and/or information divide.

Then, the most important factors which stimulate or restrain the mass–market broadband adoption and proliferation of Web-based *e*-services will be examined considering human needs and in particular demand or necessity for broadband services. In the next section, methods and tools for bridging the information divide will be studied with respect to technical factors and impact of legal regulations. Finally, some conclusions and remarks on the problems, drives and barriers which can result in or lead to the information divide will be provided, together with some recommendations as to how to better satisfy user needs for broadband access and adoption of *e*-services.

# DIGITAL OR INFORMATION DIVIDE

## Shift From Physical Access to Skills and Usage

The latest innovations, based on the application of digital technologies, and the evolution towards information and communication have led to a strong coupling between services and communications infrastructure used to deliver these services. These new services for multifaceted tele-work, tele-education and telematics (like telemedicine) can be efficiently supported by the next generation Internet capabilities in a nearly endless number of multimedia applications (Networked Media of the Future, 2007).

Today, users are interested in experiencing full virtual access to services and information and not in accessing network nodes that host just information or provide services (Hulicki, 2008b), (A Digital Agenda for Europe, 2010), i.e. one can observe a need to create an environment, where all of the human senses are engaged and where communication via technological means preserves and augments the richness and subtle characteristics of interpersonal communications. The idea of the NGN (Next Generation Network), developed with the purpose of integrating different multiple services (data, voice, video, etc.) and of facilitating the convergence of fixed and mobile networks, will enable a development of new network paradigms which will have features and capabilities to ensure the provisioning of new value-added multimedia services over broadband access technologies that can be deployed in the market. In the future, the emphasis will be on services which reflect societal needs (van Dijk, 2005), (Mathea, 2006). Increasingly such services will be produced and customized by people who will have the ability to create new services based on the integration of services and content from a multitude of services. Hence, one can expect that the future digital world will be characterized by the emergence of a social infrastructure where access to knowledge resources and services is no longer location or time dependent (Networked Media of the Future, 2007).

These trends place enormous demands on network operators, ICTs suppliers and service providers. They must cope with the constantly rising needs of end users, and simultaneously, they must create technologies which seem to be the evolutionary cornerstones of the global information society.

In the telecom/networking world where most of us live, traditionally, deployment of broadband infrastructure comes first and then demand for broadband services can originate. Of course, the viability of a business case for deployment of broadband technologies depends, among other factors, on potential demand. This first and foremost is demand for infrastructure access. Consequently, people will need to pay special attention in perfect harmony with the technological environment because the new converging ICTs can be perceived as the physical engines that make it possible to build the infrastructure necessary to support a society based on information and communication.

Global information can be used for online education, telemedicine, *e*-government, international trade and many other applications that could solve vital problems in the developing world. It is also clear that this is a field that is going to affect everybody in every walk of life, be it for access to culture and education or for leisure. Moreover, the amount of information in a digital form is continuously increasing and access to ICTs, and broadband networks, increasingly determines access to wealth and income (Marine & Blanchard, 2004), (EU policies, 2007), (A Digital Agenda for Europe, 2010). This is the case already today and will be even more so in the future as personalized media services without a central control will be pervasive (Networked Media of the Future, 2007). However, the differences in the usage of communication resources still exist and even are intensifying between countries, regions and social groups. Despite the growth in the availability of broadband services, this gap in access to and usage of ICTs has come to be known as the *"digital divide"* (Ganesa, 2008), (World Information Society Report, 2007).

The term "digital divide" initially referred to the gap in ownership of computing devices. Then, it expressed the difference in facilities for people to communicate, i.e. between those people with effective access to digital ICTs and those without, relative to their geographic location, their living standard and their level of education (van Dijk, 2005). On the other hand, unlike the traditional notion of the "digital divide" between social classes, the "global digital divide" essentially concerned a geographical division between developed and developing countries (EU policies, 2007), and still, there was only discussion about the access to the Internet (EE Report, 2010), i.e. about technological divide. Later, one could observe in the literature a redefinition of that term, focusing on skills and usage, i.e. it reflected various differences among individuals, households, businesses and geographic areas at different socio-economic levels with regard both to their opportunities to access ICTs and to their use of the Internet (Hulicki, 2008b). Moreover, in most cases people talk about the digital divide concerning the entire world, i.e. as if there only existed one and as if it had the same characteristics at any time or in any social space. This is one of the strongest aspects of the illusion behind the definition of the digital divide concept.

The digital divide would not have attracted so much attention was it not for its impact on development within a global economy increasingly based on the exchange of information and knowledge. For that reason, a new definition of that term still seems to be necessary.

Today, the most developed countries of the world with the resources to invest in and develop ICT infrastructure are reaping enormous benefits from the information age. This gap in rates of technological progress could also widen the economic disparity between developed and developing countries, thus creating a digitally fostered divide. Now, however, there is not only discussion about the Internet and ICTs, but also the usage of any communication infrastructure (e.g. mobile, broadcasting etc.) (Hulicki, 2008a). To understand a digitally comprehended divide, it is necessary to analyze fundamental aspects of that process which include an insight into the environment for the mass–market broadband adoption, i.e. social appropriation conditions of the mentioned gaps and not simply reduce comprehension to the availability of the ICT infrastructure, connectivity, and e-services.

With this approach, the concept of the digital divide incorporates three essential problems (Hulicki, 2008b): infrastructure, capacity-building, and usage of the resources. Infrastructure problems basically refer to connectivity problems and the possibility/difficulty of having computers available that are connected to the worldwide net. This also includes the problem in availability of servers and backbones, i.e. the status of broadband infrastructure that depends on the existing backbone and access networks (Luise, 2008). As one can deduce, the infrastructure does concern aspects viewed in economic terms, whereas two other problems deal with the usability and the empowerment, i.e. the "people" aspect of the above-mentioned problems. Consequently, one can assume that the notion of the digital divide includes two aspects:

- Technological
- Infrastructural

Both elements can be crucial to further stratification of the society, i.e. they may aggravate pre-existing problems, or reduce inequalities. In fact, through their ability to disseminate information efficiently, the new ICTs promise huge improvements to communication infrastructure, so that users can effectively get credible and trustworthy information to solve their own problems (Marine & Blanchard, 2004), (EU policies, 2007).

Another important aspect to be recovered from the foregoing discussion is that the access to and usage of the ICTs and communication infrastructure concern the exchange of information and knowledge (provision of e-services). It is worth emphasizing, however, that information can be comprehended as any conceptual entity that enables people to connect to the world and make sense of it (thereby removing uncertainty), whereas possessing such a conceptual entity in a structured and accessible way pertains to knowledge (Corazza, 2008). Hence, from the perspective of the above-mentioned two other problems incorporated in the divide process, one can perceive the divide not only as pertaining to technological-infrastructure, i.e. "digital" (conventional, common sense), but also as the "information divide," i.e. the separation from one's knowledge and the rest of all information. Moreover, the information divide can be considered not only as a result produced by the digital divide (e.g. the techno-economic stratification), but also caused by other factors. There are two aspects of the information divide:

- Inability to access information; and
- Inability to handle (i.e. process or understand) information.

The first information divide dimension is a result of both technological and infrastructural limitations included in the digital divide process and corresponds to the lack of means on the part of the user. The lack of power to handle information, on the other hand, is caused by two groups of factors, mainly related to the human barriers of growth. One can categorize them as follows:

- Psychological obstacles; and
- Information overload frontiers.

Both subcategories incorporate factors which reflect user skills and capacities. Thus, unlike the notion of the digital divide, the information divide seems to be the right term to describe disparities in opportunity to access information and diverse opportunities tied to this access. Besides, it describes essentially a universal division and at the same time a new dimension of social stratification.

In contrast to the digital divide, the information divide can be considered as a familiar concept. Indeed, an analysis of the earliest statistics on telecommunications (refer to Figure 1 in the previous section) indicates a clear divide between the Member States of the ITU (World Information Society Report, 2007). Such disparities have narrowed and, in some cases, even reversed over time, but other gaps have arisen. This suggests that older technologies tend to be more evenly spread out than newer ones, and the main factor underlying these inequalities is a difference in wealth between individuals, between households, or between geographic areas. Certainly, it is true that such factors have impacted the divide, but from an analytical perspective such explanation is not useful because the information divide is a dynamic concept, which includes various aspects (Hulicki, 2008a). Using the initial conceptualization of the stratification process, several questions need to be explored. What is a nature of the information divide? Why does it occur and how is to be measured? What needs to be done to alleviate it? What methods and tools can be suggested? Are the same methods used in each case?

Unfortunately, it is not easy to answer all the questions with any certainty, especially since the divide evolves over time according to complicated socio-economic processes.

## TECHNO-ECONOMIC ASPECTS OF SERVICE DEVELOPMENT

In recent years, one could observe that telecommunications and computer networking have essentially merged their activities and infrastructures into an extremely competitive and changing sector (Barbara, 2006). The Internet has re-emerged as a powerful medium for community collaboration and a virtual space where experiences are personalized and shared. Being able to access the Internet becomes a major discriminator. As it is not a receive-only system, like radio and TV broadcasting, but rather a fully interactive medium of communication, its possibilities to provide new services are vast (EE Report, 2010). On the other hand, networking and media communities have not joined forces yet, but the trend seems to have no end and they will end up integrated. This will allow a richer information (and knowledge) exchange over a true broadband infrastructure. Consequently, the overall socio-economic impact one could foresee is that the new, useful broadband services will fundamentally modify the way people relate among themselves (Hulicki, 2008b). Using new (specific) service offerings, people could improve their communication skills through experience or education. However, this requires conscious person activity and appropriate information-processing capabilities, e.g. combining both digital and face-to-face/audio-visual communication forms to improve understanding of a dialogue.

On the other hand, inequalities in the availability of broadband services discussed in an earlier section (Figure 1 and Figure 2) remain a major barrier to the development of modern society and continue to provoke intense debate on the digital divide. To understand it, it is necessary to analyze diverse aspects of that process, and in particular the social appropriation conditions of the above-mentioned gaps resulted from the information divide.

Demand for and availability of services provided over the broadband infrastructure is the main precondition for successful development of broadband in any country (Mathea, 2006), (Skowroński, 2006). Although access to the Internet via cable modems has been available since the end of 90s in many developing countries, significant development of broadband started only a few years ago, when ADSL (Asymmetric Digital Subscriber Line) became available (Gupta, 2006), (Kocher et al., 2006). Nowadays, development of broadband access and e-services in a number of developing regions is accelerating as shown in Figure 2 in an earlier section.

The Web-based e-services are provided by public institutions as well as by commercial entities. However, the penetration of broadband access lines varies by country and it is still much lower compared with most of developed economies (Ginesi, 2008), (Kuchar et al., 2006), (Luise, 2008), (EE Report, 2010). For users and non-users of broadband, a wide gap exists between households in the North/West and South/East countries (EU policies, 2007) together with a gap between rural and urban areas in both categories of the states as well as in a given country (A Digital Agenda for Europe, 2010). Non-users of Internet represent a large pool of potential broadband subscribers (Horrigan, 2008), but many are just not interested in getting online.

In most developing economies such disparities are deepening. Larger households are more likely to have broadband (Gupta, 2006), but it is still a long way to broadband for all (Skowroński, 2006). The young generation does mainly use the Internet and ICTs, shown in Figure 3, but around 50% of women and unemployed have never used them (Gupta, 2006). Figure 4 shows sources of widespread public information

*Figure 3. Internet users categorized according to the age in NMS of EU (developed and developing countries using United Nations definitions)*

*Figure 4. Obstacles and reasons not to use the Internet*

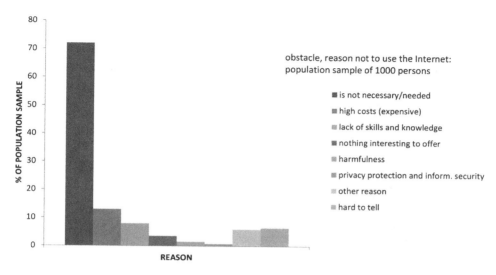

such as DTV (Digital Television), telephone services, and educational institutions that are taken for granted in developed countries. In developing countries, however, such infrastructure is seriously deficient, and this cripples users' ability to gather information (Corazza, 2008; Ginesi, 2008).

Demand for broadband services in a given country strongly depends on how well the population is prepared for using the services (Barbara, 2006), (Skowroński, 2006). In Europe however, the most popular Web-based e-services in the CE (Central European) region are the same or similar as in the other regions of the EU and include entertainment and leisure as shown in Figure 5, interpersonal communications as shown in Figure 6, and managing one's life, education, and work (Gupta, 2006). Moreover, there are a number of successful public services (e-government and e-health) in operation in that region (Hulicki, 2008b), (Kuchar et al., 2006), (Mathea, 2006) and, despite quantitative differences, the usage of online information and communication services by the ICT users in the new and the old member states of EU reveals similar trends (Barbera, 2006), (Hulicki, 2008a). Figure 7 demonstrates the information for new member states. The same conclusion can be drawn on the usage of paid online entertainment services as well as online services for e-business (e.g. commerce, banking) (Gupta, 2006), (Hulicki, 2008b), (The State of Broadband, 2016)). Also, in other regions of the world (e.g. America, Asia), despite the differences between developing and developed economies, at least a trend towards home broadband adoption looks similar (Horrigan, 2008), (Luise, 2008). Similar to disparities in the distribution of wealth items, the digital divide in ICTs and connectivity partially reflects past and existing the information divide.

*Figure 5. Users of social networks in Poland*

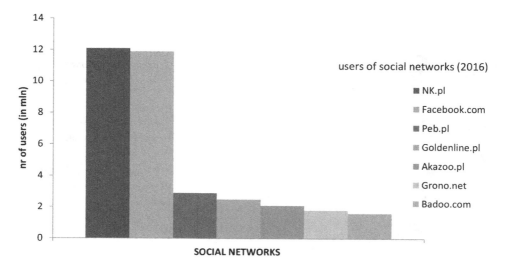

As has been already mentioned, the ICT infrastructure (fixed, mobile, and broadband) is referred to connectivity problems and the ability to promote the efficient dissemination of information and wealth of knowledge. The status of broadband infrastructure depends on the existing backbone and access networks. In many regions of the world (mainly in developed countries), optical fiber backbones employing multi-Gb/s DWDM (Dense Wavelength Division Multiplexing) technology are used (Kocher et al., 2006), (Mathea, 2006). In developing economies, access networks comprise mainly twisted copper pairs, wireless links, and cable TV networks. The remaining technologies have a marginal share of the broadband market (Kuchar et al., 2006), (World Information Society Report, 2007)). However, there are important multiplier effects from ICT investments as indicated by the experience of countries (such as India and Malaysia) that have succeeded in establishing ICT hubs (World Information Society Report, 2007).

Another aspect in the development and availability of broadband services relates to SPs (Service Providers). Until recently, new services have been introduced by overlaying individual service platforms on top of SPs' network infrastructure, leading to expensive, slow to build, and inflexible solutions (Ginesi, 2008), (Hulicki, 2008a). The competitive environment however, demands that SPs should deploy and monetize new services on a technical architecture optimized for speed, cost, and risk. Because a trend towards mass–market broadband adoption is under way (Barbera, 2006), (Gupta, 2006), (Mathea, 2006), the challenge for SPs in developing

*Figure 6. Service profile of the mobile subscriber (sample of 1000 users)*

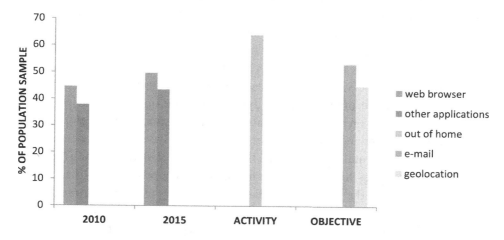

*Figure 7. Frequency of using the Internet (computer users only in NMS of EU)*

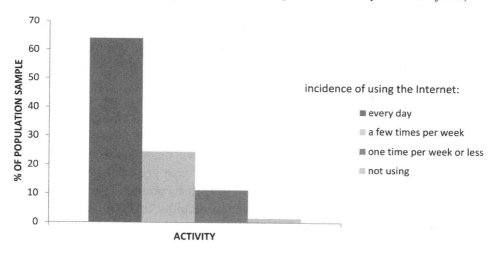

economies is finding ways to move from an early adopter stage to mass-market adoption. One can expect that SPs will play a key role both in making broadband services available to end users and in making the services affordable. Affordability of services can be another way of considering the digital divide, i.e. difference in the price and affordability of ICT services (e.g. Internet access or mobile phone service) are not as great as for higher-capacity services such as broadband (World Information Society Report, 2007).

From a methodological viewpoint, one of the hardest things to prove is the impact of policy changes and regulations. Such impact is often delayed over a few years and it is difficult to find the counter-factual. However, it is evident to observe that during the last decade telecom liberalization in the CE region has improved the provision of network access (Internet and Web-based *e*-services), first because of a further drop of service fee for telecommunication services (Hulicki, 2016). This is a result of the involvement of dynamic private operators and providers, seeking a good return on their investments. Private investments in developing both the ICT infrastructure and broadband services could drive demand for broadband access. The governmental and municipal bodies are expected to be among the major providers of e-services followed by commercial service providers (Kuchar et al., 2006). Nevertheless, the benefits of liberalization have remained limited to the urban areas, as private companies have generally considered that rural access offers little in the way of profit (Kotlarski, 2006), (Networked Media of the Future, 2007). Universal network access is therefore far from a reality in developing countries and at the same time is a challenge that the CE regulation authorities must take up. On the other hand, the market conditions determined by legislation and regulation of wholesale local loop market affect the situation on the developing markets that in turn reflects penetration of broadband access in developing economies (Hulicki, 2016). Consequently, sector reform can be a vital factor shaping both the digital and information divide.

Yet, to get broadband to the home is a complex process requiring continuous attention and effort by authorities at all levels (Kotlarski, 2006), (Marine & Blanchard, 2004), (A Digital Agenda for Europe, 2010). They must create the right competitive environment, considering a number of factors influencing broadband adoption and e-services growth. One can categorize them into three groups: technical factors, legal regulations and policy, and barriers of growth according to users themselves (Hulicki, 2008a). The first group includes: availability of ITCs and broadband infrastructure, user location – urban or rural, i.e. geographical conditions, but also costs of broadband access and services, household income and purchasing power as well as GDP (Gross Domestic Product).

According to Eurostat figures (Gupta, 2006), the income, rural, educational, and age gaps are all greater in the CE region than in the former EU-15. However, in terms of ICTs the gap is much smaller than expected (EU policies, 2007). During the past decade, ICTs have become widely available to the general public in both accessibility and cost. Generally, this trend seems to be common all over the world (Figure 2) (The State of Broadband, 2016). The digital divide in the technological sense is shrinking for most ICTs but growing in others.

In the CE countries, the main barrier to setting up telecommunication infrastructures lies in the lack of available investment (Hulicki, 2008b), (Kuchar et al., 2006). This problem is even more crucial in rural areas which are still very poorly served. Gaps remain in the use of ICTs among the population depending on factors such as age, employment status, educational level, and the degree of urbanization of the area where one lives (Skowroński, 2006). A better indicator, which gives idea of the relative importance attached to ICTs by users, is their per-income availability. On this indicator, low- and middle-income countries of the CE region are behind the old member states (Barbera, 2006). Although broadband is now available in all EU states, it remains at least ten times more expensive in the CE region than in the EU-15 and is often unavailable outside urban areas (Luise, 2008). Still high prices for broadband access with respect to the purchasing power of average citizen hinder faster development of e-services. In addition to broadband infrastructure, important indicators of the divide appear to be availability of computing devices – and potentially the availability of alternative access through TVs, mobile phones, etc. – and Internet access.

Access to ICTs and information and communication resources is increasingly considered as a basic social need in modern, highly developed societies. The Lisbon strategy considers it a driving factor behind the EU's efforts to become the leading knowledge-based economy (EU policies, 2007). Therefore, methods and tools for bridging the information divide should be discussed now.

## METHODS AND TOOLS FOR BRIDGING INFORMATION DIVIDE

The ambition of the EU to become the leading knowledge-based economy was reflected in the two successive e-Europe action plans that tried to address the above-mentioned challenges. However, the plan is seldom binding and member states are legally committed only by the provisions of the new regulatory framework for electronic communications relating to universal access and users' rights (Kotlarski, 2006).

Governmental initiatives to narrow the digital divide are referred to the policies addressed in broadband strategies. These focus on the social and regional aspects such as the provision of ICT services on multiple devices or platforms other than PC, i.e. digital TV, satellite, 3G mobile phones, etc. The mentioned aspects have been a particular focus of attention with actions being launched to cover remote and under-served areas with broadband connections (Ginesi, 2008), (Luise, 2008)).

On the other hand, because ADSL is, and in the foreseeable future will remain, the dominant technology for broadband access of end users in developing economies, it is vital for the regulators to ensure that this technology will be used as much as possible.

The importance of policy and regulatory reform needs to be underlined because the market conditions determined by legislation and regulation reflect penetration of broadband access, e.g. in the CE region of EU. The policy rationale is the social benefits to be derived from the diffusion and greater use of ICTs and related improvements to the economic activity. The liberalization of telecommunication markets and rigorous implementation of competition in developing countries can stimulate new investments and increase demand for communications access and Web-based e-services through falling prices (Horlick, 2016) and the offer of new innovative products.

Because in the developing markets forces alone are unable to provide broadband access, the governmental support (e.g. grants) – as an exception to competition law – can be allowed to use for broadband deployment. This reflects some historical prerequisites of people in many regions for provision of services to all through public funds. Moreover, because the investment in the infrastructure outside large cities has long payback periods, the state aid is necessary not only to reduce the payback period of potential investments, but also to reduce the necessary working capital for operators while a critical customer mass is being built (Hulicki, 2008a). It is also important to nurture the most promising initiatives and set up larger scale trials or pilot projects (Skowroński, 2006), (A Digital Agenda for Europe, 2010). This type of project could be usefully financed by public startup funds, possibly in partnership with private financing through Public-Private Partnership (PPP) schemes. A pilot project's essential goal must be to study the economic viability of the proposed service platforms if balanced business plans are to be drawn up. Lastly, when as many "infrastructure pieces" as possible have been set up through the pilot projects, potential investors (public or private) can commit to the large-scale deployment of infrastructures based on conventional cost-effectiveness criteria.

Much of the discussion in papers about the impact of new ICTs and social disparities has been focused on the oversimplified notion of digital divide, mainly related to the income. However, a central premise is that the ability to access, adapt, and create knowledge using ICTs is critical to social inclusion and deals with the information divide. This focus on social inclusion shifts the discussion of the digital divide from gaps to be overcome by providing equipment to social development challenges to be addressed through the effective integration of technology into communities and institutions, i.e. to the full extent of the problem covered by the information divide

(Hulicki, 2008b). More fundamentally, the information divide suggests how future divides in wealth of knowledge may take shape, as ICTs are increasingly determining the ability of users to create information and knowledge. But knowledge without experience is not wisdom (Corazza, 2008). What is most important is not so much the physical availability of ICTs and the Internet, but rather people's ability to make use of those technologies to engage in meaningful social practices. Therefore, two other aspects of the information divide will have much greater impact in the years to come, i.e. usability (usage, based on individuals who know how to use ICTs to handle information and those who do not) and usage quality (or empowerment, based on the differences between those same users) (Hulicki, 2008a).

The usability and empowerment divides can alienate huge population groups who miss out on the ICT's potential. Thus, an approach is required based primarily on usage and services, and in which the technology is not considered as an end in itself but more as a tool. There is enormous potential in this area, comprising a multitude of initiatives based on individual competences or small creative and dynamic organizations that can develop new proximity services (Kuchar et al., 2006). The public authorities will have a key role in creating conditions that favor the lasting emergence of such potential.

As considered here, the new ICTs may help to overcome some traditional divides, but simultaneously, the availability of broadband infrastructure may constitute another exclusion factor. The advanced age of elderly users added to their low income, disabilities, and their educational level can intensify their remaining at the margin of the social system. In this context, the new technologies can act as a factor of exclusion rather than one of inclusion. It is also necessary to examine barriers which reflect user skills and capacities. They include psychological obstacles and information overload frontiers, which is shown in Figure 4 in an earlier section. Both subcategories of factors influencing broadband adoption and e-services growth deal with digital literacy, education, and socialization of users, awareness and technological affinity, and incorporate also personal factors (e.g. age).

Lower (in comparison with developed countries) digital literacy of some users' groups is the Web's biggest accessibility problem in many developing regions (Hulicki, 2008a), (Networked Media of the Future, 2007). The fact that technology remains so complicated that many people couldn't use a device even if they got one for free, is a reality far worse than the economic divide, which is vanishing rapidly in industrialized countries and does not seem to be the issue in the future (World Information Society Report, 2007). Besides, many others can use ICTs, but don't achieve the modern world's full benefits because most of the available services are too difficult for them to understand (Networked Media of the Future, 2007). The usability divide will take longer to close, but at least we know how to handle it – it's simply a matter of deciding to do so. The empowerment divide, however, is the difficult challenge: even if ICTs were extraordinarily easy to use, not everybody would make full use of the opportunities that such technologies afford (van Dijk, 2005). This refers to the limitation/possibility that people have to use the resources available on the Web, and it is a common feature of any country. Consequently, a question does arise: how can one deal with a huge (or infinite) amount of information? And, can the semantic Web be sufficient to help us to overcome the information divide?

As one can deduce, the answer also concerns the development of capacities and skills required to use ICTs (capacity-building and education). Particular attention should be paid to developing policies to improve access in public institutions (local and regional government facilities, libraries, etc.) so that individuals can access ICTs at low or no cost, build familiarity, develop, strengthen, and extend skills (Gupta, 2006). Policies for making available low-cost and subsidized access in schools seek to build the future skill-base of the workforce and to enhance diffusion (Hulicki, 2008a), (EU policies, 2007). For example, in some countries of the CE region measures have also been taken to improve access for underprivileged groups, the disabled and the elderly (Networked Media of the Future, 2007), and in the whole region for rural, remote, and low-income areas, for reasons of equity and to enhance overall economic efficiency via network effects (World Information Society Report, 2007).

Given the importance of education and its close links to income, the policies to improve digital literacy and build the related skills base in educational institutions can be seen as particularly important over the long term. Besides, the concept of the information divide incorporates also the possibilities of using the technology not only to access information and knowledge, but also a new way of education to take advantage of the "new opportunities," such as the development of business, online medical servicing, telework, and enjoyment of new forms of entertainment and leisure. This aspect is also related to user awareness and technological affinity, which can potentiate such development. When a social group appropriates a technology, it is capable not only of using it to transform its own living conditions, but also transforms the technology itself by means of technological innovation processes with social identity (van Dijk, 2005). Consequently, it seems to be evident that methods and tools for bridging (or to alleviate) the information divide, and development of broadband services should include:

- Novel approaches to increase ICT penetration;
- Clear, consistent policy and legal regulations to create the right competitive environment;
- Segmented service offerings for specific user needs in developing markets that would stimulate the demand for broadband; and
- Innovative pricing schemes and service packages to extend the scope of Web-based *e*-services.

The complexity of the information divide and the possible relationship between the incorporation of the ICTs in social dynamics and the social transformation that it implies are not easy to investigate. However, to solve the problem (at least some of its aspects), it is necessary to know how to measure the information divide.

The digital divide can be measured using the ratio in penetration rates between different groups of economies. The problem is with other aspects of the information divide. Inequality in the distribution of ICTs and Web-based *e*-services can also be analyzed using mathematical techniques, such as Lorenz curve and Gini coefficient (World Information Society Report, 2007). But usage of such techniques does exceed the scope of this article and will be considered in future research.

## CONCLUSION

The chapter addresses some topics concerning the digital divide, mainly in developing countries of CE Europe, and provides a compendium of important underlying concepts and ideas. The new contribution is an insight into a concept of the information divide which can be considered not only as a result produced by the digital, i.e. the technologically-infrastructural divide, but also caused by other factors. Distinction between the digital and the information divide has been clearly specified in the article. Factors that condition the mass–market broadband adoption have been examined, and the impact of the techno-economic stratification for the development of Web-based *e*-services has also been considered, taking into account a problem of missing information, disability to find or access useful information, and barriers resulting from the limited personal interactions.

Although broadband is now available in many countries, it remains at least ten times more expensive in the low-income economies than in the high-income developed countries and is often unavailable outside urban areas. This contribution finds that home broadband adoption is driven by increasing availability of Web-based e-services but there are still many obstacles to be overcome. Using new services, people could improve both their communication skills and usage of knowledge resources which could support dialogue and understanding of interpersonal communication in the digital era. However, it needs conscious person activity and appropriate information-processing capabilities.

The barriers to faster development of broadband in developing countries are manifold and include low purchasing power of the population, unavailable broadband infrastructure in rural areas, immature regulatory environment and digital illiteracy. At the same time, continuous attention must be drawn to psychological obstacles and information overload that could make impossible the inability of users to handle (i.e. process and/or understand) the available information and knowledge. These diverse barriers can result in the techno-economic stratification of people, social groups, regions or countries. Thus, in order to better satisfy user needs and get broadband to the home some effort has to be taken that would make broadband access more diverse and attractive and increase availability of free or cheap access in public institutions, together with ICTs' education, especially to unemployed and/or elderly users. The overall impact of the techno-economic stratification of people is that the new developments in ICTs, networking infrastructure as well as in the availability and affordability of broadband services can fundamentally modify the way people relate among themselves. With only limited access to the information and knowledge, and inability to handle this information and knowledge, some users, social groups or regions (mainly in developing countries) risk being left behind in the new information economy. Though the digital (i.e. technologically-infrastructural) divide is shrinking in most regions, the information divide remains a cause for concern because the gaps are widening.

# REFERENCES

Barbera, M. (2006). Evolution scenaria for broadband services. *Proc. 3rd Forum on BB services.*

Corazza, G. (2008). Who can bridge the information divide? *Proc. UNIC Workshop.*

van Dijk, J. (2005). From digital divide to social opportunities. *Proc. 2nd Int'l Conf. for Bridging the Digital Divide.*

Ginesi, A. (2008). ESA initiatives on the digital divide. *Proc. UNIC Workshop.*

Gupta, M. (2006). User needs for broadband in Europe. *Proc. BReATH Conf.*

Horrigan, J.B. (2008). *Home broadband adoption 2008.* PEW/Internet Project Report.

Hulicki, Z. (2016). Telecommunications in Poland. Infrastructure, market and services. *Australian Journal of Telecommunications and the Digital Economy, 4*(3).

Hulicki, Z. (2008a). Drives and barriers for development of broadband access. In Proc. Summer School TSIofTNE. University of Alcala.

Hulicki, Z. (2008b). Digital divide – a myth or real challenges. In *Proc. EuroFGI workshop on socio-economic aspects of FGI.* BTH.

Kotlarski, M. (2006). Effects of the telecom market regulations. *Proc. 3rd Forum on BB services.*

Kuchar, A. (2006). Broadband development in the Czech and Slovak Republics. *Proc. BReATH Conf.*

Luise, M. (2008). EC initiatives on the digital divide and satellite fields. *Proc. UNIC Workshop.*

Mathea, K. (2006). Broadband access and integrated services. *Proc. 3rd Forum on BB services.*

Marine, S., & Blanchard, J-M. (2004). Bridging the digital divide: an opportunity for growth in the 21st century. *Alcatel Telecommun. Rev.*.

Skowroński, R. (2006). Broadband everywhere. *Proc. 3rd Forum on BB services.*

EU policies. (2007). *Bridging the 'digital divide': EU policies.* Retrieved from http://www.euractiv.com/en/infosociety/bridging-digital-divide-eu-policies/article-132315

Report, E. E. (2010). *Bridging the digital divide – Internet access in Central and Eastern Europe.* Retrieved from http://www.cdt.org/international/ceeaccess/eereport.pdf

World Information Society Report 2007. (2007). Retrieved from http://www.itu.int/osg/spu/publications/worldinformationsociety/2007/WISR07

Networked Media of the Future. (2007). *EC NM-TF Report. DG IS&M.* October. Retrieved from http://ec.europaeut/dgs/information_society/text_en.htm

A Digital Agenda for Europe. (2010). *COM(2010) 245.* Retrieved from http://ec.europa.eu/information_society/digital-agenda/documents/digital-agenda-communication-en.pdf

The State of Broadband 2016: Broadband Catalyzing Sustainable Development. (2016). Retrieved from http://broadbandcommission.org/Documents/reports/bb-annualreport2016.pdf

# Chapter 3
# Social Media:
## A Threat to Mental Health or an Opportunity to Communicate?

**Elham Mohammadi**
*University of Zanjan, Iran*

**Azam Masoumi**
*University of Zanjan, Iran*

## ABSTRACT

*This chapter examines the path of human interaction by using modern technologies. There are two sides: those in favor of using modern technologies and those who argue that modern technologies have unwanted, detrimental effects on people's lives and health. This chapter explores virtual communication's properties. It focuses on the impact that using social media instead of face-to-face interaction has on the users' health, specifically mental health. In this viewpoint, social media is not an alternative to face-to-face interaction but a complementary device that reminds us the vitality of interaction even with those who are physically unavailable to us.*

DOI: 10.4018/978-1-5225-4168-4.ch003

# INTRODUCTION

Technology marches on. As it progresses, it changes all aspects of human life, from individual thoughts, beliefs, and even personalities, to relationships in society as a whole. Progress is inevitable since movement and change bestow meaning to life. Question is "Where does technology lead us?"

Religion and science present different outlooks on using new technologies. John William Draper (1875) traces the age-old conflict between religion and science back to more than two thousand years by suggesting that "an antagonism between religion and science had existed from the earliest days of Christianity." On one hand, some religious beliefs regard new technologies as the sign of apocalypse, as Satan's favored devices, which are used for evil purposes to corrupt human soul. On the other hand, scientific perspective considers them efflorescence of humanity for experiencing more comfortable life, providing equality and fairness by making new technologies available to all social classes, spreading and improving social and cultural knowledge which can lead to the higher level of human right and democracy status, and serving creative and spiritual growth.

The other concern over the consequences of widespread technologies is ethical. Habermas (2003) presents serious debates about genetic engineering in his book "The Future of Human Nature." He discusses the controversial essence of human engineering and says:

*Eugenic programing of desirable traits and dispositions, however, gives rise to moral misgivings as soon as it commits the person concerned to a specific life-project or, in any case, puts specific restrictions on his freedom to choose a life of his own.*

Some countries are home to conservative cultures, which desperately try to prevent people from using social media, mainly because closed communities are not in favor of adapting new thoughts and attitudes from other cultures. Instead of global social networks, some countries, particularly communist ones, have developed exclusive and internal social media services with closely monitored systems. Still, many government and public services are supplied though social media. Given this, governments are not able to completely restrict the use of social media; they themselves try to use it in order to monitor their effects on their people.

Nowadays, social media make the world truly a global village. Most people who have access to the Internet find it compelling to use social media in order to satisfy a wide range of needs, from contacting their families to submitting their work and reading or watching the daily news. According to www.internetworldstats.com, on

31 Dec 2016 the number of people who have access to the Internet is 3,696,238,430. In other words, almost half of the world's population uses the Internet, which is an indication of the widespread use of social media. Using social media and exploring its relationship with different aspects of people's lives has been the target of many studies. In this chapter, the authors will try to focus on the relationship between using social media instead of face-to-face interaction and mental health.

## BACKGROUND

Virtual communication has its advocates and opponents just like any other hi-tech endeavor. Some people are against the use of social media and believe that they overload users with unimportant information and waste their time. Qualman (2009) claims that such people have not understood what social media is about, and social media users do not concern themselves with these trivial objections. Users, in fact, customize the settings of their devices to be notified of new messages. They can also turn off notifications and avoid the addictive behavior of responding to all messages instantly. Qualman maintains that it is a fundamental misunderstanding if somebody thinks that staying connected with others in social media via casual observation is a waste of time. He says, "Wasting time on Facebook and social media actually makes you more productive." He uses the example of checking on updates from social media while standing in a checkout lane in a supermarket instead of being impatient and anxious. Obviously, Qualman is a sincere advocate of social media, and many scholars, such as Dan Heath (New York Times Best Selling Author of *Made*), Dr. Stuart Levy (Professor, George Washington University), Jane Wooldridge (Award-winning journalist, The Miami Herald), and many others have praised his attitudes about social media.

On its website, the Wall Street Journal (2015) presents distinct opinions of two university professors in the form of an argumentative essay. The professors ask, "Does technology connect or disconnect us? Is technology making people less sociable?" The Wall Street Journal reports that:

*Larry Rosen, a professor of psychology at California State University, Dominguez Hills, says technology is distracting us from our real-world relationships, while Keith N. Hampton, who holds the Professorship in Communication and Public Policy at Rutgers University's School of Communication and Information, argues that technology is enriching those relationships and the rest of our social lives.*

A study about Turkish university students (Darcin, Noyan, Nurmedov, Yilmaz, and Dilbaz, 2016) introduced two factors responsible for addictive behavior towards using smartphones. The first factor is ownership and usage of a smartphone at an early age, and the second factor is perception of access to social network sites as the sole and primary purpose of using smartphones. The findings also propose that social phobia, regardless of the users' gender, and loneliness, particularly in females, put smartphone users in a more susceptible position, propelling them to more addictive usage of smartphones.

Another study focusing on 187 Malaysian mobile phone users (Lee, Tam, and Chie, 2013) represents some significant findings with regard to the openness-to-experience personality dimension, loneliness, and social anxiety. Becker, Alzahabi, and Hopwood (2013) studied the effects of media multitasking on 318 participants and claimed, "The unique association between media multitasking and the measures of psychosocial dysfunction suggests that the growing trend of multitasking with media may represent a unique risk factor for mental health problems related to mood and anxiety."

However, some empirical evidence uncovers the benefits of using social media such as improving the quality of life. For example, a study conducted by Samleo, et al. (2014) demonstrates that it is possible to provide "assistive navigation using wearable sensors and social sensors to foster situational awareness for the blind; the system acquires social media messages to gauge the relevant aspects of an event and to create alerts." Another study unfolds the benefits of embedded social media channels on hotel websites and how this enhances travelers' social gratifications of perceived social interaction (Aluri, Slevitch, and Larzelere, 2015, p. 670). In case of mental and E-mental health, one study (Martin, et al., 2011) asserts that networked communication technologies have the potential to facilitate communication between patient and health care professionals and also function as a useful addition to mental health service delivery. However, this study acknowledges that the impact and effectiveness of these technologies is inconclusive. The findings of another study (Dingwall, Puszka, Sweet, and Nagel, 2015) refer to the possibility of using e-mental health interventions to assist services in delivering evidence-based, structured interventions to improve well-being of Aboriginal and Torres Strait Islanders.

## MAIN FOCUS OF THE CHAPTER

## The Human as a Social Being and Different Types of Communication

Most of philosophers, psychologists and sociologists, from Aristotle to Marx and Hegel, believe that humans are innately social and need social interaction to maintain their physical and mental health. Humans identify themselves in communities and in company with others of their kind. How is it possible for an individual to define himself or herself while he or she lives in solitary? Aren't personality traits discoverable as a result of comparison with different characteristics of other people? In fact, humans' personality is shaped and influenced through interaction with others in society, and on a smaller scale, in the family as the nucleus of communities. It does not seem wrong to say that people's connections and relationships with others give them the motivation to move forward and accomplish what they desire and to gain a better position in society. For some though, it may cause the reverse and make them lonely and depressed. There is no doubt that people's relationships have tremendous effects on their lives, as friendship with the affluent can ease social mobility, and companionship with those involved in crime can lead an otherwise law-abiding citizen to take actions that land him or her in jail. There are many Persian proverbs about the importance of people's relationships. For instance, one says, "Tell me who your friends are, so I will tell you who you are." Another says, "If you keep a donkey and an Arabic horse together in the same stable, they won't become the same color, but they will adapt to each other's personalities." Similar sayings can be found in different languages as well.

The society and its dominant culture affect all aspects of life, including attitudes, beliefs, and life path as a whole. It is the society which determines the possible future of its children: who they can be, and who they cannot, according to the cultural, religious, and political rules and restrictions. Growing up in poverty and poor culture can prevent children from following their dreams and in result they may abandon their ambitions. The theory of cultural disadvantage suggests that children from lower social and economic backgrounds cannot perform as well as other children at school (Richards and Schmidt, 2010).

Tajfel and Turner (2004) postulate that a person's sense of self depends on the groups to which they belong. From the social-psychological perspective, Taifel and Turner argue that the necessary criteria of group membership potentially applicable to large-scale social categories are that the individuals involved define themselves and are defined by others as members of a group.

Thanks to technology, human communication has been dramatically simplified. Once, telegraphs and telephones were considered miracles. Today, using email and cellphones is ordinary. Throughout history, many human activities have involved communication with others, from painting on cave walls to different schools of contemporary painting, from the creating of writing to calligraphy, from making sound by hitting a stretched animal skin to composing symphonies. Among all types of communication, it seems that face-to-face interaction is the most satisfying way of communication because it includes all aspects of humans' sense of connection: language by sound, intonation, body language, facial gestures, and even physical contact, such as shaking hands and embracing each other. Face-to-face interaction is more than just verbal behavior; as Philip Riley (1979) maintains, "The meaning of face-to-face interaction is an amalgam of information from many channels and, in particular, the discourse structure is mainly marked non-verbally." Communication by texting on phones and computers lacks all of these aspects. Compared to speaking on the phone or writing a letter, it lies in a weaker position. Speaking on the phone has a greater value in communication, of course, after face-to-face interaction, for it transfers more information than a text by revealing emotions through specific intonation and direct interaction by turn-taking methods. Even uploading sound in social media can't replace speaking on the phone since there would be pauses in the interaction, or it can be totally unilateral. The next level belongs to writing a letter by hand, which has at least one dimension more than texting on phones, and that is the handwriting, which can reveal the writer's emotions and transfer a special feeling to the reader. The smell and texture of the paper can also serve this purpose. Finally, texting lacks most of face-to-face communication's properties. In order to satisfy users' needs to transfer their feelings better while using social media, many emoticons have been created, such as happy, angry, and surprised faces as well as many other signs to fulfill such needs. All efforts in providing visual contact through social media can be interpreted as the acceptance of face-to-face communication's superiority.

Rogers, Sharp, and Preece (2015) assert that in order to conquer the constraints of online chatting and texting through social media, interlocutors have developed and evolved some new forms of expressions, such as shorthand, abbreviations, emoticons, and emojis as compensatory tools. Emoticons consist of humorous facial gestures and smileys which became popular after people began using ASCII symbols in emails', sometimes sideways. Emojis are sets of tiny and culture-specific pictures, first were created by Shigetaka Kurita in 1995.

## The Importance of Social Interaction and Expressing Emotions

Social interaction is the direct consequence of being a social creature. The prevalence of new ideas about Individualism may convince some thinkers that humans only lived together in ancient eras in order to survive and overcome nature. However, the continuation of cohabitation has met a wider range of humans' needs, from physical ones to mental and spiritual ones. Interaction with family members is the forepart of preparation to establish good relationships in society. One of the most essential means of being successful in school, work, marriage, and more is the art of making friends and communicating effectively. People's ability to form successful relationships determines their position in society. Besides, it is vital to wisely decide on suitable friends. Another central issue is to decide on the best manner of interaction in different situations. Taking all aspects of each situation into account helps people interact more fruitfully. For instance, in formal occasions wearing appropriate attire and using proper speech and intonation will make the interaction more effective. Social interaction can give people a sense of belonging and motivate them to be more productive.

Throughout the history of humanity, no quick, significant development has occurred in isolation. Conservative communities which are thousands of years old containing hundreds of generations who have experienced and performed relatively the same traditions and rituals have corroborated this claim. In a similar way, it is more probable that isolated minds get stuck in a closed circuit of limited data resources and restricted possible paths of thinking, which may lead to staying in the same position of their ancestors. The examples of such communities in the contemporary world are primitive Indian, African, and Australian tribes. It seems that in these communities, the interaction and transaction of thoughts are confined to the members of those communities who are imprisoned by age-old binds to follow their antecedent's outlooks, and such outlooks are introduced as holy beliefs that no one is allowed to question. Who dares to fight against a God's wish in front of its worshippers?

The rate of development in conservative communities is much slower than communities that are open to new ideas and thoughts. This is the kind of difference that has made North and South Korea dramatically distinct. Of course, this doesn't mean that conservative communities don't experience any kind of development but making changes in their lifestyle is more difficult. While expanding the relationships is one of the major concerns of developed countries for commercial, educational, political, and economic purposes, conservative communities try to avoid the consequences of cultural invasion at the expense of being deprived of the positive outcomes of external communication. Of course, the seemingly apparent and hidden reasons for such resistance and fear need to be investigated before making any assertions.

The infecundity of isolated communities is so widely accepted that some people generalize it to the whole human species and prefer to attribute the magnificent accomplishments to some mysterious generous extraterrestrials who might have visited humans' forefathers. Among them is Erich von Däniken, who has written two books *Chariot of the Gods: Unsolved Mysteries of the Past* (1972) and *In Search of Ancient Gods* (1984). The ancient myth of Prometheus, a Greek god who loved humans so much that he stole fire from heaven and granted it to humans, is further evidence of such belief.

From individual perspective, even creation and imagination of isolated minds might fall in the whirlpool of repetition and erosion without receiving feedback from others. A human being mostly receives information from the world outside of his or her *noumenon*. One learns to love and hate, to respond and ignore, and to create and destroy both as the result of the outside world and through interaction with it. The authors reckon that in each human activity, there is at least one interaction that happens between human on one side and all other entities and phenomena on the other side. We interact with ourselves, including our conscience and corporeality, as well as other external stimuli which have surrounded us, including nature, culture, and society. Yet, what makes our thoughts productive and fruitful is the interaction with people and phenomena which broaden our horizons and usher in spiritual elevation and prosperity. Indeed, social interaction is one of the indispensable components of a prosperous and successful society.

As matters of life and death reveal the critical importance of something, it is interesting that a meta-analytic review of loneliness (Holt-Lunstad, Smith, and Layton, 2010) implies that "the quality and quantity of individuals' social relationships has been linked not only to mental health but also to both morbidity and mortality." This study concludes that "social relationships on risk for mortality is comparable with well-established risk factors for mortality." In another study, Hawkley and Cacioppo (2010) explain that social isolation is realized not because of being single, living alone, or residing in a remote place but as an individual's inability to start, maintain, and expand connections and relationships in society. This study defines loneliness as chronic perceived isolation, which causes deficiencies in the processes of attention, cognition, and reaction. Loneliness is highly detrimental to health through affecting the genetic, neural, and hormonal mechanisms of the body, which eventually leads one to sickness and death.

One of the main purposes of communication, which is vital for human mental health, is to share one's feelings and emotions with others. Recently, a special inclination towards the importance of human emotions can be seen in Hollywood's products, which is an obvious attempt to praise and valorize emotions. Many science fiction and fantasy animations, movies, and serials such as 9, Matrix, V, Under the Dome, Avengers, The 100, and Fringe portray the encounter between humans and emotionless aliens or hi-tech robots created by humans. These invaders are characterized as mechanical, soulless creatures who regard human emotions as the blind spot and try to overcome humanity by hurting their feelings and predicting their next moves. In the meantime, through a splendid story, which is full of excitement and suspense, the producers introduce human emotions as the most powerful source of strength and motivation which give humans the required incentive to conquer their enemies. Such insistence on the value of feelings and emotions, intentional or unintentional, encourages people to maintain and improve their emotional and, consequently, mental health while living in the era of revolutionary technology and virtual communication, which can be considered a threat to face-to-face interaction. The advertency and emphasis on the importance of emotions can be seen in all other genres, as if there is a universal attempt to remind people that their feelings are the essential properties of humanity, and people need to let their despair, anger, fear, and love be verbalized. It can be claimed that people's need to speak about their emotions is one of the most powerful motives for communication. Face-to-face interaction increases the sense of sympathy and brings people closer together by providing the chance of direct social intercourse. Speaking about feelings, in general, is of great benefit to human health. Based on this literature, the authors believe that psychiatrists who adopt the same approach in their therapy sessions substantiate the truthfulness of this assertion.

## WHAT IS HEALTH?

### Definition

Merriam Webster's definition of health is: "(a) the condition of being sound in body, mind, or spirit, (b) the general condition of the body, (c) a condition in which someone or something is thriving or doing well, which is equal to well-being."

The online encyclopedia introduces three types of health: physical, mental, and social. Experts and ordinary people give different definitions of health based on the situation.

## Classification of Health

### Physical Health

An online dictionary has defined physical health as the following:

*Physical health is essential to the complete health of an individual; this includes everything from overall well-being to physical fitness. It can also be defined as a state of physical well-being in which the individual is able to perform daily activities without problems. Physical health is achieved by maintaining fitness and health through exercise and proper nourishment. Having good physical health improves an individual's overall health and reduces the chance of becoming sick. It also helps in faster recovery when an individual has been unwell. Out of physical, emotional, social, intellectual, spiritual and environmental health, physical health is the most visible. (www.reference.com)*

Scholars have introduced some components of physical health, for instance, Koshuta (2017) in his lesson transcript on www.study.com, asserts five components:

*Physical activity, which includes strength, flexibility, and endurance; nutrition and diet, which includes nutrient intake, fluid intake, and healthy digestion; alcohol and drugs, which includes the abstinence from or reduced consumption of these substances; medical self-care, which includes addressing minor ailments or injuries and seeking emergency care as necessary; and rest and sleep, which includes periodic rest and relaxation, along with high quality sleep. (www.study.com)*

### Mental Health

Merriam Webster Dictionary defines mental health as "(a) the condition of being sound mentally and emotionally that is characterized by the absence of mental illness and by adequate adjustment especially as reflected in feeling comfortable about oneself, positive feelings about others, and the ability to meet the demands of daily life, (b) the general condition of one's mental and emotional state."

### E-Mental Health

Before defining E-mental health, there is a need to define E-health which is a relatively recent term for healthcare practice supported by electronic processes and communication (Wikipedia E-health, 2017). Its exact definition largely depends on the situation and the field of study.

E-mental health refers to the interventions and support for mental health conditions by using the internet (Bennett, Reynolds, Christensen, and Griffiths, 2010). There is a thorough definition which is provided below:

*The use of information and communication technology (ICT) – in particular the many technologies related to the Internet – when these technologies are used to support and improve mental health conditions and mental health care, including care for people with substance use and comorbid disorders. E-mental health encompasses the use of digital technologies and new media for the delivery of screening, health promotion, prevention, early intervention, treatment or relapse prevention as well as for improvement of health care delivery (e.g., electronic patient files), professional education (e-learning), and online research in the field of mental health. (Riper, et al., qtd. in Schmidt and Wykes, 2012)*

## Social Health

Social health refers to the features of a society as well as of individuals:

*A society is healthy when there is equal opportunity for all and access by all to the goods and services essential to full functioning as a citizen; the social health of individuals refers to that dimension of an individual's well-being that concerns how he gets along with other people, how other people react to him, and how he interacts with social institutions and societal mores. (Russell, 1973)*

Russell goes on to say that developing social skills is important because it can improve your relationships with others and help you make friends; it also can help you succeed in your career and experience an independent life.

## Virtual Communication's Characteristics and Effects on Users

It is completely understandable that people use their phones or computers to contact their relatives who live far from them, but what makes them do the same with people who live nearby? Is it because it satisfies their sense of individualism or merely because of laziness? Some believe that humans' indolence is the source of many inventions, such as the washing machine and remote controls for televisions. Of course, the bright side is that by inventing new machines and technologies, which provide a more convenient life, humans have more time to flourish and improve their other capabilities. Nevertheless, the habit of using social media inappropriately can be very destructive and harmful to both physical and mental health. Depending on the way we use them, they can bring us both advantages and disadvantages. Using social media can make us feel happier and more connected in a short time, but very soon we feel lonely as if we partook in an artificial communication. Any kinds of communications can meet humans' hunger for being loved and give them a sense of belonging, but not as satisfactory as face-to-face interaction. Social media can amuse us perfectly, but very soon we may realize that we are addicted to it to such an extent that we spend most of our free time or sometimes our work time using it. This, in turn, leads us to dramatically lose our productivity, which finally gives us the sense of being a failure. Social media provides us with daily news and enormous amounts of information about everything that one can imagine, but it also exposes us to misinformation, false rumors, and biased news. Social media is the best device for sharing emotions, experiences, and information. It is a wonderful platform that presents a chance to spread opinions and attitudes through an incredibly huge virtual world, but also makes us susceptible to criminals who use our personal information against us. Using social networks increases the risk of invasion of privacy and puts pressure on our minds by generating stress. The other amusing feature of social media is the possibility of hiding identity and speaking freely. For people who lack enough self-confidence to share their opinions with others, this feature is a wonderful gift. However, just like many other characteristics of social media, the ability to remain anonymous gives criminals a huge scope to deceive people as well. Not being sure about the real identity of people with whom one wants to make friends can cause stress and a sense of unreliability.

Another noticeable phenomenon is the Internet meme. Patrick Davison (2012) defines it as "a piece of culture, typically a joke, which gains influence through online transmission." According to Davison, rapidity and fidelity of form are the unique properties of Internet memes. He compares them to offline jokes, saying, "The speed of transmission is no longer limited by the movement of individuals, and the form of the joke is preserved by a medium, not memory." He also quotes from Richard Dawkins (1979), who coined the term "meme," that "much of human behavior comes not from genes but from culture (cited in Davison, 2012).

Outdated forms of communication include the town crier, estafette, and carrier pigeon. Compared to these modes, newer forms of communication such as special postal services, social media, and mobile and personal computers provide easy, quick and safe delivery of messages. These features make social media an influential device for instructional, investigational, commercial, cultural, and political issues, from distance learning and teleconferencing to introducing a new brand and propounding ethical and/or philosophical ideas.

Political usage of social media has lately received special attention. The recent virtual estimation of the 2016 United States presidential election and President Trump's messages on Twitter show how influential it can be. It is the most recent instance of a president using such an opportunity to contact his or her nation directly, in the absence of any news anchor or correspondent. Social media has eliminated the age-old distance and hindrance between leaders and followers, which mutually helps people better know their assignee, and assists the leader in fulfilling the people's wishes.

## Social Media and Mental Health

Basically, the goal of each interaction among people is the transaction of emotion and/or information. Although social media's amusing and fascinating properties can be so attractive that make people feel addicted to it" instead of " attractive that and people feel addicted, it would be naive to assume that social media makes people mentally ill. Among all kinds of mental disorders, researchers have focused on the sense of loneliness and depression and their relationship with using social media. However, none of them indicates that using social media causes mental disorders. It is more probable that people who are alone or depressed dedicate more time to using social media for consolation. They may use social media to fill their empty life, and it can be a great relief. Finally, they become addicted to it, which leads them to a deeper immersion in their undesired condition. The result of a study performed by Caplan (2003) indicated that "psychosocial health predicted levels of preference for online social interaction, which, in turn, predicted negative outcomes associated with problematic Internet use." However, it cannot be concluded that using social media makes people feel lonely or depressed. It can be misunderstood by people who tend to view this relationship as bilateral.

Being mentally healthy, in part, emanates from experiencing a good social life. A good social life can be defined as having the sense of belonging and receiving support, spiritually and materially, from the society a person is living in. Patulny and Seaman (2016) suggested that in spite of declining face-to-face communication and increasing mediated contact through phone and computer among Australians between 2002 and 2010, the perceived social support was not reduced.

A positive link between Internet use and mental health has been found among older adults by Forsman and Nordmyr (2017). They identified "(a) enhanced interpersonal interaction at individual level, (b) increased access to resources within the community, and (c) empowered social inclusion at society level as the psychosocial impacts of Internet use in later life.

A study done by the Youth Research Centre at the University of Melbourne introduces three social and economic criteria for mental health: social inclusion, freedom from discrimination, and access to economic resources (Wyn, Cuervo, Woodman and Stokes, 2005). This study finds information and communication technologies (ICTs) as provider of social inclusion, contributor to freedom from discrimination, and facilitator to access economic resources. It seems that social media is a perfect supplement for social and economic equality by providing unbiased and impartial accessibility to data resources.

Recently, social media has become a platform for some social movements, causing controversies. People with distinct attitudes call them ethical and moral disclosure, while others consider them to be immoral and destructive conspiracy. Nowadays, thanks to the Internet and mobiles equipped with video cameras, people can protect their social and human rights by recording and spreading footage of scenes that reveal political and/or financial scandals. Sometimes divulging the offending activities of people who are in charge results in public chaos and damages people's tranquility. Nevertheless, most people prefer to know the truth rather than live in mock serenity.

Even people who are opposed to the development of modern technologies in general, and social media in particular try to spread their voices through the same instrument as if they have found out that the world wouldn't stop until they change their minds. It is a curious paradox that even opponents have to utilize the same thing that they disagree with.

A very useful application of social media is telepsychiatry. McGinty, Saeed, Simmons, and Yildirim (2006) refer to the ease of accessibility to mental health care in rural, remote, and under-served areas due to telepsychiatry and e-mental health services. They further elaborate on some impediments to the extensive use of these services that need to be overcome:

*Although telepsychiatry and e-mental health offer a tremendous promise, implementation has been neither widespread nor easy to achieve. Several potential barriers to the diffusion of telepsychiatry and e-mental health have been identified. Some of the barriers are associated with the acceptance of any new technology and practice in health care. Usual impediments include cost issues, resistance to change by individuals or organizations, and technological illiteracy.*

A study under the title of *Understanding the acceptability of e-mental health - attitudes and expectations towards computerised self-help treatments for mental health problems,* (Musiat, Goldstone, and Tarrier, 2014), which was performed on 490 participants, indicates that although people know the benefits of computerized interventions and e-mental health services, such as saving time and easy access, they tend to neglect such assets. It is highly recommended that all information about e-mental health services, its various treatment options, and the merits of using them become available to people in order to enable them to take advantage of e-mental health knowledgeably.

Several studies have attested to the effectiveness and advantages of utilizing e-mental health services. Thewissen and Gunther (2015) propound that meta-analyses have repeatedly indicated the relevance of online cognitive behavior therapy (CBT) to significant reductions of measured symptoms of depression, panic disorder, and social phobia in adults.

Nonetheless, the findings of some studies like the one by Feng and Campbell (2011) reveal barriers that exist in the current methods of employing e-mental health services. In this study, the researchers demonstrate that adolescents do not often attempt to search for e-mental health resources since they are not aware of the existence of such services and information. To make the case even more complicated, searching for online help is less probable on the part of neurotic adolescents suffering from more serious conditions.

To signalize further advantages of computerized cognitive behavior therapy (cCBT) interventions in comparison with traditional delivery platforms, Musiat and Tarrier (2014) review, in a systematic way, the evidence of the cost-effectiveness, geographic flexibility, time flexibility, waiting time for treatment, stigma, therapist time, effects on help-seeking, and treatment satisfaction of cCBT interventions for mental health. The findings of this review are in line with cCBT's potential of all these added benefits. However, it is in need of "more investigation in the context of a large-scale implementation. As more evidence is corroborating the efficacy of e-mental health, future investigations, in addition to identifying the added benefits, should concentrate on the working mechanisms of these interventions."

## SOLUTIONS AND RECOMMENDATIONS

Nowadays, billions of people own computers, mobile phones, and tablets. A large proportion of them, excluding offices and companies, uses these technologies not exclusively to create, discover, produce, or research something, but to enjoy and entertain themselves. These technologies are advertised in a way that leads to commercial success, as can be witnessed in many communities where they function as toys in children's hands. Parents compete with each other to buy the most recent version of modern technologies for their children. They attempt to create the best setting for their children to thrive, neglecting the incongruity between the children's needs and such technologies. To make a long story short, there is an urgent need to inform people of how to manage their use of technologies, and specifically social media. When people buy a refrigerator, a washing machine, or even a fan, they receive an instructional paper containing the warning section, and other guidelines about their most appropriate usage. In many cases, governments attempt to improve the user's understanding of the product by broadcasting instructional programs through mass media, such as taking the precaution of installing gas-fired heaters. The operating systems of modern technologies are so user-friendly that most people don't have to attend professional courses to learn how to use them, let alone receive any complementary instruction about the consequences and impacts of using them. In fact, many people learn to operate modern technologies by trial and error, which can be a challenging and unpleasant experience.

Interestingly, software developers have produced some monitoring programs in the form of different hi-tech devices that enable parents to supervise their children's Internet usage. It is expected that adults also be engaged in self-monitoring systems in order to manage their own use of these technologies. Governmental organizations and NGOs are supposed to present illuminating information about all aspects of using technologies.

## FUTURE RESEARCH DIRECTIONS

Few studies, to date, have investigated the causal relationship between virtual communication and mental health. According to geneticists, there are many sleeping genes in the human body that are stimulated by specific chemicals. Until the special chemical have been produced or come into the body, the gene remains inactive. It does not mean that those chemicals cause the related genes, but only activate them. Does social media act as similarly to such chemicals, exacerbating the already existing mental disorders or does it create them in the first place?

Seeking answers to the following questions is also crucial: Can interaction via social media be used as remedial mental health therapy? What if the habit of using social media could present a hint to psychologists in diagnosing mental disorders? Could the time spent on social media and sending digital messages reveal any aspects of one's characteristics?

# CONCLUSION

There is no doubt that virtual communication through social networks cannot replace face-to-face interaction. However, using social networks to communicate is inevitable. After all, no one can deny social media's value with regard to the convenience that it has granted us.

In religious communities, it is argued that social media has made it easier to access unethical and immoral products, such as porn movies or brutal pictures, which are detrimental to people's virtue and mental health, which is a major source of concern for teenagers. It is also argued that criminals use social networks to more easily and quickly pursue their dishonest, illegal objectives. Such reasoning is similar to the suggestion of keeping people in prisons in order to prevent them from committing a crime! In fact, people who want to have a healthy, peaceful, and modest life try to make most of whatever is available, and those who want to follow their brutal, hateful desires will do the same; the instrument is the same, but purposes are different. People are responsible for their own choices. It would be a big mistake to blame social media for people's woes. Social media, like all other kinds of inventions, is about making life more convenient by providing faster and less expensive access to information and communication. It is up to people to decide on what they want to access, whether it is a porn movies and violent images, or a constructive, scientific data.

In the end, it depends on each individual to decide how to use social media and how much time to spend on it. It is highly suggested that everybody does some research about social media's benefits and damages before starting to use them.

# REFERENCES

Aluri, A., Slevitch, L., & Larzelere, R. (2015). The effectiveness of embedded social media on hotel websites and the importance of social interactions and return on engagement. *International Journal of Contemporary Hospitality Management*, *27*(4), 670–689. doi:10.1108/IJCHM-09-2013-0415

Becker, M. W., Alzahabi, R., & Hopwood, C. J. (2013). Media multitasking is associated with symptoms of depression and social anxiety. *Cyberpsychology, Behavior, and Social Networking*, *16*(2), 132–135. doi:10.1089/cyber.2012.0291 PMID:23126438

Bennett, K., Reynolds, J., Christensen, H., & Griffiths, K. M. (2010). E-hub: An online self-help mental health service in the community. *The Medical Journal of Australia*, *192*(11), 48–52. PMID:20528710

Caplan, S. E. (2003). Preference for online social interaction: A theory of problematic internet use and psychosocial well-being. *Communication Research*, *30*(6), 625–648. doi:10.1177/0093650203257842

Darcin, A. E., Noyan, C., Nurmedov, S., Yilmaz, O., & Dilbaz, N. (2016). Smartphone addiction in relation with social anxiety and loneliness among university students in Turkey. *Behaviour & Information Technology*, *35*(7), 520–525. doi:10.1080/01 44929X.2016.1158319

Davison, P. (2012). The language of internet memes. In M. Mandiberg (Ed.), *The social media reader* (pp. 120–134). New York University Press.

Dingwall, K., Puszka, S., Sweet, M., & Tricia Nagel, T. (2015). Like drawing into sand: Acceptability, feasibility, and appropriateness of a new e-mental health resource for service providers working with Aboriginal and Torres Strait Islander people. *Australian Psychologist*, *50*(1), 60–69. doi:10.1111/ap.12100

Draper, J. W. (1875). *History of the conflict between religion and science* (Vol. 13). New York: D. Appleton.

Feng, X. L., & Campbell, A. (2011). Understanding e-mental health resources: Personality, awareness, utilization, and effectiveness of e-mental health resources amongst youth. *Journal of Technology in Human Services, 29*, 101–119. doi:10.1 080/15228835.2011.595276

Forsman, A. K., & Nordmyr, J. (2017). Psychosocial links between internet use and mental health in later life: A systematic review of quantitative and qualitative evidence. *Journal of Applied Gerontology, 36*(12), 1471–1518. doi:10.1177/0733464815595509 PMID:26245208

Habermas, J. (2003). *The future of human nature*. Cambridge, UK: Polity Press.

Hawkley, L. C., & Cacioppo, J. T. (2010). Loneliness matters: A theoretical and empirical review of consequences and mechanisms. *Annals of Behavioral Medicine, 40*(2), . 10.1007/s12160–010–9210–8

Holt-Lunstad, J., Smith, T. B., & Layton, J. B. (2010). Social relationships and mortality risk: A meta-analytic review. *PLoS Medicine, 7*(7), e1000316. doi:10.1371/journal.pmed.1000316 PMID:20668659

Koshuta, J. (2017). *What is physical health?* Retrieved June 2, 2017, from www.study.com

Lee, S., Tam, C. L., & Chie, Q. T. (2013). *Mobile phone usage preferences: the contributing factors of personality, social anxiety and loneliness*. Springer. doi:10.100711205-013-0460-2

Martin, S., Sutcliffe, P., Griffiths, F., Sturt, J., Powell, J., Adams, A., & Dale, J. (2011). Effectiveness and impact of networked communication interventions in young people with mental health conditions: A systematic review. *Patient Education and Counseling, 85*(2), e108–e119. doi:10.1016/j.pec.2010.11.014 PMID:21239133

McGinty, K. L., Saeed, S. A., Simmons, S. C., & Yildirim, Y. (2006). Telepsychiatry and e-mental health services: Potential for improving access to mental health care. *The Psychiatric Quarterly, 77*(4), 335–342. doi:10.100711126-006-9019-6 PMID:16927161

Merriam Webster Dictionary. (n.d.). Retrieved May 18, 2017, from https://www.merriam-webster.com

Musiat, P., Goldstone, P., & Tarrier, N. (2014). Understanding the acceptability of e-mental health-attitudes and expectations towards computerized self-help treatments for mental health problems. *BMC Psychiatry, 14*(1). Retrieved 26 May 2017, from http://www.biomedcentral.com/1471-244X/14/109

Musiat, P., & Tarrier, N. (2014). *Collateral outcomes in e-mental health: A systematic review of the evidence for added benefits of computerized cognitive behavior therapy interventions for mental health. Psychological Medicine, 44, 3137–3150.* doi:10.1017/S0033291714000245

Patulny, R., & Seaman, C. (2016). 'I'll just text you': Is face-to-face social contact declining in a mediated world? *Journal of Sociology.* doi: 1440783316674358

Qualman, E. (2009). *Socialnomics: How social media transforms the way we live and do business.* Hoboken, NJ: John Wiley & Sons.

Richards, J. C., & Schmidt, R. (2010). *Longman dictionary of language teaching and applied linguistics.* Pearson Education Limited.

Riley, P. (1979). Towards a contrastive pragmalinguistics. In J. Fisiak (Ed.), *Contrastive linguistics and the language teacher* (pp. 121–146). Oxford, UK: Pergamon Press Ltd.

Riper, H., Andersson, G., Christensen, H., Cuijpers, P., Lange, A., & Eysenbach, G. (2010). Theme issue on e-mental health: A growing field in Internet research. *Journal of Medical Internet Research, 12*(5), e74. doi:10.2196/jmir.1713 PMID:21169177

Rogers, Y., Sharp, H., & Preece, J. (2015). *Interaction design: Beyond human-computer interaction.* John Wiley & Sons.

Russell, R. D. (1973). Social health: An attempt to clarify this dimension of well-being. *International Journal of Health Education, 16,* 74–82.

Samleo, L., Xiao, J., Zhang, X., Chawda, B., Narang, K., Rajput, N., ... Subramaniam, V. (2014). Being aware of the world: Toward using social media to support the blind with navigation. *IEEE Transactions on Human-Machine Systems*. doi:10.1109/THMS.2014.2382582

Schmidt, U., & Wykes, T. (2012). E-mental health: A land of unlimited possibilities. *Journal of Mental Health (Abingdon, England)*, *21*(4), 327–331. doi:10.3109/0963 8237.2012.705930 PMID:22823092

Tajfel, H., & Turner, J. C. (2004). The social identity theory of intergroup behavior. *Political Psychology*, 276–293.

The Wall Street Journal. (n.d.). *Is technology making people less sociable?* Retrieved 26 May 2017, from https://www.wsj.com/articles/is-technology-making-people-less-sociable-1431093491

Thewissen, V., & Gunther, N. (2015). E-mental health: State of the art. *Tijdschrift voor Psychotherapie*, *41*(6), 374–392. doi:10.100712485-015-0102-z

Wikipedia e-health. (2017). Retrieved 4 May 2017, from http://en.wikipedia.org/wiki/EHealth

World Internet Users Statistics and 2017 World Population Stats. (n.d.). Retrieved March 23, 2017, from www.internetworldstats.com

Wyn, J., Cuervo, H., Woodman, D., & Stokes, H. (2005). *Young people, wellbeing and communication technologies*. Retrieved May 2, 2017, from www.vichealth.vic.gov.au

# KEY TERMS AND DEFINITIONS

**Complementary Device:** An appliance or a tool that is used in addition to other devices or tools as an extra.

**Detrimental Effect:** The harmful and unwanted impact of something as a result of using or being prone to it.

**Face-to-Face Interaction:** Kind of relationship through which people meet each other in a real place and interact while they can see, speak to, hear, and touch each other simultaneously.

**Health:** The condition of wellbeing physically and mentally; when all of body's organs work properly and the mind is in peace besides the absence of any kinds of pain and sorrow.

**Modern Technology:** The novel and new devices and services that people can benefit from in their life.

**Social Media:** All kinds of instruments that can be used by most people in order to transaction and interaction.

**Virtual Communication:** Contacting people via mobile or computer using internet and in an unreal space.

# Chapter 4
# Ghostly (Re-)Semblances and Specular (Con-)Figurations:
## The Age of the Advent of Technologism and the End of Communication?

**Raymond Aaron Younis**
*Australian Catholic University, Australia*

## ABSTRACT

*Many thinkers conceptualize authentic communication in terms of an interpersonal encounter, for example between an "I" and a "you," a living subject and a living subject, unmediated by objects, electronic gadgets, or ICTs (informatics and communication technologies), or through an authentic human dialogue involving openness, choice, freedom, courage, and almost always, some risk and uncertainty. In the elevated language of Buber and Maritain one might say an existentially charged encounter between two (or more) beings involves opening up to each other, calling each to the other, face to face, thus allowing living truth to emerge.*

## INTRODUCTION

There can be little doubt that informatics and communication technologies have transformed, and some would say rendered problematic, not just such ways of thinking about relations and authenticity between human subjects, but also the very question of the possibility of such relations, especially given the global phenomenon of simulation, social media, avatars, and technologically mediated communication at almost every point of our personal, interpersonal and professional relationships in

DOI: 10.4018/978-1-5225-4168-4.ch004

the digital age. The following questions will be explored in this chapter: What are the changes to and effects of ICTs on our communicative relations in the 21st century? Is it still possible to speak of authentic interpersonal encounters in the light of the emergence of informatics and communication technologies and their proliferation in the digital age, in the paths opened up by thinkers like Buber and Heidegger (for example, 2017, 2016, 2013, 2002A, 2002B, 1998, 1984, 1982, 1976A, 1976B, 1973, 1971, 1967, 1966, 1955, among many others)? And what should one do, given the acceleration and intensification of the advent of technologism in our time?

## THE SPECIAL REALITY OF THE INTERHUMAN

### The Sphere of Interhuman Communication

Communication is a vast and intricate subject. Many thinkers have tried to give a rigorous and deep account of what it is and what constitutes it authentically. This section will focus on Martin Buber's account, with a brief critical evaluation. Buber introduced the notion of "interhuman communication" in the 1940s. He focused profoundly, and unforgettably, on the question of what it means for one human being to communicate with another human being authentically, particularly in several essays and meditations gathered into these volumes which appeared between the 1940s and the 1970s, namely, *Between Man and Man* (1947), *The Knowledge of Man* (1965), and *I and Thou* (1970).

In *The Knowledge of Man* (1965, p.74), he confronts a dominant existentialist paradigm:

*The only thing that matters is that for each of the two... the other happens as the particular other. That each becomes aware of the other and is thus related to him in such a way that he does not regard and use him as his object, but as his partner in a living event.... It is well known that some existentialists assert that the basic factor between men is that one is an object for the other. But so far as this is actually the case, the special reality of the interhuman, the fact of the contact, has been largely eliminated.*

What is striking here is the distinction Buber introduces between the other as object, and the other as a particular human being, that is, as a particular, living, conscious, free, thinking human being, the other as "partner" in the event of a living encounter. The "special reality of the interhuman" then highlights the non-objectified nature of this other human being, with whom and in whom we find a living partner, in and through communication.

But Buber went much further (1965, pp.74-75):

*We have in common with all existing beings that we can be made objects of observation. But... it is my privilege... that by the hidden activity of my being I can establish an impassable barrier to objectification. Only in partnership can my being be perceived as an existing whole.*

It is as if the threat of objectification is always present, in the eyes of the other. But the problem with objectification here is that it obscures the fact that a human being is a living whole - not a mere object to be observed or manipulated at will. Objectification can be surmounted then by the affirmation of the "special reality of the interhuman," which opens up the internal activity – thoughts, feelings, intuitions, perceptions, dispositions, choices, and so on – to another human being who is a partner in communication and participates as such as a living, responding as a whole. Such communication involves "actual happenings between [us]... whether wholly mutual or tending to grow into mutual relations" (1965, p.75). But Buber adds that the unfolding of the "sphere of the interhuman", in all such living encounters with a non-objectified other human being, is called "the dialogical" (1965, p.75), because it is mediated, for example, through genuine one-to-one communication and through a dialogue which affirms and holds one and the other in an encounter which takes the form of a relation that is "wholly mutual or tending to grow into mutual relations." So Buber argues that it is an error to try and explain the sphere of "the dialogical," or "interhuman phenomena" more broadly, as merely psychological phenomena. Buber's (lucid) reasoning is that though "the psychological" plays a role in the encounter, and in explaining the meaning of the encounter, nonetheless it is "only the hidden accompaniment to the conversation itself, the phonetic event fraught with meaning, whose meaning is to be found neither in one of the two parts nor in both together, but *only in their dialogue itself, in this 'between' which they live together"* (emphasis added; 1965, p.75). Note that once again he affirms the living, dynamic nature of the dialogue and the *dialoguers, in the fullness of their being.*

Of course, one may ask an important epistemic question at this point: How it is that one knows that it is truly the other who engages us in dialogue, in such a living interhuman encounter? Buber has a thought provoking response. He draws a distinction between "being" and "seeming" (1965, p.75). He argues that there are two types of human existence: "The one proceeds from what one really is, the other from what one wishes to seem [to be]" (1965, p.76). "Seeming" has two forms: first, "genuine seeming," "where a lad, for instance, imitates his heroic model and while he is doing so, is seized by the actuality of heroism.... In this situation there is nothing false... the mask, too, is a mask and no deceit;" and second, inauthentic seeming, "where the semblance originates from the lie and is permeated by it"

(1965, pp.76-77). It is the second form that threatens "the interhuman" "in its very existence" (1965, p.77), and this will be a focal point in this chapter.

It is not a lie about facts; it is a lie "in relation to existence itself and it attacks interhuman existence as such" (1965, pp.76-77). Buber, it needs to be noted, is uncompromising on this point: When a human being, in a dialogical encounter with another human being, lies in this way, he or she "forfeits the great chance of a true happening between I and You [as distinct from a happening between an "I" and an "It"]" (1965, p.77). It must be said that this coheres to a significant degree with philosophical trajectories in France and Germany between the 1930s and 1950s and beyond. Gabriel Marcel, for example, was writing of the extent to which we find out who we are as human beings and as persons in our relations with others (1967*)*, in the sense that we open ourselves, as an "I," to a "Thou," or in the sense that we are *co-esse,* being with other beings (1965, p.99, but see also 1973, 1966, 1963, 1952, 1951, 1949, among others).

Karl Jaspers (1955, pp.79-80) was writing of the extent to which truth and communication are interrelated:

*Truth cannot be separated from communicability. It only appears in time as a reality-through-communication. Abstracted from communication, truth hardens into an unreality. The movement of communication is at one and the same time the preservation of, and the search for, the truth.... In general then, it applies to my being, my authenticity, and my grasp of the truth that, not only factually am I for myself alone, but I cannot even become myself alone without emerging out of my being with others.*

Buber emphasizes the relation between I and You as a "true happening," in the quote above, or an inauthentic one. He illustrates the point with a vivid and germane analogy. Imagine two men, Peter and Paul, each preoccupied with appearance, or semblance, conversing face to face. At least six "configurations" are possible: we have Peter as "he wishes to appear to Paul," and vice versa; we have Peter "as he really appears to Paul, that is, Paul's image of Peter" (1965, p.77), which is not what Peter wishes Paul to see, and vice versa; moreover, we have Peter as he "appears to himself," and likewise Paul; finally we have the "bodily Peter and the bodily Paul. Two living beings and six ghostly appearances, which mingle in many ways in the conversation between the two. Where is there room for any genuine interhuman life?" (1965, p.77)

It may be asked: What does it mean to communicate truthfully then, in the context of authentic being, given the importance of the distinction between being (for example, what one is) and not seeming (for example, to be what one is not)? Buber's answer (1965, p.77) is a striking one and it deserves some consideration:

*Whatever the meaning of the word 'truth' may be in other realms, in the interhuman realm it means that men communicate themselves to one another as what they are. It does not depend on one saying to the other everything that occurs to him, but only on his letting no seeming creep in between himself and the other. It does not depend on one letting himself go before another, but on his granting to the man to whom he communicates himself a share of his being. This is a question of the authenticity of the interhuman, and where this is not to be found, neither is the human element itself authentic.*

So, the question of truth is not just an epistemic or a logical question; it is a question of communication, more precisely, *communicating authentically what one is*. Though the language here seems a little awkward, or unusual, the meaning is quite clear: When "I" communicate truthfully, and therefore authentically, to "You," the latter gets a true sense, not just of the meaning of the words, and more broadly the communication, but also of what "I" am, and of what "I" am in relation to them, and of where we stand, together, each before the other, as human beings.

Or, in other words, the communicative relation is authentic to the degree that no seeming compromises the interhuman, dialogical space and time between "I" and "You" and it is inauthentic to the degree that seeming compromises the interhuman, dialogical space and time between "I" and "You." Buber did not mean by such claims that seeming cannot take place at all in the dialogical space between two human beings; it would be difficult to imagine interhuman relations as entirely and unceasingly authentic and truthful relations, but what he was arguing is that authentic interhuman relations ought to have this form. Authenticity is a matter of a certain type of relation, and it is manifest when truth and communication intersect in dialogue in the space and time of the interhuman.

But the question of truth here is also a matter of "granting" and "sharing." "Granting" to "You" something important if "You" is to understand "I" truthfully, namely, "a share of 'I's' being," without seeming. It is clear then how seeming could obscure, compromise, problematize, or even destroy the dialogical relation in its authentic unfolding between one human being and another. Granting to "You" a *semblance* of the "I" is not an authentic relation, necessarily, for it could conceivably encompass manipulation, deceit or distortion, among other things. It could also serve to conceal "I" from "You" and therefore destroy the authentic relation between the two. Sharing one's being with "You," in a way that actualizes and promotes seeming compromises and clouds the truthfulness, and therefore also the authenticity, of the communicative relation and indeed the communicative horizon, precisely because it promotes impressions and images of what one is which are false, distorted, or misleading. The being of "I" is superseded by the image or *ghost* of the "I." So, Buber asks, "What if a man by his nature makes his life subservient to the images which he produces in others? Can he, in such a case, still become a man living from his being, can he escape from his nature?" (p.78)

To return to the analogy of Peter and Paul for a moment, Buber adds (1965, p.78) that when subservience to images or faulty representations, or the ghosts of being (rather than one's being, in terms of what one truly is, and nothing else) predominates:

*We see Peter and Paul before us surrounded by the ghosts of the semblances. A ghost can be exorcized. Let us imagine that these two find it more and more repellent to be represented by ghosts. In each of them the will is stirred and strengthened to be confirmed in their being as what they really are and nothing else. We see the forces of real life at work as they drive out the ghosts, till the semblance vanishes and the depths of personal life call to one another*

So, it is not coincidental that Buber draws an analogy between striving for authenticity and a kind of process of exorcism, at the level of the dialogical. That is, in order to understand and encounter another truthfully through communicative relation, in the sphere of the interhuman, it becomes necessary to "drive out the ghosts," to eliminate seeming as much as is possible, and to apprehend clearly the differences between the order of semblance (and by extension, the suborder of false images or representations) and the nascent sphere of the interhuman, in which "mutuality stirs" (1965, p.81). In particular, the "invasion of seeming and the inadequacy of perception" are overcome (1965, p.82). He added that because "Genuine dialogue is an ontological sphere which is constituted by the authenticity of being, *every invasion of semblance must damage it*" (emphasis added, 1965, p.86).

Finally, there are many ways according to Buber, in and through which the communicative relation with "You," can be transformed into a relation with an "It." This is the "sublime melancholy of our lot" (1970, p.68) and it has no less than six or seven characteristics. As soon as the relation "has run its course or is permeated by means, the You becomes an object among objects... assigned its measure and boundary" (1970, p.68), there is "a loss of actuality" (1970, p.68) and presumably an increase in deceptive appearances or pretense. One's "natural being" that "only now revealed itself to me in the mystery of reciprocity" becomes describable (in its entirety, since it is in an important sense, a surface, or more precisely, a surface appearance, a surface representation, a surface *effect*), becomes "analyzable" (again in its entirety as an object among objects). It also becomes "classifiable" (as an object among other objects), an "aggregate of qualities, a quantum with a shape" (1970, pp.68-69). It becomes an abstraction. In these kinds of contexts every "You" in the world is "doomed" to become an "It," to "enter into 'thinghood' again and again" (1970, p.69). The "It" represents the "chrysalis." The "You" represents the "butterfly" (not in states of alternation, to be sure, according to Buber, but often "an intricately entangled series of events that is tortuously dual" 1970, p.69). What this "series of events" opens up is the sphere of *thinghood* – a sphere that brings into view informatics, technology, and communication, in short, the age of technologism, its emergence and convergence, in which thinghood will extend to electronic and digital representation.

# THE QUESTION CONCERNING TECHNOLOGY

## Human and Machine Communication

The age of informatics is an age dominated to a very significant degree by the advent and convergence of information and communication technologies. A number of thinkers, as we have seen, have explored the communicative relation between human being and human being. Still others, no less significant, have explored the communicative relation between human beings and machines. Martin Heidegger provided what is perhaps the most wide-ranging, searching, and troubling account of this emergent, and increasingly dominant, paradigm of communication in the twentieth century. The aim here is not to give an account of his views and the manifold criticisms of these views, for that is a necessary but immense task that lies outside the scope of this chapter. Rather the aim here is to place him firmly in the context established so far and point out some of the important ways in which his project intersected with the projects of Buber (and Marcel, among others, without obscuring or forgetting the important differences between them).

Writing in the 1950s, Heidegger argued that we are "everywhere," "chained to technology," and "we remain unfree" (1977, p.4). The way it is represented to us, for example, as "something neutral" blinds us to "the essence of technology" (1977, p.4), namely, "the manufacture and utilization of equipment, tools and machines, the manufactured and used things themselves, and the needs and ends that they serve..." (1977, pp. 4-5). Note at this point that Heidegger places technology in its essence, in a space that is analogous in some respects to the space of Buber's "It:" a "neutral" thing, a tool among tools, in the space of mere objects and representations. According to this reading, "technology" is just a means to an end, and therefore something to be manipulated by human beings, at will. Technology is only related to *human activity* as an instrument is related to a human worker.

So, if this is correct, then "technology" can be mastered. The will to mastery becomes "all the more urgent the more technology threatens to slip from human control" (1977, p.5). However, this instrumentality, in respect of its causality, is not yet sufficiently examined, and so long as this state of affairs continues, "the accepted definition of technology" remains "obscure and groundless" (1977, p.7). It is crucial to see what instrumentality is, quite apart from the many representations and semblances of what it is supposed to be, especially in terms of its "primal meaning." That is in relation to the emergence of what comes to be called *causality*; what Heidegger would call the "bringing-forth in its full scope... in which the Greeks thought it" (1977, p.10) and "bringing-forth" ["*Her-vor-bringen*"] means "something concealed comes into unconcealment" (1977, p.11).

So, we must question "technology." In doing so we arrive at *alētheia,* the revealing of what was once concealed. Truth as revealing unmasks the essence of technology, according to Heidegger. Truth as revealing, though similar in one respect to Buber's relational conception, and the revealing of what one truly is to another, nonetheless stands here in a relation between a questioner and an emerging powerful instrumentality whose origins are as yet un-thought (that is, more fully) and therefore, remain unclear. What is revealed then is that instrumentality "is considered to be the fundamental characteristic of technology," and revealing opens up the question of the "possibility of all productive manufacturing" (1977, p.12). So "technology" is not a mere means; it "is a way of revealing" (1977, p.12).

If this claim is true, the "realm of revealing" is the realm of truth, and in turn, of authentic inquiry, and it is therefore opened up. This opening reveals *technē* (at the root of "technology") as the name not just "for the activities and skills of the craftsman, but also for the arts of the mind and the fine arts" (1977, p.13). It reveals *technē* as a "bringing-forth" "to *poiēsis* ("it is something poetic") (1977, p.13). However, it also opens up again the connection, affirmed by the Greeks, between two names for knowing: *technē* and *epistēme* -- "they mean to be entirely at home in something, to understand and be expert in it" (1977, p.13). So what "is decisive" in *technē,* Heidegger argues, is not making and manipulating, or means to ends, but *revealing.* It is "as revealing and not as manufacturing, that *technē* is a bringing-forth," a "mode of revealing" (1977, p.13). In other words, "technology" comes "to presence" in the very space, so to speak, where the intersection between revealing and truth, as unconcealment, "happens" (1977, p.13). Heidegger calls this the "essential domain of technology" opened up by questioning and recalling the ancient conception of truth as unconcealment. However, this leaves a "decisive question" unanswered: What is the nature of the relation between the essence of modern technology and its "putting exact science to use" (1977, p.14)?

This question opens up the conception of modern technology as a second kind of revealing, modern technology as a "challenging" (*Herausfordern*) (1977, p.14), not just as "bringing forth." It "puts to nature the unreasonable demand that it supplies energy that can be extracted and stored as such" (1977, p.14). Modern technology "sets upon" [*stellt*] nature in the sense of challenging it, namely, to produce and yield more energy, which in turn can be "released either for destruction or for peace; it is a *setting upon* that is also an expediting" [*Fördern*] for it "unlocks and exposes," again and again, aiming at a "maximum yield at the minimum expense" (1977, p.15).

A river, for example, becomes "set upon." It becomes something that exists to serve a hydroelectric plant. It is a supplier of energy. In this sense, "monstrousness reigns" for the river becomes "an object on call," and little else. It's essential task and value, according to this technocentric mode of apprehension of nature, is to serve as a means, the energy concealed within it is unlocked, "what is unlocked is transformed, what is transformed is stored up, what is stored up is, in turn, distributed, and what is distributed is switched about ever anew" (1977, p.16). All of these are "ways of revealing" which highlight "regulating" and "securing." Note the important but tacit analogy between being unfree, as thinkers, on the one hand, and being subject to the technological drive towards *regulating*, storing and by extension, *controlling*. These are all modes of "the challenging revealing" (1977, p.16). Heidegger extends the point rhetorically: "Everything is ordered to stand by, to be immediately at hand, indeed to stand there just so that it may be on call for a further ordering. We call it the standing reserve [*Bestand*]" (1977, p.17). Objects become standing-reserve, things to be ordered and exchanged for other things, readily.

Yet the unconcealment "within which ordering unfolds" is not something that "man" controls. It is not man's "handiwork" (1977, p.18). The human being is "everywhere already brought into the unconcealed." They "merely" respond "to the call of unconcealment" (1977, p.19). When they investigate, observe, "ensnare nature" "as an area" of their own "conceiving," they have "already been claimed by a way of revealing" that challenges the apprehension of nature as "an object of research." This "gathering" focuses "man upon ordering the real as standing reserve" (1977, p.19) and places him within a configuration, namely, *Ge-stell* (Enframing), a "calling forth," a "challenging," a demand that gathers "man" "to order the self-revealing as standing reserve" (1977, p.19). "Man" is "set upon," then, like nature, to reveal what is real in the mode of "standing reserve." It is the essence of modern technology to allow Enframing to "hold sway" as a mode of revealing. So, technology cannot be thought of as merely instrumental. Its "work," in the context of Enframing, reveals the real and the natural, through unconcealment, as "standing reserve."

Nature becomes a "storehouse." It becomes "entrapped" in the light of modern science "as a calculable coherent set of forces" (1977, p.21). And the "modern physical theory of nature," according to Heidegger, "prepares the way... for the essence of technology... [because] in physics the challenging gathering-together into ordering revealing" already "holds sway" (1977, p.22). It is the "herald of Enframing" (1977, p.22). The "essence of modern technology lies in Enframing" (1977, p.23). It *shows itself* in "Enframing" (1977, p.23). In other words, like *What is philosophy?* he argues that the "rise and dominance of the sciences" "puts a specific imprint on the history of mankind upon the whole earth" (1955, pp.31, 33).

The role of questioning then is to bring to light "our relationship to its essence" (1977, p.23). Its role is to show more broadly how "man stands within the essential realm of Enframing," how the "destining of revealing" comes to "hold complete sway over man" (1977, p.25). Freedom, and authenticity presumably, are achieved "only insofar as he belongs to the realm of destining and so becomes one who listens and hears, and not one who is simply constrained to obey" (1977, p.25). Freedom means "starting" "a revealing upon its way," and "all revealing comes out of the air, goes into the open and brings into the open" (1977, p.25). It is in the light of this mystery that freedom becomes possible.

Heidegger returns to an earlier argument. He argues that it is not enough to define something in terms of its causality "without ever considering the essential origin of this causality" (1977, p.26). Heidegger describes eloquently the danger of "exalting" ourselves to "the posture of lord[s] of the earth" (1977, p.27). The consequence is that "man" no longer "encounters himself…[in] his essence," Enframing holds sway, and so, "man" "fails to see himself as the one spoken to, and hence also fails in every way to hear in what respect he *ek-sists*, from out of his essence in the realm of exhortation or address, and thus *can never* encounter only himself" (1977, p.27). This means, of course, that the truth cannot come to unconcealment, cannot "come to pass" (1977, p.27). This catastrophic transformation, bound up with the essence of modern "technology," will be explored further below.

What poses the greatest danger, according to Heidegger, is not "technology" alone, but "rather the mystery of its essence" (1977, p.28), that is, as a "destining of revealing." He put this memorably (1977, p.28):

*The threat to man does not come in the first instance from the potentially lethal machines and apparatus of technology. The actual threat has already affected man in his essence. The rule of enframing threatens man with the possibility that it could be denied to him to enter into a more original revealing and hence to experience the call of a more primal truth.*

He adds that where such dangers lie, there is a "saving power" to be found. "Saving" here means bringing something back ("home") "into its essence," in order to "bring the essence for the first time into its genuine appearing" (1977, p.28). It *takes root and thrives* even as the danger unfolds through Enframing. It allows us to "ponder this arising [of the "saving power"] and that, recollecting, we watch over it." We "must catch sight of what comes to presence in technology" (1977, p.32). So long as we "represent technology as an instrument, we remain held fast in the will to master it." The task is to "ask how the instrumental comes to presence as a kind of causality" and "experience this coming to presence as the destining of a revealing" (1977, p.32), or experience this as a relation to the essence of truth. We are "needed" for the "safekeeping of the coming to presence of truth," and it is in this need and this task that the "arising of the saving power appears" (1977, p.32).

It is reflection that allows us to ponder the fact that "all saving power must be of a higher essence" (than the essence of technology) (1977, p.34). So "art" according to Heidegger is a revealing that "brings forth and hither" and belongs "within *poiēsis,*" which Enframing denies. It can hold sway, too, but only to reveal "that which shines forth most purely" (1977, p.34). Revealing "lays claim to the arts most primally, so that they may for their part expressly foster the growth of the saving power, may awaken and found anew our look into that which grants and our trust in it" (1977, p.35). This much can astound us – that the "frenziedness of technology may entrench itself everywhere to such an extent that someday throughout everything technological, the essence of technology may come to presence in the coming-to-pass of truth" (1977, p.35).

"Essential reflection" on technology and "decisive confrontation" must then take place in the domain of art, but "only if reflection on art, for its part, does not shut its eyes to the constellation of truth after which we are *questioning*" (1977, p.35). This is the way out, according to Heidegger, of the crisis precipitated by the advent of the coming to presence of technology. He writes (1977, p.35):

*The closer we come to the danger, the more brightly do the ways into the saving power begin to shine and the more questioning we become. For questioning is the piety of thought.*

## WHAT OUGHT ONE DO?

Several key points can be taken from the thinking of Buber and Heidegger in relation to the task that confronts us as netizens in the age of the advent of technologism. Buber argued, as we have seen, against processes of objectification (in which the other comes to be seen as an object, for example, to be manipulated, not a living human *partner* in a living, unfolding, authentic *interhuman event*). It is important therefore to become aware of and to overcome conditions that promote such processes of objectification (which amount largely to the same thing as the mass, and accelerated, replication of images and semblances which becomes the norm, under the reign of technologism), and this can be done by turning away wherever possible from the sphere of replication and simulation to the sphere of interhuman relations, or to authentic fully human partnership. In other words, this can be done by turning, actively, in our communicative relations, again and again, to the fullness of another's being as a human being (and nothing less).

This may sound a little unclear on a first reading, but what it suggests, strongly, is that the authentic dialogue between one human being and another, the authentic relation between one human being and another, as a true expression of the status of each as a living whole and as a disclosure of one whole being to another, creates a "between" that cannot be replicated or simulated without qualitatively transforming, eroding, or destroying the sphere of the interhuman itself. If Buber is right, we cannot live together authentically and fully, then, as images of ourselves, or of one another, nor can we relate to each other fully as human beings in the technologistic context of simulations, ghostly semblances and resemblances, or specular configurations and reconfigurations.

It is important in the age of the advent of technologism, more than ever, then, also to sound out the many forms of seeming, and associated forms of untruth or better, inauthenticity. Masks, as Buber notes, may be healthy, but they can also be false or inauthentic. They can in this sense eliminate, erode, or destroy the special nature of the interhuman that is part of the *ontological sphere* of the human being. It is important to sound out such semblances (and, of course, in the age of the advent of technologism, such *re*semblances) and the lies, secrecy, or untruth from which they originate, and which permeate them. It is important in the age of the advent of technologism, more than ever, then, also to sound out those things that degrade, erode, or destroy the sphere of interhuman being and the possibility of authentic dialogical relations, as such. In this way, two living beings can have, possibly, a genuine, full interhuman life without being haunted by ghostly, false, or misleading semblances, resemblances, and appearances, or inhuman (or indeed, unhuman) specular configurations and reconfigurations. The liberation of human beings from the accelerating sphere of the inhuman and the non-human, requires then that we become non-subservient to the advent of technologism, and to the reign of semblances and resemblances, configurations and reconfigurations that we find ourselves captive to, again and again, in the communicative modalities of the twenty-first century. In this context, it is important to see *genuine dialogue,* as Buber did, in terms of an *ontological sphere,* which is not only *constituted* by authentic human being in relation, but which impels us to resist, actively, in the words of Buber, *every invasion of semblance* (1965, p.86) that threatens the very existence of this sphere at its foundations. The other as "it," is the chrysalis, then, out of which the "I" and the "you," and their full (human) relation, may then be liberated.

In the wake of Heidegger's thinking, it becomes important to take a number of practical steps, also. He emphasized the extent to which we have become *set upon* in the age of the advent of technologism – to which we have become *objects on call,* so to speak, our value reduced to that of mere means to ends that we do not fully understand. In short, this represents a world of transformation (into objects) and distribution (as objects) in an order that is not human. If he is right, and *everything is ordered to stand by, to be immediately at hand, indeed to stand there just so that it may be on call for a further ordering* (the "standing reserve" 1977, p.17) and if the world of objects becomes a world of *standing-reserve,* then we also become objects *to be ordered and exchanged for other objects readily.* The process of transformation and objectification then must be sounded out, confronted decisively. The configuration into which we are thrust, as objects, in the age of the advent of technologism, and that *Enframing,* must be sounded out and confronted decisively so that we are not *set upon* continually and irreversibly, and so that modern technologism is confronted in its *essence.*

In order to be free or live authentically, according to Heidegger, one ought to become "one who listens and hears, and not one who is simply constrained to obey" (1977, p.25). Objectified beings obey, so to speak. They do not think for themselves or ponder their condition, so they do not encounter themselves in their essence, which means as reflective, free beings in the world, among others, enduring in the light of being and therefore alive in the "realm of exhortation or address" (1977, p.27).

So, it becomes important to resist and sound out processes by which we are constrained in the realm of objects, as objects, where the truth of our being, and its constellation, cannot emerge or come to pass (1977, p.27). It is important also to reflect essentially on technology and more importantly, technologism and its reign; what is required, by extension, of us, is a *decisive confrontation,* not just in *the domain of art,* but in the sphere in interpersonal relations and communication, and deep reflection, in which we our eyes are open again to the *constellation of truth after which we are questioning* (1977, p.35), that is, that constellation that reminds us of our being, our freedom, authentic listening and hearing, and pondering, so that we may see and free ourselves from the crisis generated and perpetuated (as the order of the "real") by the advent of the age, the *coming to presence* of, viral technologism. Our thinking as questioning, and questioners, in this respect, is not just *the piety of thought* (1977, p.35). Rather, it is an enduring mark of what makes us most human, and most authentic, as beings in the world.

## THE ADVENT OF THE AGE OF TECHNOLOGISM AND THE END OF COMMUNICATION?

The advent of the age of technologism is unlike any other in qualitative and quantitative terms. In qualitative terms, it influences and shapes to an unprecedented degree the way we communicate with each other in the 21st century, given the accelerated convergence of information and communication technologies. This applies across the globe, to be sure, even though internet penetration, for example, is almost 90%

in the USA and almost 85% in Western Europe. Nonetheless, it is just under 60% in East Asia and South East Asia. In Oceania it is almost 70% (Chaffey, 2017).

There can be no denying the genuinely global impact and penetration of such information and communication technologies, and the significance of the qualitative impact on our ways of searching for, finding and using information, and our ways of seeking, contacting, meeting and communicating with others around the globe through social media sites, web technologies and configurations. But there can be no denying the quantitative nature of these changes, either. For example, in the Asia Pacific alone, it is estimated that almost 400 million people are active users of social media on mobiles, with a 35% increase in the last 12 months alone. Mobile subscriptions globally number over eight billion users. Facebook alone has almost 90% penetration in the USA (Chaffey, 2017). It seems this is a new world order, the new emerging order of the real (not the semblance of the order of the real).

It is not uncommon to see numbers such as these in many studies and surveys. The advent of the age of technologism is evidently upon us. It is defined in terms of the emergence of human to machine or human to computer interaction, and communicative relations, as a ruling paradigm, if not the only paradigm, of communication and communicative modes in the late twentieth and early twenty first centuries. But what is the broader meaning of the work of Buber and Heidegger for such an age?

Though many have examined or been influenced by Buber's understanding of the dialogical (see for example, Mendes-Flohr 2015 and 1989; Putnam 2008; Atterton, Calarco and Friedman 2004; Crossley 1996; Bergman 1991; Silberstein 1989; Arnett 1986; Berry 1985; Theunissen 1984; Friedman 1976; Wood 1969; Matson and Montagu 1967; Diamond 1960; among many others), and though many have examined or been influenced by Heidegger's understanding of technology (see for example, Lawson 2017; Grigenti 2016; Evans 2015; Lack 2014; Skrbina 2014; Scharff 2013; Ihde 2010; Brockelman 2008; Willson 2006; Appignanesi 2003; Cooper 2002; Harman 2002; Heim 1993; Rothenberg 1993; Zimmerman 1990; Theunissen 1984; and Loscerbo 1981; among many others), still there are few detailed studies of the relation between the two and the implications of their work in the context of *technologism*. But before addressing this question, it is important to continue the critical dialogue surrounding such approaches to the interhuman and to "technology."

Buber, it has to be said, understates or overstates a number of points, notwithstanding the enduring significance and value of his thinking. For example, it is difficult to see how the encounter with the other self "as the particular other" can be "the *only thing* that matters" (1965, p.74; emphasis added). If, for each person in a dialogue, it matters that the "other happens as the particular other," as Buber argues, with some justification, then it would also matter that the particular other is revealed, and reveals themselves, in their particularity, and also (at the same time) in their wholeness. But the relation between particularity and wholeness here does need to be made coherent.

Moreover, it does not seem to be sufficient "that each becomes aware of the other... as his partner in a living event." What is required is a certain kind of awareness, namely, a *correct* awareness "of the other... as his partner in a living event." This much seems crucial, for awareness can be vague, or indistinct, or even misleading or incorrect. Correct awareness would seem to be a crucial part of the "special reality of the interhuman" (1965, p.74). In other words, there is a conscious and experiential dimension certainly, but it is difficult to see how the epistemic dimension cannot be integrally important in these kinds of relations, especially authentic ones. That Buber recognized this is clear at times, for example when he affirms elsewhere not just a happening between persons, but a "true happening." The epistemic dimension then does need further clarification and elucidation.

By logical extension, Buber's understanding of truth is thought provoking to say the least. He emphasized two persons communicating "to one another as what they are," but this is a little ambiguous. One could communicate as what one thinks one is, or as what one actually is. But the two are not (logically) the same. One might argue that it is not always clear to one what one is. The question of identity is a profound metaphysical question and though this kind of complication does not invalidate Buber's broad position, nonetheless he does take a little too much for granted on occasions, especially when he focusses on the question of what one is or of what "they are." By extension, granting to another a "share of [one's] being" need not necessarily be an authentic act. Much would depend on what "one is," whether or not what one believes one is accords with it, and just which share of one's being is granted to another, and vice versa. These are not just metaphysical and logical intricacies which ought to be disentangled further; it is important to take into consideration also the manifold existential, ontological, and phenomenological complexities of identity in the 21$^{st}$ century.

Heidegger insisted on the relation between *Enframing*, the transformation of living things into *standing-reserve* and the essence of technology. But it has to be said that it is not altogether clear that the essence of technology amounts to this alone. "Technology" refers to instruments and means, certainly, and effects, which can be catastrophic, but it also refers to phenomena and relations which can enable and transform positively, for example, in medical, diagnostic, and therapeutic contexts. It is not that Heidegger failed to understand this. The question is whether or not he was sufficiently attuned to the complexities of "technology" and the manifold ways in which human beings can relate to it as an instrument but also as a mediator, as a part of our being, as communicative creatures, and as a paradigm. If thinking is adequate to the great task of examining technology and its causality, and further, the origins of this causality in ancient Greek philosophy, it seems unlikely that the essence of technology will be a monolithic or one-dimensional matter (and the presupposition that it is so is not one that is self-evident).

*Technē* in ancient Greek thinking does not just suggest craft or skill, for example, in a professional sense, but also producing something in relation to knowledge, understanding, and reason, for as Aristotle argues in *Metaphysics* 981b: *master craftsmen are superior in wisdom, not because they can do things, but because they possess a theory and know the causes* (see also *Nicomachean Ethics,* Book VI, 1140a). It is also associated with skill in making, producing, or doing in Plato (see for example, *Charmides* and *Gorgias,* among other Platonic dialogues).

In other words, *technē,* at its origins, and in relation to its originary bond in and to "technology," tends to carry us beyond the conception of technology as *Enframing* in the context of standing reserve. It opens up also, in its originary light, contexts, arguments, crafts, and ends, but also reason, skills, and ways of doing and producing, which may promote health, well-being, good ends, and perhaps even flourishing. It is therefore difficult to see how deep and authentic thinking, or pondering, concerning the question of technology and its originary connection to ancient Greek thinking about *technē,* can neglect, evade, push aside, or exclude these complexities, contexts, constellations, and affiliations, especially when the question of the essence of technology arises, in Heidegger's words, "the bringing forth *in its full scope...* in which the Greeks thought it" (emphasis added, 1977, p.10). It remains then to think, and to bring forth, to the extent that this is even possible, *in its full scope, the essence of technology in the light of this originary and enduring heritage.*

One other question needs to be asked. It remains unclear why the "decisive confrontation" "must take place in the domain of art" (1977, p.35), and only in the domain of art. As suggested earlier, there are other meaningful possibilities of thinking and of action. Of course, the Presocratics did think poetically, but thinking poetically itself is subjective. It can be analyzed and evaluated by deep and authentic philosophical thinking. Philosophical thinking is not in any obvious way connected to thinking about being as being, alone or primarily. So, if we extend the concept of philosophical thinking to thinking about *poiēsis, technē,* and *logos,* it should become apparent that original thinking in philosophy opens up the possibility of a decisive confrontation between Heidegger's thinking about *poiēsis, technē,* and *aletheia* (truth as unconcealment) and thinking about the complexity of these terms in ancient Greek philosophy also. Certainly the "domain of art" as Heidegger understood it – that is as thoughtful, poetic and insightful, for example – needs to have a place.

But it does not follow from this proposition that the (philosophical) domain of metaphysics, or logic, or epistemology, or ethics, or philosophical thinkers cannot play a momentous and historical role in the "decisive confrontation" between "essential reflection" and the age of the advent of technologism, broadly conceived. Much work remains therefore to be done in this respect (let alone the critically important question now of the interconnection between the age of the advent of technologism, the rise of National Socialism in Germany, and its catastrophic trajectories, and the advent of nihilism). If we are to open our eyes fully to the "constellation of truth after we are questioning" (1977, p.35), it is indeed difficult to see how such intricacies, complexities, and affiliations can be underemphasised, ignored or overlooked. This much, it would seem, is required, especially if we are to "ponder" and in "recollecting" "catch sight of what comes to presence in technology" (1977, p.32) more fully and deeply.

So, finally, what is the meaning and value of Buber's and Heidegger's thinking in relation to communication in the advent of the age of technologism? Given the proliferation of representations, images, and electronic communication in the age of informatics and communication, one could be forgiven for the assertion that it is also the age of (re-)semblances, configurations, and reconfigurations. That is, not just of semblances of the human and of the person, but also semblances with an in-principle infinite capacity for reproduction and dissemination; not just of seeming on an unprecedented (global, given the interconnectedness that is characteristic of web penetration now) scale but also seeming with an in-principle infinite capacity for reproduction, replication, and dissemination.

Unlike Baudrillard's *simulacra*, however, (see 1999, 1997, 1987 and 1981 among others) (re-)semblances do not embody, paradoxically, the truth which hides the fact that there is no truth, nor do (re-)semblances belong to the order of *precession of simulacra* (Baudrillard, 1981). Rather, they belong to an order in which an in-principle infinite capacity for reproduction, replication, and dissemination is manifest, but also in which the human person is not removed, does not vanish from the symbolic or actual order, and meaning and authenticity still have some anchors, for example, in authentic dialogue, which can still be removed from the order of rhetoric, simulation, semblance, illusion, and sophistry.

Buber's emphasis on the twin obstacles of seeming and the inadequacy of perception is vital. It is difficult at the best of times to know that what one faces in social media, for example, is a person in their particularity or in their wholeness, *as what they are*, or one who is seeming to be such a person, seeming to be what they claim to be? We are confronted by the image of a person, the representation of a person, the semblance of a person, to be sure, and we hear not their voices, but the recording of their voices using multiple protocols, and configured, for example, through an electronic mail account. But the face we see is not a human face; it is a digital representation of a human face. The voices we hear are not human voices, but electronically configured and mediated voices of human beings. Indeed, it is conceivable in such cases that one could hear the voice of a machine and mistake it for a human voice, so sophisticated is the digital recording technology in the age of the advent of technologism.

The inadequacy of perception is potentially catastrophic in such contexts, for if the distinction between the human and the electronic, the human and the digital, is not recognized clearly and perceived accurately, then semblance, as Buber argued, will not only problematize the authenticity of the interhuman encounter; it could open the way for the *invasion of semblance,* which damages the ontological sphere in which one human being communicates directly and authentically with another human being, the space of the dialogical. The particularity of the person is lost as every semblance of the person can be replicated, *ad infinitum,* in theory. The authentic partner in a living event is lost as the semblance of the partner can be reiterated when the living event ends. The non-objectifiable nature of the partner is compromised as the semblance of the partner is an object in an order, potentially global, of objects among other objects, in cyberspace. The existing whole in communication with another existing whole, granting a share of their being to each other is unattainable as existing wholes are reduced to existing and recirculating representations, resemblances, images, icons and avatars in configurations which are detached from the world of actual living human beings.

It is no longer the order of the interhuman. Rather, it is the order of (re-)semblances, *ghosts* in a sense, as Buber would have it, and specular (re-)configurations that hold up electronically or digitally generated surfaces and forms, *as in a mirror.* But it is important to never forget that they are not human beings or persons, but rather the ghostly (re-)semblances that circulate in cyberspace, itself the specular analogue of the space and time that govern the sphere of the interhuman.

It is not just the images that one "produces in others" that are critical here (Buber, 1965, p.78). What is no less striking is the production, reproduction, replication, concatenation, and dissemination of the images one produces of oneself, the images one produces of others, the images others produce of oneself, and the images others produce of others. The order of communication and the horizon of communicative possibilities is not so much interhuman anymore, but rather potentially inhuman, or, more precisely, non-human and on a global scale. In one sense, it might be argued then (though this is a topic for another paper) that what we are witnessing, with increased internet and ICT penetration in our lives, is the accelerating eclipse of the sphere of the interhuman, potentially, by the rapidly emerging sphere of the nonhuman, in which the order of the digital, the electronic, and the specular, are the ruling modes.

After Heidegger, it is possible to go even further. The rapidly emerging sphere of the nonhuman, in which the order of the digital, the electronic, and the specular are the ruling modes, means that the *essence of technology* now is not just the *challenging revealing,* as Heidegger saw it, but also a challenging replication, proliferation, and dissemination of (re-)semblances, in which the non-human is sustained for electronic and digital configurations that were once elements in a person to person communicative mode.

What this means, then, is that that communicative mode becomes part of the precondition for the emergence of, and acceleration of, the process of objectification, as persons, faces, voices, and dialogues are superseded by electronic and digital traces - *ghosts,* in Buber's sense of that term. In this context, the essence of technology cannot be sufficiently explained or understood without an integral account of the revealing of the meaning, place, and function of digitalization, electronization, replication, and partly as a consequence, accelerating boundless (in a geographical sense) objectification. Under this critical category, it is not nature alone or human beings alone, in their humanity, that are set upon, but also (re-)semblances of nature, (re-)semblances of human beings, and by extension, in theory, (re-)semblances of every subject and object that is vulnerable to the order of replication, objectification, proliferation, and global dissemination. It is part of the essence of modern technology, then, not just to allow Enframing to "hold sway" as a "mode of revealing" in the realm of the natural and the human, in space, but also, it seems irreversibly, now, in the realm of electronic and digital configurations and (re-)semblances, or more broadly, the realm of proliferating (non-human) objects in the specular reconfiguration, or shadow, of space, so to speak, namely, cyberspace and virtual space.

It is not just nature and the human that are *ensnared* as Heidegger would have it, but also, often, the virtual, the digital, the electronic, the hyperreal, and the non-human. It is difficult to even imagine interpersonal communication in the 21st century, generally, in terms that exclude such categories. So, if freedom and authenticity, are achieved to the extent that we become listeners, and not beings who are just constrained to obey, as Heidegger put it (1977, p.25) and if it means "starting" "a revealing upon its way," then the revealing that is required now is one in which such categories are subject to the deepest thinking, so that the potential and actual obstacles to the interhuman, the dialogical and authentic human freedom can be seen in their true light, and so that we can encounter ourselves as we are, and each to each, in our full humanity.

## CONCLUSION

Now, it is possible to see more clearly the changes and the challenges if we return to Buber's analogy and add at least another four configurations, and multiplying (re-) semblances and specular (re)configurations and "ghosts" -- Peter's image of Peter, as he wishes it to appear *as an image*, to Paul, and vice versa, Peter's image, as it really appears, as image, to Paul, which is not the image of Peter that Peter wishes Paul to see, and vice versa, Peter's image of how he "appears to himself," and likewise Paul, and finally, the image of the "bodily Peter" and the image of the "bodily Paul" circulating beyond any boundaries that Peter or Paul may be aware of, let alone in control over. To extend Buber's point: "two living beings" and multiplying (more than seven!) "ghostly appearances, which mingle in many ways in the conversation between the two" (1965, p.77).

If there is room for "genuine interhuman life" here, and one could argue after Buber and Heidegger, among others, that there is, it is because the human being, the person, the living partner whose own face we see and whose own voice we hear in the space of the interhuman, and not the objects, (re-)semblances or (re-)configurations, that *stand for* these, or displace, or *set upon* these, endure and continue the task of thinking the event of the dialogical and the deeper and broader essence of technology.

## REFERENCES

Appignanesi, R. (2003). *The end of everything: postmodernism and the vanishing of the human: Lyotard, Haraway, Plato, Heidegger, Habermas, McLuhan*. Cambridge, UK: Icon.

Aristotle. (n.d.a). Available at: http://www.perseus.tufts.edu/hopper/text?doc=Perseus%3Atext%3A1999.01.0052%3Abook%3D1%3Asection%3D982a

Aristotle. (n.d.b). *Nicomachean Ethics*. Available at: http://www.perseus.tufts.edu/hopper/text?doc=Perseus%3Atext%3A1999.01.0054%3Abekker+page%3D1094a%3Abekker+line%3D1

Arnett, R. C. (1986). *Communication and community: implications of Martin Buber's dialogue*. Carbondale, IL: Southern Illinois University Press.

Atterton, P., Calarco, M., & Friedman, M. (Eds.). (2004). *Lévinas and Buber: dialogue and difference*. Pittsburgh, PA: Duquesne University Press.

Baudrillard, J. (1981). *Simulacra and Simulation*. University of Michigan Press Michigan.

Baudrillard, J. (1997). *Art and Artefact*. London: Sage.

Bergman, S. H. (1991). *Dialogical philosophy from Kierkegaard to Buber*. Albany, NY: State University of New York Press.

Berry, D. L. (1985). *Mutuality: the vision of Martin Buber*. Albany, NY: State University of New York Press.

Brockelman, T. (2008). *Žižek and Heidegger: the question concerning techno-capitalism Continuum*. London.

BuberM. (1947). Between Man and Man. Macmillan.

Buber, M. (1952). Images of good and evil (M. Bullock, Trans.). Routledge & Kegan.

Buber, M. (1965). *The Knowledge of Man*. London: George Allen & Unwin.

Buber, M. (1970). *I and Thou*. New York: Charles Scribner's Sons.

Buber, M. (1990). *A believing humanism: My testament, 1902-1965* (M. Friedman, Trans.). Atlantic Highlands, NJ: Humanities Press International.

Calani, M., Baranauskas, C., Liu, K., & Sun, L. (Eds.). (2016). *Socially Aware Organisations and Technologies. Impact and Challenges: 17th IFIP WG 8.1 International Conference on Informatics and Semiotics in Organisations, ICISO 2016, Campinas, Brazil, August 1-3, 2016, Proceedings*. Springer International Publishing.

Chaffey, D. (n.d.). *Global social media research summary 2017*. Available at: http://www.smartinsights.com/social-media-marketing/social-media-strategy/new-global-social-media-research/

Cooper, S. (2002). *Technoculture and critical theory: In the service of the machine*. London: Routledge. doi:10.4324/9780203167021

Crossley, N. (1996). *Intersubjectivity: the fabric of social becoming*. London: Sage.

Diamond, M. L., & Buber, M. (1960). *Jewish existentalist*. New York: Oxford University Press.

Evans, L. (2015). *Locative social media: place in the digital age*. Basingstoke, UK: Palgrave Macmillan. doi:10.1057/9781137456113

Friedman, M. S., & Buber, M. (1976). The life of dialogue. University of Chicago Press.

Grigenti, F. (2016). *Existence and Machine: The German Philosophy in the Age of Machines (1870-1960)*. Cham: Springer International Publishing. doi:10.1007/978-3-319-45366-8

Harman, G. (2002). *Tool-being: Heidegger and the metaphysics of objects*. Chicago: Open Court.

Heidegger, M. (1955). *What is Philosophy?* New Haven, CT: College and University Press.

Heidegger, M. (1966). *Discourse on thinking, a translation of Gelassenheit by John M. Anderson and E. Hans Freund*. New York: Harper & Row.

Heidegger, M. (1967). *What is a thing? Translated by W.B. Barton and Dera Deutsch*. Chicago: Regnery.

Heidegger, M. (1971). *Poetry, language, thought, translations by Albert Hofstadter*. New York: Harper & Row.

Heidegger, M. (1973). *The End of Philosophy*. Chicago: University of Chicago Press.

Heidegger, M. (1976a). *The piety of thinking: essays, translations, notes and commentary by James G. Hart and John C. Maraldo*. Bloomington, IN: Indiana University Press.

Heidegger, M. (1976b). *What is called thinking?* New York: Perennial Library.

Heidegger, M. (1982). *On the way to language* (D. Peter, Trans.). San Francisco: Hertz Harper & Row.

Heidegger, M. (1984). *Early Greek thinking* (D. F. Krell & F. A. Capuzzi, Trans.). San Francisco: Harper & Row.

Heidegger, M. (1998). *Pathmarks* (W. McNeill, Ed.). Cambridge, UK: Cambridge University Press. doi:10.1017/CBO9780511812637

Heidegger, M. (2002a). *The essence of human freedom: an introduction to philosophy* (T. Sadler, Trans.). London: Continuum.

Heidegger, M. (2002b). *The essence of truth: on Plato's cave allegory and Theaetetus* (T. Sadler, Trans.). London: Continuum.

Heidegger, M. (2013). *The event* (R. Rojcewicz, Trans.). Bloomington, IN: Indiana University Press.

Heidegger, M. (2016). *Ponderings: black notebooks 1931-1938. II-VI* (R. Rojcewicz, Trans.). Bloomington, IN: Indiana University Press.

Heidegger, M. (2017). *Ponderings. VII-XI, 1938-1939: Black notebooks* (R. Rojcewicz, Trans.). Bloomington, IN: Indiana University Press.

Heim, M. (1993). *The metaphysics of virtual reality*. New York: Oxford University Press.

Ihde, D. (2010). *Heidegger's technologies: postphenomenological perspectives*. Fordham University Press.

Jaspers, K. (1955). *Reason and Existenz*. New York: Noonday Press.

Kroker, A. (2004). *The will to technology and the culture of nihilism: Heidegger, Nietzsche and Marx*. Toronto: University of Toronto Press.

Lack, A. (2014). *Martin Heidegger on technology, ecology, and the arts*. Basingstoke, UK: Palgrave Pivot. doi:10.1057/9781137487452

Lawson, C. (2017). *Technology and isolation*. Cambridge, UK: Cambridge University Press. doi:10.1017/9781316848319

Loscerbo, J. (1981). *Being and technology: a study in the philosophy of Martin Heidegger. Kluwer*. doi:10.1007/978-94-009-8222-2

Marcel, G. (1949). *Philosophy of Existence*. New York: Philosophical Library.

Marcel, G. (1952). *Man against Mass Society*. Chicago: Regnery.

Marcel, G. (1963). *The Existential Background of Human Dignity.*. Cambridge, MA: Harvard University Press.

Marcel, G. (1965). *Being and Having*. London: Collins.

Marcel, G. (1966). *Philosophy of Existentialism*. New York: Citadel.

Marcel, G., & Man, P. (1967). Herder and Herder. London: Academic Press.

Marcel, G. (1973). *Tragic Wisdom and Beyond*. Evanston, IL: Northwestern University Press.

Maritain, J. (1932). *An introduction to philosophy*. London: Sheed & Ward.

Maritain, J. (1938). *Humanism*. Charles Scribner's Sons.

Maritain, J. (1946). *The twilight of civilization*. London: G. Bles.

Maritain, J. (1953). *The range of reason*. London: G. Bles.

Maritain, J. (1956a). *The Knowledge of Man*. London: George Allen & Unwin.

MaritainJ. (1956b). Existence and the Existent. Image Books.

Maritain, J. (1958). *The Rights of Man and Natural Law*. London: Academic Press.

Maritain, J. (1961). *On the use of philosophy: Three essays*. Princeton, NJ: Princeton U.P. doi:10.1515/9781400878284

Maritain, J. (1970). *True humanism*. Westport, CT: Greenwood Press.

Matson, F. W., & Montagu, A. (Eds.). (1967). *The human dialogue: perspectives on communication*. New York: Free Press.

Mendes-Flohr, P. (1989). *From mysticism to dialogue: Martin Buber's transformation of German social thought*. Detroit, MI: Wayne State University Press.

Mendes-Flohr, P. (2015). *Dialogue as a Trans-disciplinary Concept: Martin Buber's Philosophy of Dialogue and its Contemporary Reception*. Boston: De Gruyter. doi:10.1515/9783110402223

Plato. (n.d.a). Available at: http://www.perseus.tufts.edu/hopper/text?doc=Perseus%3Atext%3A1999.01.0176%3Atext%3DCharm

Plato. (n.d.b). Available at: http://www.perseus.tufts.edu/hopper/text?doc=Perseus%3Atext%3A1999.01.0178%3Atext%3DGorg

Putnam, H. (2008). *Jewish philosophy as a guide to life: Rosenzweig, Buber, Lévinas, Wittgenstein*. Bloomington, IN: Indiana University Press.

Rothenberg, D. (1993). *Hand's end: technology and the limits of nature*. Berkeley, CA: University of California Press.

Scharff, R. C. (2013). *Philosophy of Technology: The Technological Condition: An Anthology*. Hoboken, NJ: Wiley.

Schilpp, P. A., & Friedman, M. (Eds.). (1967). *The philosophy of Martin Buber*. Open Court, La Salle.

Schilpp, P. A., & Hahn, L. E. (Eds.). (1984). *The Philosophy of Gabriel Marcel*. Open Court Pub. Co.

Silberstein, L. J. (1989). *Martin Buber's social and religious thought: Alienation and the quest for meaning*. New York: New York University Press.

Skrbina, D. (2014). *The Metaphysics of Technology*. London: Taylor and Francis.

Theunissen, M. (1984). *The other: studies in the social ontology of Husserl, Heidegger, Sartre, and Buber*. Cambridge, MA.: MIT Press.

Willson, M. A. (2006). *Technically together: rethinking community within techno-society*. New York: Peter Lang.

Wood, R. E. (1969). *Martin Buber's ontology: An analysis of I and thou*. Evanston, IL: Northwestern University Press.

Younis, R. A. (2013). On Thinking (and Measurement). In *Selected Essays from the International Conference of the Philosophy of Education Society of Australasia*. Retrieved from https://philpapers.org/rec/YOUOT

Zimmerman, M. E. (1990). *Heidegger's confrontation with modernity: technology, politics, and art*. Bloomington, IN: Indiana University Press.

# Chapter 5
# Cyberbullying:
## A Negative Online Experience

**Michelle F. Wright**
*Pennsylvania State University, USA*

**Bridgette D. Harper**
*Auburn University – Montgomery, USA*

## ABSTRACT

*The purpose of this literature review is to describe youths' involvement in cyberbullying. The term "youths" refers to individuals in elementary school, middle school, and high school. The chapter begins by providing a description of cyberbullying and the definition of cyberbullying. The next section describes the characteristics and risk factors associated with youths' involvement in cyberbullying. The third section focuses on the psychological, social, behavioral, and academic difficulties associated with youths' involvement in cyberbullying. The chapter concludes with recommendations for schools and parents as well as recommendations for future research. The chapter draws on research utilizing quantitative, qualitative, mixed-methods, cross-sectional, longitudinal, and cross-sequential designs, and those from various disciplines, including psychology, communication, media studies, sociology, social work, and computer science.*

DOI: 10.4018/978-1-5225-4168-4.ch005

# INTRODUCTION

Millions of youths have fully embraced digital technologies such as mobile phones and the Internet, utilizing these digital technologies daily (Lenhart, 2015). Digital technologies provide many benefits to youths, including the ability to communicate with just about anyone, access to information for leisure and school purposes, and entertainment (e.g., watching videos). Although there are many benefits associated with youths' digital technology use, they are also at risk for a variety of negative experiences, such as receiving unwanted electronic content via videos, images, and text, becoming a victim of identity theft, using fake or untrue information for schoolwork, and encountering sexual predators. Another risk associated with their digital technology use is cyberbullying.

Defined as an extension of traditional bullying involving bullying behaviors using electronic technologies, including email, instant messaging, Facebook, and text messaging through mobile devices, cyberbullying involves malicious intent to cause harm to a victim or victims (Bauman, Underwood, & Card, 2013; Grigg, 2012).

The ability to remain anonymous in the cyber context offers flexibility to cyberbullies as they can harm their victims without much concern for the consequences of their actions, due to their ability to mask or hide their identity (Wright, 2014b). Anonymity can trigger the online disinhibition effect which leads some youths to do or say things that they would typically never do or say in the offline world (Suler, 2004; Wright, 2014a). Bullying through digital technologies allows cyberbullies to harm victims in a shorter amount of time. For example, cyberbullies can spread a rumor in the online world in a matter of minutes, while it could take hours for a rumor to spread in the offline world. Cyberbullies can also target victims as often as they like. Victims of offline bullying are able to escape bullying in the sanctuary of their homes, while cyberbullying often follows victims into their homes and other places they perceive as safe. Additionally, cyberbullying can involve the bully and victim only, or can additionally involve one bystander or multiple bystanders. For example, posting a video making fun of someone can receive thousands of views, whereas being bullied in the lunchroom might only be visible to the individuals paying attention to what is happening. Therefore, the nature of the cyberbullying is somewhat distinctive from traditional face-to-face bullying.

The aim of this chapter is to examine cyberbullying among youths in elementary school, middle school, and high school. The studies reviewed in this chapter are from various disciplines, including psychology, education, media studies, communication, social work, sociology, and computer science. This chapter reviews literature with cross-sectional, longitudinal, qualitative, and quantitative research designs to describe cyberbullying. In addition, the chapter draws on studies from a variety of different countries to provide a more thorough review of the literature. The chapter is organized into the following six sections:

1. **Description and Definition of Cyberbullying:** Review of the definition of cyberbullying, the types of digital technologies used, the role of anonymity, and the rates of cyberbullying perpetration and victimization
2. **Characteristics and Risk Factors Related to Youths' Involvement in Cyberbullying:** Review of the research on the predictors associated with cyberbullying among youths
3. **Consequences Associated With Youths' Involvement in Cyberbullying:** Review of the research findings regarding the social, psychological, Behavioral, and academic consequences related to youths' cyberbullying involvement
4. **Solutions and Recommendations:** Provides suggestions for prevention and intervention programs and recommendations for public policy development
5. **Future Research Directions:** Provides recommendations for future research aimed at understanding and preventing children's and adolescents' involvement in cyberbullying
6. **Conclusion:** Final remarks regarding the current nature of the literature on cyberbullying.

## BACKGROUND

Defined as youths' use of digital technologies to hostilely and intentionally harass, embarrass, and intimidate others, cyberbullying can sometimes involve repetition and an imbalance of power, like traditional forms of face-to-face bullying (Smith et al., 2013). Instrumental to the definition of cyberbullying is the hostility and intentionality of the act, which highlights the requirement that these behaviors must be intentionally and maliciously harmful to qualify as cyberbullying. Repetitiveness of cyberbullying behavior involves cyberbullies targeting a victim or group of victims multiple times by sharing humiliating video or text messages with one person or multiple people (Bauman et al., 2013). It is easier for bullies to perpetuate the cycle of cyberbullying. For example, cyberbullies can share a humiliating video or text message with one person who can then turn around and share the content additional times and with other people, and then these people can share the video or text message.

The use of digital technologies to harm others is what separates the definition of cyberbullying from the definition of traditional face-to-face bullying (Curelaru, Iacob, & Abalasei, 2009). Cyberbullying behaviors can occur through a variety of digital technologies and involve different behaviors, including sending unkind text messages and emails, theft of identity information, pretending to be someone else, making anonymous phone calls, sharing secrets about the victim by posting or sending the secret to someone else, spreading nasty rumors using social networking websites, threatening to harm someone, or uploading an embarrassing picture or video of the victim with malicious intent (Bauman et al., 2013). Other examples of cyberbullying involve behaviors that are similar to those carried out in the offline world, such as harassment, insults, verbal attacks, teasing, physical threats, social exclusion, and humiliation. Furthermore, cyberbullying can also involve the distribution of explicit or embarrassing videos through a variety of mediums, such as social networking sites, text messages, and online gaming sites. Cyberbullying can involve creating websites to defame someone else or making fake social networking profiles using someone else's identity (Rideout et al., 2005).

There are also cyberbullying behaviors that have no offline equivalent, such as happy slapping and flaming (Rideout et al., 2005). Happy slapping is when a group of people randomly insult another person while filming the incident on a mobile phone, and then these individuals will post the image(s) or video(s) online for others to see. Flaming involves posting provocative or offensive messages in a public forum with the intention of provoking an angry response or argument from members of the forum. Cyberbullying behaviors can take place through a variety of digital technologies, with the most frequently used technologies to harm others including gaming consoles, instant messaging tools, and social networking sites (Ybarra et al., 2007).

# CYBERBULLYING BEHAVIORS IN THE U.S. AND OTHER COUNTRIES

Understanding the prevalence of youths' cyberbullying involvement is important as it highlights how frequently youths are exposed to these behaviors. In one of the earliest studies on cyberbullying, Patchin and Hinduja (2006) found that 29% of children and adolescents in their sample reported that they had experienced cyber victimization and 47% indicated that they had witnessed cyberbullying. Similar rates were found by Kowalski and Limber (2007). There were 3,767 middle school students, ages 11 through 14, included in their study. Their findings indicated that 11% of the sample were cyberbullied, 4% bullied others, and 7% were classified as both cybervictim and cyberbully. Using a slightly older sample (grades 9-12th),

Goebert et al. (2011) found that 56.1% of youths in their sample from Hawaii were victims of cyberbullying. In a more recent investigation, Hinduja and Patchin (2012) examined cyberbullying behaviors within the past 30 days among 6th through 12th graders. Findings revealed that 4.9% of these youths perpetrated cyberbullying in the past 30 days. Among Canadian 10th graders, Cappadocia et al. (2013) found that 2.1% of adolescents in their study admitted to perpetrating cyberbullying, 1.9% were classified as cybervictims, and 0.6% explained that they were both cyberbullies and cyber victims. In a sample of 8th through 10th graders, Bonnanno and Hymel (2013) found that 6% admitted to being cyberbullies, 5.8% were classified as cybervictims only, and 5% were cyberbullies and cybervictims.

Cyberbullying involvement is a global problem and increasing evidence indicates that cyberbullying occurs among youths in Africa, Asia, Australia, Europe, and South America. In one study, Laftman, Modin, and Ostberg (2013) found that 5% of their large Swedish sample ($N = 22,544$, ages 15-18) were victims of cyberbullying, 4% were perpetrators of cyberbullying, and 2% were classified as both cyberbullies and cybervictims. Using a younger sample of Swedish adolescents, Beckman and colleagues (2012) found that 1.9% of their sample from 7th through 9th grade were classified as cybervictims, 2.9% as cyberbullies, and 0.6% as both cyberbullies and cybervictims. These rates were similar to those found among adolescents in Ireland. In particular, Corcoran et al. (2012) found that 6% of youths in their study, between the ages of 12 through 17, reported that they were victims of cyberbullying. Higher rates were found in Brighi et al.'s (2012) study. They found that 12.5% of Italian adolescents in their sample were classified as cybervictims. Similar rates were found by Festl and colleagues (2013). In their sample of German adolescents, Festl et al. found that 13% were classified as cyberbullies and 11% as cybervictims. Research has also focused on the rates of cyberbullying perpetration and victimization among children and adolescents from Israel. Those rates are generally higher than some European countries, but not as high as those found in India. Olenik-Shemesh et al. (2010) found that 16.5% of their participants ($N = 242$; 13-16 year olds) were cybervictims. The rate of Israeli adolescents identified as cybervictims or witnesses of cyberbullying was 32.4% of the sample ($N = 355$; 13 to 17 year olds; Lazuras et al., 2013).

A lot of research attention has focused on cyberbullying rates among Turkish youths. Estimates of cyberbullying victimization among Turkish youths vary, from 18% to 32% (Eruder-Baker, 2010; Yilmaz, 2011). Cyberbullying perpetration rates among Turkish youths also vary from 6% through 9% (Ayas & Horzum, 2012; Yilmaz, 2011). Aricak and colleagues (2008) found some of the highest rates of cyberbullying perpetration. In their sample of Turkish secondary school students, they found that 36% reported that they were cyberbullies.

Research on cyberbullying involvement among youths in Asian countries has been slower to develop. In one of the first studies on cyberbullying in Asia, Huang and Chou (2010) found that 63.4% of the Taiwanese youths in their sample had witnessed cyberbullying, 34.9% were classified as cybervictims, and 20.4% admitted to being cyberbullies. Jang, Song, and Kim (2014) examined cyberbullying involvement among 3,238 Korean adolescents. In this study, 43% of the sample were classified as perpetrators or victims of cyberbullying. These rates are similar to those of youths in China. In particular, Zhou and colleagues (2013) found that 34.8% of the 1,438 youths in their sample were classified as cyberbullies and 56.9% as cybervictims. Focusing exclusively on Facebook cyberbullying, Kwan and Skoric (2013) reported that 59.4% of Singaporean adolescents in their study experienced cyber victimization through this social media website, while 56.9% perpetrated cyberbullying. In addition, Wong and colleagues (2014) found that 12.2% of adolescents in their sample ($N =$ 1,912) were cybervictims and 13.1% were classified as cyberbullying perpetrators.

Some of the research on the prevalence of cyberbullying has focused on cross-cultural differences in youths' cyberbullying involvement. This research usually classified countries according to an independent self-construal or an interdependent self-construal. Someone with an independent self-construal views the self as separate from the social context, while someone with an interdependent self-construal views the self within the context of their social environment or society. Usually people from Western countries, like the United States, Canada, and England, are reinforced and primed for behaving in ways aligned with an independent self-construal. On the other hand, people from Eastern countries, like China, Korea, and Japan, may be reinforced and primed for behavior deemed an independent self-construal. Differences in self-construal affect people's social behaviors, particularly bullying and cyberbullying. Therefore, independent self-construal and interdependent self-construal have been used to explain these behaviors.

In their research on cross-cultural differences in cyberbullying, Barlett and colleagues (2013) found that youths from the United States self-reported higher levels of cyberbullying involvement when compared to youths from Japan. These results were also corroborated in a study examining differences in cyberbullying involvement rates among Japanese and Austrian adolescents. Austrian adolescents reported more cyberbullying perpetration and victimization than Japanese adolescents (Strohmeier, Aoyama, Gradinger, & Toda, 2013). In addition, Li (2008) found that Chinese youths engaged in less cyberbullying perpetration when compared to Canadian children and adolescents. However, Li found little differences between Chinese and Canadian youths when it came to cyberbullying victimization. In an earlier study, with a different sample, Li (2006) found that Chinese youths self-reported more cyberbullying victimization in comparison to Canadian youths. Focusing on differences in reactive (i.e., response to provocation) and proactive (i.e., to obtain some sort of goal) forms of cyberbullying, Shapka and Law found that East Asian adolescents from Canada reported more proactive cyberbullying perpetration while Canadian adolescents reported engaging in more reactive forms of cyberbullying (Shapka & Law 2013).

Little attention has been given to understanding cyberbullying involvement among youths from Africa, India, and South America. In one of the few studies to investigate cyberbullying involvement in India, Wright and colleagues (2015) found that Indian adolescents reported more cyberbullying perpetration and victimization when compared to adolescents from China and Japan, with Chinese adolescents reporting more of these behaviors in comparison to Japanese adolescents. Gender differences in cyberbullying involvement are also found to vary across countries as well. In particular, Genta and colleagues (2012) found that Italian males perpetrated more cyberbullying when compared to Spanish and English males. In Wright and colleagues' (2015) research, they found boys from India were more often involved in cyberbullying when compared to boys from China and Japan.

Taken together, this research indicates that cyberbullying perpetration and cyber victimization is a global concern, warranting additional investigation. Variations in prevalence are due to differences in samples, sampling techniques, and measures used.

## CHARACTERISTICS ASSOCIATED WITH CYBERBULLYING

After preliminary research of the prevalence of cyberbullying indicated that researchers should be concerned with these behaviors, other research focused on the characteristics associated with youths' involvement in cyberbullying. Age is one variable examined as having a role in cyberbullying. Research focused on age and cyberbullying typically reveals that cyberbullying victimization is more prevalent among early adolescents, while cyberbullying perpetration is more often carried out by older adolescents. Williams and Guerra (2007) examined cyberbullying perpetration among adolescents between 6th through 8th grades. They delineated different types of cyberbullying, with findings revealing that physical forms of cyberbullying, like hacking, peaked in middle school, while rates of physical forms of cyberbullying declined in high school. Other research has indicated that 9th graders had the highest risk of cyberbullying involvement when compared to adolescents in middle school (Wade & Beran, 2011). Consequently, age was not found to be a reliable predictor of youths' cyberbullying involvement.

Gender has also been examined as a predictor of cyberbullying involvement among youths. Some researchers have found that boys reported that they were more often the perpetrators of cyberbullying when compared to girls (Boulton et al., 2012; Li, 2007; Ybarra et al., 2007). Girls reported more cyber victimization than boys in other studies (Hinduja & Patchin, 2007; Kowalski & Limber, 2007). In contrast, some researchers (e.g., Dehue, Bolman, & Vollink, 2008; Pornari & Wood, 2010) reported that girls engaged in more cyberbullying perpetration, while boys experienced more cyber victimization (e.g., Huang & Chou, 2010; Sjurso, Fandrem, & Roland, 2016). Other researchers (e.g., Stoll & Block, 2015; Wright & Li, 2013b) have found no gender differences in children's and adolescents' involvement in these behaviors. In a recent study on the role of digital technologies and behavior in girls' and boys' cyberbullying perpetration, Wright (in press) found that it is important to consider the type of technology used and the behaviors perpetrated. In particular, boys were more likely to experience cyberbullying via gaming consoles, while girls were more likely to perpetrate relational and verbal forms of cyberbullying. Therefore, like age, gender has proven to be an inconsistent predictor of cyberbullying involvement as well.

Youths' involvement in other forms of bullying are typically examined as a risk factor associated with cyberbullying involvement. In this research, relationships are usually found between cyberbullying perpetration and traditional face-to-face bullying perpetration, cyber victimization and traditional face-to-face victimization, and traditional face-to-face victimization and cyberbullying perpetration (Barlett & Gentile, 2012; Mitchell et al., 2007; Wright & Li, 2013a; Wright & Li, 2013b).

Digital technology use is another characteristic associated with cyberbullying perpetration and victimization among youths. In this research, youths' greater use of the internet is positively correlated with their cyberbullying perpetration and victimization (Ang, 2016; Aricak et al., 2008). In addition, cybervictims are more likely to use instant messaging tools, email, blogging sites, and online game when compared to nonvictims, according to another finding suggesting the role of digital technology use in cyberbullying involvement (Smith et al., 2008). The link between digital technology use and cyberbullying involvement might be explained by some youths' greater likelihood to disclose personal information online. Disclosing personal information online, like one's geographical location or school name, increases youths' risk for cyberbullying victimization.

Both internalizing difficulties, such as depression and loneliness, and externalizing difficulties, such as alcohol and drug use, are factors related to youths' involvement in cyberbullying. To explain these associations, researchers propose that internalizing and externalizing problems reduce youths' coping strategies, making them more vulnerable to cyberbullying (Cappadocia et al., 2013; Mitchell et al., 2007). Alcohol and drug use are both associated with youths' involvement in cyberbullying as the perpetrator and victim (Cappadocia et al., 2013; Wright, in press).

Researchers have also investigated a variety of variables in relation to youths' cyberbullying involvement. In some research, higher normative beliefs (i.e., beliefs about the acceptability of behavior or behaviors) regarding face-to-face bullying and cyberbullying were related positively to cyberbullying perpetration (e.g., Burton, Florell, & Wygant, 2013; Wright, 2014b). Consequently, cyberbullies often hold favorable attitudes toward engaging in bullying behaviors, leading them to believe these behaviors are acceptable to perpetrate. In addition, holding lower levels of pro-victim attitudes, defined as the belief that bullying is unacceptable and that defending victims is valuable, lower peer attachment, less self-control and empathy, and greater moral disengagement were each correlated positively with cyberbullying perpetration (e.g., Sevcikova, Machackova, Wright, Dedkova, & Cerna, 2015; Wright, Kamble, Lei, Li, Aoyama, & Shruti, 2015).

Little attention has been given to understanding the longitudinal relationships between various characteristics and youths' cyberbullying involvement. In one of the few studies to investigate these behaviors utilizing a longitudinal design, Fanti and colleagues (2012) examined children's and adolescents' exposure to violent media, their callous and unemotional traits, and their cyberbullying involvement one year later. Media violence exposure was positively linked to adolescents' cyber victimization one year later. Wright (2014a) found that perceived stress from parents, peers, and academics/school were related to adolescents' cyberbullying perpetration one year later. Taken together, the research in this section highlights the various risk factors that increases youths' vulnerability to cyberbullying perpetration and victimization. This section also described the individual predictors associated with youths' cyberbullying involvement. The rest of this section will focus on the role of parents, schools, teachers, and peers in youths' involvement in cyberbullying.

## Parents

Some parents choose to monitor their children's activities in the online world. Mason (2008) found that 50% of children and adolescents reported that their parents did not monitor their online activities, while 80% of parents reported monitoring their children's online activities. In another study, 93% of parents reported that they set limits on their children's online activities (McQuade, Colt, & Meyer, 2009). However, only 37% of their children reported that they were given rules from their parents concerning their online activities. This could mean that parents are over reporting the amount of monitoring they engage in or that their strategies for monitoring are ineffective such that their children believe no strategies have been implemented. Parents have an important role in protecting their children against online risks. More attention should be given to how parents navigate having conversations with their children about online risks and opportunities.

Wright (2015) examined the person, either parents, teachers, or friends, who most frequently mediated youths' digital technology use. She found that parents were more likely to mediate youths' digital technology use and when they did, their children reported less cyber victimization and negative adjustment difficulties. Consequently, she concluded that parental mediation buffers against these negative psychological consequences. A possible explanation for these relationships is that parents who monitor their children's digital technology use provide more opportunities to discuss the risks associated with technology use. Furthermore, it might even increase youths' awareness that negative online behaviors are not acceptable. It could also make them think about what their parents might do if they engaged in negative online behaviors. This proposal is consistent with research finding that youths who believed that their parents would punish them for participating in negative online behaviors, like cyberbullying, were less likely to perpetrate cyberbullying (Hinduja & Patchin, 2013; Wright, 2013a). Other research has revealed that parental monitoring has no impact on youths' online risk exposure. Aoyama et al. (2011) found that parental mediation and monitoring of children's online activities were unrelated to youths' involvement in cyberbullying. They explained that some parents lack the technological skills to understand how to effectively monitor their children's online activities. Because parents lack these skills, they are not sure of how and when to intervene. Such a proposal is consistent with previous research findings in which parents reported that they were not sure how to discuss online activities with their children (Rosen, 2007). This uncertainty might mean some parents do not know to talk to their children about appropriate online behaviors.

Some parents do not follow-up on the strategies they implement for making the Internet safer for their children. Youths might develop the perception that their parents are not concerned with their online behaviors, and this could subsequently increase their risk of engaging in cyberbullying. In addition, it is important for parents to not only enforce the strategies they implement regarding digital technology use, but to also update the strategies they use as their children become older and desire more independence and privacy.

Family characteristics have also been examined in association with youths' cyberbullying involvement. Ybarra and Mitchell (2004) found that family income, parental education, and marital status of caregivers were unrelated to youths' cyberbullying perpetration or victimization. However, Arslan et al. (2012) found that parental unemployment was related to youths' cyberbullying perpetration and victimization. Neglectful parenting increased youths' risk of cyberbullying involvement when compared to youths who were not involved in cyberbullyinh (Dehue, Bolman, Vollink, & Pouwelse, 2012). Furthermore, authoritarian parenting style increased youths' experience of cyberbullying as cybervictims.

In sum, the literature reviewed in this section suggests that parents have an important role in mitigating their children's involvement in cyberbullying and other negative online behaviors. The research reviewed in the next section focuses on the role of schools and peers in youths' cyberbullying perpetration and victimization.

## Schools

The school's role in monitoring and providing sanctions for youths' cyberbullying is a topic of great debate. This is because many cyberbullying incidents occur off school grounds, making it difficult for the school to know about these cases or how to deal with such situations (deLara, 2012; Mason, 2008). Although most cyberbullying incidents occur off school grounds, many involve youths who attend the same school. This further complicates the schools' role in handling cyberbullying. Because cyberbullying typically involves youths who know each other at school, it is likely that knowledge of the incidents might spread across the school or that these individuals might engage in negative interactions while on school grounds, which could disrupt the learning process.

Although cyberbullying incidents have the potential to "spill over" onto school grounds, administrators' and teachers' perceptions of cyberbullying vary, leading some school staff to perceive these behaviors as problematic while others do not (Kochenderfer-Ladd & Pelletier, 2008). Oftentimes administrators and teachers will not perceive cyberbullying or any form of covert bullying behavior as serious or harmful (Sahin, 2010). Some teachers are more likely to encourage prevention programs designed to reduce physical forms of face-to-face bullying (Tangen & Campbell, 2010). They do not understand the harmful consequences associated with relational bullying and cyberbullying. Some teacher training does not properly inform teachers on how to recognize cyberbullying or how to deal with it. Sometimes teachers are unfamiliar with newer technologies (Cassidy et al., 2012a). This unfamiliarity makes it difficult for teachers to deal with cyberbullying as they are unsure of how to respond to the incident or which strategies to implement to alleviate the situation. If teachers are concerned about cyberbullying, there are usually few policies and programs at the school level, making it difficult to implement solutions (Cassidy, Brown, & Jackson, 2012b).

Schools must recognize the importance of implementing effective policies and professional development designed to deal effectively with cyberbullying as these behaviors impact learning (Shariff & Hoff, 2007). When youths are involved in cyberbullying, as perpetrators or victims, they are less likely to perceive their school and teachers positively when compared to uninvolved youths (Bayar &

Ucanok, 2012). Many victims of cyberbullying fear that their classmates might be cyberbullies, which disrupts their ability to concentrate on learning (Eden, Heiman, & Olenik-Shemesh, 2013). Such disruptions might reduce their academic attainment and performance. Furthermore, lower school commitment and perceptions of a negative school climate increase youths' perpetration of cyberbullying as they feel less connected to their school (Williams & Guerra, 2007).

Administrators and teachers require training to increase their awareness of cyberbullying. They also need to work together to develop policies at the school level to reduce these behaviors and implement strategies to handle cyberbullying incidents. Confidence in one's teaching abilities and having a stronger commitment to the school increases teachers' likelihood of learning about cyberbullying (Eden et al., 2013). When teachers learn about cyberbullying, they increase their awareness of these behaviors and how to effectively deal with these incidents. This awareness could help to prevent youths' involvement in cyberbullying. In particular, when teachers feel more confident, they intervene in cyberbullying incidents more often, which protects adolescents' from experiencing these behaviors (Elledge et al., 2013). Teachers' motivation for learning about cyberbullying varies such that elementary school teachers are more concerned with this behavior than middle school students. This is problematic as cyberbullying involvement increases from elementary school to middle school (Ybarra et al., 2007). Therefore, there is a need for educator training programs aimed at raising awareness of cyberbullying, particularly in middle schools.

## Peers

Peer relationships help youths learn about the social norms dictating acceptable and unacceptable behaviors within the peer group; as a consequence of this learning, youths will engage in more of these acceptable behaviors, as dictated by their peers, even if they are negative. In one study, the best predictor of cyberbullying involvement was the climate of the classroom in which these behaviors were encouraged (Festl et al., 2013). Furthermore, believing that one's friends engaged in cyberbullying predicts youths' perpetration of these behaviors (Hinduja & Patchin, 2013). The peer contagion effect potentially explains these associations, which suggests that engagement in negative behaviors perpetrated by one's friends "spread" to other children and adolescents within their social network (Sijtsema, Ashwin, Simona, & Gina, 2014).

Peer attachment is another variable which has been examined in relation to youths' involvement in cyberbullying. Peer attachment refers to youths' beliefs that their peers will be or will not be there for them when they need it. This variable directly relates to peer interactions. In one study, Burton and colleagues (2013) found that lower peer attachment was associated positively with cyberbullying perpetration and victimization. Peer rejection also increased youths' cyberbullying perpetration and cyber victimization (Sevcikova et al., 2015; Wright & Li, 2013b). To explain the connection between peer rejection and cyberbullying involvement, Wright and Li (2012) propose that peer rejection triggers negative emotional responses that lead to cyberbullying perpetration and victimization. Other research has explored the potential of cyberbullying to promote youths' social standing in their peer group, both online and offline. With digital technologies having such a prominent role in youths' lives, these technologies might be used as tools to promote or maintain youths' social standing in the peer group. Wright (2014c) found that higher levels of perceived popularity, a reputational type of popularity in the peer group, was associated positively with cyberbullying perpetration six months later among adolescents. The literature in this section suggests that it is important to consider the role of peers in youths' cyberbullying involvement.

## CONSEQUENCES ASSOCIATED WITH CYBERBULLYING INVOLVEMENT

Parents', schools', and researchers' concerns with cyberbullying involvement among youths are triggered by the various negative social, psychological, behavioral, and academic consequences associated with youths' exposure to these behaviors. Much of the research on cyberbullying reveals that this experience disrupts youths' emotional experiences. Cybervictims report lower levels of global happiness, general school happiness, school satisfaction, family satisfaction, and self-satisfaction (Toledano, Werch, & Wiens, 2015). Furthermore, cybervicitms also report that they experience anger, sadness, and fear more often than uninvolved youths (Dehue et al., 2008; Machackova, Dedkova, Sevcikova, & Cerna, 2013; Patchin & Hinduja, 2006).

Cyberbullying involvement also disrupts youths' academic performance. In particular, cyberbullies and cybervictims experience more academic difficulties, including less motivation for school, poor academic performance, lower academic attainment, and more school absences (Belae & Hall, 2007; Yousef & Bellamy, 2015). Lower school functioning, such as disruptive classroom behaviors, lower grades, and lower test scores, is associated with cyberbullying perpetration and victimization (Wright, in press).

Cyberbullies and cybervictims are also at risk for a variety of internalizing and externalizing difficulties (e.g., Mitchell, Ybarra, & Finkelhor, 2007; Patchin & Hinduja, 2006; Wright, 2014b; Ybarra, Diener-West, & Leaf, 2007). Youths involved in cyberbullying report more suicidal thoughts and attempts when compared to uninvolved youths (Bauman, Toomey, & Walker 2013). Experiencing or perpetrating cyberbullying increases youths' risk of mental health problems (Beckman et al., 2012) and psychiatric and psychosomatic problems (Sourander et al., 2010).

The research on psychological and behavioral consequences related to cyberbullying involvement usually do not take into account youths' involvement in traditional forms of bullying and victimization. Studies that consider youths' involvement in both cyber and face-to-face forms of bullying are important because these variables are highly correlated (Williams & Guerra, 2007; Wright & Li, 2013b). In one of the few studies to take these high correlations into account, Bonanno and colleagues (2013) controlled for face-to-face bullying and victimization and found that youths involved in cyberbullying experienced greater depressive symptoms and suicidal ideation. Other researchers have focused on the conjoint effects of cyber and face-to-face bullying on youths' psychological and behavioral adjustment. Gradinger and colleagues (2009) and Perren et al. (2012) found that victims of both traditional face-to-face bullying and cyberbullying reported higher levels of internalizing symptoms when compared to children and adolescents who experienced only one type of victimization. Thus, a combination of various bullying behaviors exacerbates children's and adolescents' experience of depression, anxiety, and loneliness. Such findings further support the importance of considering children's and adolescents' involvement in bullying behaviors both offline and online in an effort to understand more about these relationships and how to best intervene.

## SOLUTIONS AND RECOMMENDATIONS

Everyone in our communities should be concerned with youths' involvement in cyberbullying. School curriculum should include elements that teach youths about cyberbullying, digital literacy, and digital citizenship (Cassidy et al., 2012b). Such curriculum should also discuss the many positive uses of digital technology, pro-victim attitudes, empathy, self-esteem, and social skills. Schools should also aim to improve school climate by learning students' names, praising good behavior, and staying technologically up-to-date (Hinduja & Patchin, 2012). A code of conduct which addresses appropriate digital technology use should also be developed and adopted. It important not only to implement this code of conduct, but also for administrators, teachers, and other school staff to enforce these policies.

Parents also have a role in helping to address cyberbullying. They should partner with educators from their children's school and increase their awareness and knowledge of digital technologies (Cassidy et al., 2012a; Diamanduros & Downs, 2011). Furthermore, parents should develop more knowledge of digital technologies in an effort to understand their children's desire to be involved in the cyber context and to have an awareness of the potential risks that their children might be exposed to via digital technologies. Such knowledge can help them develop and implemental parental monitoring strategies to reduce their children's vulnerability to cyberbullying. They should also maintain an open dialogue with their children regarding appropriate digital technology use. Some parents engage in poor digital technology habits, such as using mobile phones and texting while driving or using mobile phones during dinner or special events. Parents should model appropriate online behavior in order to serve as appropriate role models for their children.

## FUTURE RESEARCH DIRECTIONS

The purpose of this literature review was to describe cyberbullying behaviors and the role of various characteristics and risk factors associated with youths' involvement in these behaviors. This review of the literature on cyberbullying involvement suggests some noticeable limitations and future directions for research. Anonymity is a prominent factor found to relate to youths' perpetration of cyberbullying. Despite such awareness, little attention has been given to this topic, particularly how anonymous beliefs about the cyber context develop and how such beliefs relate to cyberbullying. Other research should focus on non-anonymous forms of cyberbullying versus anonymous forms of cyberbullying in order to understand more about the motivators underlying these behaviors, and whether victims might experience differential adjustment difficulties following victimization by anonymous versus non-anonymous cyberbullies. More specifically, non-anonymous cyberbullying, perpetrated by a known peer, might have more of an impact on an adolescent's depressive symptoms than if he or she were to experience the same behaviors from an anonymous perpetrator.

More attention is needed to develop an understanding of the long-term impact of cyberbullying perpetration and cyber victimization across multiple age groups, particularly among young children and adults. Most studies on cyberbullying involvement focus on early and late adolescents, with little attention given to cyberbullying perpetration and cyber victimization among elementary school-aged children (Madden et al., 2013; Ybarra et al., 2007). Focusing on this younger age group makes it easier to understand the developmental trajectory of traditional face-to-face bullying and cyberbullying involvement, and it could help to answer questions about the temporal order of these bullying behaviors. This research will help to shed light on whether there is an age at which youths are most vulnerable to cyberbullying involvement. Intervention and prevention programs could be developed with consideration to the specific age group identified as the most at risk for cyberbullying involvement.

## CONCLUSION

The findings from the literature on cyberbullying underscore the need for continued investigations on cyberbullying. The earlier research on cyberbullying focused on rates of cyberbullying to understand how many youths were at risk for these behaviors. From this early research, researchers directed their attention to the causes and consequences of youths' cyberbullying involvement. Most of the research focused on the "causes" of cyberbullying utilize concurrent research designs and focus on the role of parents, schools, and peers in youths' involvement in these behaviors. More investigations need to focus on these individuals and entities, because cyberbullying is a global concern. This is important as cyberbullying affects all aspects of our society, undermining ethical and moral values. It is imperative that we unite and do our part to reduce children's and adolescents' involvement in cyberbullying together.

The aim of this chapter was to review literature on cyberbullying by providing a description and definition of these behaviors, the associated characteristics and risk factors, and the outcomes related to youths' involvement in cyberbullying. The literature reviewed in this chapter includes studies with cross-sectional, longitudinal, qualitative, and quantitative research designs. Solutions and recommendations and future research directions were also discussed.

# REFERENCES

Ang, R. P. (2016). Cyberbullying: Its prevention and intervention strategies. In D. Sibnath (Ed.), *Child safety, welfare and well-being: Issues and challenges* (pp. 25–38). Springer. doi:10.1007/978-81-322-2425-9_3

Aoyama, I., Utsumi, S., & Hasegawa, M. (2011). Cyberbullying in Japan: Cases, government reports, adolescent relational aggression and parental monitoring roles. In Q. Li, D. Cross, & P. K. Smith (Eds.), *Bullying in the global playground: Research from an international perspective.* Oxford, UK: Wiley-Blackwell.

Aricak, T., Siyahhan, S., Uzunhasanoglu, A., Saribeyoglu, S., Ciplak, S., Yilmaz, N., & Memmedov, C. (2008). Cyberbullying among Turkish adolescents. *Cyberpsychology & Behavior, 11*(3), 253–261. doi:10.1089/cpb.2007.0016 PMID:18537493

Arslan, S., Savaser, S., Hallett, V., & Balci, S. (2012). Cyberbullying among primary school students in Turkey: Self-reported prevalence and associations with home and school life. *Cyberpsychology, Behavior, and Social Networking, 15*(10), 527–533. doi:10.1089/cyber.2012.0207 PMID:23002988

Ayas, T., & Horzum, M. B. (2010). *Cyberbullying / victim scale development study.* Retrieved from: http://www.akademikbakis.org

Barlett, C. P., & Gentile, D. A. (2012). Long-term psychological predictors of cyber-bullying in late adolescence. *Psychology of Popular Media Culture, 2*, 123–135. doi:10.1037/a0028113

Barlett, C. P., Gentile, D. A., Anderson, C. A., Suzuki, K., Sakamoto, A., Yamaoka, A., & Katsura, R. (2013). Cross-cultural differences in cyberbullying behavior: A short-term longitudinal study. *Journal of Cross-Cultural Psychology, 45*(2), 300–313. doi:10.1177/0022022113504622

Bauman, S., Toomey, R. B., & Walker, J. L. (2013). Associations among bullying, cyberbullying, and suicide in high school students. *Journal of Adolescence, 36*(2), 341–350. doi:10.1016/j.adolescence.2012.12.001 PMID:23332116

Bauman, S., Underwood, M. K., & Card, N. A. (2013). Definitions: Another perspective and a proposal for beginning with cyberaggression. In S. Bauman, D. Cross, & J. Walker (Eds.), *Principles of cyberbullying research: Definitions, measures, methodology* (pp. 26–40). New York, NY: Routledge.

Bayar, Y., & Ucanok, Z. (2012). School social climate and generalized peer perception in traditional and cyberbullying status. *Educational Sciences: Theory and Practice*, *12*, 2352–2358.

Beckman, L., Hagquist, C., & Hellstrom, L. (2012). Does the association with psychosomatic health problems differ between cyberbullying and traditional bullying? *Emotional & Behavioural Difficulties*, *17*(3-4), 421–434. doi:10.1080/13632752.2012.704228

Bonanno, R. A., & Hymel, S. (2013). Cyber bullying and internalizing difficulties: Above and beyond the impact of traditional forms of bullying. *Journal of Youth and Adolescence*, *42*(5), 685–697. doi:10.100710964-013-9937-1 PMID:23512485

Boulton, M., Lloyd, J., Down, J., & Marx, H. (2012). Predicting undergraduates' self-reported engagement in traditional and cyberbullying from attitudes. *Cyberpsychology, Behavior, and Social Networking*, *15*(3), 141–147. doi:10.1089/cyber.2011.0369 PMID:22304402

Brighi, A., Guarini, A., Melotti, G., Galli, S., & Genta, M. L. (2012). Predictors of victimisation across direct bullying, indirect bullying and cyberbullying. *Emotional & Behavioural Difficulties*, *17*(3-4), 375–388. doi:10.1080/13632752.2012.704684

Burton, K. A., Florell, D., & Wygant, D. B. (2013). The role of peer attachment and normative beliefs about aggression on traditional bullying and cyberbullying. *Psychology in the Schools*, *50*(2), 103–114. doi:10.1002/pits.21663

Cappadocia, M. C., Craig, W. M., & Pepler, D. (2013). Cyberbullying: Prevalence, stability and risk factors during adolescence. *Canadian Journal of School Psychology*, *28*(2), 171–192. doi:10.1177/0829573513491212

Cassidy, W., Brown, K., & Jackson, M. (2012a). "Making kind cool": Parents' suggestions for preventing cyber bullying and fostering cyber kindness. *Journal of Educational Computing Research*, *46*(4), 415–436. doi:10.2190/EC.46.4.f

Cassidy, W., Brown, K., & Jackson, M. (2012b). "Under the radar": Educators and cyberbullying in schools. *School Psychology International*, *33*(5), 520–532. doi:10.1177/0143034312445245

Corcoran, L., Connolly, I., & O'Moore, M. (2012). Cyberbullying in Irish schools: An investigation of personality and self-concept. *The Irish Journal of Psychology*, *33*(4), 153–165. doi:10.1080/03033910.2012.677995

Curelaru, M., Iacob, I., & Abalasei, B. (2009). *School bullying: Definition, characteristics, and intervention strategies.* Lumean Publishing House.

Dehue, F., Bolman, C., & Vollink, T. (2008). Cyberbullying: Youngsters' experiences and parental perception. *CyberPscyhology & Behavior, 11*(2), 217–223. doi:10.1089/cpb.2007.0008 PMID:18422417

Dehue, F., Bolman, C., Vollink, T., & Pouwelse, M. (2012). Cyberbullying and traditional bullying in relation to adolescents' perceptions of parenting. *Journal of Cyber Therapy and Rehabilitation, 5,* 25–34.

deLara, E. W. (2012). Why adolescents don't disclose incidents of bullying and harassment. *Journal of School Violence, 11*(4), 288–305. doi:10.1080/15388220.2012.705931

Diamanduros, T., & Downs, E. (2011). Creating a safe school environment: How to prevent cyberbullying at your school. *Library Media Connection, 30*(2), 36–38.

Eden, S., Heiman, T., & Olenik-Shemesh, D. (2013). Teachers' perceptions, beliefs and concerns about cyberbullying. *British Journal of Educational Technology, 44*(6), 1036–1052. doi:10.1111/j.1467-8535.2012.01363.x

Elledge, L. C., Williford, A., Boulton, A. J., DePaolis, K. J., Little, T. D., & Salmivalli, C. (2013). Individual and contextual predictors of cyberbullying: The influence of children's provictim attitudes and teachers' ability to intervene. *Journal of Youth and Adolescence, 42*(5), 698–710. doi:10.100710964-013-9920-x PMID:23371005

Erdur-Baker, O. (2010). Cyberbullying and its correlation to traditional bullying, gender and frequent and risky usage of internet-mediated communication tools. *New Media & Society, 12*(1), 109–125. doi:10.1177/1461444809341260

Fanti, K. A., Demetriou, A. G., & Hawa, V. V. (2012). A longitudinal study of cyberbullying: Examining risk and protective factors. *European Journal of Developmental Psychology, 8*(2), 168–181. doi:10.1080/17405629.2011.643169

Festl, R., Schwarkow, M., & Quandt, T. (2013). Peer influence, internet use and cyberbullying: A comparison of different context effects among German adolescents. *Journal of Children and Media, 7*(4), 446–462. doi:10.1080/17482798.2013.781514

Goebert, D., Else, I., Matsu, C., Chung-Do, J., & Chang, J. Y. (2011). The impact of cyberbullying on substance use and mental health in a multiethnic sample. *Maternal and Child Health Journal, 15*(8), 1282–1286. doi:10.100710995-010-0672-x PMID:20824318

Gradinger, P., Strohmeier, D., & Spiel, C. (2009). Traditional bullying and cyberbullying. *The Journal of Psychology, 217*, 205–213.

Grigg, D. W. (2012). Definitional constructs of cyberbullying and cyber aggression from a triangulatory overview: A preliminary study into elements. *Journal of Aggression, Conflict and Peace Research, 4*(4), 202–215. doi:10.1108/17596591211270699

Hinduja, S., & Patchin, J. W. (2007). Offline consequences of online victimization. *Journal of School Violence, 6*(3), 89–112. doi:10.1300/J202v06n03_06

Hinduja, S., & Patchin, J. W. (2012). Cyberbullying: Neither and epidemic nor a rarity. *European Journal of Developmental Psychology, 9*(5), 539–543. doi:10.1080/17405629.2012.706448

Hinduja, S., & Patchin, J. W. (2013). Social influences on cyberbullying behaviors among middle and high school students. *Journal of Youth and Adolescence, 42*(5), 711–722. doi:10.100710964-012-9902-4 PMID:23296318

Huang, Y., & Chou, C. (2010). An analysis of multiple factors of cyberbullying among junior high school students in Taiwan. *Computers in Human Behavior, 26*(6), 1581–1590. doi:10.1016/j.chb.2010.06.005

Jang, H., Song, J., & Kim, R. (2014). Does the offline bully-victimization influence cyberbullying behavior among youths? Application of general strain theory. *Computers in Human Behavior, 31*, 85–93. doi:10.1016/j.chb.2013.10.007

Kochenderfer-Ladd, B., & Pelletier, M. (2008). Teachers' views and beliefs about bullying: Influences on classroom management strategies and students' coping with peer victimization. *Journal of School Psychology, 46*(4), 431–453. doi:10.1016/j.jsp.2007.07.005 PMID:19083367

Kowalski, R. M., & Limber, S. P. (2007). Electronic bullying among middle school students. *The Journal of Adolescent Health, 41*(6), 22–30. doi:10.1016/j.jadohealth.2007.08.017 PMID:18047942

Kwan, G. C. E., & Skoric, M. M. (2013). Facebook bullying: An extension of battles in school. *Computers in Human Behavior, 29*(1), 16–25. doi:10.1016/j.chb.2012.07.014

Laftman, S. B., Modin, B., & Ostberg, V. (2013). Cyberbullying and subjective health: A large-scale study of students in Stockholm, Sweden. *Children and Youth Services Review, 35*(1), 112–119. doi:10.1016/j.childyouth.2012.10.020

Lazuras, L., Barkoukis, V., Ourda, D., & Tsorbatzoudis, H. (2013). A process model of cyberbullying in adolescence. *Computers in Human Behavior, 29*(3), 881–887. doi:10.1016/j.chb.2012.12.015

Lenhart, A. (2015). *Teens, social media & technology overview 2015*. Retrieved from: http://www.pewinternet.org/2015/04/09/teens-social-media-technology-2015/

Li, Q. (2007). Bullying in the new playground: Research into cyberbullying and cybervictimization. *Australian Journal of Educational Technology, 23*, 435–454.

Li, Q. (2008). A cross-cultural comparison of adolescents' experience related to cyberbullying. *Educational Research, 50*(3), 223–234. doi:10.1080/00131880802309333

Machackova, H., Dedkova, L., & Mezulanikova, K. (2015). Brief report: The bystander effect in cyberbullying incidents. *Journal of Adolescence, 43*, 96–99. doi:10.1016/j.adolescence.2015.05.010 PMID:26070168

Machackova, H., Dedkova, L., Sevcikova, A., & Cerna, A. (2013). Bystanders' support of cyberbullied schoolmates. *Journal of Community & Applied Social Psychology, 23*(1), 25–36. doi:10.1002/casp.2135

Mason, K. (2008). Cyberbullying: A preliminary assessment for school personnel. *Psychology in the Schools, 45*(4), 323–348. doi:10.1002/pits.20301

McQuade, C. S., Colt, P. J., & Meyer, B. N. (2009). *Cyber bullying: Protecting kids and adults from online bullies*. Westport, CT: Praeger.

Mitchell, K. J., Ybarra, M., & Finkelhor, D. (2007). The relative importance of online victimization in understanding depression, delinquency, and substance use. *Child Maltreatment, 12*(4), 314–324. doi:10.1177/1077559507305996 PMID:17954938

Patchin, J. W., & Hinduja, S. (2006). Bullies move beyond the schoolyard: A preliminary look at cyberbullying. *Youth Violence and Juvenile Justice, 4*(2), 148–169. doi:10.1177/1541204006286288

Perren, S., Dooley, J., Shaw, T., & Cross, D. (2010). Bullying in school and cyberspace: Associations with depressive symptoms in Swiss and Australian adolescents. *Child and Adolescent Psychiatry and Mental Health, 4*(1), 1–10. doi:10.1186/1753-2000-4-28 PMID:21092266

Pornari, C. D., & Wood, J. (2010). Peer and cyber aggression in secondary school students: The role of moral disengagement, hostile attribution bias, and outcome expectancies. *Aggressive Behavior, 36*(2), 81–94. doi:10.1002/ab.20336 PMID:20035548

Rideout, V. J., Roberts, D. F., & Foehr, U. G. (2005). *Generation M: Media in the lives of 8-18-year-olds: Executive summary.* Menlo Park, CA: Henry J. Kaiser Family Foundation.

Rosen, L. D. (2007). *Me, Myspace, and I: Parenting the Net Generation.* New York: Palgrave Macmillan.

Sahin, M. (2010). Teachers' perceptions of bullying in high schools: A Turkish study. *Social Behavior and Personality, 38*(1), 127–142. doi:10.2224bp.2010.38.1.127

Sevcikova, A., Machackova, H., Wright, M. F., Dedkova, L., & Cerna, A. (2015). Social support seeking in relation to parental attachment and peer relationships among victims of cyberbullying. *Australian Journal of Guidance & Counselling, 15*, 1–13. doi:10.1017/jgc.2015.1

Shapka, J. D., & Law, D. M. (2013). Does one size fit all? Ethnic differences in parenting behaviors and motivations for adolescent engagement in cyberbullying. *Journal of Youth and Adolescence, 42*(5), 723–738. doi:10.100710964-013-9928-2 PMID:23479327

Shariff, S., & Hoff, D. L. (2007). Cyber bullying: Clarifying legal boundaries for school supervision in cyberspace. *International Journal of Cyber Criminology, 1*, 76–118.

Sijtsema, J. J., Ashwin, R. J., Simona, C. S., & Gina, G. (2014). Friendship selection and influence in bullying and defending. *Effects of moral disengagement. Developmental Psychology*, *50*(8), 2093–2104. doi:10.1037/a0037145 PMID:24911569

Sjurso, I. R., Fandream, H., & Roland, E. (2016). Emotional problems in traditional and cyber victimization. *Journal of School Violence*, *15*(1), 114–131. doi:10.1080 /15388220.2014.996718

Smith, P. K., Del Barrio, C., & Tokunaga, R. S. (2013). Definitions of bullying and cyberbullying: How useful are the terms? In S. Bauman, D. Cross, & J. Walker (Eds.), *Principles of cyberbullying research: Definitions, measures, methodology* (pp. 26–40). New York, NY: Routledge.

Smith, P. K., Mahdavi, J., Carvalho, M., Fisher, S., Russell, S., & Tippett, N. (2008). Cyberbullying: Its nature and impact in secondary school pupils. *Journal of Child Psychology and Psychiatry, and Allied Disciplines*, *49*(4), 376–385. doi:10.1111/ j.1469-7610.2007.01846.x PMID:18363945

Sourander, A., Brunstein, A., Ikonen, M., Lindroos, J., Luntamo, T., Koskelainen, M., ... Helenius, H. (2010). Psychosocial risk factors associated with cyberbullying among adolescents: A population-based study. *Archives of General Psychiatry*, *67*(7), 720–728. doi:10.1001/archgenpsychiatry.2010.79 PMID:20603453

Stoll, L. C., & Block, R. Jr. (2015). Intersectionality and cyberbullying: A study of cybervictimization in a Midwestern high school. *Computers in Human Behavior*, *52*, 387–391. doi:10.1016/j.chb.2015.06.010

Strohmeier, D., Aoyama, I., Gradinger, P., & Toda, Y. (2013). Cybervictimization and cyberaggression in Eastern and Western countries: Challenges of constructing a cross-cultural appropriate scale. In S. Bauman, D. Cross, & J. L. Walker (Eds.), *Principles of cyberbullying research: Definitions, measures, and methodology* (pp. 202–221). New York: Routledge.

Suler, J. (2004). The online disinhibition effect. *Cyberpsychology & Behavior*, *7*(3), 321–326. doi:10.1089/1094931041291295 PMID:15257832

Tangen, D., & Campbell, M. (2010). Cyberbullying prevention: One primary school's approach. *Australian Journal of Guidance & Counselling*, *20*(02), 225–234. doi:10.1375/ajgc.20.2.225

Toledano, S., Werch, B. L., & Wiens, B. A. (2015). Domain-specific self-concept in relation to traditional and cyber peer aggression. *Journal of School Violence*, *14*(4), 405–423. doi:10.1080/15388220.2014.935386

Wade, A., & Beran, T. (2011). Cyberbullying: The new era of bullying. *Canadian Journal of School Psychology*, *26*(1), 44–61. doi:10.1177/0829573510396318

Wong, D. S., Chan, H. C. O., & Cheng, C. H. (2014). Cyberbullying perpetration and victimization among adolescents in Hong Kong. *Children and Youth Services Review*, *36*, 133–140. doi:10.1016/j.childyouth.2013.11.006

Wright, M. F. (2013). The relationship between young adults' beliefs about anonymity and subsequent cyber aggression. *Cyberpsychology, Behavior, and Social Networking*, *16*(12), 858–862. doi:10.1089/cyber.2013.0009 PMID:23849002

Wright, M. F. (2014a). Cyber victimization and perceived stress: Linkages to late adolescents' cyber aggression and psychological functioning. *Youth & Society*.

Wright, M. F. (2014b). Predictors of anonymous cyber aggression: The role of adolescents' beliefs about anonymity, aggression, and the permanency of digital content. *Cyberpsychology, Behavior, and Social Networking*, *17*(7), 431–438. doi:10.1089/cyber.2013.0457 PMID:24724731

Wright, M. F. (2014c). Longitudinal investigation of the associations between adolescents' popularity and cyber social behaviors. *Journal of School Violence*, *13*(3), 291–314. doi:10.1080/15388220.2013.849201

Wright, M. F. (2015). Cyber victimization and adjustment difficulties: The mediation of Chinese and American adolescents' digital technology usage. *Cyberpsychology (Brno)*, *1*(1), 1. Retrieved from http://cyberpsychology.eu/view.php?cisloclanku=2015051102&article=1

Wright, M. F. (in press). Adolescents' cyber aggression perpetration and cyber victimization: The longitudinal associations with school functioning. *Social Psychology of Education.*

Wright, M. F., Kamble, S., Lei, K., Li, Z., Aoyama, I., & Shruti, S. (2015). Peer attachment and cyberbullying involvement among Chinese, Indian, and Japanese adolescents. *Societies (Basel, Switzerland), 5*(4), 339–353. doi:10.3390oc5020339

Wright, M. F., & Li, Y. (2012). Kicking the digital dog: A longitudinal investigation of young adults' victimization and cyber-displaced aggression. *Cyberpsychology, Behavior, and Social Networking, 15*(9), 448–454. doi:10.1089/cyber.2012.0061 PMID:22974350

Wright, M. F., & Li, Y. (2013a). Normative beliefs about aggression and cyber aggression among young adults: A longitudinal investigation. *Aggressive Behavior, 39*(3), 161–170. doi:10.1002/ab.21470 PMID:23440595

Wright, M. F., & Li, Y. (2013b). The association between cyber victimization and subsequent cyber aggression: The moderating effect of peer rejection. *Journal of Youth and Adolescence, 42*(5), 662–674. doi:10.100710964-012-9903-3 PMID:23299177

Ybarra, M. L., Diener-West, M., & Leaf, P. (2007). Examining the overlap in internet harassment and school bullying: Implications for school intervention. *The Journal of Adolescent Health, 1*(6), 42–50. doi:10.1016/j.jadohealth.2007.09.004 PMID:18047944

Ybarra, M. L., & Mitchell, K. J. (2004). Online aggressor/targets, aggressors, and targets: A comparison of associated youth characteristics. *Journal of Child Psychology and Psychiatry, and Allied Disciplines, 45*(7), 1308–1316. doi:10.1111/j.1469-7610.2004.00328.x PMID:15335350

Yousef, W. S. M., & Bellamy, A. (2015). The impact of cyberbullying on the self-esteem and academic functioning of Arab American middle and high school students. *Electronic Journal of Research in Educational Psychology, 23*(3), 463–482.

Zhou, Z., Tang, H., Tian, Y., Wei, H., Zhang, F., & Morrison, C. M. (2013). Cyberbullying and its risk factors among Chinese high school students. *School Psychology International, 34*(6), 630–647. doi:10.1177/0143034313479692

## ADDITIONAL READING

Bauman, S. (2011). *Cyberbullying: What counselors need to know*. Alexandria, VA: American Counseling Association.

Bauman, S., Cross, D., & Walker, J. (2013). *Principles of cyberbullying research: Definitions, measures, and methodology*. New York, NY: Routledge.

Hinduja, S., & Patchin, J. W. (2015). *Bullying beyond the schoolyard: Preventing and responding to cyberbullying*. Thousand Oaks, CA: Sage Publications.

Li, Q., Cross, D., & Smith, P. K. (2012). *Cyberbullying in the global playground*. Malden, MA: Blackwell Publishing. doi:10.1002/9781119954484

Menesini, E., & Spiel, C. (2012). *Cyberbullying: Development, consequences, risk and protective factors*. New York, NY: Psychology Press.

Tokunaga, R. S. (2010). Following you home from school: A critical review and synthesis of research on cyberbullying victimization. *Computers in Human Behavior*, *26*(3), 277–287. doi:10.1016/j.chb.2009.11.014

# KEY TERMS AND DEFINITIONS

**Anonymity:** The quality of being unknown or unacknowledged.

**Anxiety:** A mental health disorder which includes symptoms of worry, anxiety, and/or fear that are intense enough to disrupt one's daily activities.

**Collectivism:** A cultural value that stressed the importance of the group over individual goals and cohesion within social groups.

**Cyberbullying:** Children's and adolescents' usage of electronic technologies to hostilely and intentionally harass, embarrass, and intimidate others.

**Empathy:** The ability to understand or feel what another person is experiencing or feeling.

**Externalizing Difficulties:** Includes children's and adolescents' failure to control their behaviors.

**Individualism:** The belief that each person is more important than the needs of the whole group or society.

**Loneliness:** An unpleasant emotional response to isolation or lack of companionship.

**Normative Belief:** Beliefs about the acceptability and tolerability of a behavior.

**Parental Mediation and Monitoring:** The strategies that parents use to manage the relationship between their children and media.

**Parenting Style:** The standard strategies that parents use in their child rearing.

**Peer Attachment:** The internalization of the knowledge that their peers will be available and responsive.

**Peer Contagion:** The transmission or transfer of deviant behavior from one adolescent to another.

**Pro-Victim Attitudes:** The belief that bullying is unacceptable and that defending victims is valuable.

**Social Exclusion:** The process involving individuals or groups of people block or deny someone from the group.

**Traditional Face-to-Face Bullying:** The use of strength or influence to intimidate or physically harm someone.

# Section 2

# Chapter 6
# Facing the Challenges of a New Communication Era

**James M. Goodwin**
*Georgetown University, USA*

## ABSTRACT

*Interpersonal deception, issue acceptance, privacy and control of information, and relationship building are key challenges people face each day in their quests to communicate effectively. Conquering these challenges is important in achieving shared understanding and making interactions flow smoothly and contain feedback and communication adjustments. Uncertainty is a risk to effective communication, so this chapter offers methods to adjust behaviors, solve problems, and build trust to create and nurture communicative relationships. The literature addresses the various ways that communicators have attempted to achieve success over the years. This is followed by an explanation of the key challenges and how to address them. A flexible, full-cycle examination indicates ways to energize effective communication in both face-to-face and online interactions.*

DOI: 10.4018/978-1-5225-4168-4.ch006

## INTRODUCTION

Any successful communication activity begins and ends with shared understanding. If all parties agree on the end state, communication should flow smoothly, feedback should flow freely, and there should be energizing interactions for all concerned. But the world today challenges us. To be effective communicators in the "noise" of today, we must alleviate the uncertainty we face in interactions by aiding others during the session. Pivotal to this process is garnering meaning from interactional, nonverbal behaviors -- such as kinesics, proxemics, and paralanguage -- as part of a systems theory approach to communication (Scheflen, 1972) (Scheflen, 1973). In short, interpreting nonverbal cues and behaviors is equally critical to alleviating communication roadblocks as is deriving meaning from conversation.

We must solve problems, whether online or digitally, to be effective communicators. Communication Accommodation Theory (CAT) leads communicators in verbal and non-verbal interactions to assess the needs of the session and minimize or emphasize differences between the parties. According to the theory, success can be achieved through flexibility of approach, active listening, changing communication styles, or ongoing self-assessment.

## LITERATURE REVIEW

This chapter addresses four key challenges – interpersonal issues, issue acceptance, privacy and control of information, and relationship building. We face these challenges during interactions as we seek ways to communicate effectively.

We will focus first on an examination of the types of communication and comprehension, which continue to evolve. Taking advantage of full-process communication that is available in face-to-face interactions can suggest ways to improve digital interactions.

Full-process communication requires sender, message, receiver, *and* feedback. On the other hand, evaluating ongoing changes in the way people communicate digitally can lead to solutions that alleviate the current misperceptions and conflicts in face-to-face communication. However, the most effective communication strategy delivers the potential for success whether it is used in a face-to-face or online conversation.

One way to address communication is to master electronic technology. But electronic technology is "impoverished in social cues and shared experience" (Sproull and Kiesler, 1991). No one believes that technology can fully replace the human moment created by face-to-face interaction. Electronic communication is not the best method for building long-term trust among strangers, or a true team out of people who have never met (Olson and Olson, 2000). Experts believe it is important that people who form teams meet face-to-face first; then electronic communication can assist the process of team-building (Olson, 1999).

Social media and digital conversations are powerful activities, but they do not do enough in terms of taking advantage of the full range of the communication process. Face-to-face interactions can create stronger bonds over time than those of electronic communication. There are growing challenges in interpersonal interactions caused by the evolving intergenerational use of social media and the need to reintroduce face-to-face communications. We cannot discount social media as it defines important cultural, social, and work environment considerations. However, this power can also create a cross-cultural and cross-generation communication problem because the full range of the communication process is limited or absent.

In many cases, managers dealing with the growth of the cyber workplace cannot recognize or find adequate tools for building virtual teams. One problem is that virtual teams may struggle to find common ground if they have never met. A good face-to-face meeting allows the leader to assess the group's collective ability to employ the full communication process of sender, message, receiver, and feedback. If this need for connection is not successfully addressed, there is a likelihood that the team will not function as efficiently as possible (Brown, 2017). The danger is that there may never be a meeting of the minds, which is crucial to team and culture building.

Digital communications continue to flourish; however, leaders, managers, and supervisors have identified issues that affect communication. For instance, studies on Gen Y and Millennials -- two generations with overlapping periods of birth in the 1980s to 2000s -- demonstrate that these age groups will comprise more than 50% of the workforce by 2020 (Brown, 2017). Experts have found that both groups prefer to use instant messaging or other social media rather than stop by an office for a talk. That signals real challenges to building and nurturing a team and corporate culture.

Similarly, managers may find that using social platforms online to complete a full communication loop (sender, message, receive, feedback) is not enough when establishing meaningful and transparent relationships with external audiences. A study on how creating a human presence online in organizational digital communications revealed that a "conversational human voice" was perceived by external audiences to be higher for those organizations engaging with a human presence versus those who took a more organizational approach (Park and Lee 2013). The results point to the importance of transparency online as a means of engaging in meaningful communication that can lead to more favorable conditions for relationship building. The study's authors suggest that the use of interpersonal approaches to online communication, such as a social media manager using a photo of himself as an avatar on an organizational social platform, appear to "promote favorable organization-public relationships and positive word-of-mouth communication" (Park and Lee, 2013).

Just as managers should leverage face-to-face communication to increase communication success with internal audiences, corporations must actively pursue human-to-human communication when engaging in dialogue with stakeholders external to the organization. In other words, as people develop a sense that they are interacting with a human rather than a corporate entity, so too increases the likelihood of successful cultivation of value-based relationships between an organization and its stakeholders (Park and Lee, 2013). Undoubtedly, the intrinsic need to communicate interpersonally—especially when communicating digitally—can influence both the level of value and trust experienced during the communication, factors closely tied to a belief that the other party is not just a corporate entity, a faceless algorithm, or auto-generated reply, but is in fact human.

Two United Kingdom researchers analyzed how the presence of mobile communication technology influences the quality of face-to-face conversations (Przybylski and Weinstein, 2013). They argued that developing the interpersonal closeness and trust that is required in face-to-face communications is made difficult by the mere presence of mobile phones. These results suggest that communication difficulties are even more pronounced when discussions are of a personally meaningful nature.

A national study in 2010 by the Kaiser Family Foundation examined a sample of more than 2,000 eight- to eighteen-year-olds. The study discovered a rise in the average total time that they reported experiencing media (Rideout, Foehr et al., 2010). In the study, the average amount of media experience rose 44% over a decade, from 8 hours and 33 minutes per day in 1999 to 10 hours and 45 minutes per day in 2009. The proportion of media time spent using more than one medium concurrently increased from 16% in 1999 to 26% in 2004 to 29% in 2009 (Rideout, Foehr et al., 2010) (Pea, Nass et al., 2012). Obviously, the numbers are anticipated to be even higher now.

People now communicate online about serious topics like purchases, contracts, and even love without the benefit of verbal and/or visual cues. There is widespread consensus that the face-to-face interaction is much more effective, even than chatting via video. Only with face-to-face interaction can one use all five senses. These are important communication considerations when examining the sender, message, and receiver exchanges. As we work together to improve communication, these vital considerations suggest changing communication experience from totally online to face-to-face, or at least using a combination of the two.

We can also look to education as we try to improve communication. The world's communicators are challenged by learning and instruction that is technology-based versus in-person, demonstrated by the work of some researchers in comparing course instruction (Stacey and Wiesenberg, 2007) (Jaggars, 2014). Such comparisons are found in many academic references on trust, comparing the two methods, as well as social skills, interpersonal communication, and mobile technology (Ma, 2007) (Baek, Wojcieszak et al., 2012) (Brown, 2013) (Przybylski and Weinstein, 2013) (Gheorghiță and Pădurețu, 2014) (Carter and Fuller, 2015).

Business management communication practices also offer insight into the importance of value-driven communication in developing relationships. "C" suite senior executives across all major functional areas consistently claim that developing meaningful relationships is the most important element to their success year after year (Wallace, 2016). Still, a recent study showed that of the 89% of surveyed executives who share this attitude, only 24% make a planned effort to improve their relationship building skills (Wallace, 2016). Unsurprisingly, fewer than 5% of organizations surveyed admitted to having any specific strategies to help their professionals develop the communication skills necessary to strengthen their business relationships (Wallace, 2016). Of course, the problem most cited as to why so little effort is made in improving meaningful relationships and developing the communication skills is a preoccupation with technology and processes (Wallace, 2016).

Education is another realm where there is a need to have at least some face-to-face interaction in the online classroom. All kinds of organizations that are interested in transforming interpersonal communication and team building are turning to hybrid formats. These leaders are now adding blended interactions that combine online and face-to-face sessions for the best effect—enriched learning and sharing communities for faculty that blend information and communication technologies (Salas, 2016). Some researchers even go so far as to recommend workshops, formal discussion forums, and other similar communication opportunities as tantamount to educators' interpersonal communication growth when technology integration is being considered (Salas, 2016).

A study of East Carolina University faculty opinions regarding use of podcasting as a means of instruction in place of traditional textbooks found that the faculty users established "a community of practice that encourages social co-participation" through consistent formal and informal meetings and collaborative documentation (Salas, 2016, p. 176). Incorporating podcasts as a means of creating a hybrid learning environment led the 11 faculty members who participated in the study to regular, productive conversation about podcast best practices to enrich otherwise strictly interpersonal communication (Salas, 2016).

A 2012 study by the nonprofit ITHAKA examined quality of education that offers broadening access to higher education to more individuals while lowering costs for students.

*Our intention was to provide a rigorous side-by-side comparison of specific learning outcomes for students in this hybrid version of the statistics course and comparable students in a traditionally-taught version of the same course. (Bowen, Chingos et al., 2014)*

The study showed that hybrid-format students performed slightly better than traditional-format students on three outcomes and, while none of these differences passes traditional tests of statistical significance, there is merit in the notion of educational flexibility. Cowan and Menchaca (2014) examined hybrid online graduate education programs in terms of value creation. Their study showed importance in the hybrid environment evidenced by the 10-year success of a master's program in educational technology. Participant responses specifically mentioned the importance of problem-based learning, connections to real-world problems, a flexible learning environment relying on many newer technologies, and the critical importance of a face-to-face component in establishing community.

The other very important part of successful communication is the feedback cycle. Feedback is the part of communication that perpetuates the cyclic process that keeps the parties engaged. Senders need to know that the other party or parties interpreted the message correctly or at least that the intended value of the message is understood and shared by all parties. Feedback is important to management as leaders work through issues, both good and bad, by understanding how subordinates respond to directives and plans. Supervisors must understand how the work is progressing and they must have a sense of how employees are invested, or not invested, in the task or tasks at hand.

Deeper still, constructive feedback provided by leaders can directly impact employees' valence of emotions, sense of justice, overall mood, and motivation to perform (Sommer and Kulkarni, 2012). In other words, it is not enough to simply provide feedback to complete a communication cycle to keep parties engaged, motivated, and willing to communicate further. Instead, the implementation of positively-delivered, constructive feedback—that is, feedback that identifies acceptable behavioral standards and promotes opportunities for change to correct specific problematic behaviors—enables employees to remain approachable and self-assured in their outlooks of their positions within their organizations (Sommer and Kulkarni, 2012).

The need for a common understanding is the cornerstone of communicating as it is necessary in measuring effectiveness that is achieved. Senders always hope that the receiver understands the message in the manner intended. But great communicators keep communicating until there is a certainty that shared understanding has been achieved. Unfortunately, sometimes people assume that this agreement is reached.

Equally unfortunate is lost dialogue that occurs when people back down from crucial conversations, normally from fear of engaging in uncomfortable, emotional discourse that requires critical thinking and a check on their emotions. Crucial conversations are the day-to-day conversations we have that impact our lives in some manner (Patterson, 2011). These are tough conversations that normally involve two or more people. The stakes of the conversation are high, opinions vary, and emotions run strong (Patterson, 2011). Often, people back down from these conversations because they are afraid they will only make matters worse. Instead of engaging in value-rich exchanges, they change the subject, stop participating in the conversation, lash out against the initiator of the conversation, or engage in any number of tactics to avoid embracing the situation, pushing their emotions to the side, and failing to pay attention to the true meaning and value of the conversational topic (Patterson, 2011).

True dialogue demands a free flow of meaning (Patterson, 2011). Nothing can kill this free flow more quickly than our own fear, as well as an inability to sense fear or hesitation in those with whom we are communicating. Authors Patterson, Grenny, McMillan, and Switzler (2012) suggest communicators generate a safe environment for free-flowing dialogue by providing meaningful feedback and remembering that others normally have only our best interests in mind: "If you don't fear that you're being attacked or humiliated, you yourself can hear almost anything and not become defensive" (Patterson, 2011).

When the communication features a human, "hands-on" interchange, we can use verbal and visual cues and the five senses to achieve our goals. These tools are not all available in digital conversations. One example of the many challenges is when prospective members of a team must meet face-to-face first, then use electronic communication to assist in the process of team-building (Sproull and Kiesler, 1991) (Sproull and Kiesler, 2000) (Olson and Olson 2000).

## UNDERSTANDING KEY CHALLENGES

Armed with an overview of the pros and cons of communication, we can deal with key challenges that will allow us to achieve successful interactions. We begin with the interpersonal aspect.

Dealing with *interpersonal issues* to enhance communication is important, because participants may flourish or struggle with interpersonal control and may use interpersonal deception. Interpersonal control is one of the CAT strategies that determines how much the sender controls the receiver or how one person in an interaction controls the other. Sender and receiver roles change during communication activities and interpersonal control is a way of managing or regulating another's thoughts, feelings, or actions (Stets, 1991). When we address how people handle actual or perceived deception in face-to-face interactions, we are dealing with interpersonal deception.

Interpersonal deception can occur consciously or subconsciously. Interpersonal Deception Theory states that senders try to manipulate messages to be untruthful, causing apprehension on the part of the sender due to the concern that their false communication will be detected. At the same time, receivers try to determine the validity of the information, creating suspicion about whether the sender is being deceitful (Brown, 2017). Deceptive messages have three parts:

1. The central deceptive message, which is usually verbal,
2. The ancillary message containing verbal and non-verbal communication, often revealing how truthful the message might be, and
3. Inadvertent behaviors, which are primarily non-verbal and help demonstrate the deceit of the sender through a concept known as leakage.

Leakage occurs when non-verbal signals betray the true content of a contradictory verbal message. Facial expressions may signal deception, but they are sometimes hard to read. Non-verbal signals for deception include the following (Brown, 2017):

- Pronounced hesitations
- Pupil dilation
- Increased rate or tempo of speech
- Increased, rapid, or strained blinking
- Voice changes pitch
- Sweating

Nuanced non-verbal cues not only signal a person's true intentions but can also serve in helping those adept at mastering giving and receiving nonverbal cues to negotiate the social world—a form of "disguise and conquer"— when they leave open multiple possibilities for interpretation (Keating, 2016, p. 33). Proponents of nonverbal communication theories often conclude that an inaccuracy in human expression can be used strategically to control desired messages sent and received, such as being a "hard read" during a game of poker (Keating, 2016). In this regard, leakage becomes a means to determine a person's true intent beyond the intended deception. Understanding this nuanced aspect of communication is significant when research shows that up to 65% of the message intended for delivery is communicated through nonverbal behaviors (Uzun, 2017).

When dealing with *issue acceptance*, we can look at the challenges as a form of conflict. Acceptance or rejection of the issue is caused by positive or negative influences. Conflict happens, but it can be positive or negative. There is positive conflict when communication is increased, stored feelings are released, problems are solved, performance is improved, or the relationship grows (Brown, 2017). There is negative conflict when parties do not address real issues or problems, when people become uncooperative, or when the relationship between the parties is damaged or disrupted. We can also categorize conflict as expressive, rooted in a desire to release tension, or as instrumental, stemming from a difference in goals or practices (Knapp, 1983). An integrating style of communication that demonstrates concern for self and others is most effective in these situations.

Group dynamics in communication networks can determine the best social and psychological tone of the interactive relationships and can address the relative acceptance or rejection that group members feel (Muchinsky, 1977) (Guzley, 1992) (Atkinson and Frechette, 2009). In other words, is the environment conducive to discussion, feedback, and decision? Leaders should seek commitment from all parties to get individual buy-in for a common purpose and achievement of the communication goal or goals. Leaders can begin meetings with motivational moments or reviews of successes and can stress shared achievements and rewards. Building networks that transmit in downward, upward, horizontal, diagonal, or through the grapevine methods is very effective (Lunenburg, 2011). The networks function to help group members grow, decide, and build relationships.

Networks face an added challenge when relying on technology to facilitate meetings virtually. Satisfaction levels decrease as the level of virtuality increases (Marlow, Lacerenza et al., 2017). What's more, communication volume does not necessarily equate to more successful collaboration between team members, regardless of whether a group meets in person or relies on increasingly faster, more mobile digital technologies to facilitate communication (Marlow, Lacerenza et al., 2017). Undoubtedly, organizations are relying more on virtual teamwork to achieve organizational goals, especially where more flexible work schedules, such as teleworking, are offered and encouraged. Since virtual work teams are interdependent work relationships by their very nature (Leonard, 2011), minimizing communication frequency through sorting out which communication is irrelevant can help virtual teams build trust, grow working relationships, and achieve goals (Marlow, Lacerenza et al., 2017). Still, minimizing communication regularity virtually and settling on only the most meaningful interactions requires a balancing act between communicating too much or too little. Relatedly, higher communication frequency is thought to contribute to team development, but only when all team members contribute beneficially to collective understanding and increase overall team functioning.

Addressing *privacy and control of information* provides a sense of security in communication leading to trust. Communication privacy management theory focuses on important methods people can use to process information. It supposes that people have private information, private boundaries, and control and ownership about the information, and that they control it with rule-based management and privacy management dialectics. Privacy management dialectics focus on the tension between communication aspects that are private/concealing and public/revealing, and this tension shows itself because of people deciding what to reveal or not reveal when exchanging information. One expert says that privacy and disclosure are opposing conditions existing in a symbiotic relationship (Petronio, 2012):

*...disclosing implies that we are giving up some measure of privacy. However, disclosure cannot occur if there exists no private information that can be told to others. Correspondingly, CPM also accepts the contention that there is interactive unity for privacy-disclosure. Thus, privacy is a necessary condition that one protects or gives up through disclosure. (p. 14)*

*Relationship building* in communications requires that communicators seek out people with whom they share values so that the engagement has value. Interactivity in communication allows the sender to align values and build trust to create two-way, cyclic interactions that address mutually beneficial concerns and responsibilities. Social capital is created through active listening to ensure all parties give and receive feedback. The reward should be rich relationships to generate and receive tangible social, psychological, emotional, and economic benefits in short or long terms.

Interactive listening can then occur and it is helpful to define steps that will assist all communication using a social media benchmarking study (Brown, Alkadry et al., 2013):

- Go beyond simply connecting with people and focus on building meaningful relationships that will endure;
- Develop a strong capability to listen to and understand all audiences;
- Trust and empower the communication partner(s) and strive for increased transparency in the interaction;
- Coordinate your messages and goals to make them clear and concise;
- Seek and return meaningful feedback at every opportunity;

- Identify, call out, and seek clarification of nonverbal cues that may threaten communication integrity;
- Be flexible to adapt to and respond to receivers in real time; and
- Seek and answer questions about the receiver's interest and satisfaction with the communication.

Communication done right builds social capital and lasting relationships. It allows leaders to be flexible and enables them to send the right message on the right platform at the right time.

Most importantly, carefully assess the people you share with, and then assess them again. In your social networking activities, you might use a "friend of a friend" system for vetting people. If they know or are connected to someone in your network that you trust and respect, then maybe you can accept connecting with them. Without that, it might not be wise to accept someone you have not met. Having said all of that, you might want to take some risks. There are just too many people involved in the social networking adventure who are too compelling to ignore, delete, refuse, or turn away from. Once the adventure has captured your full attention, push forward with privacy controls (Brown and Schario 2014).

## CONCLUSION

This chapter addresses four key challenges people face during interactions and then attempts to find ways to communicate effectively.

1. Deal with interpersonal deception;
2. Adjust to communication partners who seek or avoid the issue at hand;
3. Protect privacy and control information; and
4. Create and nurture long-term relationships.

This certainly is not an exhaustive list. However, it is a list that serves to start, or continue, the conversation. Good communication needs continuing and new research to get it right. The benefits of face-to-face and online interactions must be combined for the best impact. The format with the most tangible benefits, and therefore the greatest chances for success, is face-to-face based on the current examination. Still, the "conversation" is by no means finished.

# REFERENCES

Atkinson, T., & Frechette, H. (2009). *Creating a Positive Organizational Climate in a Negative Economic One Improving Organizational Climate to Transform Performance*. Retrieved from http://www. trainingindustry. com/media/2505214/creatingpositiveorgclimate_us_aug09. pdf

Baek, Y. M., Wojcieszak, M., & Delli Carpini, M. X. (2012). Online versus face-to-face deliberation: Who? Why? What? With what effects? *New Media & Society*, *14*(3), 363–383. doi:10.1177/1461444811413191

Baker, W. E. (2000). *Achieving success through social capital: tapping the hidden resources in your personal and business networks*. San Francisco: Jossey-Bass.

Bowen, W. G., Chingos, M. M., Lack, K. A., & Nygren, T. I. (2014). Interactive learning online at public universities: Evidence from a six-campus randomized trial. *Journal of Policy Analysis and Management*, *33*(1), 94–111. doi:10.1002/pam.21728

Brown, C. (2013). *Are We Becoming More Socially Awkward? An Analysis of the Relationship Between Technological Communication Use and Social Skills in College Students*. Academic Press.

Brown, M. Sr. (2013). Social Networking and Individual Perceptions: Examining Predictors of Participation. *Public Organization Review*, 1–20.

Brown, M. A. Sr. (2017). *Solutions for High-Touch Communications in a High-Tech World*. Hershey, PA: IGI Global. doi:10.4018/978-1-5225-1897-6

Brown, M. A. Sr, & Schario, T. A. (2014). *Social Media 4EVR: Identifying, Achieving, & Nurturing Social Capital*. Yorktown, VA: CreateSpace Independent Publishing Platform.

Carter & Fuller. (2015). *Symbolic interactionism*. Academic Press.

Cowan, J. E., & Menchaca, M. P. (2014). Investigating value creation in a community of practice with social network analysis in a hybrid online graduate education program. *Distance Education*, *35*(1), 43–74. doi:10.1080/01587919.2014.893813

Gallois, C., & Giles, H. (2015). *Communication Accommodation Theory. The International Encyclopedia of Language and Social Interaction.* John Wiley & Sons, Inc.

Gheorghiță & Pădurețu. (2014). Social Networks And Interpersonal Communication. *System, 2*(3), 5.

Guzley, R. M. (1992). Organizational climate and communication climate predictors of commitment to the organization. *Management Communication Quarterly, 5*(4), 379–402. doi:10.1177/0893318992005004001

Jaggars, S. S. (2014). Choosing Between Online and Face-to-Face Courses: Community College Student Voices. *American Journal of Distance Education, 28*(1), 27–38. doi:10.1080/08923647.2014.867697

Keating, C. (2016). The life and times of nonverbal communication theory and research: Past, present, and future. APA handbook of nonverbal communication, 17-42.

Knapp, M. L. (1983). *Interpersonal communication and human relationships.* Boston: Allyn and Bacon.

Leonard, B. (2011). Managing Virtual Teams. *HRMagazine,* 38–42.

Lunenburg, F. C. (2011). Network Patterns and Analysis: Underused Sources to Improve Communication Effectiveness. *National Forum Of Educational Administration And Supervision Journal.*

Ma, L. (2007). "I'll trust you if I expect you to trust me": An analysis of interpersonal trust, friends, and social interactions within social networks. Tufts University.

Marlow, S. L., Lacerenza, C. N., & Salas, E. (2017). Communication in virtual teams: A conceptual framework and research agenda. *Human Resource Management Review, 27*(4), 575–589. doi:10.1016/j.hrmr.2016.12.005

Muchinsky, P. M. (1977). Organizational communication: Relationships to organizational climate and job satisfaction. *Academy of Management Journal, 20*(4), 592–607. doi:10.2307/255359

Olson, G. M., & Olson, J. S. (2000). Distance matters. *Human-Computer Interaction, 15*(2), 139–178. doi:10.1207/S15327051HCI1523_4

Park, H., & Lee, H. (2013). Show us you are real: The effect of human-versus-organizational presence on online relationship building through social networking sites. *Cyberpsychology, Behavior, and Social Networking, 16*(4), 265–271. doi:10.1089/cyber.2012.0051 PMID:23363228

Patterson, K. (2011). *Crucial conversations: tools for talking when stakes are high.* New York: McGraw-Hill Professional.

Pea, R., Nass, C., Meheula, L., Rance, M., Kumar, A., Bamford, H., ... Zhou, M. (2012). Media use, face-to-face communication, media multitasking, and social well-being among 8-to 12-year-old girls. *Developmental Psychology, 48*(2), 327–336. doi:10.1037/a0027030 PMID:22268607

Petronio, S. (2012). *Boundaries of privacy: Dialectics of disclosure.* SUNY Press.

Przybylski, A. K., & Weinstein, N. (2013). Can you connect with me now? How the presence of mobile communication technology influences face-to-face conversation quality. *Journal of Social and Personal Relationships, 30*(3), 237–246. doi:10.1177/0265407512453827

Rideout, V. J. (2010). *Generation M²: Media in the Lives of 8-to 18-Year-Olds.* Henry J. Kaiser Family Foundation.

Salas, A. (2016). Literature Review of Faculty-Perceived Usefulness of Instructional Technology in Classroom Dynamics. *Contemporary Educational Technology, 7*(2), 174–186.

Scheflen, A. E. (1972). Body Language and the Social Order; Communication as Behavioral Control. In How behavior means. Interface.

Sommer, K. L., & Kulkarni, M. (2012). Does constructive performance feedback improve citizenship intentions and job satisfaction? The roles of perceived opportunities for advancement, respect, and mood. *Human Resource Development Quarterly, 23*(2), 177–201. doi:10.1002/hrdq.21132

Sproull, L., & Kiesler, S. (1991). *Connections: new ways of working in the networked organization.* Cambridge, MA: MIT Press.

Stacey, E., & Wiesenberg, F. (2007). A study of face-to-face and online teaching philosophies in Canada and Australia. *International Journal of E-Learning & Distance Education, 22*(1), 19–40.

Stets, J. E. (1991). Psychological aggression in dating relationships: The role of interpersonal control. *Journal of Family Violence, 6*(1), 97–114. doi:10.1007/BF00978528

Uzun, T. (2017). Development of the nonverbal communication skills of school administrators scale (NCSSAS): Validity, reliability and implementation study. *Educational Research Review, 12*(7), 442–455.

Wallace, E. (2016). *The Relationship Engine: Connecting with the People who Power Your Business.* AMACOM Div American Mgmt Assn.

# Chapter 7
# Virtual Happiness:
## ICT, FtF Communication, and Wellbeing

**Tihana Brkljačić**
*Institute of Social Sciences Ivo Pilar, Croatia*

**Ljiljana Kaliterna Lipovčan**
*Institute of Social Sciences Ivo Pilar, Croatia*

**Zvjezdana Prizmić-Larsen**
*Washington University in St. Louis, USA*

## ABSTRACT

*This chapter examines characteristics of information and communication technology (ICT) and face-to-face communication and their associations with subjective wellbeing among students. The participants were N=500 students who reported average time they spent in face-to-face (FtF) and ICT communications. They also reported dominant communication in two types of communication contexts (communication purpose and persons involved in communication) and estimated their happiness and life satisfaction. Students spent more time in FtF communication than in ICT. Those who spent more time in FtF communication with friends were happier and more satisfied with their lives. FtF communication was dominant when meeting new people, for personal talk, and for flirting, while ICT communication was dominant for casual and informative chat. Students most frequently communicated with close persons FtF. Students who use dominantly FtF communication for personal talk and with people from their private lives (i.e., parents, friends, partners) were happier and more satisfied with their lives.*

DOI: 10.4018/978-1-5225-4168-4.ch007

# INTRODUCTION

Every significant change in communication technologies, such as the invention of the radio and the invention of television, has significantly impacted human daily lives and consequently affected the quality of human lives. In the last few decades, information and communication technology (ICT) has grown rapidly, influencing all domains of humans' lives. It has considerably changed the way people learn, work, and socialize. It has also influenced the way people deal with everyday tasks, such as shopping, receiving information, and paying bills. It has made these activities faster and easier, therefore leaving more time for leisure activities. Because ICT offers endless possibilities of entertainment, it also occupies the time that was previously spent on other activities.

Internet world statistics (2017) report that over 80% of Europeans, and over 88% of Americans use the Internet. Therefore, it is not surprising that internet usage makes a significant impact society and everyday life (Jelfs, & Richardson, 2012).

Using the Internet is found to be related to higher levels of well-being (e.g. Kavetsos, & Koutroumpis, 2011; Ford, & Ford, 2009). Penard, Poussing and Suire (2013) found that people who don't use the Internet are less satisfied in their lives than Internet users. The positive influence of Internet use was stronger for younger people and for those not satisfied with their income. Poushter (2015) studied attitudes towards the Internet among people in 32 emerging and developing nations, such as Croatia. Most of the participants considered the increasing use of the Internet to be a good influence in the realms of education, personal relationships, and the economy, but considered it to be a negative influence on morality.

Hall (2016) revealed three components of Internet use: time spent on the Internet, use of the Internet for information gathering, and use of the Internet for affective expression. Hall found that time spent on the Internet was negatively related to happiness. Information gathering was positively related to happiness. Affective expression was unrelated to happiness.

# PURPOSE AND ROLE OF THE ICT COMMUNICATION

Some research suggests that during '90s the Internet was used mostly for entertainment such as surfing and playing games (Valkenburg, & Soeters, 2001). However, with the new millennium it has become increasingly used for interpersonal communication in the forms of chat, e-mails, forums, blogs, and especially social networks (Gross, 2004; Lenhart, Madden, & Hitlin, 2005). Poushter (2015) found that in emerging and developing countries, the Internet is most often used for social networking and staying in touch with friends and family. Sinkkonen, Puhakka and Merilainen

(2014) investigated Internet use among Finnish adolescents and found that for the majority, the most common reasons for using the Internet were entertainment and social interaction.

In recent years the web has become an important mechanism for creating, enhancing, and maintaining communication and social contacts. In everyday social interactions, ICT devices play important role. There are lot of concerns regarding detachment from real world and slipping into virtual one. However, it does not seem that Internet communication is overtaking face-to-face communication. For example, Gallardo-Echenique, Bullen and Marqués-Molias (2016) found that students prefer face-to-face communication for both academic and social communication. Similarly, Morreale, Staley, Stavrositu and Krakowiak (2015) who studied first-year college students born after 1990 and their attitudes toward communication technologies in formal and personal situations, found that students preferred face-to-face communication across all ten different communication situations.

Given the increasingly prominent role the Internet plays in daily life, deeper insight into the relation between online and face-to-face communication, as well as online communication's influence on individual well-being, is crucial.

## BACKGROUND

In this study, we are interested in the association between online and offline communication and its relation to well-being. The Internet allows easy contact with different people and instant communication with almost everyone on the planet. Computer mediated communication (CMC) has some undoubtable benefits. For instance, it enables people to stay in touch with friends and family members in situations where physical distance or other obstacles prevent face-to-face communication. It also enables people to communicate with others with similar interests across the world. Still, recent comprehensive review on online communication, social media, and adolescent wellbeing (Best, Manktelow, & Taylor, 2014) reveals that different studies report different and sometimes even contradictory results, and therefore further research is needed.

### The Concept of Well-Being

Subjective well-being has become one of the most studied concepts in psychology in the last few decades (Diener, 2017). While objective well-being comprises elements such as objective health, financial status, and standard of living, subjective well-being is defined as satisfaction with life as a whole (Diener, 2017). Objective indicators of well-being can only give a partial account of what it means to live well. Subjective well-being encompasses both affective and cognitive aspects, and it is usually defined in terms of frequent positive affect (pleasant mood and emotions), infrequent negative affect (unpleasant mood and emotions), and high life satisfaction – individual's appraisal of life as a whole (Diener, 2017). Subjective well-being depends on many factors and differs markedly across nations. There are many instruments available to assess specific aspects of well-being (e.g. positive emotions, depression, flourishing) or general well-being. Single-item measures of general well-being are often used (e.g. European Value Survey, Eurobarometer) since these are more convenient for respondents to perform and produce the same results as multiple item measures (Cheung & Lucas, 2014). Studies in Croatia usually report moderately positive well-being levels with averages between 6 and 7 (e.g. Brajša-Žganec et al., 2017; Kaliterna Lipovčan et al., 2016) on a 0-10 scale where higher values indicate greater well-being.

Although there are many factors that may influence subjective well-being, social affiliation and activity is one of its strongest predictors. All prominent theories and models of human well-being stress the significance of social relationships (e.g. Diener & Saligman, 2002; Baumeister & Leary, 1995), and importance of social connections has been confirmed without exception throughout decades of research around the world. Furthermore, extroverted people report higher levels of happiness and adults are typically happier when living with a spouse than when they are single (Veenhoven, 2014). Since communication is a crucial part of (and origin of) all social contacts, its features are inevitably associated with well-being. As the nature of communication has changed significantly over the last few decades, much research has been conducted to explore how these changes affect people's lives, well-being, and relationships (Goodman-Deane et al, 2015). In the following section, we will present some of the main theories and findings.

## Online and Face-To-Face Communication

Internet communication could have an important effect on a person's social life, since it provides new possibilities of social contact with distant as well as close friends, family members, colleagues, and strangers. Most importantly, it allows instant and affordable personal or public communication regardless of physical barriers. On the other hand, everyone's time is limited, so time spent in online communication reduces the amount of time that would otherwise be used for something else, possibly face-to-face communication. These opposing views are the foundations of two prominent theories: displacement and stimulation theories, which we will describe in the next section.

## Displacement Theory

The displacement theory assumes that people require real-life face-to-face communication to be happy and satisfied, while the Internet is an inadequate alternative. According this theory, communication time is displaced from in-person to online settings. Results of several studies conducted at the turn of the century support this theory. People who were using Internet often were found to spend less time with family and friends, and felt lonelier and more depressed (Nie, Hillygus, & Erbring, 2002). The subjects' online social relationships were found to be weaker than real-life relations (Parks & Roberts, 1998). Additionally, people generally consider electronic mail (email) less valuable for building and sustaining close social relationships than other means, such as face-to-face contact and telephone conversations (Cummings, Butler, & Kraut, 2002). More recently, Ramirez, Dimmick, Feaster, and Lin (2008) showed that instant messaging displaced e-mail and landline telephones, while Masur, Reinecke, Ziegele, & Quiring (2014) reported that people's offline social activities have decreased since they started using social networks. Additionally, as Internet use has continued to grow over the past decade, the amount of time allocated to face-to-face socializing has decreased slightly (Bureau of Labor Statistics, 2014).

## Stimulation Theory

Adherents of the stimulation theory argue that online communication might enhance social contact and therefore improve well-being (Bryant, Sanders-Jackson, & Smallwood, 2006). Valkenburg and Peter (2007a) tested both theories, and found support for the stimulation hypothesis, but not for the displacement hypothesis. In another study, positive relationship between frequency of social contact and online communication with other people and well-being was found (Carr, 2004). Other research supported this theory and showed that Internet use is positively related to the time spent with friends (Kraut et al., 2002), to the closeness of friendships (Valkenburg & Peter, 2007b), and to well-being (Kraut et al., 2002; Morgan & Cotten, 2003; Shaw & Gant, 2002). Blight, Jagiello and Ruppel (2015) studied support seeking on Facebook and found cumulative effect for online and offline support. Their participants received more total support than they would if they had only sought support offline. Dienlin, Masur, and Trepte (2017) found that social networking and instant messaging reinforce one another and that social network communication reinforces face-to-face communication and slightly increases life satisfaction.

Displacement and stimulation theories are not necessarily incompatible. Since different studies have yielded inconclusive results, it seems that sometimes online communication reinforces face-to-face communication and contributes to well-being, but in some other situations this effect is non-existent or even opposite. One reason for mixed findings may be that in many studies various Internet activities were not analysed separately (Baym, Zhang, & Lin, 2004). For example, in the study of Shen and Williams (2011) it was shown that negative or positive outcomes of Internet use were largely dependent on the purposes and context of situation, and individual characteristics of users. Hence, it seems that online communication is a complex phenomenon, determined by many individual and situational factors, and therefore it shouldn't be operationalized as general concept.

Following this rationale, we chose not to study online communication as a general concept, but to differ between communication mode, purpose of conversation, and communication with different persons.

## ICT AND COMMUNICATION CONTEXT IN PREDICTION OF WELL-BEING

People communicate using different ICT modes such as text messages, phone calls, and social networking. Communication is furthermore characterized by communication context which, as we define it, depends on purpose of communication and collocutor. A large body of research found benefits of online communication for subjective well-being (e.g. Ellison, Vitak, Gray, & Lampe, 2014; Reinecke, Vorderer, & Knop, 2014, Burke, & Kraut, 2014, 2016, Verduyn, Ybarra, Résibois, Jonides, & Kross, 2017). On the other hand, several studies have provided evidence for the negative association between online communication and well-being, (e.g., Pea et al., 2012, Farahani, Kazemi, Aghamohamadi, Bakhtiarvand, & Ansari, 2011; Lin et al., 2016; Sampasakanyinga, & Lewis, 2015). So it seems that relationship between online communication and well-being is not straightforward, but it is mediated by individual features such as personality traits (Weigin, Campbell, Kimpton, Wozencroft, & Orel, 2016), and communication context such as the nature of the message or the closeness of communication partners (Burke, & Kraut, 2014). In this study we are interested in the latter. For the purposes of this research we defined communication context as (a) purpose of communication (e.g. casual, informative, personal) and (b) relation to the collocutor (e.g. friend, colleague).

People use online communication for different purposes. For instance, one may use Internet chat just to exchange information, or to chat casually. On the other hand, a person can use Internet communication for deeper relations, such as talking about feelings, attitudes, or values. Young people often use new technologies to enhance communication with friends and family, make plans, and maintain social contact (Grinter, Palen, & Eldridge, 2006; Lenhart, Madden, & Hitlin, 2005; Lenhart, Rainie, & Lewis, 2001; Schneider, Sperling, Schell, Hemmer, Glauer, & Silberhorn, 2004; Valkenburg, & Peter, 2007b). It seems that youth prefer face-to-face communication for conversations in which they anticipate high levels of self-disclosure (Ruppel, 2015).

Bessière, Kiesler, Kraut and Boneva (2008) examined how frequently participants used the Internet for different purposes: communicating with friends and family, communicating in online groups and to meet people, retrieving and using information, seeking entertainment, shopping, and acquiring health information or talking about health. Researchers demonstrated that differentiating these types of Internet use suited the data better than a model that assumed use reflected a single dimension ranging from light use to heavy use. Selfhout and colleagues (Selfhout, Branje, Delsing, Bogt, & Meeus, 2009) showed that Internet use for communication purposes had beneficial effects on depression for adolescents who report having poor friendships, while Internet use for non-communication purposes had detrimental effects on adolescents' depression. Furthermore, well-being was related to the specific purpose of Internet use: use of the Internet for finding information, for entertainment, or for commerce was not associated with greater changes in depression but use for communication was.

Selfhout et al. (2009) found that more online communication with friends and family was associated with declines in depression, while communication with weaker ties was associated with increases in depression. When communicating with existing friends, online communication can enhance the interaction between users, promote closeness, and therefore increase well-being (Morgan, & Cotten, 2003; Shaw, & Gant, 2002). Valkenburg and Peter (2007b) found a moderating effect of type of online communication on adolescents' well-being. Instant messaging, which was mostly used to communicate with friends, positively predicted well-being via the mediating variables such as the time spent with friends and the quality of friendships. On the other hand, chat in a public chat-room, which was relatively often used to talk with strangers, had no effect on adolescents' well-being via the mediating variables. Kraut and Burke (2015) present an overview of the research on Internet use and psychological well-being. They conclude that communicating with close friends online was related to improvements in social support and decrease of depression, while talking with strangers was not. They argued that increased use of the Internet, especially for communication with close persons, would increase the amount of social support and consequently reduce depression, stress, and loneliness, while improving mood and even physical health.

## RATIONALE FOR THIS RESEARCH

This short review suggests that the relation between well-being and use of online communication may depend on a number of factors. Therefore, research should focus on specific functions of Internet use, and not the Internet as a generalized whole. Following this rationale, the main purpose of the current study was to examine relationship between well-being and communication mode, taking into account specific features of communication situation such as purpose of communication and relationship with collocutor.

## MAIN FOCUS OF THE CHAPTER

This research was designed to contribute to better understanding of association between different characteristics of ICT and face-to-face communication and subjective well-being among the students. The present study explored the time students spent in different types of communication (ICT communication and face-to-face communication), their frequency of use of different communication contexts, as well as their relationship with well-being variables. Specifically, the aims of the study were threefold:

1.  To examine the amount of time students spend in ICT communications and face-to-face communication, and their interrelationships.
2.  To examine the dominant communication type depending on communication contexts. Communication context was defined (1) by communication purposes (meeting new people, personal talk, flirting, informative chat, and casual chat) and (2) by the person with whom speaker is communicating (parents, friends, partner, colleagues, and teacher).
3.  The third aim was to explore the relationships between well-being variables (happiness and life satisfaction) and (a) the amount of time spent in various types of ICT and face-to-face communications and (b) dominant communication type in two communication contexts.

## METHOD

- **Participants:** The research was conducted on the sample of N= 500 students from the Faculty of Electrical Engineering and Computing at the University of Zagreb. There were 112 (22.4%) women. Age range was 18-32 years, with M= 20 years, while dominant age was 19 years.
- **Procedure:** Participation in the study was voluntary and anonymous. Participants completed a questionnaire that took 15-20 minutes. The questionnaire was administrated during regular class time.
- **Communication Measures:** Since various communication situations may have different effect on well-being, we decided to investigate them separately. Thus, we opted to study communication involving (a) various modes (types) of ICT tools; (b) various purposes of communication; and (c) various collocutors. Using these separate assessments enabled us to study the relationship between well-being and specific communication situations.
- **Time Spent in Different Modes of Communication:** Participants had to report how much time they spent in each different mode of communication. They estimated time spent in ICT communication, e.g. how many minutes per day they spent talking on the phone, online chatting, writing e-mails, social networking, and on average how many text messages they sent per day. They also estimated time spent in face-to-face communication with family, with friends, and with partners.

Since previous research suggested that various ICT communication modes could be associated with face-to-face communication and well-being in different manners, we decided to assess time in various online communication modes separately. We expected this method to provide more accurate data since it may be easier for the participant to assess time spent in a particular activity (and not time spent in ICT communication in general). However, this method doesn't allow us to assess total time spent in (ICT) communication since various communications may happen at the same time, so overall time would be overestimated. However, in this research we are not interested in total amount of time spent in online/offline communication, so possible overlaps do not affect the results.

- **Communication Modes and Communication Context:** Participants were given a list of six different modes of communication. Five of them were ICT communication (phone/mobile talk, text messaging, online chat, e-mail, and social networking) and the last one was face-to-face communication. They had to indicate the dominant communication mode they used in two communication contexts.

The first element of context was defined by *communication purposes,* which included meeting new people, personal talk, flirting, informative chat, and casual chat. Participants had to check the dominant communication mode for each of the communication purposes. The second element of context was defined by *person to whom the participant is communicating*, which included parents, friends, partner, colleagues, and teachers. Participants had to check the dominant communication mode for each option.

- **Well-Being Measures:** Well-being was defined as happiness and positive evaluation of one's life in general (Diener et al., 1999). In order to make our questionnaire as simple as possible for the participants, we used two single-question measures of well-being: happiness and life-satisfaction. Single-item measures perform very similarly compared to the multiple-item measures and produce virtually identical answers to substantive questions (Cheung, & Lucas, 2014).
- **Happiness:** Overall happiness was measured by the question, "In general, how happy do you feel?" This is a standard question in the World Value Survey. Participants rated their answers on the 10-point scale ranging from 1, "extremely unhappy," to 10, "extremely happy."
- **Life Satisfaction:** Life satisfaction was measured by the question, "All things considered, how satisfied are you with your life as a whole nowadays?" This is a standard question in Eurobarometer. Participants rated their answers on the 10-point scale ranging from 1, "extremely dissatisfied," to 10, "extremely satisfied."
- **Data Analyses:** To analyse the associations between different communications, Pearson's correlation coefficients were calculated. Chi-square tests were used to test the differences in the percentage of use of different modes of communication in two communication contexts.

Differences in happiness and life satisfaction between those who dominantly use face-to-face communication, and those who dominantly use ICT communication were tested by t-tests for independent samples.

## RESULTS

The first examination is about the time spent and association between different modes of communication. The average time students spent in ICT and face-to-face communications is presented in Table 1.

## Time Spent in Different Communications Per Day (N=500)

Overall, students spent the most time socializing offline with friends (over two hours per day), and those in relationships spent the most time with partner (almost two and a half hours per day). Face-to-face communication with family took about one and a half hour per day, while online chatting and social networking took about 1 hour per day. Talking on the phone took less than 30 minutes, while writing e-mails and text messages was even less popular. Lenhart, Madden, Smith and Macgill (2007) reported that youth aged 12–17 spent an average of 10.3 hours a week with friends doing social activities outside of school, which is less than participants in our research did. The difference can be contributed to the difference in age. Our participants were older, and of the age where friends are the most important social ties.

Results indicated that time spent with a partner was not "taken" at the expense of other socializations, as those in a relationship did not differ from singles regarding amount of time spent with friends (t=1.1, p>.01), while they spent even more time with family (t=2.27, p<.05). However, there might be an overlap between time spent with partner and time spent with friends.

*Table 1. Communication time by mode/method*

| | Mean | SD |
|---|---|---|
| Number of SMS per day | 8.8 | 22.23 |
| Talking on mobile or phone | 25 min. | 34 min |
| Online chatting | 1 h 9 min | 1h 24 min |
| Writing e-mails | 12 min. | 27 min |
| Social networking | 1 h 12 min. | 1h 32 min |
| Face-to-face with family | 1h 31 min. | 1h 38 min |
| Face-to-face with friends | 2h 11 min. | 1h 47min |
| Face-to-face with partner (just for those with a partner; N=310) | 2h 24 min. | 2 h |

Overall results showed that the Internet was integrated into the social lives of students, but face-to-face remained dominant in interpersonal communication.

The associations between ICT and face-to-face communications are presented in Table 2. All significant correlations were positive and low in magnitude (bellow .30). The only higher association (r=.44) was found between social networking and online chatting, which is probably due to the fact that social networks are often platforms for online chatting. Still, these two activities share only 20% of common variance, confirming that overlap is low to moderate at most. Moreover, as we already mentioned, in this research we were not interested in assessing total amount of time in online/offline communication, so possible overlaps do not affect the results.

## Pearson's Correlations Between Time Spent in Different Modes of Communication (N=500)

Students who spent more time with friends spent more time with family and with partners, while correlation between time spent with family and time spent with partners didn't yield any level of significance.

Time spent with family and time spent with friends showed the same correlations. Students who spent more time with family and friends also spent more time chatting online and using social networking.

Time spent with partners showed a somewhat different pattern of correlation. Students who spent more time with a partner also spent more time in phone/mobile talks and writing e-mails.

*Table 2. Research correlation summary*

|  | 1 | 2 | 3 | 4 | 5 | 6 | 7 |
|---|---|---|---|---|---|---|---|
| 1. Number of SMS per day | - |  |  |  |  |  |  |
| 2. Talking on mobile or phone | .24** | - |  |  |  |  |  |
| 3. Online chatting | .18** | .17** | - |  |  |  |  |
| 4. Writing e-mails | .06 | .15** | .22** | - |  |  |  |
| 5. Social networking | .07 | .13** | .44** | .16** | - |  |  |
| 6. Face-to-face with family | .04 | -.03 | .16** | .06 | .21** | - |  |
| 7. Face-to-face with friends | .03 | -.01 | .10* | .06 | .16** | .28** | - |
| 8. Face-to-face with partner (N=310) | .01 | .13* | .05 | .19** | .11 | .11 | .22** |

Note: *p<.05; **p<.01

Next is an examination of communication contexts and dominant modes of interaction focusing on communication purposes. Dominant communication was examined in two communication contexts. The first one of these was dependent on communication purposes and the second on particular person to whom the participant was communicating.

The percentages of dominant communication (phone/mobile talk, text message, online chat, e-mail, social networking, and face-to-face communication) for different communication purposes (meeting new people, personal talk, flirting, informative chat, and causal chat) that students indicated are presented in Table 3.

## Percentages of Students Indicating Dominant Communication for Each Communication Purposes (N=500)

Chi-squares for all communication purposes were significant, indicating that modes of communication were not equally distributed across the different communication purposes. While face-to-face communication was used most frequently for meeting new people (90%), personal talk (88%), and flirting (63%), casual and informative chats were predominantly communicated using ICT communication (74%, and 65%, respectively).

*Table 3. Dominant communication mode by percentage*

| | Meeting New People | Personal Talk | Flirt | Informative Chat | Casual Chat |
|---|---|---|---|---|---|
| Face-to-face | 90.2 | 88.0 | 62.8 | 33.8 | 24.8 |
| All ICT communications | 9.2 | 11.4 | 34.4 | 64.8 | 73.8 |
| *Specific ICT communications:* | | | | | |
| Talking on mobile/ phone | .2 | 4.6 | 2.4 | 14.0 | 5.8 |
| SMS | .2 | 1.4 | 12.6 | 3.2 | 3.4 |
| Online chatting | 1.4 | 2.6 | 7.6 | 6.6 | 23.2 |
| Writing e-mails | .6 | 2.2 | 3.2 | 11.6 | 20.0 |
| Social networks | 6.8 | .6 | 8.6 | 29.3 | 21.4 |
| Chi-square (df) | 1973.23 (5) | 1850.81 (5) | 825.83 (5) | 234.53 (5) | 132.69 (5) |

Results indicated that specific ICT communications were in use for specific communication purposes. Thus, phone talk was most popular for sharing information, SMS for flirting, chat for casual talks, and e-mail for both casual and informative chat. Social networking was mostly used for seeking or sharing information and casual chat.

Personal talks and meeting new people were two communication purposes that most of the participants did face-to-face. Only a very small portion of participants decided to make first contact on social networks (6.8%), or to engage in personal talk on the phone (4.6%). When all five modes of communication purposes were taken together, 60% of students preferred face-to-face communication (although this varies from 90% for meeting new people to 25% for casual chat).

The study also examined the differences in communication based on the person or person involved. The percentages of modes of communication (phone/mobile talk, text message, online chat, e-mail, social networking, and face-to-face communication) used with different persons (parents, friends, partner, colleagues, and teachers) reported by students are presented in Table 4.

Chi-squares for all collocutors were significant, indicating that frequencies of dominant communication weren't evenly distributed. Face-to-face communication was the most frequently used, regardless of the collocutor's relation to the student.

Although most of the participants dominantly communicated with all relevant others in a face-to-face manner, it is interesting to note that for about 10% of students, phone talks were the dominant mode of interaction with parents. Online communication, especially e-mail, was found to be important part of academic life, since for 37% of students it was the dominant mode of communication with teachers. For 12% of students, e-mail surpassed face-to-face and other ICT communication devices when communicating with colleagues.

## Percentages of Students Indicating Dominant Communication With Different Persons (N=500)

The Table 4 data showed that students used face-to-face communication more frequently with persons with whom they were in close or intimate relationships (partner, parents, or friends), compared to persons with whom they were in formal relationships (colleagues and teachers).

The study yielded well-being variables based on mode of communication. As expected, happiness and life satisfaction were highly inter-correlated, sharing almost 70% of common variance (r=.83, p<.01). The results showed that students were mostly satisfied with their lives (M=7.7, SD=1.92), and generally felt quite happy (M=7.5, SD=1.96). These results are in accordance with previous research on students in Croatia (e.g. Brkljačić, & Kaliterna Lipovčan, 2010). Students in romantic

*Table 4. Dominant communication mode by person*

|  | Parents | Friends | Partner | Colleagues | Teachers |
|---|---|---|---|---|---|
| Face-to-face | 84.6 | 80.8 | 85.4 | 66.2 | 57.6 |
| All ICT communications | 14.6 | 18.8 | 12 | 33.4 | 41.5 |
| *Specific ICT communication:* |  |  |  |  |  |
| Phone/mobile | 10.6 | 5.4 | 4.0 | 5.2 | .8 |
| SMS | .8 | .8 | 2.2 | 3.2 | .8 |
| Chat | .2 | 4.0 | .8 | 4.6 | 0 |
| e-mail | 2.6 | 4.2 | 3.8 | 12.0 | 37.4 |
| Social networks | .4 | 4.4 | 1.2 | 8.4 | 1.8 |
| Chi-square (df) | 1704,74 (5) | 1493,4 (5) | 1770,86 (5) | 904,24 (5) | 707,45 (4) |

Note: $*p<.05$; $**p<.01$

relationships outscored single students at both well-being measures, showing higher life satisfaction (t= 4.34, p<.01) and happiness (t=4.26, p<.01).

Our first step was to correlate the amount of time spent in different forms of communication with the indicators of well-being. Next, Table 5 shows Pearson's correlations for all students, and separately for students who were involved in a romantic relationship (with a partner) and those who weren't.

Pearson's correlations between times spend in different communications and well-being for the whole sample, and separately for those with and without a partner.

When considering the whole sample, we noticed there was a weak negative association between time spent in online chatting and happiness, while positive associations were found between both well-being indicators and face-to-face communication with friends and partners. However, when students were divided into two groups (single vs. in a romantic relationship) time with partner ceased to be significantly related to well-being, indicating that just being in a relationship, per se, is responsible for observed association at the whole sample. After separation of the groups, online chatting also ceased to be significantly related to well-being, but this was probably due to the initially small value -- we required a larger sample to achieve a level of significance. Interestingly, time with friends was significantly associated with both well-being indicators, but only for students in a romantic relationship, while for others this relation was close to zero. For the students who were not involved in a romantic relationship the only mode of communication associated with well-being was writing e-mails: students who spent more time in this activity showed significantly lower levels of both happiness and life satisfaction.

*Table 5. Pearson's correlations*

| | All Students (N=500) | | With a Partner (N=310) | | Without a Partner (N=190) | |
|---|---|---|---|---|---|---|
| | Happiness | Life Satisfaction | Happiness | Life Satisfaction | Happiness | Life Satisfaction |
| Happiness | 1 | .83** | 1 | .80** | 1 | .89** |
| Life Satisfaction | .83** | 1 | .80** | 1 | .86** | 1 |
| Chat | -.09* | -.08 | -.10 | -.07 | -.08 | -.09 |
| Mail | -.05 | -.08 | .06 | .02 | -.22** | -.25** |
| Mobile/ Phone | .06 | .06 | .07 | .10 | -.04 | -.07 |
| SMS (Text Message) | .06 | .04 | .02 | -.01 | .09 | .06 |
| Social Networking | -.03 | -.02 | -.08 | -.01 | .02 | -.05 |
| Face-to-face with Family | .04 | .06 | .02 | .04 | .03 | .05 |
| Face-to-face with Friends | .11* | .13** | .16** | .20** | .03 | .01 |
| Face-to-face with Partner | - | - | .11 | .08 | - | - |

Note: *p<.05; **p<.01

To test the differences in well-being between those who dominantly use ICT communication and those who dominantly communicate face-to-face in a particular communication context, the participants were divided into two groups. One group consisted of those who dominantly utilized face-to-face communications, and the other group comprised all modes of ICT communications. Descriptive statistics (M, SD) for each group and results of t-tests for independent samples are now presented in Table 6.

Differences in happiness and life satisfaction (LS) in those who dominantly use face-to-face communication versus those who use ICT communication (N=500)

The difference on both well-being indicators proved to be significant only for personal communication. Students who talked about personal issues face-to-face were happier and more satisfied with their lives, and so were those who mostly communicated face-to-face with people from private life (parents, friends, and partner). Additionally, students who flirt using face-to-face communication were

*Table 6. Differences in happiness and life satisfaction*

|  |  | M±SD Mostly Face-to-Face | M±SD Mostly ICT | t-Value |
|---|---|---|---|---|
| Making first contact | Happiness | 7.5±1.94 (N=451) | 7.0±2.16 (N=46) | 1.61 |
|  | LS | 7.8±1.89 (N=451) | 7.2±2.22 (N=46) | 1.71 |
| Casual talks | Happiness | 7.7±1.87 (N=124) | 7.4±2.00 (N=369) | 1.29 |
|  | LS | 7.8±1.92 (N=124) | 7.7±1.92 (N=369) | 0.23 |
| Personal talks | Happiness | 7.6±1.92 (N=440) | 6.9±2.23 (N=57) | 2.20* |
|  | LS | 7.8±1.84 (N=440) | 7.00±2.34 (N=57) | 2.65** |
| Informative talks | Happiness | 7.6±1.92 (N=169) | 7.4±1.99 (N=324) | 1.39 |
|  | LS | 7.9±1.77 (N=169) | 7.6±1.99 (N=324) | 1.41 |
| Flirting | Happiness | 7.7±1.90 (N=314) | 7.2±2.01 (N=172) | 2.30* |
|  | LS | 7.9±1.85 (N=314) | 7.6±1.95 (N=172) | 1.71 |
| Communicating with parents | Happiness | 7.6±1.85 (N=423) | 6.9±2.37 (N=73) | 2.53* |
|  | LS | 7.8±1.82 (N=423) | 7.1±2.27 (N=73) | 2.55* |
| Communicating with friends | Happiness | 7.6±1.86 (N=404) | 7.0±2.31 (N=94) | 2.36* |
|  | LS | 7.9±1.78 (N=404) | 7.2±2.36 (N=94) | 2.53* |
| Communicating with partner | Happiness | 7.6±1.84 (N=427) | 6.6±2.39 (N=60) | 3.11** |
|  | LS | 7.9±1.80 (N=427) | 7.00±2.31 (N=60) | 2.80** |
| Communicating with colleagues | Happiness | 7.6±1.68 (N=331) | 7.2±1.91 (N=167) | 2.56* |
|  | LS | 7.8±1.91 (N=331) | 7.5±1.93 (N=167) | 1.87 |
| Communicating with teachers | Happiness | 7.7±1.90 (N=288) | 7.2±2.05 (N=204) | 2.64** |
|  | LS | 7.9±1.84 (N=288) | 7.5±2.02 (N=204) | 1.64 |

Note: *p<.05; **p<.01, LS= Life Satisfaction

happier, as were those who communicated with their colleagues and teachers in the same manner. The greatest difference between the groups (1 point on 10-point scale) was found for communicating with partner, where students who communicated with partner face-to-face were significantly happier. If students didn't have a partner at the time, they were supposed to assess the dominant type of communication with a partner on the basis of their previous relationships

## DISCUSSION

The main purpose of this study was to examine the use of different modes of communication (ICT and face-to-face) in different contexts, and their relation to subjective well-being in the sample of students (N=500).

Our first goal was to assess the average time students spent in various modes of ICT and face-to-face communication.

Although the time spent in different modes of ICT communication indicated that this is important mode of interaction between students, the major part of communication happened in the real face-to-face environment, which is consistent with findings of Baym et al. (2004). Baym conducted two studies to compare college students' interpersonal interactions online, face-to-face, and on the telephone. In the first study, they assessed a relative amount of social interactions via communication diary. The second study was a survey to explore students' most recent significant social interactions (online, face-to-face, or telephone). Results of the first study showed that the Internet was used almost as often as the telephone, but face-to-face remained a far more frequently used means of communication. The second study showed that use of the Internet was positively correlated with the use of other modes of interpersonal communication, and that it was integrated into students' social lives.

Our participants were electronic engineering students, a segment of the population that has had ICT integrated into their social world from an early age. It is also necessary for their daily university task. They spent a lot of time using different ICT communications (mostly chat and social networking), supporting previous findings that youth are actively using the Internet as an important form of social interaction (Brignall, & Valey, 2005). Pempek, Yermolayeva and Calvert (2009) reported that the amount of time that students spent daily on social networks varied a lot, with an average of about 50 minutes per day. Compared to these results, our participants reported more time spent on social networks, 70 minutes per day. On the other hand, percentage of e-mail usage was low (only 12 minutes per day), indicating that other modes of ICT communication substituted this tool. Ten years ago, e-mail was very popular communication mode, but recently the online communication is shifting from slow, such as e-mail, towards faster and contextually richer devices, such as social networks (Boase, Horrigan, Wellman, & Rainie, 2006; Fallows, 2004; Kraut et al., 2002).

Students who spent more time in social networking also spent more time with family and friends. According to Franzen (2000) positive associations between amount of time spent in ICT communication and face-to-face communication suggested that the Internet offered an additional technology for both engaging in social interaction and coordination of social activities. Negative associations, would, as Nie and Hillygus (2002) argued, imply that the more time people sit in front of a computer screen, the less time they have for interacting directly with family and friends. These authors surveyed over 4,000 randomly selected Internet users and found that the Internet was responsible for decreased time spent with family members and friends for 9% of the participants. Our results showed weak but positive correlations between time spent in online chatting and social networking and face-to-face communication with family and friends. Furthermore, those who spent more time in writing e-mails and talking on the phone spent more times in face-to-face communication with a partner. Those significant correlations pointed toward the positive relation between time spent in online communication and time spent with significant others.

The second aim was to explore specific relation of different modes of communication and communication context. Communication context in this research was defined via purposes of communication and persons involved in communication. The results confirmed that face-to-face communication was the dominant mode for meeting new people, personal talk, and flirting, while casual and informative talks were predominantly communicated via new technologies. The results indicated that distinct ICT communications were dominant for various communication purposes: phone talk was the most popular for sharing information, text messages for flirting, chat for casual talks, and e-mail for both casual and informative chat. Social networking was mostly used for seeking or sharing information, and for casual chat. Personal talks and meeting new people were two situations that almost all of our participants did face-to-face. It appears that modern technologies have the advantage when casual or informative chats are in question, but when it comes to personal issues, face-to-face is still the preferred mode of communication.

When all five modes of ICT communication were taken together, 60% of students preferred face-to-face communication, which is in accordance with the findings of Baym et al. (2004). Examining frequencies of significant voluntary social interactions conducted face-to-face, on the telephone, and on the Internet, they found that out of the 851 interactions, most were face-to-face (64%), while Internet and telephone interactions were similar in amount: 16.1% Internet interactions and 18.4% telephone calls.

However, unlike in their research, our results showed that various modes of Internet communication dominated telephone communication, with almost 30% of students preferring online interaction, and only about 10% choosing phone talks or text messaging. This discrepancy can be attributed to the period of more than 10 years that passed since the Baym et al. (2004) research was conducted. In that time, Internet communication, especially social networking, has achieved remarkable expansion.

Regarding communication context, we further explored dominant mode of interaction in relation to the collocutor. Face-to-face communication proved to prevail as a dominant mode, regardless of collocutor. Higher percentages of preference of face-to-face communication were related to higher level of intimacy with collocutor. Subrahmanyam and colleagues (Subrahmanyam, Reich, Waechter, & Espinoza, 2008) argued that emerging adults used social networking sites to establish intimate relationships by forming and maintaining interconnections with the people in their lives. However, our results suggested that intimate relationships, such as with partner, parents, or friends, were rarely dominantly preceded online.

Finally, we examined the relationship between time spent in various modes of ICT and face-to-face communication and well-being. We found a positive correlation between time spent with friends and well-being, just as in the previous research that has almost without exception demonstrated positive relation between various social activities and well-being (e.g. Diener, & Seligman, 2002; Hartup, & Stevens, 1999; Reis, Sheldon, Gable, Roscoe, & Ryan, 2000, Lee at al, 2011). Moreover, Larson, Mannell and Zuzanek's (1986) finding that people were happiest with their friends, followed by family members, and the least happy if they were alone, is also in the line with our finding that time spend in face-to-face communication with friends is associated with higher levels of well-being. Online chatting showed weak negative relation to well-being, which is not in line with the results of Selfhout, Branje, Delsing, Bogt and Meeus (2009), who reported a decrease in depression among Dutch adolescents who used the Internet for chatting with friends.

In exploring the relationship between subjective well-being and use of different modes of communication in various communication contexts, it was found that students who dominantly used ICT communication tended to have lower happiness and life satisfaction. This difference was significant when personal issues and close persons were involved, confirming the importance of contextual cues in communication. Our findings were not in accordance with the results of Bessière and colleagues (Bessière, Kiesler, Kraut, & Boneva, 2008) or Shen and Williams (2011), who found that Internet use negatively affects psychosocial health when it is used to meet new people online. Furthermore, Gross, Juvonen and Gable (2002) found that participants who reported feeling lonely or socially anxious were more likely to communicate through instant messaging with strangers. In our research, those who dominantly used internet devices to meet new people didn't differ in happiness or life satisfaction from those who used traditional a face-to-face approach. These results were in line with the findings of Valkenburg and Peter (2007a), who didn't find an effect of chat in a public chat room, which was relatively often used to talk with strangers, on adolescents' well-being.

The relation between use of the Internet, various modes of online communication, and well-being represents a field of research that has grown drastically in the last 20 years. As we already mentioned, two prominent theories with opposite predictions try to explain the relation between online communication and well-being. Stimulation theory foresees positive outcomes, while displacement theory anticipates negative outcomes on well-being. The results of this study can give some insights that might be relevant for further analyses of these two theories.

Valkenburg and Peter (2007a) confronted these theories, assessing time spent in two different ICT communications (instant messaging and chat in public chatrooms), time spent with existing friends, the quality of friendship, and well-being. They found that time spent in instant messaging was positively related to the time spent with existing friends, but neither messaging nor chat use was directly related to well-being. However, instant messaging positively predicted well-being via the mediating variables (a) time spent with existing friends and (b) the quality of these friendships. On the other hand, no relation was found between well-being and chat in a public chatroom. Valkenburg and Peter (2007a) attributed the differences in findings for instant messaging and chatting to the effect of collocutor. Namely, instant messaging was mostly used with existing friends, while public chatrooms were often used to talk with strangers.

Valkenburg and Peter's (2007b) study design differed from ours, as they studied only two ICT communication modes, and unlike us, they assessed the quality of friendships. However, there are some similarities in the findings of both studies. First, we confirmed that time spent in face-to-face socialization with friends is positively related to well-being, and secondly, time spent in socialization with significant others was positively related to time spent in ICT supported communication. On the other hand, our research showed some negative associations between well-being and ICT communication that were not observed in Valkenburg and Peter's (2007b) research. Namely, time spent chatting online was negatively associated with happiness in our research, although this correlation was low.

According to displacement theory, people who use the Internet for communication dislocate interaction in an inappropriate manner, because online communication lacks some important features typical in face-to-face communication (such as physical closeness, body language, etc.). However, the importance of these features depends on communication context, i.e. face-to-face communication is presumed to be more important when discussing more intimate issues, and with closer collocutors. We found that those who dominantly communicated intimate issues (such as personal talks and flirting) in a face-to-face manner expressed higher levels of well-being. In addition, people who dominantly communicated with different persons face-to-face showed higher well-being, compared to those who dominantly used ICT communication.

Expected, but still interesting, is the finding that the difference between well-being among groups who dominantly utilize ICT and face-to-face communication was proportional to the closeness to the person they communicated with, and the privacy of the topic. The more private the theme of discussion, and the more intimate their relationship, the more often a negative relation between ICT communication and well-being was apparent. This finding is in line with Ruppel (2015) who found that participants self-disclosed with less breadth and depth when they used reduced-cue communication technologies than when they used face to face communication, and preferred face-to-face communication for conversations in which they anticipated high levels of self-disclosure.

In summary, although we found some weak positive associations between the amount of time spent in online and in-person communication, most of our findings go in line with the displacement theory, suggesting that online communication is an inappropriate substitution for in-person interaction. It seems that for casual or informative talks, mode of communication it is not really important, but when personal issues and close persons are involved, face-to-face communication becomes essential.

## SOLUTIONS AND RECOMMENDATIONS

This study is among the first to explore the relation between subjective well-being and the use of different modes of communication in various communication contexts. It has been conducted on a relatively large sample (N=500).

Despite these strengths, the results of this study should be viewed in light of some limitations. First, the sample in this study was a homogeneous group of students from the Faculty of Electrical Engineering and Computing, who had high knowledge and use of computers, so the results may be partially biased. However, since our aim was to detect participants for whom ICT communication was dominant mode of communication, we needed to have a sample consisting of heavy users. Therefore, unlike previous research, in this study we were able to select participants for whom ICT communication prevailed over face-to-face communication and to explore their well-being.

The main finding of this research is related to the importance of communication context. This research suggests that the relation between well-being and dominant mode of communication may partially depend on *our relation to the person to whom we communicate* and *the purpose of communication*. Face-to-face contact seems to be important when people are communicating with close persons and talking about personal issues. On the other hand, in the case of formal, superficial, and casual communication, face-to-face communication can be replaced with ICT without serious impact on one's well-being.

Therefore, people should be encouraged to use ICT for faster and more efficient exchange of information, and even for entertainment, but the importance of face-to-face contact should be stressed when communication involves close relations and emotions.

## FURTHER RESEARCH DIRECTIONS

Correlations between times spent in different modes of communication showed some ambiguity. For example, those who spent more time in online chatting also spent more time with family and friends, but while chatting online negatively predicted well-being, time spent with friends predicted well-being in a positive manner. Therefore, we speculate that positive relation between time spent in ICT and face-to-face communication could be mediated by the total amount of free time. This assumption, however, needs further validation.

Furthermore, in this research we did not examine the quality of time spent with relatives, friends, and partners. Rather, we examined the total amount of time and dominant mode of communication. More detailed research should explore the quality of time spent with important persons.

## CONCLUSION

Our results indicated that ICT communication was an integral part of the daily lives of our participants, though they spent on average more time in face-to-face communications. Face-to-face communication was dominant when it comes to communicating with different people, regardless of collocutor. However, the more formal the relation to collocutor was, the more participants choose ICT over face-to-face communication. Regarding association between well-being and different modes of communication, it was found that spending more time in face-to-face communication with friends was related to being happier and more satisfied with life. In addition, dominant use of face-to-face communication for personal talks and with people from private life was related to better well-being. In summary, our results are more in line with displacement theory, but stress the importance of contextual cues and showing that for discussing personal issues, and for communication with close persons, well-being is lower for those who dominantly use ICT.

# REFERENCES

Baumeister, R. F., & Leary, M. R. (1995). The need to belong: Desire for interpersonal attachments as a fundamental human motivation. *Psychological Bulletin, 117*(3), 497–529. doi:10.1037/0033-2909.117.3.497 PMID:7777651

Baym, N., Zhang, Y. B., & Lin, M. C. (2004). Social interactions across media: Interpersonal communication on the Internet, telephone and face-to-face. *New Media & Society, 6*(3), 41–60. doi:10.1177/1461444804041438

Bessiere, K., Kiesler, S., Kraut, R., & Boneva, B. (2008). Effects of Internet use and social resources on changes in depression. *Information Communication and Society, 11*(1), 47–70. doi:10.1080/13691180701858851

Best, P., Manktelow, R., & Taylor, B. (2014). Online communication, social media and adolescent wellbeing: A systematic narrative review. *Children and Youth Services Review, 41*, 27–36. doi:10.1016/j.childyouth.2014.03.001

Blight, M. G., Jagiello, K., & Ruppel, E. K. (2015). "Same stuff different day:" A mixed-method study of support seeking on Facebook. *Computers in Human Behavior, 53*, 366–373. doi:10.1016/j.chb.2015.07.029

Boase, J., Horrigan, J. B., Wellman, B., & Rainie, L. (2006). *The Strength of Internet Ties* (pp. 1–52). Washington, D.C.: Pew Internet & American Life Project.

Brajša-Žganec, A., Kaliterna-Lipovčan, Lj., Prizmić-Larsen, Z., Glavak-Tkalić, R., Sučić, I., Tadić Vujčić, M., . . . Lučić, L. (2017). CRO-WELL: Well-being and life events - preliminary analysis. *Abstract Book - 15th ISQLS Annual Conference.*

Brignall, T. W. III, & Valey, T. V. (2005). The impact of Internet communication on social interaction. *Sociological Spectrum, 25*(3), 335–348. doi:10.1080/02732170590925882

Brkljačić, T., & Kaliterna-Lipovčan, L. (2010). Life satisfaction and feeling of happiness among students. *Suvremena Psihologija, 13*(2), 189–201.

Bryant, J. A., Sanders-Jackson, A., & Smallwood, A. K. (2006). IMing, Text Messaging, and Adolescent Social Networks. *Journal of Computer-Mediated Communication, 11*(2), 577–592. doi:10.1111/j.1083-6101.2006.00028.x

Bureau of Labor Statistics. (2014). *American Time Use Survey.* Retrieved from http://www.bls.gov/tus/

Burke, M., & Kraut, R. (2014). Growing closer on Facebook: Changes in tie strength through site use. *ACM CHI 2014: Conference on Human Factors in Computing Systems*, 4187-4196. 10.1145/2556288.2557094

Burke, M., & Kraut, R. (2016). The relationship between Facebook use and well-being depends on communication type and tie strength. *Journal of Computer-Mediated Communication*, *21*(4), 265–281. doi:10.1111/jcc4.12162

Carr, A. (2004). *Positive psychology: The science of happiness and human strengths*. Hove: Brunner-Routledge.

Cheung, F., & Lucas, R. E. (2014). Assessing the validity of single-item life satisfaction measures: Results from three large samples. *Quality of Life Research: An International Journal of Quality of Life Aspects of Treatment, Care and Rehabilitation*, *23*(10), 2809–2818. doi:10.100711136-014-0726-4 PMID:24890827

Cummings, J. N., Butler, B., & Kraut, R. (2002). The quality of online social relationships. *Communications of the ACM*, *47*(7), 103–108. doi:10.1145/514236.514242

Diener, E., Pressman, S. D., Hunter, J., & Delgadillo-Chase, D. (2017). If, Why, and When Subjective Well-Being Influences Health, and Future Needed Research. *Applied Psychology. Health and Well-Being*, *9*(2), 133–167. doi:10.1111/aphw.12090 PMID:28707767

Diener, E., & Seligman, M. E. (2002). Very happy people. *Psychological Science*, *13*(1), 81–84. doi:10.1111/1467-9280.00415 PMID:11894851

Diener, E., Suh, E. M., Lucas, R. E., & Smith, H. L. (1999). Subjective well-being: Three decades of progress. *Psychological Bulletin*, *12*(2), 276–302. doi:10.1037/0033-2909.125.2.276

Dienlin, T., Masur, P., & Trepte, S. (2017). Reinforcement or displacement? The reciprocity of FtF, IM, and SNS communication and their effects on loneliness and life satisfaction. *Journal of Computer-Mediated Communication*, *22*(2), 71–87. doi:10.1111/jcc4.12183

Ellison, N. B., Vitak, J., Gray, R., & Lampe, C. (2014). Cultivating social resources on social network sites: Facebook relationship maintenance behaviors and their role in social capital processes. *Journal of Computer-Mediated Communication*, *19*(4), 855–870. doi:10.1111/jcc4.12078

Fallows, D. (2004). *The Internet and daily life: Many Americans use the Internet in everyday activities, but traditional offline habits skill dominate.* Retrieved August 26, 2008, from http://www.pewInternet.org/pdfs/pip_college_report.pdf

Farahani, H. A., Kazemi, Z., Aghamohamadi, S., Bakhtiarvand, F., & Ansari, M. (2011). Examining mental health indices in students using Facebook in Iran. *Procedia: Social and Behavioral Sciences, 28,* 811–814. doi:10.1016/j.sbspro.2011.11.148

Franzen, A. (2000). Does the Internet Make Us Lonely. *European Sociological Review, 16*(4), 427–438. doi:10.1093/esr/16.4.427

Gallardo-Echenique, E., Bullen, M., & Marqués-Molias, L. (2016). Student communication and study habits of first-year university students in the digital era. *Canadian Journal of Learning and Technology, 42*(1), 2–21. doi:10.21432/T2D047

Goodman-Deane, J. A., Mieczakowski, A., Johnson, D., Goldhaber, T., & Clarkson, P. J. (2015). The impact of communication technologies on life and relationship satisfaction. *Computers in Human Behavior, 57,* 219–229. doi:10.1016/j.chb.2015.11.053

Gross, E. F. (2004). Adolescent Internet use: What we expect, what teens report. *Journal of Applied Developmental Psychology, 25*(6), 633–649. doi:10.1016/j.appdev.2004.09.005

Gross, E. F., Juvenon, J., & Gable, S. L. (2002). Internet use and well-being in adolescence. *The Journal of Social Issues, 58*(1), 75–90. doi:10.1111/1540-4560.00249

Hall, R. H. (2016) Internet Use and Happiness. *Third International Conference on HCI in Business, Government and Organizations: eCommerce and Innovation,* 37-45.

Hartup, W. W., & Stevens, N. (1999). Friendships and adaptation across the life span. *Current Directions in Psychological Science, 8*(3), 76–79. doi:10.1111/1467-8721.00018

Internet World Stats. (2017). *Internet usage statistics. The Internet Big Picture World Internet Users and 2017 Population Stats.* Retrieved November 2017: http://www.internetworldstats.com/stats.htm

Jelfs, A., & Richardson, J. T. E. (2012). The use of digital technologies across the adult life span in distance education. *British Journal of Educational Technology*, *44*(2), 338–351. doi:10.1111/j.1467-8535.2012.01308.x

Kaliterna Lipovčan, Lj., Babarović, T., Brajša-Žganec, A., & Bejaković, P., & Japec, L. (2016). Trendovi u kvaliteti života Hrvatska: 2007. – 2012. s naglaskom na subjektivno blagostanje. *Radno pravo*, *11*(9), 69–75.

Kraut, R., & Burke, M. (2015). Internet use and psychological well-being: Effects of activity and audience. *Communications of the ACM*, *58*(12), 94–100. doi:10.1145/2739043

Kraut, R., Kiesler, S., Boneva, B., Cummings, J. N., Helgeson, V., & Crawford, A. (2002). The Internet paradox revisited. *The Journal of Social Issues*, *58*(1), 49–74. doi:10.1111/1540-4560.00248

Larson, R., Mannell, R., & Zuzanek, J. (1986). Daily well-being of older adults with friends and family. *Psychology and Aging*, *1*(2), 117–126. doi:10.1037/0882-7974.1.2.117 PMID:3267387

Lee, P. S. N., Leung, L., Lo, V., Xiong, C., & Wu, T. (2011). Internet communication versus face-to-face interaction in quality of life. *Social Indicators Research*, *100*(3), 375–389. doi:10.100711205-010-9618-3

Lenhart, A., Madden, M., & Hitlin, P. (2005). *Teens and Technology: Youth are Leading the Transition to a Fully Wired and Mobile Nation*. Washington, DC: Pew Internet & American Life Project.

Lenhart, A., Rainie, L., & Lewis, O. (2001). *Teenage life online: The rise of the instant- message generation and the internet's impact on friendships and family relationships*. Washington, DC: Pew Internet and American Life Project.

Lin, L. Y., Sidani, J. E., Shensa, A., Radovic, A., Miller, E., Colditz, J. B., ... Primack, B. A. (2016). Association between social media use and depression among U.S. young adults. *Depression and Anxiety*, *33*(4), 323–331. doi:10.1002/da.22466 PMID:26783723

Masur, P. K., Reinecke, L., Ziegele, M., & Quiring, O. (2014). The interplay of intrinsic need satisfaction and Facebook specific motives in explaining addictive behavior on Facebook. *Computers in Human Behavior*, *39*, 376–386. doi:10.1016/j. chb.2014.05.047

Morgan, C., & Cotten, S. R. (2003). The relationship between Internet activities and depressive symptoms in a sample of college freshmen. *Cyberpsychology & Behavior*, *6*(2), 133–141. doi:10.1089/109493103321640329 PMID:12804025

Morreale, S., Staley, C., Stavrositu, C., & Krakowiak, M. (2015). First-year college students' attitudes toward communication technologies and their perceptions of communication competence in the 21st century. *Communication Education*, *64*(1), 107–131. doi:10.1080/03634523.2014.978799

Nie, N., Hillygus, D. S., & Erbring, L. (2002). Internet use, interpersonal relations, and sociability: A time diary study. In B. Wellman & C. Haythornthwaite (Eds.), *The Internet in Everyday Life* (pp. 215–243). Oxford, UK: Blackwell. doi:10.1002/9780470774298.ch7

Nie, N., & Hillygus, S. (2002). The impact of internet use on Sociability: Time-diary findings. *IT & Society*, *1*(1), 1–20.

Parks, M. R., & Roberts, L. D. (1998). Making MOOsic: The development of personal relationships on-line and a comparison to their offline counterparts. *Journal of Social and Personal Relationships*, *15*(4), 517–538. doi:10.1177/0265407598154005

Pea, R., Nass, C., Meheula, L., Rance, M., Kumar, A., Bamford, H., & Zhou, M. (2012). Media use, face-to-face communication, media multitasking, and social well-being among 8- to 12-year-old girls. *Developmental Psychology*, *48*(2), 327–336. doi:10.1037/a0027030 PMID:22268607

Pempek, T. A., Yermolayeva, Y. A., & Calvert, S. L. (2009). College students' social networking experiences on facebook. *Journal of Applied Developmental Psychology*, *30*(3), 227–238. doi:10.1016/j.appdev.2008.12.010

Penard, T., Poussing, N., & Suire, R. (2013). Does the Internet make people happier? *Journal of Socio Economics, Elsevier*, *46*, 105–116.

Poushter, J. (2015). *Internet Seen as Positive Influence on Education but Negative on Morality in Emerging and Developing Nations*. Retrieved from: http://assets. pewresearch.org/wp-content/uploads/sites/2/2015/03/Pew-Research-Center-Technology-Report-FINAL-March-19-20151.pdf

Ramirez, A. Jr, Dimmick, J., Feaster, J., & Lin, S.-F. (2008). Revisiting interpersonal media competition: The gratification niches of instant messaging, e-mail, and the telephone. *Communication Research, 35*(4), 529–547. doi:10.1177/0093650208315979

Reinecke, L., Hartmann, T., & Eden, A. (2014). The guilty couch potato: The role of ego depletion in reducing recovery through media use. *Journal of Communication, 64*(4), 569–589. doi:10.1111/jcom.12107

Reis, H. T., Sheldon, K. M., Gable, S. L., Roscoe, J., & Ryan, R. M. (2000). Daily well-being: The role of autonomy, competence, and relatedness. *Personality and Social Psychology Bulletin, 26*(4), 419–435. doi:10.1177/0146167200266002

Ruppel, E. K. (2015). Use of communication technologies in romantic relationships: Self-disclosure and the role of relationship development. *Journal of Social and Personal Relationships, 32*(5), 667–686. doi:10.1177/0265407514541075

Sampasakanyinga, H., & Lewis, R. F. (2015). Frequent Use of social networking sites is associated with poor psychological functioning among children and adolescents. *Cyberpsychology, Behavior, and Social Networking, 18*(7), 380–385. doi:10.1089/cyber.2015.0055 PMID:26167836

Schneider, D., Sperling, S., Schell, G., Hemmer, K., Glauer, R., & Silberhorn, D. (2004). *Instant Messaging - Neue Räume im CyberspaceNutzertypen, Gebrauchsweisen, Motive, Regeln*. München: Verlag Reinhard Fischer.

Selfhout, M. W., Branje, S. T., Delsing, M., Bogt, T. T., & Meeus, W. J. (2009). Different types of Internet use, depression, and social anxiety: The role of perceived friendship quality. *Journal of Adolescence, 32*(4), 819–833. doi:10.1016/j.adolescence.2008.10.011 PMID:19027940

Shaw, L. H., & Gant, L. M. (2002). In defense of the Internet: The relationship between Internet communication and depression, loneliness, self-esteem, and perceived social support. *Cyberpsychology & Behavior*, *5*(2), 157–170. doi:10.1089/109493102753770552 PMID:12025883

Shen, C., & Williams, D. (2011). Unpacking Time Online: Connecting Internet and Massively Multiplayer Online Game Use with Psychosocial Well-being. *Communication Research*, *38*(1), 123–149. doi:10.1177/0093650210377196

Sinkkonen, H. M., Puhakka, H., & Merilainen, M. (2014). Internet use and addiction among Finnish Adolescents (15–19 years). *Journal of Adolescence*, *37*(2), 123–131. doi:10.1016/j.adolescence.2013.11.008 PMID:24439618

Subrahmanyam, K., Reich, S. M., Waechter, N., & Espinoza, G. (2008). Online and offline social networks: Use of social networking sites by emerging adults. *Journal of Applied Developmental Psychology*, *29*(6), 420–433. doi:10.1016/j.appdev.2008.07.003

Valkenburg, P. M., & Peter, J. (2007a). Online communication and adolescent well-being: Testing the stimulation versus the displacement hypothesis. *Journal of Computer-Mediated Communication*, *12*(4), 2. doi:10.1111/j.1083-6101.2007.00368.x

Valkenburg, P. M., & Peter, J. (2007b). Preadolescents' and adolescents' online communication and their closeness to friends. *Developmental Psychology*, *43*(2), 267–277. doi:10.1037/0012-1649.43.2.267 PMID:17352538

Valkenburg, P. M., & Soeters, K. (2001). Children's positive and negative experiences with the Internet. *Communication Research*, *2*, 653–676.

Veenhoven, R. (2014) What we have learnt about happiness classic qualms in the light of recent research. In A Life Devoted to Quality of Life, Festschrift in Honor of Alex C. Michalos. Springer.

Verduyn, P., Ybarra, O., Résibois, M., Jonides, J., & Kross, E. (2017). Do social network sites enhance or undermine subjective well-being? A critical review. *Social Issues and Policy Review*, *11*(1), 274–302. doi:10.1111ipr.12033

Weigin, E. L., Campbell, M., Kimpton, M., Wozencroft, K., & Orel, A. (2016). Social capital on Facebook: The impact of personality and online communication behaviors. *Journal of Educational Computing Research*, *54*(6), 747–748. doi:10.1177/0735633116631886

## KEY TERMS AND DEFINITIONS

**Communication Context:** Is in this study defined as specific features of communication including (1) purpose of communication and (2) relation between persons in the communication.

**Displacement Theory:** Postulates that online communication is an inadequate alternative for face-to-face communication and therefore has harmful effects on wellbeing.

**Face-to-Face Communication:** Is the social interaction between two or more persons without mediating technology.

**ICT:** Is information and communication technology including devices such as phones, smartphones, and computers.

**Life Satisfaction:** Is the way persons evaluate their lives.

**Stimulation Theory:** Postulates that online communication enhances social contacts and therefore improves peoples' wellbeing.

# Chapter 8
# Communication Accommodation Theory:
## Finding the Right Approach

**James M. Goodwin**
*Georgetown University, USA*

## ABSTRACT

*A lack of face-to-face interactions affects society while digital influences on the world create and sustain communications characterized by limited feedback, incomplete information, tentative connections, and misunderstandings. Thousands of digital messages lack the full communication components—sender-receiver-feedback—creating barriers to communication completion. The ability to adapt to the receiver and the medium is enhanced in face-to-face communication, as defined within communication accommodation theory (CAT). CAT allows all parties to emphasize or minimize differences in verbal and non-verbal conversations.*

DOI: 10.4018/978-1-5225-4168-4.ch008

## INTRODUCTION

Globally, modern society is challenged by a lack of direct, face-to-face interactions and digital influences, resulting in broken communications characterized by limited feedback, incomplete information, tentative connections, and misunderstandings. Without effective sender-receiver-feedback, the thousands of digital messages exchanged daily results in barriers to complete communication. Senders who can adapt messages to be more likely accurately understood by the receiver, often through use of the appropriate medium, are more likely to experience success in those interactions. Communication Accommodation Theory (CAT) posits that successful communication is often determined by each party's ability to emphasize or minimize verbal and non-verbal interaction disconnects. The theory maintains that people adjust speech, vocal patterns, and gestures to help promote mutual understanding in communication (Gallois and Giles 2015).

In business situations, leaders must adapt their approach to interpersonal and group communication to the information exchange situation at hand. This accommodation and flexibility increases understanding, which makes interactions more powerful. Great communicators listen and learn on the fly to adjust to each participant's emotions, risk, and feedback and ensure successful interactions. Approaches are tailored in the group atmosphere to adjust to challenges of the location or time of the interaction.

Communicators must not only adapt, they must use visual and verbal cues to ensure the adaptations are right for each situation. This is important because communication adjustments that fail can lead to dissatisfying, problematic, or even adversarial experiences (Gallois, Giles & Ogay 2005).

There are many ways personal and social identity affect our interactions and CAT is a way to ensure success in making these adjustments (Giles 2008). CAT demonstrates that people accommodate communication partners by adjusting to their gestures, vocal patterns, and speech when dealing with social encounters, interactions, or negotiations (Gallois and Giles 2015). Minimizing or emphasizing differences with interaction partners is normal and often occurs without sender or receiver realizing it. CAT assists with verbal and non-verbal challenges and helps communicators navigate the path to understanding that is filled with considerations of language, context, identity, interpersonal factors, and intergroup factors.

## CONVERGENCE AND DIVERGENCE

CAT contains the key factors of convergence and divergence. Convergence refers to individual strategies employed to adapt to another person's communication behavior. Divergence is when people stress and manage speech and non-verbal differences between themselves and others.

In group settings, facilitators ensure a collective comprehension, making sure to remain flexible and willing to change phrases or terms used. There might be other needs for change that involve altering the tempo of the presentation, employing repetition to drive home a point, or changing the rate of their speech.

The accommodation suggested by the theory includes ways to emphasize or minimize verbal and non-verbal interaction differences with other people. Such accommodation is achieved through the use and adjustment of language, context, identity, and intergroup and interpersonal factors. When using convergence and divergence, social differences are reduced by changing the interactive environment, as well as the communication behaviors in the ways that best suit the parties involved (Ayoko, Härtel et al. 2002). Convergence is the way people adapt to communicative behaviors to reduce social differences. People highlight speech and non-verbal differences to arrive at ways to adjust for success. Senders should be careful when using convergence because too much accommodation can lead to a receiver interpreting the sender's intended message to seem condescending. They should also avoid communication breakdowns by getting consensus on task processes and by managing discourse to make sure it is healthy and productive. A 2002 study on discourse management found that productive conflict was the result of increased use of discourse management strategies (Ayoko, Härtel et al.). These strategies were applied to achieve common ground and remove roadblocks to communication. Senders and receivers will be more effective when using the accommodation theory's valuable resources.

CAT strategies include team building, interpersonal control, interpretability, discourse management, and emotional expression. Interpersonal control enhances communication abilities by determining how much the sender controls the receiver, or how one party in an interaction controls another. Parties to the communication change sender-receiver roles throughout the process, so interpersonal control is a way of managing or regulating another's thoughts, feelings, or actions (Stets 1991).

Interpretability is a strategy used to allow the receiver additional help in understanding the message (Jones, Woodhouse et al. 2007). This involves using a receiver's emotions, visual cues, and other characteristics to ensure message delivery and to start and sustain feedback. As a dialogue non-approximation strategy, interpretability may equate to a communicator using slower or more simple speech, use of questions to provide feedback, as well as choosing co-familiar topics to discuss to ensure messages are understood and communication is successful (Gallois, Giles et al. 2005).

Discourse management is used to organize information in the best way for the intended audience. Discourse management is adjusting communication activities to ensure effectiveness in information exchange. The skills required to manage discourse include good eye contact, taking turns so each person can be heard, and paying attention to and addressing nonverbal behaviors. Communicators make sure to repair any difficulties or breaks in information sharing and seek common ground where the interaction will be most effective.

Similarly, people express, regulate, experience, and influence emotions in many ways during communication. This strategy is called emotional expression and it requires thoroughly understanding and managing one's emotions and the emotions of others during a communicative interaction. Emotional expressions are observable, resulting in verbal and non-verbal behaviors that include facial movements, audible sounds, and obvious emotional reactions such as laughing, crying, smiling, or scowling (Gallois, Giles et al. 2005). A discussion of receiver activity levels provides context and relevance for group communication. CAT also requires that senders identify effective and ineffective activities.

## SENDER-RECEIVER RELATIONSHIP

A 2007 study examining effective nurse to patient communication found that effective communication was accommodative and more interpersonal while ineffective communication was generally under-accommodative and more intergroup (Jones, Woodhouse et al. 2007). These findings suggest that group dynamics are enhanced when perceptions of effective and ineffective communication are analyzed. The findings also point to effective communication that can be derived from shared management of the interaction, as well as the appropriate support and reassurance of the nurses. Ineffective communication was characterized by under-accommodation and more intergroup exchanges. Study participants believed that the communication was more effective when the interaction was more balanced (Jones, Woodhouse et al. 2007).

Additional findings from the study are important for the current discussion. For instance, participants mentioned discourse management and emotional expression most often when highlighting successful and valued verbal communication that involved informal chatting. Many participants mentioned interpretability (inconsistent, vague, conflicting, indirect, or confusing information) as a contributor to ineffective communication. Undoubtedly, groups can benefit from the ability to discover and correct issues during collaborations when feedback is readily available.

CAT strategies from the nurse communication study are useful to evaluate relationships as people realize activity levels in each strategy as shown in Table 1. Senders and receivers can view communication as a balancing act, where high or low activity levels may not bring the best outcome. In fact, when moderate activity levels are applied, CAT provides the most communication rewards for the effort given.

*Table 1. Adapted from "Coding System for Communication Strategies," Effective nurse parent communication: A study of parents' perceptions in the NICU environment, (Jones, Woodhouse et al. 2007) (Brown 2017).*

| Sender-Receiver Relationships – Activity Comparisons | | | |
|---|---|---|---|
| | Receiver Activity Level: How Much Does Receiver Engage With Message and Sender? | | |
| **Strategy** | **High** | **Moderate** | **Low** |
| Interpersonal Control | • Emphasis on personal power or position <br> • Too formal <br> • Lack of connection to or acceptance of the message | • Genuinely interested in the message <br> • Participates in feedback <br> • Polite <br> • Respectful <br> • Encouraging | • In awe of the sender <br> • Failure to share information or feedback <br> • Surrenders too much authority to the sender |
| Interpretability | • Vague or ambiguous responses <br> • Confusing or inaccurate information <br> • No explanations | • Clear, direct, honest <br> • Straightforward and to the point <br> • Plenty of explanations <br> • Verify understanding of the message | • Topic is too simple to hold your interest <br> • "Talking down to" someone <br> • May give receiver feelings of inferiority |
| Discourse Management | • Dominate the conversation <br> • Fails to listen <br> • Does not let others speak | • Ask questions <br> • Ask opinions <br> • Open to new ideas and topics <br> • Listen first, talk second <br> • "Chat" relationship | • Responds only when asked <br> • Allows sender to determine what is discussed |
| Emotional Expression | • Hostile <br> • Unsupportive | • Show empathy <br> • Establish caring interaction <br> • Give message reassurances | • Too much sympathy <br> • Lack of real information exchange |

For each strategy, the table demonstrates how and why receiver activity level is high, moderate, or low. Moderate levels of activity are more accepting of the message, possibly leading to greater understanding. Increased feedback due to a clear and understandable message would be the best outcome.

How could this table be helpful? Consider a digital conversation so technical that it is overbearing in how the information is presented. There is no real attempt at feedback because the sender is trying to dominate dialogue with their level of expertise. Another digital conversation might be so simple that it disrespects the intelligence of the receiver. The receiver might feel that they are being "talked down to," or might consider the information so simplified that it is insulting. Still, feedback is not normally exchanged when the receiver has these negative beliefs.

Face-to-face conversation is best conducted with a moderate activity level where the sender caters to the receiver. This type of conversation is flexible and is characterized by clear and direct information sharing that is straightforward and to the point with plenty of explanation. This approach generally creates feedback that makes necessary adjustments and value creation very easy for all parties involved.

Well-structured organizational dynamics are characterized by continual efforts and adjustments to get people to collaborate and communicate. A good start is active listening that ensures senders *and* receivers are constantly tuned, using feedback and visual and verbal cues to adjust. Senders listen for relevant information, possible disconnects in detail, or misunderstandings that slow down or stop the communication. Senders then model the appropriate behavior to establish positive norms, creating freedom of expression in interaction partners and ensuring that all parties have clear expectations. Likewise, style diversity is a skill that ensures an openly collaborative, creative culture, offering parties an ongoing self-assessment to examine how well the communication is progressing and to determine what might interfere with effectiveness.

How do adjustments in communication work to accommodate participants? The sender accommodates the receiver or receivers by paying attention to four keys: body language, shared meaning, engagement, and efficiency. The sender accommodates participants by paying attention to body language; both good and bad. If the receiver is smiling or leaning toward the sender, the sender should continue the type and tone of the communication to take advantage of the interaction bond he or she is creating. If the receiver is frowning or turns their body partially or fully away from the sender, the sender should take time to find out why. Once the sender knows why the message is not getting through, he or she can accommodate the receiver by changing the type or tone, or even the time, of the interaction.

Using the principles of EVR to find shared meaning is another way of accommodating the receiver. EVR stands for Expectation, Value, and Return on the investment of time, attention, and energy of communication participants (Brown 2016). EVR relies on three key principles for communication success (Brown 2016). First is the ability to get useful help in a two-way arrangement.

Second is the opportunity for a valued information exchange (Brown 2016). The third benefit to EVR is getting and giving recognition that matters to others (Brown 2016). Paying attention to EVR leads to shared meaning because every member of the communication is fully aware of their role and of the value they will receive from the interaction.

The next way to ensure good communication accommodation is to make sure that the receiver or receivers are fully engaged (Brown 2016). It is not enough to have shared meaning; communicators must take advantage of face-to-face meetings to ensure that everyone is listening or decoding the information. Communication success is the result of getting and giving feedback that enriches and continues the conversation (Brown 2016).

The fourth and final way to accommodate receivers is to conduct efficient face-to-face interactions (Brown 2016). Each meeting should have an agenda that begins with a purpose that leads to achievement of a goal. Effective communicators should determine a good start time and reasonable duration for the meeting and then stay on track with purpose and goal. They must also avoid getting sidetracked.

Unexpectedly, body language, shared meaning, engagement, and efficiency require and promote flexibility to accommodate communication participants (Brown 2016). But there is more to flexible communications; the use of CAT strategies should start with ensuring active listening. The use of effective listening approaches such as questioning, paraphrasing, and summarizing can encourage conversation about ideas (Gallois, Giles et al. 2005).

There are few hidden agendas when the parties to the communication are truly energized. Achieve an open, effective environment by modeling good communication behaviors and by establishing norms for the interactions. If sender and receiver are on the same page, everyone feels free to express their feelings. These actions create clear expectations and allow the communication to flow more freely.

Style diversity allows communication regardless of the social or cultural differences of the parties. Finally, ongoing self-assessment is about revisiting both successful and unsuccessful interactions to enhance strengths and mitigate weaknesses.

## MODIFYING COMMUNICATION BEHAVIOR

Investing in positive communication behaviors ensures that sender and receiver share meaning. Several communication behaviors were suggested in a 2017 study examining how employee engagement enhances supportive communication behaviors and reduces turnover intentions (Kang and Sung). Mentioning or supporting the goal signals acceptance of full participation in the communication, while collecting information provides the necessary details to facilitate full-cycle communication that includes feedback. Sharing information provides opportunities for open evaluation, inspection, or assessment to facilitate discussion. Building networks creates linkages between people in various interactions to increase information availability. Modeling good communication behaviors, as Figure 1 suggests, should make the interaction more valuable.

*Figure 1. Communication Behaviors rely on supporting a goal, collecting information, sharing information, and building networks*
© *Can Stock Photo Inc / michaeldb*

Beyond the behaviors mentioned, effective communicators will bring authenticity and trustworthiness to their interactions. Authenticity is how well a person exudes their true self or characteristics when communicating (Reinecke and Trepte 2014).

There are four dimensions of authenticity: (1) Awareness, which refers to being knowledgeable about one's own inner motives, feelings, goals, strengths, and weaknesses and motivated to learn more about such self-relevant aspects, (2) unbiased processing of self-relevant information, which describes the willingness and ability to assess one's positive and negative self-aspects honestly and objectively without denying or exaggerating externally based evaluative information, (3) behavior, which refers to acting self-determined, deliberately, and in accordance with one's needs and goals, and (4) relational orientation, which describes the motivation to act and communicate sincerely and truthfully in one's close relationships.

The basis of authenticity is that a person's goals, feelings, and motives are the motivators to act in concert with the "true self" (Reinecke and Trepte 2014). Being authentic in communication means having a strategy to make your purpose clear, building character by being clear in what you say and how you say it, fostering relationships to promote trust in the interaction, and setting the example with a consistent voice and exemplary behavior.

Trustworthiness is another construct that is relative to communication accommodation activities. Trustworthiness is best established at the beginning of communication activities because initial impressions come from the cues that can be seen in facial expressions and other nonverbal characteristics, called surface cues. This initial assessment involves subjective impressions that a receiver has the right characteristics such as ability, benevolence, or integrity, to be a worthy communication partner (Holtz 2015). A basic evaluation of the findings of a 2013 study indicates that early impressions of trustworthiness continue to affect communications and may possibly outweigh trust and fairness-related factors that come into play later in the interaction (Holtz 2015).

## UNDERSTANDING BARRIERS TO COMMUNICATION

Senders should work to ensure genuine communication because every relevant metric shows that people are interacting at breakneck speed and frequency through social media. Society is attempting to create relationships and make decisions when 93% of the communication context is stripped away by digital communications that may or may not have feedback. So, people are often left with phrases, abbreviations, snippets, or emoticons which may or may not be accurate representations of the truth.

Social media has the potential to make people less social since digital communication can be a surrogate for the real thing. All parties bear a responsibility to be genuine, accurate, and not allow social media to replace human contact altogether. This makes social media a truly effective communication vehicle.

Everyone knows that electronic communication has surpassed face-to-face methods. Today's splintered business communications and the lack of comfort with traditional interpersonal communication contributes to the rise of digital communication. Some experts attribute this move to the influence of Gen Y and Millennials, two generations that share significant overlap of those born in the 1980s and 90s. Many believe that these generations will comprise more than half of the workforce by 2020 (Brown 2017). These generations tend to favor the instant kind of messaging afforded by social media and digital applications over face-to-face interaction. This reality causes a gap in communication ability and actuality that characterizes communications between Boomers and their younger colleagues.

One barrier that communicators face is the need to create cultural compatibility or find common ground. Senders can foster long-standing, mutually beneficial relationships by achieving shared values in their communication. This enhances shared understanding.

Another barrier, one that exists in face-to-face and online interactions, is resistance to participate based on fear, disbelief, and underestimation of the benefits of communication; lack of a sense of return on investment of time and effort; misunderstanding; and misperception. In face-to-face communication, use of verbal and visual cues allow the sender to get a sense of the resistance barrier and work to determine which of the reasons stated is at work. This activity is much harder, or impossible, in online communication because the receiver must reveal the issue. Certainly, if the receiver does not respond, there is an issue, but the reason for the communication breakdown can be hard to determine.

Other barriers are not new. Senders must deal effectively with the pace of communication to ensure that information exchange is timely and holds the receiver's interest. Both face-to-face and digital communications require attention to physical barriers. In direct interactions, the setting must allow a level of comfort for participants to enter and remain in the interaction. Online interactions require that the physical surroundings of the sender are conducive to getting the message across. All communicators deal with attitudes and language in their own way. Lack of common experience and information overload are other barriers at play in any kind of communication. There are other barriers to communication, but the ones mentioned here are most relevant for our examination.

Communication should be an agile, flexible activity that keeps the sender and receiver in tune to the goals of the interaction. Sensemaking theory posits that communicators should pay attention to the creation of meaning and to the perceived role each member believes they accept. This is another central principle to addressing barriers to communication. The social activity of decoding messages by drawing upon a common language and managing the actions in which we engage is the focus of sensemaking theory (Brown 2017).

The communicating parties need to work through each step in the process, using cues to explain what is happening and to adjust to changes or difficulties in the activity. Communicators also use cues to create stories that match the encoded message and allow action and learning to take place (Brown 2017). Sensemaking helps people attach meaning to their world when faced with ambiguity and complexity (Brown 2017). For instance, social dilemmas and tension are created when organizations participate in corporate social responsibility (CSR). CSR is when companies take measures to be accountable for their effects on social and environmental well-being. CSR activities are felt inside and outside organizations, bringing new experiences to employees based on their role in the community and in the world at large (Aguinis and Glavas 2017). Senders are responsible for accommodating receivers to help with the sensemaking process (Brown 2017).

There are seven sensemaking properties that provide tools to help with the communication process (Mills and Mills 2000). The properties are: identity, retrospective, enactment, social context, ongoing events, salient cues, and plausibility. These were originally described by Karl Weick (1995, Schwandt 2005) and are explained below.

1.   **Identity:** Socially-constructed meanings are assigned to events because of assessing the receiver's social identity in context with that of the sender.
2.   **Retrospective:** Using experience to create meaning in the present situation.
3.   **Enactment:** People must act to create a meaningful environment to fully understand the communication.
4.   **Social Context:** Meaning is not created in a vacuum; the internal decision to act relies on collective action of all parties that can be used to create and test meaning.
5.   **Ongoing Events:** Sensemaking is a cycle of starts, stops, and restarts, attempting to allow people to find shared meaning.
6.   **Salient Cues:** Indicators come from environmental context, language, noticing, search strategies, and organizational vocabularies.
7.   **Plausibility:** Rather than focusing on accuracy, sensemaking is about seeking a kind of constructed reality that is plausible, pragmatic, coherent, reasonable, creative, and inventive (Starbuck and Milliken 1988).

Communication barriers are also addressed through the emotional intelligence of the parties involved, with participants working to recognize, respect, and value honesty, energy, feedback, and intuition in the communication. Additional emotional intelligence features that are relevant to communication are emotional fitness (authenticity, resilience, and renewal of message and idea), emotional depth (assessing character of the parties involved and seeking commitment, drive, initiative, and/ or accountability), and emotional alchemy (using all resources to transform lesser ideas into greater ones through the communication activity) (Mayer, Salovey et al. 2011). These considerations are important to addressing communication barriers, but so is common sense. For instance, senders should make sure their message has value and pay careful attention to finding the right key words, language, and tone to get their message across. They should transmit the message using the most appropriate communication vehicle for the communication participant, and help the receiver accept and decode the message. Senders should stay attached to the communication to ensure that the receiver can provide feedback, which signals that two-way communication has begun and can continue.

The key consideration in terms of barriers to communication is that the sender must recognize them and address them when and if they interfere with the interaction. Barriers often drive receivers away from the communication, causing them to either not fully understand the message or not stay long enough to provide the valuable feedback that keeps communication alive as a cyclical process. Effective communications feature shared understanding between the participants, which cannot be taken for granted. Senders must pay attention to any signs or signals to determine whether the message reaches its target. The communication goal is simple: encode, send, decode, and provide feedback. Senders must accept responsibility for this whole process, and for continued communications. Face-to-face interactions give the sender a chance to directly face the receiver and adjust in real time. Online communicators must look much deeper, but the signs and signals are still there, albeit harder to identify.

In face-to-face communications, the sender has many tools with which to change the communication in progress by using verbal and visual cues. That same capability doesn't fully exist in online communication. What is more telling about online communications is that they happen so fast that the sender often has no time to even consider adjusting, before the conversation has moved on to the next communication. Such speed in the communication process often presents a challenging barrier to successful communication.

## TRUST AND COMMITMENT

All leaders and all organizations need trust; they need to be continuously engaged in building and maintaining trust. Interpersonal communication is important because the emphasis should always be on the individual as a performing and valuable part of the group. Effective communicators never let any person disappear when dealing with the group. They make comments all-inclusive at every opportunity. This builds trust, fosters belonging, and reduces the noise in the channel. Noise refers to distractions in the communication. The significance of noise in this context is in its interference with message delivery: as the frequency of attempted message deliver increases, so to increases the potential for a message to be altered by a sender from its original meeting. An all-inclusive delivery promotes a one-goal, one-voice approach to communicating.

The way to ensure the message is delivered efficiently is to create a communication zone that provides the best environment for the interaction. A communication zone is the place where social bonding takes place to create close ties and exchange feedback. Participants in the communication zone agree to a "contract" of paying attention and responding to messages (Nardi and Whittaker 2002). The "zone" is typically a physical environment that allows participants to understand each other's state of work in an attempt to find common reference points and common orientations (Leinonen, Järvelä et al. 2005). The communication zone can be created virtually, but face-to-face meetings tend to be much more powerful and interactive.

Exchanging feedback and agreeing to the "contractual" sharing of information can be considered a two-pronged approach to communication zones. The value of the face-to-face interaction cannot be ignored, according to two researchers who argue that there is a rich body of research listing this as the most information-rich medium (Nardi and Whittaker 2002). Relationships grow and trust develops when the parties exchange expressions of commitment to a communication. This allows teams to create an environment where members interact freely regardless of the message and where feedback is the norm and not the exception.

Closely related to the communication zone approach is social bonding, which is engaging sender and receiver in social interaction and using informal conversation. Effective social bonding is about awareness and having a sense of the other person's "presence," which includes their physical appearance, body language, and facial expressions (Brown 2017). Skilled communicators will also have a sense of the other person's makeup, jewelry, hair style, and clothing, because they all say something about the person. Additional pluses come from off-the-cuff conversation such as family questions, gossip, jokes, or just idle chat. Social bonding is an invaluable way to empower all communication participants.

Personal values and expectations can cause problems in a communication. This is because people can get wrapped up in their own point of view. Common ground is the key to overcoming this barrier. If each party can work to understand the other's point of view, they can work toward adjustments that make message delivery and receipt easier. Shared understanding can also help to ensure that no person's values are negatively affected by the interaction.

Personality differences can be overcome by taking special care not to create or escalate an emotionally-charged topic. People see things differently based on their personality and other factors, so it is sometimes best to avoid topics that create an uncomfortable atmosphere. If an emotionally-charged topic must be discussed, ensure that you have an agreement on the shared expectations by all parties and that the session can be stopped or rescheduled should problems occur.

Another barrier has to do with hierarchy between communicators and can be overcome by increasing and improving daily communication between upper and lower levels of an organization. Such organizational communications must also ensure that each person's skills and knowledge are valued, and that each voice is heard. In one-on-one situations that require a participative decision, try to meet somewhere other than the higher-ranking person's office. A neutral place, maybe the break room or a coffee shop, can be a great choice.

When dealing with disruptive behavior, effective communicators are deliberate in their approach and professional in their actions. They let the other person know up front that the behavior will not be tolerated. They do not continue the communication until the other person commits to the change in behavior and they stop the communication if the person reverts to the disruptive behavior. It is important to be consistent with these actions whenever dealing with disruptive behavior.

A difference in language and jargon is an especially challenging barrier to communication. The best way to address this is to prepare in advance. Effective communicators find out about their subject or subjects to determine whether this will be a problem. If the problem is a difference in language, they schedule an interpreter. If the problem is one of semantics or dialect based on the cultural leanings of participants, it might help to agree on some terms of reference that will come up in the conversation. The way to address jargon is to make a conscious attempt to avoid it. When it creeps in, participants in the conversation must define what is really being discussed.

Fears of diluted professional identity are really about people worrying that something that is said or done in the communication will affect their standing or their career. The key here is open and honest communication that allows each participant equal standing. A culture of professional courtesy is also helpful in putting people at ease.

When people are treated differently in terms of accountability and rewards, it hinders the communication process (Brown 2017). Whether it's a one-on-one or multiple relationship interaction, every person must have the same accountability for the discussion and the outcome. At the same time, every person must have an equal opportunity to be rewarded and the reward process must be specific and transparent.

The final barrier that is commonly encountered is emphasis on rapid decision making. There is often no time to address other barriers when the decision must be made rapidly. The best approach is to let everyone know up front that there will be limited discussion before the final decision. If possible, one should inform the people or the group about why the decision must be made so rapidly. The key to overcoming this communication barrier is to have a professional, collaborative, trusting culture that will help everyone through what could be a difficult action. Setting up a person or a team in a collaborative agreement and then deciding without collaborating is risky, but this is sometimes a necessary action for a leader or an organization.

Barriers to communication are always a part of interactions in some way. The best way to ensure that they are being addressed is to have an organizational climate that is conducive to managing all issues. For instance, the organization should have a unifying philosophy of open and honest communication. Members should be committed to the common goal of collaboration and should be willing to share responsibilities. The organization must have an established process for negotiation of goals and roles as the work evolves. The organization should also have a process for resolving conflicts between team members. In addition, all team members should be aware of the organization's complaint or grievance process. All these actions prepare the team for the dynamics of organizational change.

All good relationships either are built on trust or grow and strengthen because of it. Trust is built when people or groups who are vulnerable to each other participate in open communication. If they are willing to admit mistakes, acknowledge weaknesses, applaud strengths, and lean on each other for help, they can build trust. Leaders and managers increase their own trustworthiness when they trust their team. This is certainly not easy to achieve since trust is a contract that requires taking risks, such as putting one's faith or a pending decision in the hands of someone a person may not have confidence in.

There are several ways to build trust. Senders should start by being patient as receivers adjust to the messages and the communication process. It is also important to collaborate and make the course of action or decisions seem more like suggestions than direct orders. When possible, effective communicators keep communications secure by managing risk. They also raise comfort levels by helping people understand and adjust to the activity.

Trust can also be built through acknowledging and confronting risk by explaining what is at stake, analyzing available options, and providing a safety net. Shared values, shared interests, and shared responsibility create trust because everyone's point of view is considered and is accommodated when possible (Denhardt and Denhardt 2007). It is important to find common ground for values, beliefs, and even cultural background, emphasizing "we" more than "I." Effective communicators care about others by making sure their actions are good for everyone involved. They might have to sacrifice their own wants and desires at times to allow other interests to prevail for the good of the communication.

## CONCLUSION

Effective communicators use their skills and competence to manage communication; they may have to relinquish control to address issues that threaten progress. It is a helpful policy to "under promise and over deliver" to ensure communicating from a position of integrity and predictability. Finally, over-communication is helpful because communication should be timely and candid so that the benefits of thinking outside the box can be realized.

Lynne Zucker, an American professor and researcher, identified three central modes of trust production: institutional-based, characteristic-based, and process-based trust (1986). Institutional-based trust is influenced by formal societal structures that depend on individual or organization-specific attributes. Characteristic-based trust is about a person's ethnicity, culture, and background. Process-based, or personal, trust is created through face-to-face contact and is important because relationships begin with this kind of trust.

At the interpersonal level, people must deal with uncertainty based on relationships (work and personal), group issues, and work requirements. Collecting information as direct requests or observations from a variety of internal and external sources is valuable in managing uncertainty (Kramer 2015). Former interactions can be used to assess the degree of uncertainty that is associated with current communications. This is a way to ensure successful message delivery.

Good communicators build trust and address uncertainty through commitment, giving time and attention to the interaction, constantly checking to ensure success with the message, telling the truth, seeking shared value, and staying engaged to seek feedback. These challenging tasks of trust and uncertainty can pay great rewards because they can help people be responsive. This happens because they feel that they are communicating with someone who is in tune with them. The key is to understand and address a person's needs and be accessible and accountable. Taking these meaningful steps will ensure that people respond and want to be a part of your team.

# REFERENCES

Aguinis, H., & Glavas, A. (2017). On Corporate Social Responsibility, Sensemaking, and the Search for Meaningfulness Through Work. *Journal of Management*.

Ayoko, O. B., Härtel, C. E., & Callan, V. J. (2002). Resolving the puzzle of productive and destructive conflict in culturally heterogeneous workgroups: A communication accommodation theory approach. *International Journal of Conflict Management, 13*(2), 165–195. doi:10.1108/eb022873

Brown, M. A. Sr. (2017). *Solutions for High-Touch Communications in a High-Tech World*. Hershey, PA: IGI Global. doi:10.4018/978-1-5225-1897-6

Denhardt, J. V., & Denhardt, R. B. (2007). *The new public service: Serving, not steering*. ME Sharpe.

Gallois, C., & Giles, H. (2015). *Communication Accommodation Theory. In The International Encyclopedia of Language and Social Interaction*. John Wiley & Sons, Inc.

Giles, H. (2008). *Communication accommodation theory*. Sage Publications, Inc. doi:10.1002/9781405186407.wbiecc067

Holtz, B. C. (2015). From First Impression to Fairness Perception: Investigating the Impact of Initial Trustworthiness Beliefs. *Personnel Psychology, 68*(3), 499–546. doi:10.1111/peps.12092

Jones, L., Woodhouse, D., & Rowe, J. (2007). Effective nurse parent communication: A study of parents' perceptions in the NICU environment. *Patient Education and Counseling, 69*(1), 206–212. doi:10.1016/j.pec.2007.08.014 PMID:17936549

Kang, M., & Sung, M. (2017). How symmetrical employee communication leads to employee engagement and positive employee communication behaviors: The mediation of employee-organization relationships. *Journal of Communication Management, 21*(1), 82–102. doi:10.1108/JCOM-04-2016-0026

Kramer, M. W. (2015). *Uncertainty and Communication in Organizations. In The International Encyclopedia of Interpersonal Communication*. John Wiley & Sons, Inc.

Leinonen, P., Järvelä, S., & Häkkinen, P. (2005). Conceptualizing the Awareness of Collaboration: A Qualitative Study of a Global Virtual Team. *Comput Supported Coop Work Computer Supported Cooperative Work, 14*(4), 301–322. doi:10.100710606-005-9002-z

Mayer, J. D., Salovey, P., Caruso, D. R., & Cherkasskiy, L. (2011). Emotional intelligence. The Cambridge handbook of intelligence, 528-549. doi:10.1017/CBO9780511977244.027

Mills, J. H., & Mills, A. J. (2000). *Sensemaking and the Gendering of Organizational Culture*. Montreal, Canada: ASAC-IFSAM Conference.

Nardi & Whittaker. (2002). *The place of face-to-face communication in distributed work*. Distributed work: 83-110.

Reinecke, L., & Trepte, S. (2014). Authenticity and well-being on social network sites: A two-wave longitudinal study on the effects of online authenticity and the positivity bias in SNS communication. *Computers in Human Behavior, 30*, 95–102. doi:10.1016/j.chb.2013.07.030

Schwandt, D. R. (2005). When Managers Become Philosophers: Integrating Learning with Sensemaking. *Academy of Management Learning & Education, 4*(2), 176–192. doi:10.5465/AMLE.2005.17268565

Starbuck & Milliken. (1988). *Executives' perceptual filters: What they notice and how they make sense*. Academic Press.

Stets, J. E. (1991). Psychological aggression in dating relationships: The role of interpersonal control. *Journal of Family Violence, 6*(1), 97–114. doi:10.1007/BF00978528

Weick, K. E. (1995). *Sensemaking in organizations*. Thousand Oaks, CA: Sage.

Zucker, L. G. (1986). *Production of trust: Institutional sources of economic structure. In Research in organisational behaviour* (p. 8). Greenwich, CT: JAI.

Chapter 9
# New Communication Technology Integration:
## Recommendations for Public Sector Change

**Leigh Nanney Hersey**
*University of Louisiana at Monroe, USA*

**Gayla Schaefer**
*Schaefer Communications, USA*

## ABSTRACT

*Communication is key in the public sector as governments aim to interact with and respond to their residents. Citizens often participated in government through face-to-face communication like town meetings. Today, digital communication has become increasingly important to improving government-citizen relations. The authors explore how governments are using Web 2.0 and mobile government (m-government) to spread information quickly. As governments implement these new communication tools, they must also consider ethical implications associated with technology. The research identifies the elements that lead to successful integration and the biggest barriers that government employees are facing during the transition.*

DOI: 10.4018/978-1-5225-4168-4.ch009

## INTRODUCTION

Communication innovations have historically played an important role in transforming cultures and governments. As the invention of the printing press led toward the Protestant Reformation, current information and communications technology (ICT) innovations are transforming how people interact with the public and nonprofit sectors (Shirky, 2008; Gore, 2007). Coming quickly upon the heels of the E-government (EG) service transformation of the 1990s, the more recent Web 2.0 and mobile government (m-government) innovations are once again challenging standard practices, structures, and policies (GAO, 2011; Shareef, Archer & Duda, 2012). New opportunities must be carefully balanced with ethical responsibilities to protect confidential information collected and stored online (GAO, 2011). The questions to be addressed here are as follows: What are the elements that lead toward successful new technology integration? How do organizational policies, management, and human resource structures impact the change?

Transformational ICTs, such as those used in e-government and Web 2.0, have increased access to information, resulting in greater public expectations for transparency and engaged participation, while also providing increased abilities for public outreach, advocacy, education, collaboration, service provision, and volunteer and financial support (Shirky, 2008; Pynes, 2009). Additionally, this technology can improve skill levels, lead to new business models, expand organizational capabilities, as well as create a culture that supports change and innovation (Ceric, 2015). The speed of innovation and the associated costs of keeping up with it have left many organizations struggling through an organizational digital divide caused by outdated or underutilized technology, restrictive cultures, and vague policies, especially at the local and state levels (Greene, 2011). However, as noted by the U.S. Chief Information Officer, the successful integration of the new technology tools will provide a large return on investment with even greater innovations in service provision and engagement (VanRoekel, 2011). Integrating such a large change calls for investments in system upgrades and focus on the development of new organizational policies and strategic human resources management cultures that embrace constant training and feedback (Bolman & Deal, 2008; VanRoekel, 2011). Successful technology implementation and communications transformation can only be realized with consistent leadership.

## LITERATURE REVIEW

There are many reasons public administrators should understand the important differences between EG, 2.0 technology capabilities, and public opinion as they navigate organizational ICT changes and integration into organizational culture.

### Changes and Challenges

The EG movement began in the 1990s as a function of expanded IT departments into service provision (Grönlund & Horan, 2004). In 2009, President Barack Obama called for government agencies to embrace new social media technologies for transparency, public participation, and inter-agency collaboration (Presidential Documents, 2009). Online government thus shifted towards a more participatory communications function, ushering in the Governance 2.0 and M-government era. The Pew Internet & American Life Project Government Online Survey (Smith, 2010) subsequently revealed that 61% of all American adults had sought information or completed transactions on government websites that year even though online services were still not universally accessible. Populations of the elderly, impoverished, less educated, non-English speakers, and residents of rural areas lacking technology infrastructure remain more likely to be negatively impacted by this "digital divide" of the population (Emerson, Menkus & Van Ness, 2011; Kruger & Gilroy, 2011).

The EG transformation was only the beginning of the communications shift. Government interactions have since moved beyond static websites to include a range of new media technologies for citizen engagement such as social networking, blogs, and mobile device access (Smith, 2010). The public now expects organizations to maintain communications that require comment moderation, timely feedback, and information curation while maintaining system security, interoperability, and sensitive information protection (Howard, 2011).

While it is commonly accepted that younger, highly educated, and more affluent people are most likely to engage with government websites, the Pew Internet & American Life Project Government Online survey conducted in 2009 found minority groups prefer new media. African Americans and Latinos use blogs, social networking sites, and online video to monitor and interact with government agencies at the same rate as other demographic groups. These minorities are also more likely to say it is "very important" that agencies use social mediums (Smith, 2010). Accordingly, in a survey of 53 national advocacy groups, Obar, Zube, and Lampe (2011) found that leaders believe the new mediums play an essential and cost effective advocacy role by strengthening communication speed, outreach, and feedback. Gore (2007) further notes that unlimited online participation and access to information has the potential to make government agencies more responsive and citizens more educated and engaged.

## Systems and Tools

Crowdsourcing capabilities offer many opportunities. Crowdsourcing is the strategy of using an online platform to call for input from a large group of people or communities to contribute to knowledge gathering or finding solutions to complex problems (Briggs, 2009; Mergel, 2011). High speed interconnection is reinvigorating engaged citizen participation in a virtual town hall where problems and solutions can be quickly resolved through group participation (Gore, 2007; Mergel, 2011). Aaker and Smith (2010) recommend storytelling across the variety of web platforms to emotionally engage stakeholders with such calls to action. Web 2.0 tools also offer a low cost solution to traditional public/nonprofit sector disadvantages by lowering communications barriers to reach previously underserved or out of reach populations (Pallotta, 2008; Leighninger, 2011).

Since public safety managers can greatly improve service provision with better resource deployment through new ICT, Sherman (2011) calls for organizations to implement new communications technology before the onset of a crisis. Eighty percent of the general public surveyed by the American Red Cross in 2011 now expects national emergency response organizations to regularly use and monitor social media for crisis communications (Walker, 2011). For example, FEMA and the New York City Mayor's office made reactionary use of new ICT when the city website crashed under the volume of residents seeking emergency information during a natural disaster. Offering a glimpse into the type of changes occurring, a new form of public/private partnership quickly evolved out of necessity to mirror site data on a privately managed cloud platform while the city worked to restore its official website (Walker, 2011).

The ability of the public sector to manage this response is critical. User-generated content is an important aspect of social media strategy. O'Hearn and Kahle (2013) define user-generated content as "original contributions that are created by users, are expressed in a number of different media... and are widely shared with other users and/or with firms" (p. 23). User-generated content during a crisis can provide increased awareness of the situation during a crisis, often from an eyewitness perspective. However, as noted by Hager (2012) rumors are easily spread on social media and have the potential to spread misinformation, creating additional challenges for emergency management personnel. For example, Gupta, et al (2013) collected nearly 1.8 million tweets between October 20 and November 1, 2012, related to Hurricane Sandy in the northeast United Sates. Of these, more than 10,000 of the tweets contained fake images from the storm's damage. These fake images spread quickly, with 86% of the 10,000 tweets being retweets of the images.

## Human Resources, Culture and Structure

An important question for public administrators is whether social media is a communications tool to be managed by communications/public affairs offices or whether it remains part of the infrastructure managed by IT departments. Orlikowski and Scott (2008) report little direction is to be found on how to formalize technological responsibility structures in the organization studies literature despite the undeniable impact of technology. The authors divide the literature into two distinct groups: those which view technology as the domain of discrete entities and those that frame it under more mutually dependent teams. Orlikowski and Scott (2008) recommend research into reframing conventional organization structures in favor of social and technical connections across departmental boundaries. Lam (2005) found 17 barriers related e-government integration under the broad categories of strategy that prevented integrating, insufficient technology, policy concerns, and organizational capacity.

Organization leadership's understanding of how online engagement brings value and their support for modifications of organizational structure and professional development to embrace new ICT leads to more successful integration (Leighninger, 2011). In corporations, governance strategy often corresponds to the communication model embraced by leadership. Those managers who emphasized a one-way dialogic communication model often believed in a centralized communication structure that closely controls the message and messengers. On the other hand, those more supportive of a two-way dialogic model allow more freedom on who posts for the corporation and the messages they share (van den Berg and Verhoeven, 2017). Web 1.0 EG projects receive more funding currently than social media projects, but rarely attract the same level of public participation as ICT crowdsourcing projects (Mergel, 2011; Leighninger, 2011). Budgetary support shifts are needed to discourage the frequent practice of uploading complex data to official websites without mechanisms for public participation or useful interaction (Leighninger, 2011).

## The Role of Policy, Transparency, and Privacy Concerns

Technological advances have become a wildcard for the development of the sector (Salamon, 2003). Although organization leaders may have been quick to see the benefits of social networking, many still lack the human resource staffing and knowledge needed (Pope, Isely, & Asamoa-TuTu, 2009). Many public managers mistake e-government transaction portals and reports posted online for transparency as sufficient public engagement. Unintended consequences may result, however, from placing complex bureaucratic reports not written to web standards on websites without thought to how citizens may interpret, share, or respond to them (Leighninger, 2011).

The critical questions for managers, then, are as follows: How can they integrate existing e-government services and data transparency on static websites securely with interactive social media functions? How can they promote two-way participation and conversation in productive ways?

As the public has become more accustomed to conducting government transactions online, filing for permits and renewing licenses for example, the database of private sensitive information flowing through government computer systems has greatly increased (Emerson, Menkus, & Van Ness, 2011).

New media ICT has thus created a great challenge for ethically competent managers and organizations to maintain sensitivity, due diligence and respect for the treasured information on government servers (Menzel, 2010). Policies and procedures should be crafted to protect privacy without discouraging engagement by employees or end-users (Sherman, 2011).

Ojoa, Esteveza, and Janowskia (2010) provide recommendations for government semantic interoperability problems associated with integration of 2.0 ICT. Only the governments of the United States and the United Kingdom have explicit strategies and initiatives for harnessing the benefits of social media to transform service delivery and open government (Ojoa, Esteveza, & Janowskia, 2010). However, online writing abilities and information mapping standards vary dramatically by organization. Plain language and web writing guidelines for federal government websites offer guides for the rest of the public/nonprofit sectors who must also adapt to the new mediums.

Adding to the ICT integration confusion is the plethora of different types of website content management systems (CMS) used by agencies and organizations. Variations in CMS capabilities because of age, type, and complexity can limit institutional collaboration (HowTo.Gov, 2011). Although agencies are using social media more frequently, examinations of 24 major agencies by the GAO indicated disjointed progress in setting social media policies to deal with new challenges to record keeping, privacy protections, and federal computer system security (GAO, 2011). Only half of the agencies had policies for record keeping and updated privacy policies. Only eight had completed the recommended risk assessment and just seven had documented security risks and outlined policies to address them (GAO, 2011).

## Elements of Successful Integration Models

Organizations can no longer be one-way communicators and viewed as part of the democratic community (Shirky, 2008; Leighninger, 2011). New media ICT has changed public opinion toward transparency and engagement by governments as social media sites draw citizens whose comments are easily visible and shared (Bertot, Jaeger, & Grimes, 2010; Right Now Government, 2010). Access to Internet information and the ability to interact in the online public sphere are now considered by many, including the United Nations, as a basic human right (Kurczy, 2010; Lester, 2010; La Rue, 2011). Public and nonprofit managers, while not in complete agreement regarding the value or objectives inherent in 2.0 technologies, are still advised to craft practical policies guiding their use.

Public/private and interagency collaboration is essential in the 2.0 era. Dawes, Cresswell and Pardopublic (2009) promote knowledge networking as a new solution for external and interagency management problems that often plague the sector. Organizational collaborative structures, policies, and open dialogue about assumptions and expectations, rather than fixed IT solutions, encourage adaptation (Dawes, Cresswell & Pardopublic, 2009). Change leadership that embraces open innovation mechanisms to promote crowdsourcing of ideas and solutions can lead to increased transparency, accountability, and social capital (Mergel, 2011). To further transform public sector silos and reduce rigid hierarchies, Linden (2010) posits that integration of new media technology to institutionalize collaboration by crossing boundaries between employees, agencies, stakeholders, and customers. Such collaborations will lead to greater creativity, lateral communications, increased speed, flexibility, and creation of loosely connected communities of interest (Linden, 2010).

Since many laws and organizational policies were written before the advent of Web 2.0 online interactions, a comprehensive evaluation of the legal framework for open meetings, social media, advisory committees, and other aspects of participation is needed (Leighninger, 2011). Bertot, Jaeger, and Hansen (2011) examine how the rapid pace of technology adoption has outpaced bureaucratic policymaking and note that pre-existing federal regulatory frameworks still provide useful guiding principles. Since many public managers may be hesitant to embrace new communication technology while unclear of the legalities involved, policy development and support from upper management is warranted. Although disagreements exist about the value of open participation in the online social conversation, comparative analysis of options by teams of experts representing diverse fields should provide a method for continuous incremental changes in the absence of agreed upon theory (Lindblom, 1959).

Klischewski and Abubakr (2010) note that dedicated integration goals and implementation rules should guide such efforts. Using Egypt as a case study, the authors conclude that technology-first approaches can lead to wasted time and resources because of delays in collaborative organizational learning. They recommend careful selection of technology upfront to streamline organizational discourse and development of consistent strategies and policies (Klischewski & Abubakr, 2010).

Fernandez and Rainey (2006) provide public managers with strategies to successfully lead through changes such as adopting a new technology and an interactive culture. The factors are as follows: ensure and communicate the need, provide a plan for implementing change, build internal support and overcome resistance by encouraging stakeholder participation, ensure top management support and commitment, build external support from key political overseers and external stakeholders, provide sufficient resources for the process, institutionalize changes, and pursue comprehensive change across sub-systems. Important structural, human resources, and political frameworks such as organization capacity, stakeholder support, public approval, and bureaucratic resistance to change must be considered along with focus on clear internal communication and stakeholder support (Fernandez & Rainey, 2006; Menzel, 2010).

Tan, Stockdale, and Vasa (2011) provide a useful program model for higher education online engagement programs based on the experiences of two Australian university programs. Their research demonstrates the need for managed strategic online communication plans to avoid disjointed efforts and systematic evaluation of success based on community member benefit.

Yanosky and McCredie (2008) provide another useful university-based model for public sector IT management. Among the elements they ascribe to successful programs are: active governance design, ability of users to describe the governance properly, frequency of participation to provide input by stakeholders, and incorporation of a formal evaluation measurement program (Yanosky & McCredie, 2008). Ojoa, Esteveza, and Janowskia (2010) provide more specific recommendations and architecture for governments seeking to merge function with expectation. They propose that the change process guide not only policy, governance, and organizational and technical capabilities, but also communication context, protocols, message, contents, and domains associated with system conflicts. Ojoa, Esteveza, and Janowskia (2010) further note that successful implementation of the technological sea-change depends on factors within each organization. In a case study based on a nonprofit organization's strategic use of social media, Schaefer and Hersey (2017) found that one of key factors to successful integration of social media sites was the shift in organizational culture. Once the organization began encouraging experimentation and data-based decision-making, the pieces began to come together to create a planned use of social media and to restructure human and financial resources in support of this tactic. Public leaders are advised to take time to consider new options and perspectives to meet constituent needs and accomplish organization goals (Lester, 2010). The long range benefits of adoption of new technology often exceeds initial expectations, therefore organizations should consider reframing cultures to support a flexible innovation process, constant communication, experimentation, and training (Atkinson & McCay, 2007; Bolman & Deal, 2008).

## METHODOLOGY

Since public sector research into the integration impact of Web 2.0 ICT through organizational institutionalization is still in its early stages, the existing literature is limited. Previous research has focused primarily on quantifying reach and qualifying end-user impact with a limited scope of analysis on the role of organizational change and structure. Consequently, the methodology here begins with analysis of structures, capabilities, and related policies to determine impact to answer the research question of how public and nonprofit organizations are integrating social media into their infrastructure.

Drawing upon the burgeoning literature for secondary data analysis, a cross-sectional research survey design was used to create a snapshot of the current state of public sector institutionalization of new ICT in order to identify relationships and trends. The resulting findings only depict what exists at one point in time, as technology will undoubtedly continue to evolve. The survey research design was crafted to gather information on organizational knowledge, attitudes, and behavior from a large, geographically dispersed population in order to identify hypotheses, stimulate exploratory research, and create practical recommendations for managers in the field.

Data collection and research included survey data collection and analysis to uncover organizational policies, frameworks, and technological challenges impacting new ICT adoption in the public sector. A 38-question research survey distributed online was used to gather data on public sector ICT policies and managing structures, social media integration with existing content management systems, and organization cultural experiences.

The anonymous survey was distributed online through social networks, online professional groups, and via email to target populations of government, nonprofit, and university professionals involved with website administration and public communications. The nature of distribution makes it impossible to accurately measure the targeted sample size. The survey sample included members of online government and nonprofit social media discussion groups on GovLoop, Twitter, and LinkedIn, as well as followers of various relevant Twitter hashtags. The survey, hosted on Qualtrics.com, was accessible during late fall of 2011. None of the answers were required for advancement through the survey, resulting in a 57% completion rate. Analysis concentrated on organizational staff structures, technology, and policies.

## Findings and Results

A total of 46 people responded to the survey, representing the following types of public sector organizations: federal, state, or local government (44%); national, state, or local/community nonprofits (24%); universities (11%); and other (24%). The respondents were experienced in their field, with 54% of all respondents having more than 15 years' professional experience, and only 20% having five years of experience or less. Respondents primarily represented Communications (22%), Senior Management (20%), and Other (28%) job categories. About half of the respondents (52%) reported having IT staff onsite. The highest percentage of respondents (41%) reported living in a community of 500,000 to 999,999 residents. Respondents were most likely to represent organizations that are very large (more than 500 employees) or very small (less than 10), with 32% of the respondents in each of these categories.

Analysis of descriptive statistics and cross-tabulations identified connections related to: the age of content management systems and the level of social media engagement, disjointed policy implementation for ICT usage, and institutionalization by sector, size, and responsible department. Results indicate a clear positive impression from participants that social media has enhanced their organization's ability to increase general public engagement (67%). Thirty-eight percent of respondents credited Web 2.0 integration as having increasing public opinion, transparency, and involvement from key stakeholders, while 25% reported little discernible impact. As the breadth and depth of social media engagement was not explored with regard to staff skill, comparison of platforms, or strategies for allowing discourse, no trends regarding strategic implementation impact can be identified.

As to the impact on technology integration by organizational policies, human resources, and structure, the findings varied by professional level and organizational levels of social media use as reported by respondents. Of the 15% of respondents who indicated that their organizations were not utilizing social media at all, 43% identified firewalls and lack of staff time as primary causes. It is also worth noting that 29% of these respondents noted a lack of management support as a primary deterrent as well.

Regarding technology in place, results indicate several levels of new ICT adoption. Findings mirrored the diversity of the Federal Web Managers Council's federal agency content management systems list of more than 25 different systems (HowTo.Gov, 2012) with survey respondents listing 16 different CMS platforms. The broad range of technologies being used in the sector is clearly identifiable even within this small sample and supports the call for more research into inter-agency system interoperability and security concerns. More than 75% of all respondents indicated staff training in new ICT was conducted less than 2 times per year, while 77% of government respondents reported training at least 1-2 times per year. Seventy-eight percent of nonprofits reported CMS platforms did not integrate social media. Interestingly, 100% of nonprofits reported IT departments on site, yet 57% reported no new ICT training in the past three years and none of the respondents reported responsibility for social media was the domain of communications staff (57% indicated development and 29% said administration had primary responsibility). Thirty-eight percent of government respondents had content management systems in place for more than three years (18% for more than 6 years and 12% for more than 10 years) with 65% reporting that web CMS did not integrate social media. All respondents reported having at least one policy in place for social media, with some organizations reporting have all nine listed on the survey. The most common policies involved who was responsible for writing online content (75%), who could post materials to the website and social media accounts (61%), and what materials could be posted (50%).

More respondents indicated that the addition of staff or calls for greater online interaction by constituent stakeholders would impact ICT integration rather than system updates or policy change. Despite holding true across groups, this finding may be skewed since a greater proportion of respondents had 11 years or more of professional experience. This finding may indicate a lack of clear leadership support at the executive level to proactively institutionalize change.

Although the number of respondents indicating updated CMS as a key strategy toward integrating new technologies was fewer than expected, subsequent questions may provide further insight. Of the 25 respondents who answered both questions about online communication frequency and likelihood of Web 2.0 integration with updated CMS autopost capabilities, 64% indicated CMS with automatic social media integration would definitely or probably enhance their efforts at such communications. Follow up social media communication management from autoposted website content was not specifically addressed.

## CONCLUSION

Proper integration of emerging communications technologies for public engagement should lead to increased transparency, increased public trust, better policymaking, and greatly enhanced service provision. Comparison of survey results with the existing literature demonstrates that organizational policies and human resources structures impacts ICT integration for participatory citizen engagement in several ways. First and most importantly, consistent leadership from the top down is recommended. Additional organizational culture elements that can increase ICT integration include stakeholder buy-in and management support for funding, experimentation, training, innovation, and technology system upgrades.

Rapid technological changes have drastically altered the field of public administration during the past few decades. Emphasis is quickly evolving from the development of new EG services and information transparency toward developing transformational government practices interacting with participatory citizens (Oasis eGov, 2010). Public managers will have to lead their organizations through the change with great attention to crafting policies that support structural changes, workforce development, technological interoperability, and changing public and employee perceptions and norms.

Survey primary data analysis and secondary analysis contained in the literature review have identified relationships which inform future research hypotheses exploring the impact on technology integration resulting from division of duty and hierarchy structures within organizational departments tasked with IT and communications related tasks, system interoperability and online security issues related to the various CMS programs in use, policies for mandating and guiding online interactions, and organizational needs assessments focused on full and efficient integration of existing technological capabilities versus the addition of more or better trained staff. One question worthy of further research and deliberative practical consideration moving forward is whether specialized additional staff is required in addition to updated systems, better trained existing staff, and policy creation. Results of the research survey, supported by the GAO report (2011) clearly indicate, however, a lack of clear organizational policies to guide managers and employees as to online communication legalities, transparent web writing standards and information presentation options, and information security.

The ICT transformation defines this snapshot in time. Analysis has provided future research suggestions and strategic management recommendations that can be applied through the continuing evolution. Practicing public administrators would benefit from further research into how best to inventory technology capabilities and requirements in order to assess human resources needs. Planned organizational change to incorporate focus on online service provision as well as participation from constituents will require a sea-change in the way public managers view communication, transparency, the web, client service, and accountability. As such, it is important that public serving organization leaders develop the support culture, human resource structure, and policies to adapt to the changing environment. Such a complex socio-technical issue should be examined holistically, taking policy, organization, and management into account.

# REFERENCES

Aaker, J., & Smith, A. (2010). *The dragonfly effect: Quick, effective, and powerful ways to use social media to drive social change.* San Francisco, CA: Jossey-Bass.

Atkinson, R. D., & McKay, A. S. (2007). *Digital prosperity: Understanding the economic benefits of the information technology revolution.* The Information Technology and Innovation Foundation. Retrieved from http://www.itif.org/files/digital_prosperity.pdf

Bertot, J., Jaeger, P., & Grimes, J. (2010). Using ICTs to create a culture of transparency: Egovernment and social media as openness and anti-corruption tools for societies. *Government Information Quarterly, 27*(3), 264–271. doi:10.1016/j.giq.2010.03.001

Bertot, J., Jaeger, P., & Hansen, D. (2011). The impact of polices on government social media usage: Issues, challenges, and recommendations. *Government Information Quarterly.* doi:10.1016/j.giq.2011.04.004

Bolman, L. G., & Deal, T. E. (2008). *Reframing Organizations: Artistry, Choice, and Leadership* (4th ed.). San Francisco, CA: Jossey-Bass.

Boyd, D., & Ellison, N. (2007). Social network sites: Definition, history, and scholarship. *Journal of Computer-Mediated Communication, 13*(1), 210–230. doi:10.1111/j.1083-6101.2007.00393.x

Briggs, M. (2009). *Journalism next: A practical guide to digital reporting and publishing.* Washington, DC: CQ Press.

Ceric, A. (2015). Bringing together evaluation and management of ICT value: A systems theory approach. *The Electronic Journal of Information Systems Evaluation, 18*(1), 19–35.

Dawes, S., Cresswell, A., & Pardo, T. (2009). From "need to know" to "need to share": Tangled problems, information boundaries, and the building of public sector knowledge networks. *Public Administration Review, 69*(3), 63–84. doi:10.1111/j.1540-6210.2009.01987_2.x

Documents, P. (2009). Transparency and open government: Memorandum for the heads of executive departments and agencies. *Federal Register, 74*(15), 4685–4686. Retrieved from http://edocket.access.gpo.gov/2009/pdf/E9-1777.pdf

Emerson, S., Menkus, R., & Van Ness, K. (2011). *The Public Administrator's Companion: A Practical Guide.* Washington, DC: CQ Press.

Fernandez, S., & Rainey, H. (2006). Managing successful organizational change in the public sector. *Public Administration Review*, *66*(2), 168–176. doi:10.1111/j.1540-6210.2006.00570.x

Franklin, M. I. (2011). Decolonising the future: Not to go where cyborgs have gone before? In *Interoperabel Nederland* (pp. 23–41). Den Haag, the Netherlands: Dutch Ministry of Economic Affairs. Retrieved from http://www.forumstandaardisatie.nl/fileadmin/os/publicaties/01.1_Franklin.pdf

GAO. (2011). *Social Media: Federal Agencies Need Policies and Procedures for Managing and Protecting Information They Access and Disseminate* (Report to Congressional Requesters). United States Government Accountability Office (GAO). Retrieved from http://www.gao.gov/new.items/d11605.pdf

Gore, A. (2007). *The Assault on Reason*. New York, NY: Penguin Books.

Greene, S. (2001). Astride the digital divide. *The Chronicle of Philanthropy.*, *13*(6), 18–19.

Grönlund, A., & Horan, T. A. (2004). Introducing e-gov: History, definitions, and issues. *Communications of the Association for Information Systems*, *15*, 713–729. Retrieved from http://www.cips.org.in/public-sector-systems-governmentinnovations/documents/Introducing_e_governance.pdf

Gupta, A., Lamba, H., Kumaraguru, P., & Joshi, A. (2013, May). Faking Sandy: characterizing and identifying fake images on Twitter during Hurricane Sandy. In *Proceedings of the 22nd international conference on World Wide Web companion* (pp. 729-736). International World Wide Web Conferences Steering Committee. 10.1145/2487788.2488033

Hager, C. (2013). Crisis informatics: Perspectives of trust – is social media a mixed blessing? *Student Research Journal, 2*(2). Retrieved from http://scholarworks.sjsu.edu/slissrj/vol2/iss2/2

Howard, A. (2011). 2011 Gov 2.0 year in review: A look at the Gov 2.0 themes, moments and achievements that made an impact in 2011. *O'Reilly Radar.* Retrieved from http://radar.oreilly.com/2011/12/2011-gov2-year-in-review.html

HowTo.Gov. (2012). *Content management systems used by government agencies.* Retrieved from http://www.howto.gov/tech-solutions/agency-cms-products

Klischewski, R., & Abubakr, R. (2010). Can e-Government adopters benefit from a technologyfirst approach? The case of Egypt embarking on service-oriented architecture. *43rd Hawaii International Conference on System Sciences*, 1-10.

Kruger, L., & Gilroy, A. (April 12, 2011). *Broadband Internet Access and the Digital Divide: Federal Assistance Programs* (Report Prepared for Members of Congress). Congressional Research Service. 7-5700. RL30719.

Kurczy, S. (2010). Is internet access a human right? *The Christian Science Monitor.* Retrieved from http://www.csmonitor.com/World/Global-News/2010/0309/Is-Internet-access-a-human-right-Top-10-nations-that-say-yes

La Rue, F. (2011). *Report of the Special Rapporteur on the promotion and protection of the right to freedom of opinion and expression.* Human Rights Council; United Nations General Assembly. 17th session: Agenda Item 3. A/HRC/17/27. Retrieved from http://www2.ohchr.org/english/bodies/hrcouncil/docs/17session/A.HRC.17.27_en.pdf

Lam, W. (2005). Barriers to e-government integration. *Journal of Enterprise Information Management, 18*(5/6), 511–530. doi:10.1108/17410390510623981

Leighninger, M. (2011). Citizenship and governance in a wild, wired world: How should citizens and public managers use online tools to improve democracy? *National Civic Review, 100*(2), 20–29. doi:10.1002/ncr.20056

Lester, A. (2010). Gladwell: the revolution will not be tweeted. *The Nonprofit Quarterly.* Retrieved from http://www.nonprofitquarterly.org/index.php?option=com_content&view=article&id=6096:gladwell-the-revolution-will-not-be-tweeted&catid=153:features&Itemid=336

Lindblom, C. (1959). The science of "muddling through." *Public Administration Review, 19*(2), 79–88. doi:10.2307/973677

Linden, R. (2010). *Leading across boundaries: Creating collaborative agencies in a networked world.* San Francisco, CA: Jossey-Bass.

Menzel, D. (2010). *Ethics moments in government: Cases and controversies.* Boca Raton, FL: Taylor & Francis.

Mergel, I. (2011). Crowdsourced ideas make participating in government cool again. *PA Times, 34*(4), 4,6.

Norris, D., Fletcher, P., & Holden, S. (2001). *Is your local government plugged in? Highlights of the 2000 Electronic Government Survey.* Washington, DC: International City/County Management Association.

O'Hearn, M. S., & Kahle, L. R. (2013). The empowered customer: User-generated content and the future of marketing. *Global Economics and Management Review, 18*(1), 22–30. doi:10.1016/S2340-1540(13)70004-5

O'Leary, R., Van Slyke, D., & Kim, S. (Eds.). (2010). *The future of public administration around the world: The Minnowbrook perspective.* Washington, DC: Georgetown University Press.

Oasis eGov Member Section. (2010). *Avoiding the pitfalls of eGovernment: 10 lessons learnt from eGovernment deployments.* Retrieved from: http://www.oasis-egov.org/sites/oasisegov.org/files/eGov_Pitfalls_Guidance%20Doc_v1.pdf

Obar, J., Zube, P., & Lampe, C. (2011). *Advocacy 2.0: An analysis of how advocacy groups in the United States perceive and use social media as tools for facilitating civic engagement and collective action* (Working Paper Series). Social Science Research Network. Retrieved from: http://ssrn.com/abstract=1956352

Ojoa, A., Esteveza, E., & Janowskia, T. (2010). Semantic interoperability architecture for governance 2.0. *Information Polity, 15,* 105–123. doi 10.3233/IP-2010-0199

Orlikowski, W., & Scott, S. (2009). Sociomateriality: Challenging the separation of technology, work and organization. *The Academy of Management Annals, 2*(1), 433–474. doi:10.1080/19416520802211644

Pallotta, D. (2008). *Uncharitable.* Medford, MA: Tufts University Press.

Pope, J., Isely, A., & Asamoa-Tutu, F. (2009, April). Developing a marketing strategy for nonprofit organizations: An exploratory study. *Journal of Nonprofit & Public Sector Marketing, 21*(2), 184–201. doi:10.1080/10495140802529532

Pynes, J. (2009). *Human resources management for public and nonprofit organizations.* San Francisco, CA: Jossey-Bass.

Right Now Government. (2010). *Citizen service meets social media: Best practices for citizen engagement* (White Paper). RightNow Technologies, Inc. Retrieved from http://api.ning.com/files/Fkoi1sHp00bvHPs84maiIXkGot-*6ZcAf0xkCm qadr7P1hcFegPmZl2cdEAo5YS*ceIUoAF7bWjEYdPyYmbKLFVtxQroFMw/RightNowGovernmentSocialContactCenterWhitePaper6.pdf

Salamon, L. (2003). *The resilient sector.* Washington, DC: Brookings Institution Press.

Schaefer, G., & Hersey, L. N. (2015). Cat Videos for a Cause: A Nonprofit Social Media. In H. Asencio & R. Sun (Eds.), *Cases on Strategic Social Media Utilization.* Hershey, PA: IGI Global. doi:10.4018/978-1-4666-8188-0.ch005

Shareef, M., Archer, N., & Dutta, S. (2012). *E-Government service maturity and development: Cultural, organizational and technological perspectives.* Hershey, PA: IGI Global; doi:10.4018/978-1-60960-848-4

Sherman, A. (2011). How law enforcement agencies are using social media to better serve the public. *Mashable*. Retrieved from: http://mashable.com/2011/08/31/law-enforcementsocial-media-use/

Shirky, C. (2008). *Here comes everybody: The power of organizing without organizations*. New York, NY: Penguin Books.

Smith, A. (2010). *Government online* (Report). Pew Internet & American Life Project. Retrieved from http://www.pewinternet.org/Reports/2010/Government-Online/Summaryof-Findings.aspx

Tan, F., Stockdale, R., & Vasa, R. (2011). *Leveraging emerging web technologies for community engagement project success in higher education*. European Conference of Information Systems. Retrieved from http://is2.lse.ac.uk/asp/aspecis/20110211.pdf

van den Berg, A. C., & Verhoeven, J. W. (2017). Understanding social media governance: Seizing opportunities, staying out of trouble. *Corporate Communications*, *22*(1), 149–164. doi:10.1108/CCIJ-06-2015-0035

VanRoekel, S. (2011). *An Evening with Steven VanRoekel, Chief Information Officer of the United States. Remarks as prepared for delivery*. PARC. Retrieved from www.whitehouse.gov/sites/default/files/svr_parc_speech_final_0.pdf

Walker, M. (2011). Disaster response increasingly linked to social media. *FierceGovernmentIT*. Retrieved from: http://www.fiercegovernmentit.com/story/disaster-response-increasinglylinked-social-media/2011-08-31#ixzz1eyTSaWhn

Yanosky, R., & McCredie, J. (2008). *Process and politics: IT governance in higher education* (Research Study 5). Boulder, CO: EDUCAUSE Center for Applied Research. Retrieved from http://www.educause.edu/ecar

# Chapter 10
# Emotional Intelligence and Empathy:
## A Prosocial Approach to Leadership Communication

**Michael A. Brown Sr.**
*Florida International University, USA*

## ABSTRACT

*The rise of emotional intelligence (EI) and the continuing growth of online interactions work together to demonstrate the importance of participatory decision making as a motivational technique. However, participation in decisions requires that the leader act in a prosocial manner, focusing on outcomes that are beneficial to more than just the leader. A prosocial attitude leads to creation of buy-in through shared value and good management of emotions, requiring skill in both EI and empathetic approaches. EI is about connecting with one's own emotions and those of others to enable effective leadership communication. Empathy is the ability to understand someone else's emotions, feel them as if they were yours, and even to take some action in support or mitigation of those feelings. The lack of feedback or agreements on shared value in online interactions are highlighted when people are forced into face-to-face interactions and are subsequently unable to find these important communication tools. This chapter offers a new approach to leadership communication.*

DOI: 10.4018/978-1-5225-4168-4.ch010

## INTRODUCTION

In today's communicative environment, leaders need more than Emotional Intelligence (EI). Empathy is an important trait that must be mastered to achieve the best in communication, whether face-to-face or online. This is important because emphasis on EI and the continuing growth of online interactions work together to demonstrate the importance of participatory decision making as a motivational technique. However, participation in decisions requires that the leader create buy-in through shared value and good management of emotions, requiring skill in both EI and empathetic approaches.

EI is about connecting with one's own emotions and those of others to enable effective leadership communication. Empathy is the ability to understand someone else's emotions, feel them as if they were your own, and even to take some action in support or mitigation of those feelings. The lack of feedback or agreements on shared value in online interactions is highlighted when people are forced into face-to-face interactions and are subsequently unable to find these important communication tools. Mastering these abilities will give leaders ways to build a collaborative culture, emphasize everyone's strengths, and work to improve weaknesses. The literature review begins with an examination of leadership styles with emphasis on democratic/ participative style and servant leadership.

## LITERATURE REVIEW

There are nine leadership styles that are commonly recognized by experts studying the subject, so it is appropriate to review them in this work. The focus of this article is on the relevance of democratic or participative leadership and an understanding of servant leadership. Democratic/participative leaders must be adept at getting input and creating collaboration to get a final decision that has everyone's buy-in. The chance to participate at this level normally delivers high job satisfaction and great creativity. The participative approach requires patience to work, because deliberations tend to be slow. This is not the best approach if you need quick decisions.

Servant-leadership is present when leadership and team members share authority by addressing and prioritizing personal needs while collective decision-making is encouraged. This approach should bring high morale and promote diversity. Critics of the approach point to conflicts of interest that can arise when business objectives take a back seat to employee interests and suggest the leader lacks authority. The other seven styles, in no particular order, are (Anderson & Sun, 2017, pp. 77-79):

- **Transformational:** Effective communication happens because the leader energizes the intellect of those who follow by thinking outside of the box. Grand ideas often come from this kind of motivation and this leader can build confidence in others to groom the next leader.

- **Transactional:** This is based on transactions where task and reward are tied tightly together in an approach focused on the makeup of the group. The transaction is when actions result in rewarding good performance and punishing bad behaviors or outcomes. Some experts say this approach stifles creative potential (De Hoogh, Greer, & Den Hartog, 2015, p. 688; Den Hartog & Belschak, 2016, p. 412).

- **Charismatic:** This style is like transactional leadership and is driven by the personality and positive or negative charm of the leader. The downside is that the leader must be present to achieve success and the whole organization can fail when the leader moves on.

- **Autocratic:** This leader exercises tight controls over all aspects of decision making with little or no chance for employee inputs or delegation. Absenteeism and high turnover can result because not many staff members appreciate being ruled with an iron fist. Creativity can suffer since all decisions are made with virtually no discussion (Van Vugt, Jepson, Hart, & De Cremer, 2004). Military units commonly operate this way based on tradition and this style is considered most effective, or necessary, in routine jobs that require limited skills. One study concluded that group members subjected to autocratic leadership were concerned that they lacked personal control over the decision-making process and the result was that many left the group (Van Vugt et al., 2004). These findings demonstrate autocratic leadership may negatively affect team performance and psychological safety in certain circumstances.

- **Laissez-Faire:** This is a "go with the flow" approach that can be effectively utilized when you have a very experienced workforce, allowing the leader to employ a hands-off approach. Specific instructions and expectations as well as performance monitoring are required to ensure standards are met.

- **Bureaucratic:** Administrative or other highly-regulated environments lend themselves to this approach that relies on a defined hierarchy and adherence to the organization's rules. Health and safety organizations can thrive on this approach if leaders understand that they may be hindering creativity and innovation.

- **Situational:** The leader uses cues in the situation and adapts the style for the best result. The cues are typically the type of task, the kind of group, the timeline, and other factors that would indicate how to best get the job done. Management experts Paul Hersey and Ken Blanchard developed this theory in 1969 (Bates, 2016, p. 44), stating that the best leaders employ a range of different styles depending on the environment.

Transactional leadership has a place in the discussion in that it signals the need for leaders to stay in tune with workers' needs and emotions. It can be easy to reward initiative and leaders should set the example by supporting and encouraging their staff. However, leaders must recognize that people may be motivated and creative without being the best performers. They may be doing well but their level of skill may not put them in the top one percent of the organization. Creativity can suffer if these individuals don't feel that the boss is listening to their ideas, or that they are not permitted to suggest or make changes, or that they are punished without good reason (Den Hartog & Belschak, 2016, p. 412). These are issues for all leaders to consider.

This examination of leadership now leads to EI, empathy, and emotion in communication. These are hot topics for researchers searching to engage in new conversations and analyses that are starting around the globe. In addition to the definitions of EI and empathy offered earlier, it is necessary to understand and evaluate emotions to facilitate full discovery. Regulating emotions should be less about control and more about influencing performance and behavior of the staff by managing the range of activity between relationships:

*...the expression and the impropriety threshold. We have also drawn to the attention of practicing managers that the consistency followers seek in leaders does not mean that leaders need to act in the same way across situations... (Jordan & Lindebaum, 2015, p. 597).*

The research points to the importance of collaboration, participation, and situational thinking in good leadership communication. Research also continues to address relational empathy and working definitions of emotion (Frijda, 1986; Jordan & Lindebaum, 2015). The emphasis for discovery is understanding the way that emotions have very different meanings to various researchers. Researchers view emotions as much more than feelings. Some describe emotion as individual-centered processes that establish, maintain, or disrupt the interaction between people and their internal or external environment (Barrett & Campos, 1987; Frijda, 1986). One leadership study demonstrated that when the leader's emotion can be in harmony with that of employees, positive reactions are triggered that can improve performance (Agote, Aramburu, & Lines, 2016, p. 50). Another view characterizes emotion as the "attempt by the person to establish, maintain, change, or terminate the relation between the self and the environment on matters of personal significance" (Campos, Campos, & Barrett, 1989; Main, Walle, Kho, & Halpern, 2017, p. 359).

These definitions of emotions arm the leader with three processes that deliver significance to the observer:

*... (a) the relevance of an event to the goals and strivings of the person; (b) the emotional communication from significant others, such as their facial, vocal, and gestural actions; and (c) the hedonic nature of certain types of stimulation (that is, whether an event intrinsically hurts, soothes, or produces pleasure). Thus, cognitive factors such as object permanence, mirror self-recognition, and short-term memory are not, in themselves, affectogenic; for cognition to produce emotion, the cognition must be about significant events. To postulate cognition alone in emotion elicitation and emotion regulation is to miss half of the tale. (Campos et al., 1989)*

Emotions are important to leaders for several reasons. One is the importance that leaders put on the way a person deals with the environment and with other members of the team. A second consideration for leaders is how people feel. This is not just about autonomic or facial feedback; it is about leaders creating and nurturing a bond that allows them to observe and diagnose emotional cues. Finally, what significance do people attach to both regular and high-stakes issues? Leaders who can treat these considerations with equal emphasis have great opportunities to succeed in communicating with their people.

Several theories or points of view are relevant in taking a closer look at the importance of emotions. The relational view of emotions is energized by, for example, systems theory, ethology, and possibly the organizational approach to emotional development (Campos et al., 1989). Systems theory studies society as a complex collection of elements and combines people and their beliefs to view them, e.g., a country. Ethology is a theory that focuses on "communication, ecological niches, and the functions that actions serve" (Campos et al., 1989). An organizational development focus could show the leader how the same event could spark varying emotional reactions, and that there can be differing responses that have the same underlying meaning. All these viewpoints provide some insight into the need for the leader's involvement in emotions.

Emotions are relevant to the work of public managers, for instance, because they are a vital part of the human condition and the interaction with leaders (Berman, 2008; Eisenbeiss & Knippenberg, 2015; Goleman, 1995, 1998a; Hughes, 2005; Huy, 1999; Mathew & Gupta, 2015). Leaders need opportunities to find harmony between the feelings of themselves and others, to understand their strengths and weaknesses and how they relate to those of their employees, to come to grips with their own negative emotions and adaptability, and to improve their communication and relationship skills.

Managers can be more committed and enthusiastic when there is an atmosphere of understanding and acceptance (Goldsmith, 2004; Griffith, Connelly, Thiel, & Johnson, 2015; Light, 2005; Sosik, 1999). Managers need more than a notion of "people skills;" they need to understand what these skills are and what they mean in terms of emotional considerations. Emotions are common in the workplace, arising out of work practices, policies, and the workplace environment. Understanding emotions allows managers to be successful in norming and shaping their motivational interactions with employees, especially when working human resource (HR) management issues or agendas. Evan Berman and Jonathan West (2008) argued that "acknowledging the place of emotional content in administrative scholarship and practice is not new, but its significance has often been relegated to secondary status, if not ignored." It is time to put EI at the forefront to help managers understand it and use it to their best advantage.

Numerous researchers have demonstrated frameworks for workplace relationships between managers and those they employ and motivate, examining how organizational policies and practices affect the emotional skills of managers in various organizations (Barrett & Campos, 1987; Berman, 2008; De Hoogh et al., 2015; Griffith et al., 2015; Martin-Raugh, Kell, & Motowidlo, 2016). For instance, one study addressed managing EI in U.S. cities, studying the social skills of public managers (Berman, 2008). The researchers argued in favor of the need for better integration of emotions in management theory based on the range and salience of organizational efforts found in their research. Public managers, however, are not the only potential beneficiaries of improved awareness and capability in EI.

EI's foundation is self-awareness, the ability to recognize your own emotions and to have a strong sense of your own tendencies and abilities. It is important to develop people skills, which typically include active listening, acknowledging others, and mindful speaking (Goleman, 2006, 2001). Through EI, managers can use self-awareness to identify and express their emotions while understanding that being attuned to one's feelings can also be a source of feedback that helps people focus on their strengths, weaknesses, and values, hopefully resulting in self-confidence (Gowing, 2001; Jacobs, 2001; Macaleer, 2002; Martin-Raugh et al., 2016). Self-management also includes keeping disruptive emotions in check, thinking clearly under difficult or stressful conditions, having flexibility and adaptability to avoid being rigid in responding to others, and taking tough or unpopular positions on issues (Caudron, 1999; Dearborn, 2002; Smigla, 2000).

The ability to read others – to be aware of their needs and feelings – and to anticipate and address the needs of others is part of social awareness. Social awareness also includes verbalizing emotions experienced by others, acknowledging sensitivity to and consideration for the perspectives of others, and staying in touch with others' feelings. The concept of social awareness is basic to creating environments where diverse people can thrive. A related concept is relationship management, which is the ability to build bonds of alignment, appreciation, and support. Effective relationship management requires communication, teamwork, conflict management skills, and the ability to help people work toward common objectives (Macaleer, 2002).

Self-awareness, social awareness, and relationship management are key management skills and activities, which highlight various behaviors and skills that relevant literature mentions and uses for assessment and measurement. The study of EI acknowledges that although emotions are non-cognitive in nature, people can learn to recognize what they feel (Berman, 2008). People can develop courses of action that consider a rational dialogue about their own feelings and those of others. Studies show that EI increases with age as a result of learning (Bar-On, 2005). Training programs in the workplace allow managers to improve their EI skills (Cherniss, 2001; Sala, 2000) by, for example, recognizing a broader range of emotions in themselves and others and by distinguishing sincere kindness from false smiles (Ekman, 2004).

EI and self-awareness are important in helping leaders understand empathy, and that understanding leads to prosocial behavior, which will be discussed in a later section of this article. An article on narcissism in coaches makes the point that leaders have trouble supporting autonomy in their people if they exhibit low levels of empathetic concern (Matosic et al., 2017, p. 259). When leaders can share and experience the feelings of those they lead, they are better equipped to help in productivity, buy-in, feedback, and even stretching for larger goals. Empathy requires that leaders not only care how people feel, but that they include what they know about those feelings in their decisions.

In 2017, for instance, a group of researchers observed a lack of empathy on the part of American business leaders and engaged in research on the dilemma (Holt, Marques, Hu, & Wood, 2017). Empathy has been increasingly included as a primary skill for effective leadership in research literature for decades. Researchers believe that emotional sensitivity to people positively links the leader with improved relationships and creates stronger networks (Bass, 1973). Leaders need this ability to step outside of themselves and see the world as other people do (Riggio & Reichard, 2008).

When leaders apply EI, empathy, and emotion, they can use these constructs to develop an ability to change with the situation and the environment. The presence of negative emotions can create significant problems that indicate the need for adaptability or change. When that happens, radical change in the organization could be an important dynamic to consider.

Emotion, for instance, affects radical change when the process is viewed in separate components. Achieving radical change requires addressing three critical steps: receptivity, mobilization, and learning (Huy, 1999). A person's willingness to consider change is receptivity and it is characterized as both a state and a process. At any fixed point in time, a person can accept the need for the proposed change if there is an interpretive, attitudinal state on the cognitive and emotional level.

Mobilization is defined as rallying and propelling different segments of the organization to undertake joint action and to realize common change goals (Huy, 1999). When a person takes concrete action in the direction of change, they are involved in mobilization. Third, people can learn from the changes they create, thinking and then acting based on goal achievement and feedback. Learning and change are stimulated when there is a conflict or mismatch between a person's comparison of their expectations and a newly perceived reality.

Beyond receptivity leading to mobilization, individuals and organizations can learn from the outcomes of the changes they enact. A person learns by thinking then acting. Emotion provides the primary feedback mechanism that alerts the person that various goals are not being achieved, and this in turn motivates behavior. Emotion arouses dissatisfaction with the present when a person compares the newly perceived reality unfavorably with his or her prior expectations. This stimulates learning and change.

Quy Huy (1999, p. 325) calls these steps emotional dynamics, which involve ways in which leaders have the ability to "acknowledge, recognize, monitor, discriminate, and attend" to the emotions of people and to include these considerations in the organization's rules and norms (Schein, 1985). Leaders can develop this kind of emotional capability over time without having many EI-savvy surrogates in influential positions to assist.

There are many definitions of motivation, so it is important to review some of those. Using a nonacademic definition, we can say that motivation is the degree to which an individual wants and tries to do well at a particular task or job (Mitchell, 1982). Online dictionaries tend to describe motivation as an impetus to action. Social scientists suggest a more technical definition where motivation refers to the psychological processes that cause the arousal, direction, and persistence of behavior (Atkinson, 1964; Campbell, Dunnette, Lawler, & Weick, 1970; Huse & Bowditch, 1977; Kast & Rosenzweig, 1979; Korman, 1974; Luthans, 1977; Martin-Raugh et al., 2016; Naseem, 2018). Motivation can be understood to include emphasis on goal direction or some voluntary aspect. So, motivation can be viewed as a word for the psychological processes that cause the arousal, direction, and persistence of voluntary actions that are goal directed (Mitchell, 1982).

Mitchell (1982) thus provides a clear definition of motivation that is appropriate for our analysis. The researcher says that motivation is the degree to which an individual wants and chooses to engage in certain specified behaviors and contends that there is consensus about some underlying properties of motivation. Motivation is an individual phenomenon. It is intentional and, it is multifaceted, and it can predict behavior. Leaders should focus on degree of motivation because there may never be enough emphasis on it, or there will be times when there is so much focus on motivation that it stifles initiative and accountability. Leaders need to find a balance, increasing the level of intensity of motivation to achieve team goals. There is a hierarchy of emphasis where one motivates people to be good team members followed by agreeing to contribute to a winning team. Leaders who are fully in touch with their teams tend to motivate them to the "championship," even building a culture of excellence where the organization is the industry leader. This hierarchy should be used to achieve critical success factors and then to move on to finding ways to set the industry standard.

## FOCUS ON EMOTIONAL INTELLIGENCE

EI is the ability to sense, understand, and effectively apply the power and acumen of emotions as a source of human energy, information, trust, creativity, and influence (Cooper, 1997; Martin-Raugh et al., 2016; Mayer, Caruso, & Salovey, 2016; Serrat, 2017). Leaders who improve their EI can more effectively acknowledge and value feelings in themselves and in others and can respond to those feelings in an effective way. Paying attention to emotions can save the leader time by directing energies more effectively and expanding opportunities. EI has three driving forces: building trusting relationships, increasing energy and effectiveness, and creating the future. Research shows that EI far outweighs IQ and raw brain power as the primary success factor in decision making, creating dynamic organizations, and achieving lifestyle satisfaction and success (Cooper, 1997).

The core capacities of EI are drawn together and put into action in the workplace through the framework of the Four Cornerstone Model of Emotional Intelligence, first envisioned by Ayman Sawaf of Advance Intelligence Technologies (Cooper, 1997). The cornerstones are: emotional literacy, emotional fitness, emotional depth, and emotional alchemy.

1.  Emotional literacy involves developing a clear and useful vocabulary to allow recognizing, respecting, and valuing the inherent wisdom of feelings. Emotional honesty, emotional energy, emotional feedback, and practical intuition contribute to emotional literacy.
2.  Emotional fitness has trust as one of its key characteristics. Emotional fitness also includes authenticity, resilience, renewal, and constructive discontent. Trust is an actionable emotional strength – something we must feel and act on.
3.  Emotional depth has to do with calling forth your core character, identifying and advancing the unique potential and purpose that define your destiny, manifesting commitment, drive, initiative, conscience, and accountability, applying integrity, and increasing your influence beyond authority, rank, and title.
4.  Emotional alchemy is a blending of forces that enable us to discover creative opportunities and transform lesser ideas into greater ones.

Leaders should examine emotional literacy closely. Emotional literacy is the ability to recognize, understand, and appropriately express our emotions. Just as verbal literacy is the basic building-block for reading and writing, emotional literacy is the basis for perceiving and communicating emotions. Becoming emotionally literate is akin to learning the alphabet, grammar, and vocabulary of our emotional lives.

There are a variety of definitions of EI, but most scholars define it as a multifaceted concept that involves a broad range of skills and behaviors. For instance, Goleman (1995) describes EI as a leader's ability to recognize emotions in self and others and to use this information to gain improvements in self-management and relationships with others. Fundamentally, EI is a process of gaining awareness by recognizing personal emotions and those of others. Once emotions are brought to a state of consciousness, EI leads people to use this awareness, or information, skillfully and intelligently in deliberate, purposeful decision-making activities. Berman and West (2008) advance the notion that typically, EI skills and behaviors involve the domains of self-awareness, self-management, social awareness, and relationship management (Cherniss, 2001; Druskat, 2001; Hood, 2004). EI is relevant to workplace settings, though its influence extends far beyond the workplace.

## FOCUS ON EMPATHY

Successful interactions can be obtained by mastering the art of three components of empathy: perspective taking, emotional contagion, and empathetic concern. Perspective taking is the leader's ability to assess and adopt someone else's viewpoint (Stiff & et al., 1987). Leaders who understand the significance of another's point of view can handle disconnects in contextual factors, allowing them to find accurate matches through feedback. Use of that feedback improves the empathetic process which requires that input from the person and at the same time that the leader's continuing curiosity is necessary to complete the interaction (Main et al., 2017, pp. 368-369).

Leaders must have an ability to consider all sides of issues being considered.

When the leader experiences an emotional response resulting from, and like, that of another, then emotional contagion is created. This can bring thoughts and feelings of various people in line with each other. Empathic concern is defined as "(1) a general concern and regard for the welfare of others and (2) the stipulation that the affect is not parallel to that of the target person" (Stiff & et al., 1987). In other words, emotional contagion is a "sharing" of the emotion to find common ground, while empathic concern is an acknowledgement that while the leader is concerned, the points of view of the parties differ. "For example, the observation of a person in distress should activate a parallel, negative response (emotional contagion) and a positive, nonparallel response (empathic concern)" (Stiff & et al., 1987). Many theorists believe that determining another person's perspective leads to the creation of emotional contagion. These experts believe that empathetic concern naturally follows the other two components in succession.

Daniel Goleman (1998) pointed out that there are positive and negative aspects of empathy. Realistic self-assessment, self-awareness, and improved ability to make decisions are related, according to Goleman. "While the arrogant, tuned-out leader protects him or herself with blind spots, effective leaders know their strengths, their limits, and their weaknesses" (Goleman, 1998, pp. 21-22). To be effective, leaders need more than self-awareness to read the emotions of others. They need empathy because people don't just volunteer information about their feelings as is shown in newer research (Jordan & Lindebaum, 2015; Main et al., 2017; Martin-Raugh et al., 2016; Wang & Seibert, 2015). Instead, this information is often revealed, or at least available to be discovered, through facial expressions, tone of voice, gestures, or pacing.

Organizational communication can present problems when it involves self-interested people whose primary concern is how they as the leader can improve their own situation. Once in the lead, these individuals don't serve as stewards of the mission and team members; they serve as stewards of their own path to success. The absence of empathy can subject people to disrespect or contempt. Without a remedy, these people may tune out or turn to inappropriate measures of protest like absenteeism, malingering, or violence against others. "The signs of damage won't be immediately visible; they're silent, insidious, and create a ripple of dysfunction around that leader" (Goleman, 1998, p. 23).

Leaders must communicate via clear channels, putting aside their own agendas and connecting with those around them. By determining what's important to your team, and which of the "big picture" issues or responsibilities have buy-in, the leader improves the communication channels. Sensing unstated feelings in interactions and making sure they have a chance to be articulated is a winning formula in organizational communication.

Finally, positive empathy fosters workplace diversity because it enhances teaching and coaching through familiarity. If you know you people, you can determine the best ways to achieve communication success based on their needs balanced with the needs of the organization and the leader. Empathetic connections based on EI principles are vital to good communication.

Combining the communication benefits of EI and the three components of empathy leads to prosocial behavior that can help any leader in any situation.

## FOCUS ON BEING PROSOCIAL

Prosocial behavior covers the broad range of actions intended to benefit one person or more other than oneself—actions such as helping, comforting, sharing, and cooperation (Batson & Powell, 2003). This is a fundamental of democratic/

participative leadership. A leader's participative style should be one that allows the team to meet objectives with a plan of action that is personally rewarding in a nurturing, comfortable environment created by the leader; this is effectiveness (Iqbal, Anwar, & Haider, 2015, p. 5). There are common prosocial rules that we take for granted, like stopping when the traffic light is red or paying taxes. These actions may be motivated by empathetic concerns like protecting everyone's rights, acting in a manner consistent with one's reputation or social status, or pursuing general levels of fairness in interactions.

Prosocial leaders bring people together by showing them order and fairness in dealing with the team. It also helps teams seek a culture of good order and discipline. In the early 1980s, prosocial behavior was generally connected with developing desirable traits in children; however, the late 1980s saw a movement to add adult behaviors to the classification (Stiff & et al., 1987). These ideas take us back to the 1950s with democratic self-assertion and Motivation-Hygiene Theory.

R. Stagner (1950) stated that the problem of industrial harmony would not be solved until there was a realization that both executives and workers want democratic self-assertion. In 1952, J. Tiffin disputed that workers were simply "hired hands." He argued that four factors affect a worker's morale: how the person feels about the job, how the boss regards the employee, social factors, and working conditions. These factors relate directly to empathy.

Another idea favorable to combining EI and components of empathy comes from Lewin (1951), who proposed a general model of change consisting three phases, "unfreezing, change, refreezing" in *Field Theory in Social Science*. This model would become the conceptual frame for organization development. Clearly, the emphasis on workers and their behavior and needs relates well to Lewin's arguments in terms of identifying what exists, making changes, and instituting new policies.

Motivation-Hygiene Theory addresses factors that affect job attitudes, shown in Table 1 below.

*Table 1. Motivation Hygiene Factors*

| Intrinsic:<br>Leading to Satisfaction | Extrinsic:<br>Leading to Dissatisfaction |
| --- | --- |
| Achievement | Company policy |
| Recognition | Supervision |
| The work itself | Relationship with the boss |
| Responsibility | Work conditions |
| Advancement | Salary |
| Growth | Relationship with peers |

Frederick Herzberg (1966) introduced intrinsic and extrinsic motivators in his Motivation-Hygiene Theory, explaining that motivation is created by intrinsic motivators when they are present, and that motivation is reduced by extrinsic motivators when they are absent. Intrinsic motivators tend to be more emotional and less tangible: recognition, growth potential, relationships, and challenging work. Extrinsic motivators, on the other hand, are tangible and basic: salary, fringe benefits, job security, and status. Herzberg further classified our actions and how and why we do them. For example, if you perform a work-related action because you *have* to, then that is classed as movement, but if you perform a work related action because you *want* to then that is classed as motivation (Herzberg, 1959; Sachau, 2007).

The key for leaders is that motivation can be increased with intrinsic motivators because there is rarely an expectation that they will be guaranteed. However, people expect to "receive" extrinsic motivators and when they are not present, or are removed, motivation is decreased or eliminated entirely. These factors are independent, so how one affects people does not increase at the same rate that the other decreases. The leader's task then is to establish an ongoing connection so that she or he can provide intrinsic motivators when more job satisfaction is needed or provide extrinsic motivators when less job dissatisfaction is needed.

Ultimately, this is about leadership communication that creates job satisfaction. Leaders should not just add meaningless tasks to a job that leaves workers unmotivated. They should try to ensure that the new tasks are at a higher level than the current ones and that they enrich the job. If you can't add higher-level tasks, you should at least ensure the new tasks or responsibilities are more difficult than the current ones. Explain how the new tasks relate to the current ones and how they figure in the organization's big picture. Provide greater challenges and allow more feedback, then step back and let individuals enjoy their newfound freedom and authority.

Leaders must allow workers to stretch themselves by thinking outside the box or by participating in activities not directly related to work. Are there instances when the company needs a solution to a difficult problem or situation and employees are given ownership to find the solution or remedy? How many employees are encouraged by the company to pursue their education? Does the company provide any assistance? How many people are given the opportunity to participate in community events on company time?

This is a leadership and management balancing act. The way to be good at analyzing the communication task is to employ the skills and knowledge of EI and empathy components. This creates and nurtures an ongoing "sense" of the people we are dealing with and how they are feeling and operating.

## LIMITATIONS IN RESEARCHING DIGITAL EI

This examination of EI focuses on face-to-face interactions and that is a limitation in terms of giving leaders a full range of skills with which to communicate. Leaders who are successfully using EI in face-to-face (FTF) interactions can have problems translating those skills to online situations. Research in this area is ongoing and deserves to be addressed, but it is not part of this examination. The focus here is on face-to-face communication with an intent to create conversations that will lead to the digital world. In my book, *Solutions for High-Touch Communication in a High-Tech World* (Brown, 2017), the communication comparisons between FTF and online are addressed in an organizational frame. While there is not room to continue that discovery in this work, it is my hope that conversations created today will give answers tomorrow.

Those conversations can help leaders determine the correct approach – FTF or online – for communicating and being empathetic with their teams. FTF interaction requires that the leader form the message with the team member's thoughts and emotions in mind, paying special attention to physiological barriers, language, structural design, verbal/visual cues, and the risk of information overload. Online communications require the leader's agility to quickly form the concept of the message and then use any hints, such as shares, likes, retweets, reposts, etc., to demonstrate connections that lead to shared value. These are new approaches that deserve future research based on the continuing evolution of the digital space.

## WHAT DOES IT ALL MEAN?

A prosocial approach combining EI and components of EI is a great way that leaders can improve communication with their team. Some of the references used are a bit dated, but that shows that the journey to improving leadership never ends. Those early references, combined with new discoveries over the last 10 years or so, are necessary to give leaders a variety of avenues to improve their skills. Participative approaches that lead to better decisions and create prosocial leaders lead to improved quality of work life, high morale, and an atmosphere of creativity. In this approach, leaders work to view the world using the eyes of their employees to achieve shared value and empathetic interactions.

When developing new leaders, this approach can be the formula for essential training in achieving objectives through collaboration and communication. But this is by no means the final answer. This article is part of the overall initiative of this book to suggest additional research to allow organizations to find new and better ways to care for and motivate employees. Any research needs to start with EI and empathy in search of shared value and good management of emotions. The lack of feedback or agreements on shared value in online interactions is highlighted when people are forced into face-to-face interactions and are subsequently unable to find these important communication tools. This chapter offers a new approach to communication based on participative interactions that lead to prosocial behavior that is focused on EI, empathy, and emotions.

## REFERENCES

Agote, L., Aramburu, N., & Lines, R. (2016). Authentic leadership perception, trust in the leader, and followers' emotions in organizational change processes. *The Journal of Applied Behavioral Science, 52*(1), 35–63. doi:10.1177/0021886315617531

Anderson, M. H., & Sun, P. Y. T. (2017). Reviewing Leadership Styles: Overlaps and the Need for a New 'Full-Range' Theory. *International Journal of Management Reviews, 19*(1), 76–96. doi:10.1111/ijmr.12082

Atkinson, J. W. (1964). *An Introduction to Motivation.* Princeton, NJ: Van Nostrand.

Bar-On, R. (2005). The Bar-On Model of Emotional-Social Intelligence. *Psichothema, 17*(SI).

Barrett, K. C., & Campos, J. J. (1987). *Perspectives on emotional development II: A functionalist approach to emotions.* Academic Press.

Bass, B. M. (1973). *Leadership, psychology, and organizational behavior.* Westport, CT: Greenwood Press.

Bates, C. (2016). A methodology study of Hersey and Blanchard situational leadership theory. *Int J Adv Eng Technol Manage Appl Sci, 3*(11), 42–48.

Batson, C. D., & Powell, A. A. (2003). *Altruism and Prosocial Behavior.* In Handbook of Psychology. John Wiley & Sons, Inc. doi:10.1002/0471264385.wei0519

Berman, E. M., & West, J. P. (2008). Managing Emotional Intelligence in U.S. Cities: A Study of Social Skills among Public Managers. *Public Administration Review, 68*(4), 742–758. doi:10.1111/j.1540-6210.2008.00912.x

Brown, M. A. Sr. (2017). *Solutions for High-Touch Communications in a High-Tech World.* Hershey, PA: IGI Global. doi:10.4018/978-1-5225-1897-6

Campbell, J. P., Dunnette, M. D., Lawler, E. E. III, & Weick, K. E. Jr. (1970). *Managerial Behavior, Performance and Effectiveness.* New York: McGraw-Hill.

Campos, J. J., Campos, R. G., & Barrett, K. C. (1989). Emergent themes in the study of emotional development and emotion regulation. *Developmental Psychology, 25*(3), 394–402. doi:10.1037/0012-1649.25.3.394

Caudron, S. (1999). The Hard Case for Soft Skills. *Workforce, 78*(7), 60–66.

Cherniss, C., & Goleman, D. (2001). *The Emotionally Intelligent Workplace: How to Select for, Measure, and Improve Emotional Intelligence in Individuals, Groups, and Organizations.* San Francisco: Jossey-Bass.

Cooper, R. K. (1997). Applying Emotional Intelligence in the Workplace. *Training & Development*, *51*(12), 31–38.

De Hoogh, A. H., Greer, L. L., & Den Hartog, D. N. (2015). Diabolical dictators or capable commanders? An investigation of the differential effects of autocratic leadership on team performance. *The Leadership Quarterly*, *26*(5), 687–701. doi:10.1016/j.leaqua.2015.01.001

Dearborn, K. (2002). Studies in Emotional Intelligence Redefine Our Approach to Leadership Development. *Public Personnel Management*, *31*(4), 523–530. doi:10.1177/009102600203100408

Den Hartog, D. N., & Belschak, F. D. (2016). Leadership and employee proactivity. *Proactivity at Work: Making Things Happen in Organizations*, 411.

Druskat, U., & Wolff, S. (2001). Building the Emotional Intelligence of Groups. *Harvard Business Review*, *79*(3), 81–90. PMID:11246926

Eisenbeiss, S. A., & Knippenberg, D. (2015). On ethical leadership impact: The role of follower mindfulness and moral emotions. *Journal of Organizational Behavior*, *36*(2), 182–195. doi:10.1002/job.1968

Ekman, P. (2004). *Emotions Revealed: Recognizing Faces and Feelings to Improve Communication and Emotional Life*. New York: Henry Holt.

Evan, M., & Berman, J. P. W. (2008). Managing Emotional Intelligence in U.S. Cities: A Study of Social Skills among Public Managers. *Public Administration Review*, *68*(4), 742–758. doi:10.1111/j.1540-6210.2008.00912.x

Frijda, N. H. (1986). *The emotions*. Cambridge University Press.

Goldsmith, S., & Eggers, W. D. (2004). *Governing by Network: The New Shape of the Public Sector*. Washington, DC: Brookings Institute Press.

Goleman, D. (1995). *Emotional Intelligence*. New York: Bantam.

Goleman, D. (1998). The emotional intelligence of leaders. *Leader to Leader*, (10): 21–22.

Goleman, D. (1998a). *Working with Emotional Intelligence*. New York: Bantam.

Goleman, D. (Ed.). (2001). *The Emotionally Intelligent Workplace* (Vol. 27-44). San Francisco: Jossey-Bass.

Goleman, D. (2006). *Social Intelligence*. New York: Bantam.

Gowing, M. K. (Ed.). (2001). *The Emotionally Intelligent Workplace*. San Francisco: Jossey-Bass.

Griffith, J., Connelly, S., Thiel, C., & Johnson, G. (2015). How outstanding leaders lead with affect: An examination of charismatic, ideological, and pragmatic leaders. *The Leadership Quarterly*, *26*(4), 502–517. doi:10.1016/j.leaqua.2015.03.004

Herzberg, F. (1959). *The motivation to work*. New York: Wiley.

Herzberg, F. (1966). *Work and the nature of man*. Cleveland, OH: World Pub. Co.

Holt, S., Marques, J., Hu, J., & Wood, A. (2017). Cultivating empathy: New perspectives on educating business leaders. *The Journal of Values Based Leadership*, *10*(1), 3. doi:10.22543/0733.101.1173

Hood, C., & Lodge, M. (2004). Competency, Bureaucracy, and Public Management Reform: A Competency Analysis. *Governance: An International Journal of Policy, Administration and Institutions*, *17*(3), 313–333. doi:10.1111/j.0952-1895.2004.00248.x

Hughes, J. (2005). Bringing Emotion to Work: Emotional Intelligence, Employee Resistance and the Reinvention of Character. *Work, Employment and Society*, *19*(3), 603–625. doi:10.1177/0950017005055675

Huse, E. F., & Bowditch, J. L. (1977). *Behavior in Organizations: A Systems Approach to Managing*. Reading, MA: Addison-Wesley.

Huy, Q. N. (1999). Emotional Capability, Emotional Intelligence, and Radical Change. *Academy of Management Review*, *24*(2), 325–345.

Iqbal, N., Anwar, S., & Haider, N. (2015). Effect of leadership style on employee performance. *Arabian Journal of Business and Management Review, 5*(5).

Jacobs, R. L. (Ed.). (2001). *The Emotionally Intelligent Workplace*. San Francisco: Jossey-Bass.

Jordan, P. J., & Lindebaum, D. (2015). A model of within person variation in leadership: Emotion regulation and scripts as predictors of situationally appropriate leadership. *The Leadership Quarterly*, *26*(4), 594–605. doi:10.1016/j.leaqua.2015.05.004

Kast, E. F., & Rosenzweig, J. E. (1979). *Organization and Management: A Systems Approach*. New York: McGraw-Hill.

Korman, A. K. (1974). *The Psychology of Motivation*. Englewood Cliffs, NJ: Prentice-Hall.

Light, P. C. (2005). *The Four Pillars of High Performance: How Robust Organizations Achieve Extraordinary Results*. New York: McGraw-Hill.

Luthans, F. (1977). *Organizational Behavior*. New York: McGraw-Hill.

Macaleer, W. D., & Shannon, J. B. (2002). Emotional Intelligence: How Does it Affect Leadership? *Employment Relations Today, 29*(3), 9–19. doi:10.1002/ert.10047

Main, A., Walle, E. A., Kho, C., & Halpern, J. (2017). The interpersonal functions of empathy: A relational perspective. *Emotion Review, 9*(4), 358–366. doi:10.1177/1754073916669440

Martin-Raugh, M. P., Kell, H. J., & Motowidlo, S. J. (2016). Prosocial knowledge mediates effects of agreeableness and emotional intelligence on prosocial behavior. *Personality and Individual Differences, 90*, 41–49. doi:10.1016/j.paid.2015.10.024

Mathew, M., & Gupta, K. (2015). Transformational leadership: Emotional intelligence. *SCMS Journal of Indian Management, 12*(2), 75.

Matosic, D., Ntoumanis, N., Boardley, I. D., Sedikides, C., Stewart, B. D., & Chatzisarantis, N. (2017). Narcissism and coach interpersonal style: A self-determination theory perspective. *Scandinavian Journal of Medicine & Science in Sports, 27*(2), 254–261. doi:10.1111ms.12635 PMID:26689999

Mayer, J. D., Caruso, D. R., & Salovey, P. (2016). The ability model of emotional intelligence: Principles and updates. *Emotion Review, 8*(4), 290–300. doi:10.1177/1754073916639667

Mitchell, T. R. (1982). Motivation: New Directions for Theory, Research, and Practice. *Academy of Management Review, 7*(1), 80–88.

Naseem, K. (2018). Job Stress, Happiness and Life Satisfaction: The Moderating Role of Emotional Intelligence Empirical Study in Telecommunication Sector Pakistan. *J. Soc. Sci, 4*(1), 7–14.

Riggio, R. E., & Reichard, R. J. (2008). The emotional and social intelligences of effective leadership: An emotional and social skill approach. *Journal of Managerial Psychology, 23*(2), 169–185. doi:10.1108/02683940810850808

Sachau, D. (2007). Resurrecting the Motivation-Hygiene Theory: Herzberg and the Positive Psychology Movement. *Human Resource Development Review, 6*(4), 377–393. doi:10.1177/1534484307307546

Sala, F. (2000). *Do Programs Designed to Increase Emotional Intelligence at Work - Work?* Retrieved from http://www.eiconsortium.org/reports/do_ei_programs_work.html

Schein, E. H. (1985). *Organizational culture and leadership*. San Francisco: Jossey-Bass Publishers.

Serrat, O. (2017). *Understanding and developing emotional intelligence. In Knowledge Solutions* (pp. 329–339). Springer.

Smigla, J. E., & Pastoria, G. (2000). Emotional Intelligence: Some Have It, Others Can Learn. *The CPA Journal, 70*(6), 60–61.

Sosik, J. J., & Megerian, L. E. (1999). Understanding Leader Emotional Intelligence and Performance. *Group & Organization Management, 24*(3), 367–390. doi:10.1177/1059601199243006

Stiff, J. B. (1987). *Empathy, Communication, and Prosocial Behavior*. Retrieved from http://ezproxy.fiu.edu/login?url=http://search.ebscohost.com/login.aspx?direct=true&db=eric&AN=ED294266&site=eds-live

Van Vugt, M., Jepson, S. F., Hart, C. M., & De Cremer, D. (2004). Autocratic leadership in social dilemmas: A threat to group stability. *Journal of Experimental Social Psychology, 40*(1), 1–13. doi:10.1016/S0022-1031(03)00061-1

Wang, G., & Seibert, S. E. (2015). The impact of leader emotion display frequency on follower performance: Leader surface acting and mean emotion display as boundary conditions. *The Leadership Quarterly, 26*(4), 577–593. doi:10.1016/j.leaqua.2015.05.007

# Compilation of References

A Digital Agenda for Europe. (2010). *COM(2010) 245*. Retrieved from http://ec.europa.eu/information_society/digital-agenda/documents/digital-agenda-communication-en.pdf

Aaker, J., & Smith, A. (2010). *The dragonfly effect: Quick, effective, and powerful ways to use social media to drive social change*. San Francisco, CA: Jossey-Bass.

Agote, L., Aramburu, N., & Lines, R. (2016). Authentic leadership perception, trust in the leader, and followers' emotions in organizational change processes. *The Journal of Applied Behavioral Science*, *52*(1), 35–63. doi:10.1177/0021886315617531

Aguinis, H., & Glavas, A. (2017). On Corporate Social Responsibility, Sensemaking, and the Search for Meaningfulness Through Work. *Journal of Management*.

Akerlof, G. A. (1970). The Market for "Lemons": Quality Uncertainty and the Market Mechanism. *The Quarterly Journal of Economics*, *84*(3), 488–500. doi:10.2307/1879431

Aldridge, J., & Décary-Hétu, D. (2014). Not an "EBay for Drugs": The Cryptomarket "Silk Road" as a Paradigm Shifting Criminal Innovation. *SSRN Electronic Journal*. Retrieved May 12, 2017, from https://papers.ssrn.com/sol3/papers.cfm?abstract_id=2436643

Aluri, A., Slevitch, L., & Larzelere, R. (2015). The effectiveness of embedded social media on hotel websites and the importance of social interactions and return on engagement. *International Journal of Contemporary Hospitality Management*, *27*(4), 670–689. doi:10.1108/IJCHM-09-2013-0415

Anderson, M. H., & Sun, P. Y. T. (2017). Reviewing Leadership Styles: Overlaps and the Need for a New 'Full-Range' Theory. *International Journal of Management Reviews*, *19*(1), 76–96. doi:10.1111/ijmr.12082

Ang, R. P. (2016). Cyberbullying: Its prevention and intervention strategies. In D. Sibnath (Ed.), *Child safety, welfare and well-being: Issues and challenges* (pp. 25–38). Springer. doi:10.1007/978-81-322-2425-9_3

Aoyama, I., Utsumi, S., & Hasegawa, M. (2011). Cyberbullying in Japan: Cases, government reports, adolescent relational aggression and parental monitoring roles. In Q. Li, D. Cross, & P. K. Smith (Eds.), *Bullying in the global playground: Research from an international perspective*. Oxford, UK: Wiley-Blackwell.

Appignanesi, R. (2003). *The end of everything: postmodernism and the vanishing of the human: Lyotard, Haraway, Plato, Heidegger, Habermas, McLuhan*. Cambridge, UK: Icon.

Aricak, T., Siyahhan, S., Uzunhasanoglu, A., Saribeyoglu, S., Ciplak, S., Yilmaz, N., & Memmedov, C. (2008). Cyberbullying among Turkish adolescents. *Cyberpsychology & Behavior*, *11*(3), 253–261. doi:10.1089/cpb.2007.0016 PMID:18537493

Aristotle. (n.d.a). Available at: http://www.perseus.tufts.edu/hopper/text?doc=Perseus%3Atext%3A1999.01.0052%3Abook%3D1%3Asection%3D982a

Aristotle. (n.d.b). *Nicomachean Ethics*. Available at: http://www.perseus.tufts.edu/hopper/text?doc=Perseus%3Atext%3A1999.01.0054%3Abekker+page%3D1094a%3Abekker+line%3D1

Arnett, R. C. (1986). *Communication and community: implications of Martin Buber's dialogue*. Carbondale, IL: Southern Illinois University Press.

Arslan, S., Savaser, S., Hallett, V., & Balci, S. (2012). Cyberbullying among primary school students in Turkey: Self-reported prevalence and associations with home and school life. *Cyberpsychology, Behavior, and Social Networking*, *15*(10), 527–533. doi:10.1089/cyber.2012.0207 PMID:23002988

Atkinson, R. D., & McKay, A. S. (2007). *Digital prosperity: Understanding the economic benefits of the information technology revolution*. The Information Technology and Innovation Foundation. Retrieved from http://www.itif.org/files/digital_prosperity.pdf

Atkinson, T., & Frechette, H. (2009). *Creating a Positive Organizational Climate in a Negative Economic One Improving Organizational Climate to Transform Performance*. Retrieved from http://www. trainingindustry. com/media/2505214/creatingpositiveorgclimate_us_aug09. pdf

Atkinson, J. W. (1964). *An Introduction to Motivation*. Princeton, NJ: Van Nostrand.

Atterton, P., Calarco, M., & Friedman, M. (Eds.). (2004). *Lévinas and Buber: dialogue and difference*. Pittsburgh, PA: Duquesne University Press.

Ayas, T., & Horzum, M. B. (2010). *Cyberbullying / victim scale development study*. Retrieved from: http://www.akademikbakis.org

Ayoko, O. B., Härtel, C. E., & Callan, V. J. (2002). Resolving the puzzle of productive and destructive conflict in culturally heterogeneous workgroups: A communication accommodation theory approach. *International Journal of Conflict Management*, *13*(2), 165–195. doi:10.1108/eb022873

Baek, Y. M., Wojcieszak, M., & Delli Carpini, M. X. (2012). Online versus face-to-face deliberation: Who? Why? What? With what effects? *New Media & Society*, *14*(3), 363–383. doi:10.1177/1461444811413191

Baker, W. E. (2000). *Achieving success through social capital: tapping the hidden resources in your personal and business networks*. San Francisco: Jossey-Bass.

Barbera, M. (2006). Evolution scenario for broadband services. *Proc. 3rd Forum on BB services*.

Barlett, C. P., & Gentile, D. A. (2012). Long-term psychological predictors of cyber-bullying in late adolescence. *Psychology of Popular Media Culture*, *2*, 123–135. doi:10.1037/a0028113

Barlett, C. P., Gentile, D. A., Anderson, C. A., Suzuki, K., Sakamoto, A., Yamaoka, A., & Katsura, R. (2013). Cross-cultural differences in cyberbullying behavior: A short-term longitudinal study. *Journal of Cross-Cultural Psychology*, *45*(2), 300–313. doi:10.1177/0022022113504622

Bar-On, R. (2005). The Bar-On Model of Emotional-Social Intelligence. *Psichothema*, *17*(SI).

Barratt, M. J., Ferris, J. A., & Winstock, A. R. (2014). Use of Silk Road, the Online Drug Marketplace, in the United Kingdom, Australia and the United States: Silk Road Global Survey. *Addiction (Abingdon, England)*, *109*(5), 774–783. doi:10.1111/add.12470 PMID:24372954

Barrett, K. C., & Campos, J. J. (1987). *Perspectives on emotional development II: A functionalist approach to emotions*. Academic Press.

Bass, B. M. (1973). *Leadership, psychology, and organizational behavior*. Westport, CT: Greenwood Press.

Bates, C. (2016). A methodology study of Hersey and Blanchard situational leadership theory. *Int J Adv Eng Technol Manage Appl Sci*, *3*(11), 42–48.

Batson, C. D., & Powell, A. A. (2003). *Altruism and Prosocial Behavior*. In Handbook of Psychology. John Wiley & Sons, Inc. doi:10.1002/0471264385.wei0519

Baudrillard, J. (1981). *Simulacra and Simulation*. University of Michigan Press Michigan.

Baudrillard, J. (1997). *Art and Artefact*. London: Sage.

Bauman, S., Toomey, R. B., & Walker, J. L. (2013). Associations among bullying, cyberbullying, and suicide in high school students. *Journal of Adolescence*, *36*(2), 341–350. doi:10.1016/j.adolescence.2012.12.001 PMID:23332116

Bauman, S., Underwood, M. K., & Card, N. A. (2013). Definitions: Another perspective and a proposal for beginning with cyberaggression. In S. Bauman, D. Cross, & J. Walker (Eds.), *Principles of cyberbullying research: Definitions, measures, methodology* (pp. 26–40). New York, NY: Routledge.

Baumeister, R. F., & Leary, M. R. (1995). The need to belong: Desire for interpersonal attachments as a fundamental human motivation. *Psychological Bulletin*, *117*(3), 497–529. doi:10.1037/0033-2909.117.3.497 PMID:7777651

Bayar, Y., & Ucanok, Z. (2012). School social climate and generalized peer perception in traditional and cyberbullying status. *Educational Sciences: Theory and Practice*, *12*, 2352–2358.

Baym, N., Zhang, Y. B., & Lin, M. C. (2004). Social interactions across media: Interpersonal communication on the Internet, telephone and face-to-face. *New Media & Society*, *6*(3), 41–60. doi:10.1177/1461444804041438

Becker, M. W., Alzahabi, R., & Hopwood, C. J. (2013). Media multitasking is associated with symptoms of depression and social anxiety. *Cyberpsychology, Behavior, and Social Networking*, *16*(2), 132–135. doi:10.1089/cyber.2012.0291 PMID:23126438

Beckman, L., Hagquist, C., & Hellstrom, L. (2012). Does the association with psychosomatic health problems differ between cyberbullying and traditional bullying? *Emotional & Behavioural Difficulties*, *17*(3-4), 421–434. doi:10.1080/13632752.2012.704228

Bennett, K., Reynolds, J., Christensen, H., & Griffiths, K. M. (2010). E-hub: An online self-help mental health service in the community. *The Medical Journal of Australia*, *192*(11), 48–52. PMID:20528710

Bergman, S. H. (1991). *Dialogical philosophy from Kierkegaard to Buber*. Albany, NY: State University of New York Press.

Berman, E. M., & West, J. P. (2008). Managing Emotional Intelligence in U.S. Cities: A Study of Social Skills among Public Managers. *Public Administration Review*, *68*(4), 742–758. doi:10.1111/j.1540-6210.2008.00912.x

Berry, D. L. (1985). *Mutuality: the vision of Martin Buber*. Albany, NY: State University of New York Press.

Bertot, J., Jaeger, P., & Grimes, J. (2010). Using ICTs to create a culture of transparency: Egovernment and social media as openness and anti-corruption tools for societies. *Government Information Quarterly*, *27*(3), 264–271. doi:10.1016/j.giq.2010.03.001

Bertot, J., Jaeger, P., & Hansen, D. (2011). The impact of polices on government social media usage: Issues, challenges, and recommendations. *Government Information Quarterly*. doi:10.1016/j.giq.2011.04.004

Bessiere, K., Kiesler, S., Kraut, R., & Boneva, B. (2008). Effects of Internet use and social resources on changes in depression. *Information Communication and Society*, *11*(1), 47–70. doi:10.1080/13691180701858851

Best, P., Manktelow, R., & Taylor, B. (2014). Online communication, social media and adolescent wellbeing: A systematic narrative review. *Children and Youth Services Review*, *41*, 27–36. doi:10.1016/j.childyouth.2014.03.001

Blight, M. G., Jagiello, K., & Ruppel, E. K. (2015). "Same stuff different day:" A mixed-method study of support seeking on Facebook. *Computers in Human Behavior*, *53*, 366–373. doi:10.1016/j.chb.2015.07.029

Boase, J., Horrigan, J. B., Wellman, B., & Rainie, L. (2006). *The Strength of Internet Ties* (pp. 1–52). Washington, D.C.: Pew Internet & American Life Project.

Bolman, L. G., & Deal, T. E. (2008). *Reframing Organizations: Artistry, Choice, and Leadership* (4th ed.). San Francisco, CA: Jossey-Bass.

Bonanno, R. A., & Hymel, S. (2013). Cyber bullying and internalizing difficulties: Above and beyond the impact of traditional forms of bullying. *Journal of Youth and Adolescence*, *42*(5), 685–697. doi:10.100710964-013-9937-1 PMID:23512485

Borgatti, S. P., & Feld, S. L. (1994). How to test the strength of weak ties theory. *Connections*, *17*(1), 45–46.

Boulton, M., Lloyd, J., Down, J., & Marx, H. (2012). Predicting undergraduates' self-reported engagement in traditional and cyberbullying from attitudes. *Cyberpsychology, Behavior, and Social Networking*, *15*(3), 141–147. doi:10.1089/cyber.2011.0369 PMID:22304402

Bowen, W. G., Chingos, M. M., Lack, K. A., & Nygren, T. I. (2014). Interactive learning online at public universities: Evidence from a six-campus randomized trial. *Journal of Policy Analysis and Management, 33*(1), 94–111. doi:10.1002/pam.21728

Boyd, D., & Ellison, N. (2007). Social network sites: Definition, history, and scholarship. *Journal of Computer-Mediated Communication, 13*(1), 210–230. doi:10.1111/j.1083-6101.2007.00393.x

Brajša-Žganec, A., Kaliterna-Lipovčan, Lj., Prizmić-Larsen, Z., Glavak-Tkalić, R., Sučić, I., Tadić Vujčić, M., . . . Lučić, L. (2017). CRO-WELL: Well-being and life events - preliminary analysis. *Abstract Book - 15th ISQLS Annual Conference.*

Briggs, M. (2009). *Journalism next: A practical guide to digital reporting and publishing.* Washington, DC: CQ Press.

Brighi, A., Guarini, A., Melotti, G., Galli, S., & Genta, M. L. (2012). Predictors of victimisation across direct bullying, indirect bullying and cyberbullying. *Emotional & Behavioural Difficulties, 17*(3-4), 375–388. doi:10.1080/13632752.2012.704684

Brignall, T. W. III, & Valey, T. V. (2005). The impact of Internet communication on social interaction. *Sociological Spectrum, 25*(3), 335–348. doi:10.1080/02732170590925882

Brkljačić, T., & Kaliterna-Lipovčan, L. (2010). Life satisfaction and feeling of happiness among students. *Suvremena Psihologija, 13*(2), 189–201.

Brockelman, T. (2008). *Žižek and Heidegger: the question concerning techno-capitalism Continuum.* London.

Brown, C. (2013). *Are We Becoming More Socially Awkward? An Analysis of the Relationship Between Technological Communication Use and Social Skills in College Students.* Academic Press.

Brown, M. A. Sr. (2017). *Solutions for High-Touch Communications in a High-Tech World.* Hershey, PA: IGI Global. doi:10.4018/978-1-5225-1897-6

Brown, M. A. Sr., (Ed.). (2017a). *Social Media Performance Evaluation and Success Measurements.* Hershey, PA: IGI Global. doi:10.4018/978-1-5225-1963-8

Brown, M. A. Sr, & Schario, T. A. (2014). *Social Media 4EVR: Identifying, Achieving, & Nurturing Social Capital.* Yorktown, VA: CreateSpace Independent Publishing Platform.

Brown, M. Sr. (2013). Social Networking and Individual Perceptions: Examining Predictors of Participation. *Public Organization Review,* 1–20.

Brown, M., & Sr, A. (2018). *Motivationally Intelligent Leadership: Emerging Research and Opportunities*. Hershey, PA: IGI Global. doi:10.4018/978-1-5225-3746-5

Bryant, J. A., Sanders-Jackson, A., & Smallwood, A. K. (2006). IMing, Text Messaging, and Adolescent Social Networks. *Journal of Computer-Mediated Communication*, *11*(2), 577–592. doi:10.1111/j.1083-6101.2006.00028.x

Buber, M. (1947). *Between Man and Man*. Macmillan.

Buber, M. (1952). Images of good and evil (M. Bullock, Trans.). Routledge & Kegan.

*Buber, Martin, The Knowledge of Man*. (1965). London: George Allen & Unwin.

Buber, M. (1970). *I and Thou*. New York: Charles Scribner's Sons.

Buber, M. (1990). *A believing humanism: My testament, 1902-1965* (M. Friedman, Trans.). Atlantic Highlands, NJ: Humanities Press International.

Bureau of Labor Statistics. (2014). *American Time Use Survey*. Retrieved from http://www.bls.gov/tus/

Burke, M., & Kraut, R. (2014). Growing closer on Facebook: Changes in tie strength through site use. *ACM CHI 2014: Conference on Human Factors in Computing Systems*, 4187-4196. 10.1145/2556288.2557094

Burke, M., & Kraut, R. (2016). The relationship between Facebook use and well-being depends on communication type and tie strength. *Journal of Computer-Mediated Communication*, *21*(4), 265–281. doi:10.1111/jcc4.12162

Burton, K. A., Florell, D., & Wygant, D. B. (2013). The role of peer attachment and normative beliefs about aggression on traditional bullying and cyberbullying. *Psychology in the Schools*, *50*(2), 103–114. doi:10.1002/pits.21663

Buxton, J., & Bingham, T. (2015). The Rise and Challenge of Dark Net Drug Markets. *Policy Brief*, *7*. Retrieved from http://www.drugsandalcohol.ie/23274/1/Darknet%20Markets.pdf

Cabral, L. (2012). Reputation on the Internet. In M. Peitz & J. Waldfogel (Eds.), *The Oxford Handbook of the Digital Economy* (pp. 344–354). Oxford, UK: Oxford University Press.

Calani, M., Baranauskas, C., Liu, K., & Sun, L. (Eds.). (2016). *Socially Aware Organisations and Technologies. Impact and Challenges: 17th IFIP WG 8.1 International Conference on Informatics and Semiotics in Organisations, ICISO 2016, Campinas, Brazil, August 1-3, 2016, Proceedings*. Springer International Publishing.

Campbell, J. P., Dunnette, M. D., Lawler, E. E. III, & Weick, K. E. Jr. (1970). *Managerial Behavior, Performance and Effectiveness*. New York: McGraw-Hill.

Campos, J. J., Campos, R. G., & Barrett, K. C. (1989). Emergent themes in the study of emotional development and emotion regulation. *Developmental Psychology*, *25*(3), 394–402. doi:10.1037/0012-1649.25.3.394

Caplan, S. E. (2003). Preference for online social interaction: A theory of problematic internet use and psychosocial well-being. *Communication Research*, *30*(6), 625–648. doi:10.1177/0093650203257842

Cappadocia, M. C., Craig, W. M., & Pepler, D. (2013). Cyberbullying: Prevalence, stability and risk factors during adolescence. *Canadian Journal of School Psychology*, *28*(2), 171–192. doi:10.1177/0829573513491212

Carr, A. (2004). *Positive psychology: The science of happiness and human strengths*. Hove: Brunner-Routledge.

Carter & Fuller. (2015). *Symbolic interactionism*. Academic Press.

Cassidy, W., Brown, K., & Jackson, M. (2012a). "Making kind cool": Parents' suggestions for preventing cyber bullying and fostering cyber kindness. *Journal of Educational Computing Research*, *46*(4), 415–436. doi:10.2190/EC.46.4.f

Cassidy, W., Brown, K., & Jackson, M. (2012b). "Under the radar": Educators and cyberbullying in schools. *School Psychology International*, *33*(5), 520–532. doi:10.1177/0143034312445245

Caudron, S. (1999). The Hard Case for Soft Skills. *Workforce*, *78*(7), 60–66.

Caulkins, J., & Reuter, P. (2010). How Drug Enforcement Affects Drug Prices. *Crime and Justice*, *39*(1), 213–271. doi:10.1086/652386

Celestini, A., Me, G., & Mignone, M. (2016). Tor Marketplaces Exploratory Data Analysis: The Drugs Case. In H. Jahankhani, A. Carlile, D. Emm, A. Hosseinian-Far, G. Brown, G. Sexton, & A. Jamal (Eds.), *Global Security, Safety and Sustainability - The Security Challenges of the Connected World* (Vol. 630, pp. 218–229). Cham: Springer International Publishing. doi:10.1007/978-3-319-51064-4_18

Ceric, A. (2015). Bringing together evaluation and management of ICT value: A systems theory approach. *The Electronic Journal of Information Systems Evaluation*, *18*(1), 19–35.

Chaffey, D. (n.d.). *Global social media research summary 2017*. Available at: http://www.smartinsights.com/social-media-marketing/social-media-strategy/new-global-social-media-research/

Chen, A. (2011). The Underground Website Where You Can Buy Any Drug Imaginable. *Gawker*. Retrieved May 8, 2017, from http://gawker.com/the-underground-website-where-you-can-buy-any-drug-imag-30818160

Cherniss, C., & Goleman, D. (2001). *The Emotionally Intelligence Workplace: How to Select for, Measure, and Improve Emotional Intelligence in Individuals, Groups, and Organizations*. San Francisco: Jossey-Bass.

Cheung, F., & Lucas, R. E. (2014). Assessing the validity of single-item life satisfaction measures: Results from three large samples. *Quality of Life Research: An International Journal of Quality of Life Aspects of Treatment, Care and Rehabilitation*, *23*(10), 2809–2818. doi:10.100711136-014-0726-4 PMID:24890827

Christin, N. (2013). Traveling the Silk Road: A Measurement Analysis of a Large Anonymous Online Marketplace. In *Proceedings of the 22nd International Conference on World Wide Web* (pp. 213–224). ACM. Retrieved May 8, 2017, from http://dl.acm.org/citation.cfm?id=2488408

Cooper, R. K. (1997). Applying Emotional Intelligence in the Workplace. *Training & Development*, *51*(12), 31–38.

Cooper, S. (2002). *Technoculture and critical theory: In the service of the machine*. London: Routledge. doi:10.4324/9780203167021

Corazza, G. (2008). Who can bridge the information divide? *Proc. UNIC Workshop*.

Corcoran, L., Connolly, I., & O'Moore, M. (2012). Cyberbullying in Irish schools: An investigation of personality and self-concept. *The Irish Journal of Psychology*, *33*(4), 153–165. doi:10.1080/03033910.2012.677995

Cowan, J. E., & Menchaca, M. P. (2014). Investigating value creation in a community of practice with social network analysis in a hybrid online graduate education program. *Distance Education*, *35*(1), 43–74. doi:10.1080/01587919.2014.893813

Crossley, N. (1996). *Intersubjectivity: the fabric of social becoming*. London: Sage.

Cummings, J. N., Butler, B., & Kraut, R. (2002). The quality of online social relationships. *Communications of the ACM*, *47*(7), 103–108. doi:10.1145/514236.514242

Curelaru, M., Iacob, I., & Abalasei, B. (2009). *School bullying: Definition, characteristics, and intervention strategies*. Lumean Publishing House.

Darcin, A. E., Noyan, C., Nurmedov, S., Yilmaz, O., & Dilbaz, N. (2016). Smartphone addiction in relation with social anxiety and loneliness among university students in Turkey. *Behaviour & Information Technology*, *35*(7), 520–525. doi:10.1080/0144929X.2016.1158319

Dark Web News. (2017). *Darknet Markets*. Retrieved May 7, 2017, from https://darkwebnews.com/market-comparison-chart/

Davison, P. (2012). The language of internet memes. In M. Mandiberg (Ed.), *The social media reader* (pp. 120–134). New York University Press.

Dawes, S., Cresswell, A., & Pardo, T. (2009). From "need to know" to "need to share": Tangled problems, information boundaries, and the building of public sector knowledge networks. *Public Administration Review*, *69*(3), 63–84. doi:10.1111/j.1540-6210.2009.01987_2.x

De Hoogh, A. H., Greer, L. L., & Den Hartog, D. N. (2015). Diabolical dictators or capable commanders? An investigation of the differential effects of autocratic leadership on team performance. *The Leadership Quarterly*, *26*(5), 687–701. doi:10.1016/j.leaqua.2015.01.001

Dearborn, K. (2002). Studies in Emotional Intelligence Redefine Our Approach to Leadership Development. *Public Personnel Management*, *31*(4), 523–530. doi:10.1177/009102600203100408

Dehue, F., Bolman, C., & Vollink, T. (2008). Cyberbullying: Youngsters' experiences and parental perception. *CyberPscyhology & Behavior*, *11*(2), 217–223. doi:10.1089/cpb.2007.0008 PMID:18422417

Dehue, F., Bolman, C., Vollink, T., & Pouwelse, M. (2012). Cyberbullying and traditional bullying in relation to adolescents' perceptions of parenting. *Journal of Cyber Therapy and Rehabilitation*, *5*, 25–34.

deLara, E. W. (2012). Why adolescents don't disclose incidents of bullying and harassment. *Journal of School Violence*, *11*(4), 288–305. doi:10.1080/15388220.2012.705931

Dellarocas, C. (2002). Goodwill Hunting: An Economically Efficient Online Feedback Mechanism for Environments with Variable Product Quality. In J. Padget, O. Shehory, D. Parkes, N. Sadeh, & W. E. Walsh (Eds.), *Agent-Mediated Electronic Commerce IV. Designing Mechanisms and Systems* (pp. 238–252). Berlin: Springer Berlin Heidelberg. doi:10.1007/3-540-36378-5_15

Den Hartog, D. N., & Belschak, F. D. (2016). Leadership and employee proactivity. *Proactivity at Work: Making Things Happen in Organizations*, 411.

Denhardt, J. V., & Denhardt, R. B. (2007). *The new public service: Serving, not steering*. ME Sharpe.

Department of Justice. (2017). *AlphaBay, the Largest Online "Dark Market," Shut Down.* Retrieved November 8, 2017, from https://www.justice.gov/opa/pr/alphabay-largest-online-dark-market-shut-down

Diamanduros, T., & Downs, E. (2011). Creating a safe school environment: How to prevent cyberbullying at your school. *Library Media Connection, 30*(2), 36–38.

Diamond, M. L., & Buber, M. (1960). *Jewish existentalist.* New York: Oxford University Press.

Diener, E., Pressman, S. D., Hunter, J., & Delgadillo-Chase, D. (2017). If, Why, and When Subjective Well-Being Influences Health, and Future Needed Research. *Applied Psychology. Health and Well-Being, 9*(2), 133–167. doi:10.1111/aphw.12090 PMID:28707767

Diener, E., & Seligman, M. E. (2002). Very happy people. *Psychological Science, 13*(1), 81–84. doi:10.1111/1467-9280.00415 PMID:11894851

Diener, E., Suh, E. M., Lucas, R. E., & Smith, H. L. (1999). Subjective well-being: Three decades of progress. *Psychological Bulletin, 12*(2), 276–302. doi:10.1037/0033-2909.125.2.276

Dienlin, T., Masur, P., & Trepte, S. (2017). Reinforcement or displacement? The reciprocity of FtF, IM, and SNS communication and their effects on loneliness and life satisfaction. *Journal of Computer-Mediated Communication, 22*(2), 71–87. doi:10.1111/jcc4.12183

Dingwall, K., Puszka, S., Sweet, M., & Tricia Nagel, T. (2015). Like drawing into sand: Acceptability, feasibility, and appropriateness of a new e-mental health resource for service providers working with Aboriginal and Torres Strait Islander people. *Australian Psychologist, 50*(1), 60–69. doi:10.1111/ap.12100

Documents, P. (2009). Transparency and open government: Memorandum for the heads of executive departments and agencies. *Federal Register, 74*(15), 4685–4686. Retrieved from http://edocket.access.gpo.gov/2009/pdf/E9-1777.pdf

Dolliver, D. S. (2015). Evaluating Drug Trafficking on the Tor Network: Silk Road 2, the Sequel. *The International Journal on Drug Policy, 26*(11), 1113–1123. doi:10.1016/j.drugpo.2015.01.008 PMID:25681266

Dolliver, D. S., & Kenney, J. L. (2016). Characteristics of Drug Vendors on the Tor Network: A Cryptomarket Comparison. *Victims & Offenders, 11*(4), 600–620. doi:10.1080/15564886.2016.1173158

Draper, J. W. (1875). *History of the conflict between religion and science* (Vol. 13). New York: D. Appleton.

Druskat, U., & Wolff, S. (2001). Building the Emotional Intelligence of Groups. *Harvard Business Review*, *79*(3), 81–90. PMID:11246926

Duxbury, S. W., & Haynie, D. L. (2017). The Network Structure of Opioid Distribution on a Darknet Cryptomarket. *Journal of Quantitative Criminology*. doi:10.100710940-017-9359-4

Eden, S., Heiman, T., & Olenik-Shemesh, D. (2013). Teachers' perceptions, beliefs and concerns about cyberbullying. *British Journal of Educational Technology*, *44*(6), 1036–1052. doi:10.1111/j.1467-8535.2012.01363.x

Eisenbeiss, S. A., & Knippenberg, D. (2015). On ethical leadership impact: The role of follower mindfulness and moral emotions. *Journal of Organizational Behavior*, *36*(2), 182–195. doi:10.1002/job.1968

Ekman, P. (2004). *Emotions Revealed: Recognizing Faces and Feelings to Improve Communication and Emotional Life*. New York: Henry Holt.

Elledge, L. C., Williford, A., Boulton, A. J., DePaolis, K. J., Little, T. D., & Salmivalli, C. (2013). Individual and contextual predictors of cyberbullying: The influence of children's provictim attitudes and teachers' ability to intervene. *Journal of Youth and Adolescence*, *42*(5), 698–710. doi:10.100710964-013-9920-x PMID:23371005

Ellison, N. B., Vitak, J., Gray, R., & Lampe, C. (2014). Cultivating social resources on social network sites: Facebook relationship maintenance behaviors and their role in social capital processes. *Journal of Computer-Mediated Communication*, *19*(4), 855–870. doi:10.1111/jcc4.12078

Emerson, S., Menkus, R., & Van Ness, K. (2011). *The Public Administrator's Companion: A Practical Guide*. Washington, DC: CQ Press.

Erdur-Baker, O. (2010). Cyberbullying and its correlation to traditional bullying, gender and frequent and risky usage of internet-mediated communication tools. *New Media & Society*, *12*(1), 109–125. doi:10.1177/1461444809341260

EU policies. (2007). *Bridging the 'digital divide': EU policies*. Retrieved from http://www.euractiv.com/en/infosociety/bridging-digital-divide-eu-policies/article-132315

Evans, L. (2015). *Locative social media: place in the digital age*. Basingstoke, UK: Palgrave Macmillan. doi:10.1057/9781137456113

Fallows, D. (2004). *The Internet and daily life: Many Americans use the Internet in everyday activities, but traditional offline habits skill dominate.* Retrieved August 26, 2008, from http://www.pewInternet.org/pdfs/pip_college_report.pdf

Fanti, K. A., Demetriou, A. G., & Hawa, V. V. (2012). A longitudinal study of cyberbullying: Examining risk and protective factors. *European Journal of Developmental Psychology*, *8*(2), 168–181. doi:10.1080/17405629.2011.643169

Farahani, H. A., Kazemi, Z., Aghamohamadi, S., Bakhtiarvand, F., & Ansari, M. (2011). Examining mental health indices in students using Facebook in Iran. *Procedia: Social and Behavioral Sciences*, *28*, 811–814. doi:10.1016/j.sbspro.2011.11.148

Feng, X. L., & Campbell, A. (2011). Understanding e-mental health resources: Personality, awareness, utilization, and effectiveness of e-mental health resources amongst youth. *Journal of Technology in Human Services, 29*, 101–119. doi:10.1080/15228835.2011.595276

Fernandez, S., & Rainey, H. (2006). Managing successful organizational change in the public sector. *Public Administration Review*, *66*(2), 168–176. doi:10.1111/j.1540-6210.2006.00570.x

Festl, R., Schwarkow, M., & Quandt, T. (2013). Peer influence, internet use and cyberbullying: A comparison of different context effects among German adolescents. *Journal of Children and Media*, *7*(4), 446–462. doi:10.1080/17482798.2013.781514

Forsman, A. K., & Nordmyr, J. (2017). Psychosocial links between internet use and mental health in later life: A systematic review of quantitative and qualitative evidence. *Journal of Applied Gerontology*, *36*(12), 1471–1518. doi:10.1177/0733464815595509 PMID:26245208

Fox-Brewster, T. (2015, April 1). Tor Hidden Services and Drug Markets Are Under Attack, But Help Is on The Way. *Forbes*. Retrieved May 7, 2017, from https://www.forbes.com/sites/thomasbrewster/2015/04/01/tor-hidden-services-under-dos-attack/#758e66fb758e

Franklin, M. I. (2011). Decolonising the future: Not to go where cyborgs have gone before? In *Interoperabel Nederland* (pp. 23–41). Den Haag, the Netherlands: Dutch Ministry of Economic Affairs. Retrieved from http://www.forumstandaardisatie.nl/fileadmin/os/publicaties/01.1_Franklin.pdf

Franzen, A. (2000). Does the Internet Make Us Lonely. *European Sociological Review*, *16*(4), 427–438. doi:10.1093/esr/16.4.427

Friedman, M. S., & Buber, M. (1976). The life of dialogue. University of Chicago Press.

Frijda, N. H. (1986). *The emotions*. Cambridge University Press.

Gallardo-Echenique, E., Bullen, M., & Marqués-Molias, L. (2016). Student communication and study habits of first-year university students in the digital era. *Canadian Journal of Learning and Technology, 42*(1), 2–21. doi:10.21432/T2D047

Gallois, C., & Giles, H. (2015). *Communication Accommodation Theory. In The International Encyclopedia of Language and Social Interaction*. John Wiley & Sons, Inc.

Gallois, C., & Giles, H. (2015). *Communication Accommodation Theory. The International Encyclopedia of Language and Social Interaction*. John Wiley & Sons, Inc.

GAO. (2011). *Social Media: Federal Agencies Need Policies and Procedures for Managing and Protecting Information They Access and Disseminate* (Report to Congressional Requesters). United States Government Accountability Office (GAO). Retrieved from http://www.gao.gov/new.items/d11605.pdf

Gheorghiță & Pădurețu. (2014). Social Networks And Interpersonal Communication. *System, 2*(3), 5.

Giles, H. (2008). *Communication accommodation theory*. Sage Publications, Inc. doi:10.1002/9781405186407.wbiecc067

Ginesi, A. (2008). ESA initiatives on the digital divide. *Proc. UNIC Workshop*.

Goebert, D., Else, I., Matsu, C., Chung-Do, J., & Chang, J. Y. (2011). The impact of cyberbullying on substance use and mental health in a multiethnic sample. *Maternal and Child Health Journal, 15*(8), 1282–1286. doi:10.100710995-010-0672-x PMID:20824318

Goldsmith, S., & Eggers, W. D. (2004). *Governing by Network: The New Shape of the Public Sector*. Washington, DC: Brookings Institute Press.

Goleman, D. (1995). *Emotional Intelligence*. New York: Bantam.

Goleman, D. (1998). The emotional intelligence of leaders. *Leader to Leader*, (10): 21–22.

Goleman, D. (1998a). *Working with Emotional Intelligence*. New York: Bantam.

Goleman, D. (2006). *Social Intelligence*. New York: Bantam.

Goleman, D. (Ed.). (2001). *The Emotionally Intelligent Workplace* (Vol. 27-44). San Francisco: Jossey-Bass.

Gollnick, C., & Wilson, E. (2016). *Separating Fact from Fiction: The Truth About the Dark Web*. Baltimore, MD: Terbium Labs.

Goodman-Deane, J. A., Mieczakowski, A., Johnson, D., Goldhaber, T., & Clarkson, P. J. (2015). The impact of communication technologies on life and relationship satisfaction. *Computers in Human Behavior*, *57*, 219–229. doi:10.1016/j.chb.2015.11.053

Gore, A. (2007). *The Assault on Reason*. New York, NY: Penguin Books.

Gradinger, P., Strohmeier, D., & Spiel, C. (2009). Traditional bullying and cyberbullying. *The Journal of Psychology*, *217*, 205–213.

Greenberg, A. (2014, November 7). Global Web Crackdown Arrests 17, Seizes Hundreds of Dark Net Domains. *Wired*. Retrieved May 7, 2017, from https://www.wired.com/2014/11/operation-onymous-dark-web-arrests/

Greenberg, A. (2013, August 13). An Interview with A Digital Drug Lord: The Silk Road's Dread Pirate Roberts. *Forbes*.

Greene, S. (2001). Astride the digital divide. *The Chronicle of Philanthropy.*, *13*(6), 18–19.

Griffith, J., Connelly, S., Thiel, C., & Johnson, G. (2015). How outstanding leaders lead with affect: An examination of charismatic, ideological, and pragmatic leaders. *The Leadership Quarterly*, *26*(4), 502–517. doi:10.1016/j.leaqua.2015.03.004

Grigenti, F. (2016). *Existence and Machine: The German Philosophy in the Age of Machines (1870-1960)*. Cham: Springer International Publishing. doi:10.1007/978-3-319-45366-8

Grigg, D. W. (2012). Definitional constructs of cyberbullying and cyber aggression from a triangulatory overview: A preliminary study into elements. *Journal of Aggression, Conflict and Peace Research*, *4*(4), 202–215. doi:10.1108/17596591211270699

Grönlund, A., & Horan, T. A. (2004). Introducing e-gov: History, definitions, and issues. *Communications of the Association for Information Systems*, *15*, 713–729. Retrieved from http://www.cips.org.in/public-sector-systems-governmentinnovations/documents/Introducing_e_governance.pdf

Gross, E. F. (2004). Adolescent Internet use: What we expect, what teens report. *Journal of Applied Developmental Psychology*, *25*(6), 633–649. doi:10.1016/j.appdev.2004.09.005

Gross, E. F., Juvenon, J., & Gable, S. L. (2002). Internet use and well-being in adolescence. *The Journal of Social Issues*, *58*(1), 75–90. doi:10.1111/1540-4560.00249

Gupta, M. (2006). User needs for broadband in Europe. *Proc. BReATH Conf.*

Gupta, A., Lamba, H., Kumaraguru, P., & Joshi, A. (2013, May). Faking Sandy: characterizing and identifying fake images on Twitter during Hurricane Sandy. In *Proceedings of the 22nd international conference on World Wide Web companion* (pp. 729-736). International World Wide Web Conferences Steering Committee. 10.1145/2487788.2488033

Guzley, R. M. (1992). Organizational climate and communication climate predictors of commitment to the organization. *Management Communication Quarterly*, *5*(4), 379–402. doi:10.1177/0893318992005004001

Habermas, J. (2003). *The future of human nature*. Cambridge, UK: Polity Press.

Hager, C. (2013). Crisis informatics: Perspectives of trust – is social media a mixed blessing? *Student Research Journal*, *2*(2). Retrieved from http://scholarworks.sjsu.edu/slissrj/vol2/iss2/2

Hall, R. H. (2016) Internet Use and Happiness. *Third International Conference on HCI in Business, Government and Organizations: eCommerce and Innovation*, 37-45.

Hardy, R. A., & Norgaard, J. R. (2016). Reputation in the Internet Black Market: An Empirical and Theoretical Analysis of the Deep Web. *Journal of Institutional Economics*, *12*(03), 515–539. doi:10.1017/S1744137415000454

Harman, G. (2002). *Tool-being: Heidegger and the metaphysics of objects*. Chicago: Open Court.

Hartup, W. W., & Stevens, N. (1999). Friendships and adaptation across the life span. *Current Directions in Psychological Science*, *8*(3), 76–79. doi:10.1111/1467-8721.00018

Hawkley, L. C., & Cacioppo, J. T. (2010). Loneliness matters: A theoretical and empirical review of consequences and mechanisms. *Annals of Behavioral Medicine*, *40*(2), . 10.1007/s12160–010–9210–8

Heidegger, M. (1955). *What is Philosophy?* New Haven, CT: College and University Press.

Heidegger, M. (1966). *Discourse on thinking, a translation of Gelassenheit by John M. Anderson and E. Hans Freund*. New York: Harper & Row.

Heidegger, M. (1967). *What is a thing? Translated by W.B. Barton and Dera Deutsch.* Chicago: Regnery.

Heidegger, M. (1971). *Poetry, language, thought, translations by Albert Hofstadter.* New York: Harper & Row.

Heidegger, M. (1973). *The End of Philosophy.* Chicago: University of Chicago Press.

Heidegger, M. (1976a). *The piety of thinking: essays, translations, notes and commentary by James G. Hart and John C. Maraldo.* Bloomington, IN: Indiana University Press.

Heidegger, M. (1976b). *What is called thinking?* New York: Perennial Library.

Heidegger, M. (1982). *On the way to language* (D. Peter, Trans.). San Francisco: Hertz Harper & Row.

Heidegger, M. (1984). *Early Greek thinking* (D. F. Krell & F. A. Capuzzi, Trans.). San Francisco: Harper & Row.

Heidegger, M. (1998). *Pathmarks* (W. McNeill, Ed.). Cambridge, UK: Cambridge University Press. doi:10.1017/CBO9780511812637

Heidegger, M. (2002a). *The essence of human freedom: an introduction to philosophy* (T. Sadler, Trans.). London: Continuum.

Heidegger, M. (2002b). *The essence of truth: on Plato's cave allegory and Theaetetus* (T. Sadler, Trans.). London: Continuum.

Heidegger, M. (2013). *The event* (R. Rojcewicz, Trans.). Bloomington, IN: Indiana University Press.

Heidegger, M. (2016). *Ponderings: black notebooks 1931-1938. II-VI* (R. Rojcewicz, Trans.). Bloomington, IN: Indiana University Press.

Heidegger, M. (2017). *Ponderings. VII-XI, 1938-1939: Black notebooks* (R. Rojcewicz, Trans.). Bloomington, IN: Indiana University Press.

Heim, M. (1993). *The metaphysics of virtual reality.* New York: Oxford University Press.

Herzberg, F. (1959). *The motivation to work.* New York: Wiley.

Herzberg, F. (1966). *Work and the nature of man.* Cleveland, OH: World Pub. Co.

Hinduja, S., & Patchin, J. W. (2007). Offline consequences of online victimization. *Journal of School Violence*, *6*(3), 89–112. doi:10.1300/J202v06n03_06

Hinduja, S., & Patchin, J. W. (2012). Cyberbullying: Neither and epidemic nor a rarity. *European Journal of Developmental Psychology*, *9*(5), 539–543. doi:10.10 80/17405629.2012.706448

Hinduja, S., & Patchin, J. W. (2013). Social influences on cyberbullying behaviors among middle and high school students. *Journal of Youth and Adolescence*, *42*(5), 711–722. doi:10.100710964-012-9902-4 PMID:23296318

Holt-Lunstad, J., Smith, T. B., & Layton, J. B. (2010). Social relationships and mortality risk: A meta-analytic review. *PLoS Medicine*, *7*(7), e1000316. doi:10.1371/journal.pmed.1000316 PMID:20668659

Holt, S., Marques, J., Hu, J., & Wood, A. (2017). Cultivating empathy: New perspectives on educating business leaders. *The Journal of Values Based Leadership*, *10*(1), 3. doi:10.22543/0733.101.1173

Holt, T. J., & Lampke, E. (2010). Exploring Stolen Data Markets Online: Products and Market Forces. *Criminal Justice Studies*, *23*(1), 33–50. doi:10.1080/14786011003634415

Holtz, B. C. (2015). From First Impression to Fairness Perception: Investigating the Impact of Initial Trustworthiness Beliefs. *Personnel Psychology*, *68*(3), 499–546. doi:10.1111/peps.12092

Hood, C., & Lodge, M. (2004). Competency, Bureaucracy, and Public Management Reform: A Competency Analysis. *Governance: An International Journal of Policy, Administration and Institutions*, *17*(3), 313–333. doi:10.1111/j.0952-1895.2004.00248.x

Horrigan, J.B. (2008). *Home broadband adoption 2008*. PEW/Internet Project Report.

Howard, A. (2011). 2011 Gov 2.0 year in review: A look at the Gov 2.0 themes, moments and achievements that made an impact in 2011. *O'Reilly Radar*. Retrieved from http://radar.oreilly.com/2011/12/2011-gov2-year-in-review.html

HowTo.Gov. (2012). *Content management systems used by government agencies*. Retrieved from http://www.howto.gov/tech-solutions/agency-cms-products

Huang, Y., & Chou, C. (2010). An analysis of multiple factors of cyberbullying among junior high school students in Taiwan. *Computers in Human Behavior*, *26*(6), 1581–1590. doi:10.1016/j.chb.2010.06.005

Hughes, J. (2005). Bringing Emotion to Work: Emotional Intelligence, Employee Resistance and the Reinvention of Character. *Work, Employment and Society*, *19*(3), 603–625. doi:10.1177/0950017005055675

Hulicki, Z. (2008a). Drives and barriers for development of broadband access. In *Proc. Summer School TSIofTNE*. University of Alcala.

Hulicki, Z. (2008b). Digital divide – a myth or real challenges. In *Proc. EuroFGI workshop on socio-economic aspects of FGI*. BTH.

Hulicki, Z. (2016). Telecommunications in Poland. Infrastructure, market and services. *Australian Journal of Telecommunications and the Digital Economy, 4*(3).

Huse, E. F., & Bowditch, J. L. (1977). *Behavior in Organizations: A Systems Approach to Managing*. Reading, MA: Addison-Wesley.

Huy, Q. N. (1999). Emotional Capability, Emotional Intelligence, and Radical Change. *Academy of Management Review, 24*(2), 325–345.

Ihde, D. (2010). *Heidegger's technologies: postphenomenological perspectives*. Fordham University Press.

Internet World Stats. (2017). *Internet usage statistics. The Internet Big Picture World Internet Users and 2017 Population Stats*. Retrieved November 2017: http://www.internetworldstats.com/stats.htm

Iqbal, N., Anwar, S., & Haider, N. (2015). Effect of leadership style on employee performance. *Arabian Journal of Business and Management Review, 5*(5).

Jaggars, S. S. (2014). Choosing Between Online and Face-to-Face Courses: Community College Student Voices. *American Journal of Distance Education, 28*(1), 27–38. doi:10.1080/08923647.2014.867697

Janetos, N., & Tilly, J. (2017). *Reputation Dynamics in a Market for Illicit Drugs*. Retrieved May 7, 2017, from https://arxiv.org/abs/1703.01937

Jang, H., Song, J., & Kim, R. (2014). Does the offline bully-victimization influence cyberbullying behavior among youths? Application of general strain theory. *Computers in Human Behavior, 31*, 85–93. doi:10.1016/j.chb.2013.10.007

Jaspers, K. (1955). *Reason and Existenz*. New York: Noonday Press.

Jelfs, A., & Richardson, J. T. E. (2012). The use of digital technologies across the adult life span in distance education. *British Journal of Educational Technology, 44*(2), 338–351. doi:10.1111/j.1467-8535.2012.01308.x

Jones, L., Woodhouse, D., & Rowe, J. (2007). Effective nurse parent communication: A study of parents' perceptions in the NICU environment. *Patient Education and Counseling, 69*(1), 206–212. doi:10.1016/j.pec.2007.08.014 PMID:17936549

Jordan, P. J., & Lindebaum, D. (2015). A model of within person variation in leadership: Emotion regulation and scripts as predictors of situationally appropriate leadership. *The Leadership Quarterly*, *26*(4), 594–605. doi:10.1016/j.leaqua.2015.05.004

Joshua, G. (2015, April 20). *Interview with AlphaBay Market Admin*. Retrieved May 8, 2017, from https://www.deepdotweb.com/2015/04/20/interview-with-alphabay-admin/

Kaliterna Lipovčan, Lj., Babarović, T., Brajša-Žganec, A., & Bejaković, P., & Japec, L. (2016). Trendovi u kvaliteti života Hrvatska: 2007. – 2012. s naglaskom na subjektivno blagostanje. *Radno pravo*, *11*(9), 69–75.

Kang, M., & Sung, M. (2017). How symmetrical employee communication leads to employee engagement and positive employee communication behaviors: The mediation of employee-organization relationships. *Journal of Communication Management*, *21*(1), 82–102. doi:10.1108/JCOM-04-2016-0026

Kast, E. F., & Rosenzweig, J. E. (1979). *Organization and Management: A Systems Approach*. New York: McGraw-Hill.

Keating, C. (2016). The life and times of nonverbal communication theory and research: Past, present, and future. APA handbook of nonverbal communication, 17-42.

Klischewski, R., & Abubakr, R. (2010). Can e-Government adopters benefit from a technologyfirst approach? The case of Egypt embarking on service-oriented architecture. *43rd Hawaii International Conference on System Sciences*, 1-10.

Knapp, M. L. (1983). *Interpersonal communication and human relationships*. Boston: Allyn and Bacon.

Kochenderfer-Ladd, B., & Pelletier, M. (2008). Teachers' views and beliefs about bullying: Influences on classroom management strategies and students' coping with peer victimization. *Journal of School Psychology*, *46*(4), 431–453. doi:10.1016/j.jsp.2007.07.005 PMID:19083367

Korman, A. K. (1974). *The Psychology of Motivation*. Englewood Cliffs, NJ: Prentice-Hall.

Koshuta, J. (2017). *What is physical health?* Retrieved June 2, 2017, from www.study.com

Kotlarski, M. (2006). Effects of the telecom market regulations. *Proc. 3rd Forum on BB services*.

Kowalski, R. M., & Limber, S. P. (2007). Electronic bullying among middle school students. *The Journal of Adolescent Health*, *41*(6), 22–30. doi:10.1016/j.jadohealth.2007.08.017 PMID:18047942

Kramer, M. W. (2015). *Uncertainty and Communication in Organizations*. In The *International Encyclopedia of Interpersonal Communication*. John Wiley & Sons, Inc.

Kraut, R., & Burke, M. (2015). Internet use and psychological well-being: Effects of activity and audience. *Communications of the ACM*, *58*(12), 94–100. doi:10.1145/2739043

Kraut, R., Kiesler, S., Boneva, B., Cummings, J. N., Helgeson, V., & Crawford, A. (2002). The Internet paradox revisited. *The Journal of Social Issues*, *58*(1), 49–74. doi:10.1111/1540-4560.00248

Kroker, A. (2004). *The will to technology and the culture of nihilism: Heidegger, Nietzsche and Marx*. Toronto: University of Toronto Press.

Kruger, L., & Gilroy, A. (April 12, 2011). *Broadband Internet Access and the Digital Divide: Federal Assistance Programs* (Report Prepared for Members of Congress). Congressional Research Service. 7-5700. RL30719.

Kuchar, A. (2006). Broadband development in the Czech and Slovak Republics. *Proc. BReATH Conf.*

Kurczy, S. (2010). Is internet access a human right? *The Christian Science Monitor*. Retrieved from http://www.csmonitor.com/World/Global-News/2010/0309/Is-Internet-access-a-human-right-Top-10-nations-that-say-yes

Kwan, G. C. E., & Skoric, M. M. (2013). Facebook bullying: An extension of battles in school. *Computers in Human Behavior*, *29*(1), 16–25. doi:10.1016/j.chb.2012.07.014

La Rue, F. (2011). *Report of the Special Rapporteur on the promotion and protection of the right to freedom of opinion and expression*. Human Rights Council; United Nations General Assembly. 17th session: Agenda Item 3. A/HRC/17/27. Retrieved from http://www2.ohchr.org/english/bodies/hrcouncil/docs/17session/A.HRC.17.27_en.pdf

Lack, A. (2014). *Martin Heidegger on technology, ecology, and the arts*. Basingstoke, UK: Palgrave Pivot. doi:10.1057/9781137487452

Laftman, S. B., Modin, B., & Ostberg, V. (2013). Cyberbullying and subjective health: A large-scale study of students in Stockholm, Sweden. *Children and Youth Services Review*, *35*(1), 112–119. doi:10.1016/j.childyouth.2012.10.020

Lam, W. (2005). Barriers to e-government integration. *Journal of Enterprise Information Management*, *18*(5/6), 511–530. doi:10.1108/17410390510623981

Larson, R., Mannell, R., & Zuzanek, J. (1986). Daily well-being of older adults with friends and family. *Psychology and Aging*, *1*(2), 117–126. doi:10.1037/0882-7974.1.2.117 PMID:3267387

Lawson, C. (2017). *Technology and isolation.* Cambridge, UK: Cambridge University Press. doi:10.1017/9781316848319

Lazuras, L., Barkoukis, V., Ourda, D., & Tsorbatzoudis, H. (2013). A process model of cyberbullying in adolescence. *Computers in Human Behavior*, *29*(3), 881–887. doi:10.1016/j.chb.2012.12.015

Lee, P. S. N., Leung, L., Lo, V., Xiong, C., & Wu, T. (2011). Internet communication versus face-to-face interaction in quality of life. *Social Indicators Research*, *100*(3), 375–389. doi:10.100711205-010-9618-3

Lee, S., Tam, C. L., & Chie, Q. T. (2013). *Mobile phone usage preferences: the contributing factors of personality, social anxiety and loneliness.* Springer. doi:10.100711205-013-0460-2

Leighninger, M. (2011). Citizenship and governance in a wild, wired world: How should citizens and public managers use online tools to improve democracy? *National Civic Review*, *100*(2), 20–29. doi:10.1002/ncr.20056

Leinonen, P., Järvelä, S., & Häkkinen, P. (2005). Conceptualizing the Awareness of Collaboration: A Qualitative Study of a Global Virtual Team. *Comput Supported Coop Work Computer Supported Cooperative Work*, *14*(4), 301–322. doi:10.100710606-005-9002-z

Lenhart, A. (2015). *Teens, social media & technology overview 2015.* Retrieved from: http://www.pewinternet.org/2015/04/09/teens-social-media-technology-2015/

Lenhart, A., Madden, M., & Hitlin, P. (2005). *Teens and Technology: Youth are Leading the Transition to a Fully Wired and Mobile Nation.* Washington, DC: Pew Internet & American Life Project.

Lenhart, A., Rainie, L., & Lewis, O. (2001). *Teenage life online: The rise of the instant- message generation and the internet's impact on friendships and family relationships.* Washington, DC: Pew Internet and American Life Project.

Leonard, B. (2011). Managing Virtual Teams. *HRMagazine*, 38–42.

Lester, A. (2010). Gladwell: the revolution will not be tweeted. *The Nonprofit Quarterly*. Retrieved from http://www.nonprofitquarterly.org/index.php?option=com_content &view=article&id=6096:gladwell-the-revolution-will-not-be-tweeted&catid=153 :features&Itemid=336

Light, P. C. (2005). *The Four Pillars of High Performance: How Robust Organizations Achieve Extraordinary Results*. New York: McGraw-Hill.

Lindblom, C. (1959). The science of "muddling through." *Public Administration Review, 19*(2), 79–88. doi:10.2307/973677

Linden, R. (2010). *Leading across boundaries: Creating collaborative agencies in a networked world*. San Francisco, CA: Jossey-Bass.

Lin, L. Y., Sidani, J. E., Shensa, A., Radovic, A., Miller, E., Colditz, J. B., ... Primack, B. A. (2016). Association between social media use and depression among U.S. young adults. *Depression and Anxiety, 33*(4), 323–331. doi:10.1002/da.22466 PMID:26783723

Li, Q. (2007). Bullying in the new playground: Research into cyberbullying and cybervictimization. *Australian Journal of Educational Technology, 23*, 435–454.

Li, Q. (2008). A cross-cultural comparison of adolescents' experience related to cyberbullying. *Educational Research, 50*(3), 223–234. doi:10.1080/00131880802309333

Loscerbo, J. (1981). *Being and technology: a study in the philosophy of Martin Heidegger. Kluwer*. doi:10.1007/978-94-009-8222-2

Luise, M. (2008). EC initiatives on the digital divide and satellite fields. *Proc. UNIC Workshop*.

Lunenburg, F. C. (2011). Network Patterns and Analysis: Underused Sources to Improve Communication Effectiveness. *National Forum Of Educational Administration And Supervision Journal*.

Lunenburg, F. C. (2010). Communication: The process, barriers, and improving effectiveness. *Schooling, 1*(1), 1–11.

Luthans, F. (1977). *Organizational Behavior*. New York: McGraw-Hill.

Ma, L. (2007). "I'll trust you if I expect you to trust me": An analysis of interpersonal trust, friends, and social interactions within social networks. Tufts University.

Macaleer, W. D., & Shannon, J. B. (2002). Emotional Intelligence: How Does it Affect Leadership? *Employment Relations Today, 29*(3), 9–19. doi:10.1002/ert.10047

Machackova, H., Dedkova, L., & Mezulanikova, K. (2015). Brief report: The bystander effect in cyberbullying incidents. *Journal of Adolescence, 43*, 96–99. doi:10.1016/j.adolescence.2015.05.010 PMID:26070168

Machackova, H., Dedkova, L., Sevcikova, A., & Cerna, A. (2013). Bystanders' support of cyberbullied schoolmates. *Journal of Community & Applied Social Psychology*, *23*(1), 25–36. doi:10.1002/casp.2135

Main, A., Walle, E. A., Kho, C., & Halpern, J. (2017). The interpersonal functions of empathy: A relational perspective. *Emotion Review*, *9*(4), 358–366. doi:10.1177/1754073916669440

*Marcel, G. (1963). The Existential Background of Human Dignity.*. Cambridge, MA: Harvard University Press.

Marcel, G., & Man, P. (1967). Herder and Herder. London: Academic Press.

Marcel, G. (1949). *Philosophy of Existence*. New York: Philosophical Library.

Marcel, G. (1952). *Man against Mass Society*. Chicago: Regnery.

Marcel, G. (1965). *Being and Having*. London: Collins.

Marcel, G. (1966). *Philosophy of Existentialism*. New York: Citadel.

Marcel, G. (1973). *Tragic Wisdom and Beyond*. Evanston, IL: Northwestern University Press.

Marine, S., & Blanchard, J-M. (2004). Bridging the digital divide: an opportunity for growth in the 21st century. *Alcatel Telecommun. Rev.*.

Maritain, J. (1938). Humanism. Charles Scribner's Sons.

*Maritain, J. (1956a). The Knowledge of Man*. London: George Allen & Unwin.

Maritain, J. (1956b). *Existence and the Existent*. Image Books.

Maritain, J. (1958). The Rights of Man and Natural Law. London: Academic Press.

Maritain, J. (1932). *An introduction to philosophy*. London: Sheed & Ward.

Maritain, J. (1946). *The twilight of civilization*. London: G. Bles.

Maritain, J. (1953). *The range of reason*. London: G. Bles.

Maritain, J. (1961). *On the use of philosophy: Three essays*. Princeton, NJ: Princeton U.P. doi:10.1515/9781400878284

Maritain, J. (1970). *True humanism*. Westport, CT: Greenwood Press.

Markopoulos, P., Xefteris, D., & Dellarocas, C. (2015). *Manipulating Reviews in Dark Net Markets to Reduce Crime*. Retrieved May 7, 2017, from http://www.teis-workshop.org/papers/2016/TEIS_2016_1_Dellarocas.pdf

Marlow, S. L., Lacerenza, C. N., & Salas, E. (2017). Communication in virtual teams: A conceptual framework and research agenda. *Human Resource Management Review, 27*(4), 575–589. doi:10.1016/j.hrmr.2016.12.005

Martin, J. (2014). *Drugs on the Dark Net: How Cryptomarkets are Transforming the Global Trade in Illicit Drugs.* London: Palgrave Macmillan UK. doi:10.1057/9781137399052

Martin-Raugh, M. P., Kell, H. J., & Motowidlo, S. J. (2016). Prosocial knowledge mediates effects of agreeableness and emotional intelligence on prosocial behavior. *Personality and Individual Differences, 90,* 41–49. doi:10.1016/j.paid.2015.10.024

Martin, S., Sutcliffe, P., Griffiths, F., Sturt, J., Powell, J., Adams, A., & Dale, J. (2011). Effectiveness and impact of networked communication interventions in young people with mental health conditions: A systematic review. *Patient Education and Counseling, 85*(2), e108–e119. doi:10.1016/j.pec.2010.11.014 PMID:21239133

Mason, K. (2008). Cyberbullying: A preliminary assessment for school personnel. *Psychology in the Schools, 45*(4), 323–348. doi:10.1002/pits.20301

Masur, P. K., Reinecke, L., Ziegele, M., & Quiring, O. (2014). The interplay of intrinsic need satisfaction and Facebook specific motives in explaining addictive behavior on Facebook. *Computers in Human Behavior, 39,* 376–386. doi:10.1016/j.chb.2014.05.047

Mathea, K. (2006). Broadband access and integrated services. *Proc. 3rd Forum on BB services.*

Mathew, M., & Gupta, K. (2015). Transformational leadership: Emotional intelligence. *SCMS Journal of Indian Management, 12*(2), 75.

Matosic, D., Ntoumanis, N., Boardley, I. D., Sedikides, C., Stewart, B. D., & Chatzisarantis, N. (2017). Narcissism and coach interpersonal style: A self-determination theory perspective. *Scandinavian Journal of Medicine & Science in Sports, 27*(2), 254–261. doi:10.1111ms.12635 PMID:26689999

Matson, F. W., & Montagu, A. (Eds.). (1967). *The human dialogue: perspectives on communication.* New York: Free Press.

Mayer, J. D., Salovey, P., Caruso, D. R., & Cherkasskiy, L. (2011). Emotional intelligence. The Cambridge handbook of intelligence, 528-549. doi:10.1017/CBO9780511977244.027

Mayer, J. D., Caruso, D. R., & Salovey, P. (2016). The ability model of emotional intelligence: Principles and updates. *Emotion Review, 8*(4), 290–300. doi:10.1177/1754073916639667

McGinty, K. L., Saeed, S. A., Simmons, S. C., & Yildirim, Y. (2006). Telepsychiatry and e-mental health services: Potential for improving access to mental health care. *The Psychiatric Quarterly, 77*(4), 335–342. doi:10.100711126-006-9019-6 PMID:16927161

McQuade, C. S., Colt, P. J., & Meyer, B. N. (2009). *Cyber bullying: Protecting kids and adults from online bullies*. Westport, CT: Praeger.

Mendes-Flohr, P. (1989). *From mysticism to dialogue: Martin Buber's transformation of German social thought*. Detroit, MI: Wayne State University Press.

Mendes-Flohr, P. (2015). *Dialogue as a Trans-disciplinary Concept: Martin Buber's Philosophy of Dialogue and its Contemporary Reception*. Boston: De Gruyter. doi:10.1515/9783110402223

Menzel, D. (2010). *Ethics moments in government: Cases and controversies*. Boca Raton, FL: Taylor & Francis.

Mergel, I. (2011). Crowdsourced ideas make participating in government cool again. *PA Times, 34*(4), 4,6.

Merriam Webster Dictionary. (n.d.). Retrieved May 18, 2017, from https://www.merriam-webster.com

Mills, J. H., & Mills, A. J. (2000). *Sensemaking and the Gendering of Organizational Culture*. Montreal, Canada: ASAC-IFSAM Conference.

Mitchell, K. J., Ybarra, M., & Finkelhor, D. (2007). The relative importance of online victimization in understanding depression, delinquency, and substance use. *Child Maltreatment, 12*(4), 314–324. doi:10.1177/1077559507305996 PMID:17954938

Mitchell, T. R. (1982). Motivation: New Directions for Theory, Research, and Practice. *Academy of Management Review, 7*(1), 80–88.

Morgan, C., & Cotten, S. R. (2003). The relationship between Internet activities and depressive symptoms in a sample of college freshmen. *Cyberpsychology & Behavior, 6*(2), 133–141. doi:10.1089/109493103321640329 PMID:12804025

Morreale, S., Staley, C., Stavrositu, C., & Krakowiak, M. (2015). First-year college students' attitudes toward communication technologies and their perceptions of communication competence in the 21st century. *Communication Education, 64*(1), 107–131. doi:10.1080/03634523.2014.978799

Mounteney, J., Bo, A., & Oteo, A. (2016). *The Internet and Drug Markets*. Luxembourg: European Monitoring Centre for Drugs and Drug Addiction.

Muchinsky, P. M. (1977). Organizational communication: Relationships to organizational climate and job satisfaction. *Academy of Management Journal, 20*(4), 592–607. doi:10.2307/255359

Musiat, P., Goldstone, P., & Tarrier, N. (2014). Understanding the acceptability of e-mental health-attitudes and expectations towards computerized self-help treatments for mental health problems. *BMC Psychiatry, 14*(1). Retrieved 26 May 2017, from http://www.biomedcentral.com/1471-244X/14/109

Musiat, P., & Tarrier, N. (2014). *Collateral outcomes in e-mental health: A systematic review of the evidence for added benefits of computerized cognitive behavior therapy interventions for mental health. Psychological Medicine, 44, 3137–3150.* doi:10.1017/S0033291714000245

Nardi & Whittaker. (2002). *The place of face-to-face communication in distributed work*. Distributed work: 83-110.

Naseem, K. (2018). Job Stress, Happiness and Life Satisfaction: The Moderating Role of Emotional Intelligence Empirical Study in Telecommunication Sector Pakistan. *J. Soc. Sci*, *4*(1), 7–14.

Networked Media of the Future. (2007). *EC NM-TF Report. DG IS&M*. October. Retrieved from http://ec.europaeut/dgs/information_society/text_en.htm

Nie, N., Hillygus, D. S., & Erbring, L. (2002). Internet use, interpersonal relations, and sociability: A time diary study. In B. Wellman & C. Haythornthwaite (Eds.), *The Internet in Everyday Life* (pp. 215–243). Oxford, UK: Blackwell. doi:10.1002/9780470774298.ch7

Nie, N., & Hillygus, S. (2002). The impact of internet use on Sociability: Time-diary findings. *IT & Society*, *1*(1), 1–20.

Norris, D., Fletcher, P., & Holden, S. (2001). *Is your local government plugged in? Highlights of the 2000 Electronic Government Survey*. Washington, DC: International City/County Management Association.

O'Hearn, M. S., & Kahle, L. R. (2013). The empowered customer: User-generated content and the future of marketing. *Global Economics and Management Review*, *18*(1), 22–30. doi:10.1016/S2340-1540(13)70004-5

O'Leary, R., Van Slyke, D., & Kim, S. (Eds.). (2010). *The future of public administration around the world: The Minnowbrook perspective*. Washington, DC: Georgetown University Press.

O'Neill, P. H. (2017, February 3). *Dark Net Markets Moving to Adopt Bug Bounty Programs*. Retrieved May 11, 2017, from https://www.cyberscoop.com/dark-net-markets-bug-bounty-programs/

Oasis eGov Member Section. (2010). *Avoiding the pitfalls of eGovernment: 10 lessons learnt from eGovernment deployments*. Retrieved from: http://www.oasis-egov.org/sites/oasisegov.org/files/eGov_Pitfalls_Guidance%20Doc_v1.pdf

Obar, J., Zube, P., & Lampe, C. (2011). *Advocacy 2.0: An analysis of how advocacy groups in the United States perceive and use social media as tools for facilitating civic engagement and collective action* (Working Paper Series). Social Science Research Network. Retrieved from: http://ssrn.com/abstract=1956352

Ojoa, A., Esteveza, E., & Janowskia, T. (2010). Semantic interoperability architecture for governance 2.0. *Information Polity, 15,* 105–123. doi 10.3233/IP-2010-0199

Olson, G. M., & Olson, J. S. (2000). Distance matters. *Human-Computer Interaction, 15*(2), 139–178. doi:10.1207/S15327051HCI1523_4

Online, B. D. (2016, June 16). Shedding Light on the Dark Web. *The Economist*. Retrieved May 8, 2017, from http://www.economist.com/news/international/21702176-drug-trade-moving-street-online-cryptomarkets-forced-compete

Orlikowski, W., & Scott, S. (2009). Sociomateriality: Challenging the separation of technology, work and organization. *The Academy of Management Annals, 2*(1), 433–474. doi:10.1080/19416520802211644

Pallotta, D. (2008). *Uncharitable*. Medford, MA: Tufts University Press.

Park, H., & Lee, H. (2013). Show us you are real: The effect of human-versus-organizational presence on online relationship building through social networking sites. *Cyberpsychology, Behavior, and Social Networking, 16*(4), 265–271. doi:10.1089/cyber.2012.0051 PMID:23363228

Parks, M. R., & Roberts, L. D. (1998). Making MOOsic: The development of personal relationships on-line and a comparison to their offline counterparts. *Journal of Social and Personal Relationships, 15*(4), 517–538. doi:10.1177/0265407598154005

Patchin, J. W., & Hinduja, S. (2006). Bullies move beyond the schoolyard: A preliminary look at cyberbullying. *Youth Violence and Juvenile Justice, 4*(2), 148–169. doi:10.1177/1541204006286288

Patterson, K. (2011). *Crucial conversations: tools for talking when stakes are high.* New York: McGraw-Hill Professional.

Patulny, R., & Seaman, C. (2016). 'I'll just text you': Is face-to-face social contact declining in a mediated world? *Journal of Sociology.* doi: 1440783316674358

Paul, I. (2014, October 31). Facebook Says You Can Be Social and Secure, Acquires. Onion Address for Tor Users. *PCWorld.* Retrieved November 11, 2017, from https://www.pcworld.com/article/2841822/facebook-says-you-can-be-social-and-secure-acquires-onion-address-for-tor-users.html

Pea, R., Nass, C., Meheula, L., Rance, M., Kumar, A., Bamford, H., ... Zhou, M. (2012). Media use, face-to-face communication, media multitasking, and social well-being among 8-to 12-year-old girls. *Developmental Psychology, 48*(2), 327–336. doi:10.1037/a0027030 PMID:22268607

Pearson, J., & Franceschi-Bicchierai, L. (2015, March 19). There's a Bitcoin Bounty Out on Those Alleged "Evolution" Drug Market Scammers. *Motherboard.* Retrieved May 11, 2017, from https://motherboard.vice.com/en_us/article/theres-a-bitcoin-bounty-out-on-those-alleged-evolution-drug-market-scammers

Pempek, T. A., Yermolayeva, Y. A., & Calvert, S. L. (2009). College students' social networking experiences on facebook. *Journal of Applied Developmental Psychology, 30*(3), 227–238. doi:10.1016/j.appdev.2008.12.010

Penard, T., Poussing, N., & Suire, R. (2013). Does the Internet make people happier? *Journal of Socio Economics, Elsevier, 46,* 105–116.

Perren, S., Dooley, J., Shaw, T., & Cross, D. (2010). Bullying in school and cyberspace: Associations with depressive symptoms in Swiss and Australian adolescents. *Child and Adolescent Psychiatry and Mental Health, 4*(1), 1–10. doi:10.1186/1753-2000-4-28 PMID:21092266

Petronio, S. (2012). *Boundaries of privacy: Dialectics of disclosure.* SUNY Press.

Plato. (n.d.a). Available at: http://www.perseus.tufts.edu/hopper/text?doc=Perseus%3Atext%3A1999.01.0176%3Atext%3DCharm

Plato. (n.d.b). Available at: http://www.perseus.tufts.edu/hopper/text?doc=Perseus%3Atext%3A1999.01.0178%3Atext%3DGorg

Pope, J., Isely, A., & Asamoa-Tutu, F. (2009, April). Developing a marketing strategy for nonprofit organizations: An exploratory study. *Journal of Nonprofit & Public Sector Marketing*, *21*(2), 184–201. doi:10.1080/10495140802529532

Pornari, C. D., & Wood, J. (2010). Peer and cyber aggression in secondary school students: The role of moral disengagement, hostile attribution bias, and outcome expectancies. *Aggressive Behavior*, *36*(2), 81–94. doi:10.1002/ab.20336 PMID:20035548

Poushter, J. (2015). *Internet Seen as Positive Influence on Education but Negative on Morality in Emerging and Developing Nations*. Retrieved from: http://assets.pewresearch.org/wp-content/uploads/sites/2/2015/03/Pew-Research-Center-Technology-Report-FINAL-March-19-20151.pdf

Przybylski, A. K., & Weinstein, N. (2013). Can you connect with me now? How the presence of mobile communication technology influences face-to-face conversation quality. *Journal of Social and Personal Relationships*, *30*(3), 237–246. doi:10.1177/0265407512453827

Putnam, H. (2008). *Jewish philosophy as a guide to life: Rosenzweig, Buber, Lévinas, Wittgenstein*. Bloomington, IN: Indiana University Press.

Pynes, J. (2009). *Human resources management for public and nonprofit organizations*. San Francisco, CA: Jossey-Bass.

Qualman, E. (2009). *Socialnomics: How social media transforms the way we live and do business*. Hoboken, NJ: John Wiley & Sons.

Ramirez, A. Jr, Dimmick, J., Feaster, J., & Lin, S.-F. (2008). Revisiting interpersonal media competition: The gratification niches of instant messaging, e-mail, and the telephone. *Communication Research*, *35*(4), 529–547. doi:10.1177/0093650208315979

Redman, J. (2016, July 16). *Dark Net Markets Are Booming from Better Quality and Safety*. Retrieved May 8, 2017, from https://news.bitcoin.com/dark-net-market-quality-safety/

Redman, J. (2017, April 5). *Darknet Market Operators Who Stole 40 Thousand BTC Face Prison Time*. Retrieved May 4, 2017, from https://news.bitcoin.com/darknet-market-operators-who-stole-40-thousand-btc-face-prison-time/

Reinecke, L., Hartmann, T., & Eden, A. (2014). The guilty couch potato: The role of ego depletion in reducing recovery through media use. *Journal of Communication*, *64*(4), 569–589. doi:10.1111/jcom.12107

Reinecke, L., & Trepte, S. (2014). Authenticity and well-being on social network sites: A two-wave longitudinal study on the effects of online authenticity and the positivity bias in SNS communication. *Computers in Human Behavior*, *30*, 95–102. doi:10.1016/j.chb.2013.07.030

Reis, H. T., Sheldon, K. M., Gable, S. L., Roscoe, J., & Ryan, R. M. (2000). Daily well-being: The role of autonomy, competence, and relatedness. *Personality and Social Psychology Bulletin*, *26*(4), 419–435. doi:10.1177/0146167200266002

Report, E. E. (2010). *Bridging the digital divide – Internet access in Central and Eastern Europe*. Retrieved from http://www.cdt.org/international/ceeaccess/eereport.pdf

Rhumorbarbe, D., Staehli, L., Broséus, J., Rossy, Q., & Esseiva, P. (2016). Buying Drugs on a Darknet Market: A Better Deal? Studying the Online Illicit Drug Market Through the Analysis of Digital, Physical and Chemical Data. *Forensic Science International*, *267*, 173–182. doi:10.1016/j.forsciint.2016.08.032 PMID:27611957

Richards, J. C., & Schmidt, R. (2010). *Longman dictionary of language teaching and applied linguistics*. Pearson Education Limited.

Rideout, V. J. (2010). *Generation M²: Media in the Lives of 8-to 18-Year-Olds*. Henry J. Kaiser Family Foundation.

Rideout, V. J., Roberts, D. F., & Foehr, U. G. (2005). *Generation M: Media in the lives of 8-18-year-olds: Executive summary*. Menlo Park, CA: Henry J. Kaiser Family Foundation.

Riggio, R. E., & Reichard, R. J. (2008). The emotional and social intelligences of effective leadership: An emotional and social skill approach. *Journal of Managerial Psychology*, *23*(2), 169–185. doi:10.1108/02683940810850808

Right Now Government. (2010). *Citizen service meets social media: Best practices for citizen engagement* (White Paper). RightNow Technologies, Inc. Retrieved from http://api.ning.com/files/Fkoi1sHp00bvHPs84maiIXkGot-*6ZcAf0xkCm qadr7P1hcFegPmZl2cdEAo5YS*ceIUoAF7bWjEYdPyYmbKLFVtxQroFMw/RightNowGovernmentSocialContactCenterWhitePaper6.pdf

Riley, P. (1979). Towards a contrastive pragmalinguistics. In J. Fisiak (Ed.), *Contrastive linguistics and the language teacher* (pp. 121–146). Oxford, UK: Pergamon Press Ltd.

Riper, H., Andersson, G., Christensen, H., Cuijpers, P., Lange, A., & Eysenbach, G. (2010). Theme issue on e-mental health: A growing field in Internet research. *Journal of Medical Internet Research*, *12*(5), e74. doi:10.2196/jmir.1713 PMID:21169177

Rogers, Y., Sharp, H., & Preece, J. (2015). *Interaction design: Beyond human-computer interaction.* John Wiley & Sons.

Rosen, L. D. (2007). *Me, Myspace, and I: Parenting the Net Generation.* New York: Palgrave Macmillan.

Rothenberg, D. (1993). *Hand's end: technology and the limits of nature.* Berkeley, CA: University of California Press.

Ruppel, E. K. (2015). Use of communication technologies in romantic relationships: Self-disclosure and the role of relationship development. *Journal of Social and Personal Relationships, 32*(5), 667–686. doi:10.1177/0265407514541075

Russell, R. D. (1973). Social health: An attempt to clarify this dimension of well-being. *International Journal of Health Education, 16,* 74–82.

Sachau, D. (2007). Resurrecting the Motivation-Hygiene Theory: Herzberg and the Positive Psychology Movement. *Human Resource Development Review, 6*(4), 377–393. doi:10.1177/1534484307307546

Sahin, M. (2010). Teachers' perceptions of bullying in high schools: A Turkish study. *Social Behavior and Personality, 38*(1), 127–142. doi:10.2224bp.2010.38.1.127

Sala, F. (2000). *Do Programs Designed to Increase Emotional Intelligence at Work - Work?* Retrieved from http://www.eiconsortium.org/reports/do_ei_programs_work.html

Salamon, L. (2003). *The resilient sector.* Washington, DC: Brookings Institution Press.

Salas, A. (2016). Literature Review of Faculty-Perceived Usefulness of Instructional Technology in Classroom Dynamics. *Contemporary Educational Technology, 7*(2), 174–186.

Samleo, L., Xiao, J., Zhang, X., Chawda, B., Narang, K., Rajput, N., ... Subramaniam, V. (2014). Being aware of the world: Toward using social media to support the blind with navigation. *IEEE Transactions on Human-Machine Systems.* doi:10.1109/THMS.2014.2382582

Sampasakanyinga, H., & Lewis, R. F. (2015). Frequent Use of social networking sites is associated with poor psychological functioning among children and adolescents. *Cyberpsychology, Behavior, and Social Networking, 18*(7), 380–385. doi:10.1089/cyber.2015.0055 PMID:26167836

Schaefer, G., & Hersey, L. N. (2015). Cat Videos for a Cause: A Nonprofit Social Media. In H. Asencio & R. Sun (Eds.), *Cases on Strategic Social Media Utilization.* Hershey, PA: IGI Global. doi:10.4018/978-1-4666-8188-0.ch005

Scharff, R. C. (2013). *Philosophy of Technology: The Technological Condition: An Anthology*. Hoboken, NJ: Wiley.

Scheflen, A. E. (1972). Body Language and the Social Order; Communication as Behavioral Control. In How behavior means. Interface.

Schein, E. H. (1985). *Organizational culture and leadership*. San Francisco: Jossey-Bass Publishers.

*Schilpp, P. A., & Hahn, L. E.* (Eds.). (1984). *The Philosophy of Gabriel Marcel*. Open Court Pub. Co.

Schilpp, P. A., & Friedman, M. (Eds.). (1967). *The philosophy of Martin Buber*. Open Court, La Salle.

Schmidt, U., & Wykes, T. (2012). E-mental health: A land of unlimited possibilities. *Journal of Mental Health (Abingdon, England)*, *21*(4), 327–331. doi:10.3109/0963 8237.2012.705930 PMID:22823092

Schneider, D., Sperling, S., Schell, G., Hemmer, K., Glauer, R., & Silberhorn, D. (2004). *Instant Messaging - Neue Räume im CyberspaceNutzertypen, Gebrauchsweisen, Motive, Regeln*. München: Verlag Reinhard Fischer.

Schwandt, D. R. (2005). When Managers Become Philosophers: Integrating Learning with Sensemaking. *Academy of Management Learning & Education*, *4*(2), 176–192. doi:10.5465/AMLE.2005.17268565

Selfhout, M. W., Branje, S. T., Delsing, M., Bogt, T. T., & Meeus, W. J. (2009). Different types of Internet use, depression, and social anxiety: The role of perceived friendship quality. *Journal of Adolescence*, *32*(4), 819–833. doi:10.1016/j.adolescence.2008.10.011 PMID:19027940

Serrat, O. (2017). *Understanding and developing emotional intelligence. In Knowledge Solutions* (pp. 329–339). Springer.

Sevcikova, A., Machackova, H., Wright, M. F., Dedkova, L., & Cerna, A. (2015). Social support seeking in relation to parental attachment and peer relationships among victims of cyberbullying. *Australian Journal of Guidance & Counselling*, *15*, 1–13. doi:10.1017/jgc.2015.1

Shapka, J. D., & Law, D. M. (2013). Does one size fit all? Ethnic differences in parenting behaviors and motivations for adolescent engagement in cyberbullying. *Journal of Youth and Adolescence*, *42*(5), 723–738. doi:10.100710964-013-9928-2 PMID:23479327

Shareef, M., Archer, N., & Dutta, S. (2012). *E-Government service maturity and development: Cultural, organizational and technological perspectives.* Hershey, PA: IGI Global; doi:10.4018/978-1-60960-848-4

Shariff, S., & Hoff, D. L. (2007). Cyber bullying: Clarifying legal boundaries for school supervision in cyberspace. *International Journal of Cyber Criminology*, *1*, 76–118.

Shaw, L. H., & Gant, L. M. (2002). In defense of the Internet: The relationship between Internet communication and depression, loneliness, self-esteem, and perceived social support. *Cyberpsychology & Behavior*, *5*(2), 157–170. doi:10.1089/109493102753770552 PMID:12025883

Shen, C., & Williams, D. (2011). Unpacking Time Online: Connecting Internet and Massively Multiplayer Online Game Use with Psychosocial Well-being. *Communication Research*, *38*(1), 123–149. doi:10.1177/0093650210377196

Sherman, A. (2011). How law enforcement agencies are using social media to better serve the public. *Mashable.* Retrieved from: http://mashable.com/2011/08/31/law-enforcementsocial-media-use/

Shirky, C. (2008). *Here comes everybody: The power of organizing without organizations.* New York, NY: Penguin Books.

Sijtsema, J. J., Ashwin, R. J., Simona, C. S., & Gina, G. (2014). Friendship selection and influence in bullying and defending. *Effects of moral disengagement. Developmental Psychology*, *50*(8), 2093–2104. doi:10.1037/a0037145 PMID:24911569

Silberstein, L. J. (1989). *Martin Buber's social and religious thought: alienation and the quest for meaning.* New York: New York University Press.

Sinkkonen, H. M., Puhakka, H., & Merilainen, M. (2014). Internet use and addiction among Finnish Adolescents (15–19 years). *Journal of Adolescence*, *37*(2), 123–131. doi:10.1016/j.adolescence.2013.11.008 PMID:24439618

Sjurso, I. R., Fandream, H., & Roland, E. (2016). Emotional problems in traditional and cyber victimization. *Journal of School Violence*, *15*(1), 114–131. doi:10.1080/15388220.2014.996718

Skowroński, R. (2006). Broadband everywhere. *Proc. 3rd Forum on BB services.*

Skrbina, D. (2014). *The Metaphysics of Technology.* London: Taylor and Francis.

Smigla, J. E., & Pastoria, G. (2000). Emotional Intelligence: Some Have It, Others Can Learn. *The CPA Journal*, *70*(6), 60–61.

Smith, A. (2010). *Government online* (Report). Pew Internet & American Life Project. Retrieved from http://www.pewinternet.org/Reports/2010/Government-Online/Summaryof-Findings.aspx

Smith, P. K., Del Barrio, C., & Tokunaga, R. S. (2013). Definitions of bullying and cyberbullying: How useful are the terms? In S. Bauman, D. Cross, & J. Walker (Eds.), *Principles of cyberbullying research: Definitions, measures, methodology* (pp. 26–40). New York, NY: Routledge.

Smith, P. K., Mahdavi, J., Carvalho, M., Fisher, S., Russell, S., & Tippett, N. (2008). Cyberbullying: Its nature and impact in secondary school pupils. *Journal of Child Psychology and Psychiatry, and Allied Disciplines, 49*(4), 376–385. doi:10.1111/j.1469-7610.2007.01846.x PMID:18363945

Sommer, K. L., & Kulkarni, M. (2012). Does constructive performance feedback improve citizenship intentions and job satisfaction? The roles of perceived opportunities for advancement, respect, and mood. *Human Resource Development Quarterly, 23*(2), 177–201. doi:10.1002/hrdq.21132

Sosik, J. J., & Megerian, L. E. (1999). Understanding Leader Emotional Intelligence and Performance. *Group & Organization Management, 24*(3), 367–390. doi:10.1177/1059601199243006

Soska, K., & Christin, N. (2015). *Measuring the Longitudinal Evolution of the Online Anonymous Marketplace Ecosystem.* Washington, DC: USENIX Association.

Sourander, A., Brunstein, A., Ikonen, M., Lindroos, J., Luntamo, T., Koskelainen, M., ... Helenius, H. (2010). Psychosocial risk factors associated with cyberbullying among adolescents: A population-based study. *Archives of General Psychiatry, 67*(7), 720–728. doi:10.1001/archgenpsychiatry.2010.79 PMID:20603453

Sproull, L., & Kiesler, S. (1991). *Connections: new ways of working in the networked organization.* Cambridge, MA: MIT Press.

Stacey, E., & Wiesenberg, F. (2007). A study of face-to-face and online teaching philosophies in Canada and Australia. *International Journal of E-Learning & Distance Education, 22*(1), 19–40.

Starbuck & Milliken. (1988). *Executives' perceptual filters: What they notice and how they make sense.* Academic Press.

Stets, J. E. (1991). Psychological aggression in dating relationships: The role of interpersonal control. *Journal of Family Violence, 6*(1), 97–114. doi:10.1007/BF00978528

Stiff, J. B. (1987). *Empathy, Communication, and Prosocial Behavior.* Retrieved from http://ezproxy.fiu.edu/login?url=http://search.ebscohost.com/login.aspx?direct=true&db=eric&AN=ED294266&site=eds-live

Stoll, L. C., & Block, R. Jr. (2015). Intersectionality and cyberbullying: A study of cybervictimization in a Midwestern high school. *Computers in Human Behavior, 52*, 387–391. doi:10.1016/j.chb.2015.06.010

Strohmeier, D., Aoyama, I., Gradinger, P., & Toda, Y. (2013). Cybervictimization and cyberaggression in Eastern and Western countries: Challenges of constructing a cross-cultural appropriate scale. In S. Bauman, D. Cross, & J. L. Walker (Eds.), *Principles of cyberbullying research: Definitions, measures, and methodology* (pp. 202–221). New York: Routledge.

Subrahmanyam, K., Reich, S. M., Waechter, N., & Espinoza, G. (2008). Online and offline social networks: Use of social networking sites by emerging adults. *Journal of Applied Developmental Psychology, 29*(6), 420–433. doi:10.1016/j.appdev.2008.07.003

Suler, J. (2004). The online disinhibition effect. *Cyberpsychology & Behavior, 7*(3), 321–326. doi:10.1089/1094931041291295 PMID:15257832

Tajfel, H., & Turner, J. C. (2004). The social identity theory of intergroup behavior. *Political Psychology*, 276–293.

Tan, F., Stockdale, R., & Vasa, R. (2011). *Leveraging emerging web technologies for community engagement project success in higher education.* European Conference of Information Systems. Retrieved from http://is2.lse.ac.uk/asp/aspecis/20110211.pdf

Tangen, D., & Campbell, M. (2010). Cyberbullying prevention: One primary school's approach. *Australian Journal of Guidance & Counselling, 20*(02), 225–234. doi:10.1375/ajgc.20.2.225

The State of Broadband 2016: Broadband Catalyzing Sustainable Development. (2016). Retrieved from http://broadbandcommission.org/Documents/reports/bb-annualreport2016.pdf

The Wall Street Journal. (n.d.). *Is technology making people less sociable?* Retrieved 26 May 2017, from https://www.wsj.com/articles/is-technology-making-people-less-sociable-1431093491

Theunissen, M. (1984). *The other: studies in the social ontology of Husserl, Heidegger, Sartre, and Buber.* Cambridge, MA.: MIT Press.

Thewissen, V., & Gunther, N. (2015). E-mental health: State of the art. *Tijdschrift voor Psychotherapie, 41*(6), 374–392. doi:10.100712485-015-0102-z

Toledano, S., Werch, B. L., & Wiens, B. A. (2015). Domain-specific self-concept in relation to traditional and cyber peer aggression. *Journal of School Violence, 14*(4), 405–423. doi:10.1080/15388220.2014.935386

Uzun, T. (2017). Development of the nonverbal communication skills of school administrators scale (NCSSAS): Validity, reliability and implementation study. *Educational Research Review, 12*(7), 442–455.

Valkenburg, P. M., & Peter, J. (2007a). Online communication and adolescent well-being: Testing the stimulation versus the displacement hypothesis. *Journal of Computer-Mediated Communication, 12*(4), 2. doi:10.1111/j.1083-6101.2007.00368.x

Valkenburg, P. M., & Peter, J. (2007b). Preadolescents' and adolescents' online communication and their closeness to friends. *Developmental Psychology, 43*(2), 267–277. doi:10.1037/0012-1649.43.2.267 PMID:17352538

Valkenburg, P. M., & Soeters, K. (2001). Children's positive and negative experiences with the Internet. *Communication Research, 2*, 653–676.

van den Berg, A. C., & Verhoeven, J. W. (2017). Understanding social media governance: Seizing opportunities, staying out of trouble. *Corporate Communications, 22*(1), 149–164. doi:10.1108/CCIJ-06-2015-0035

van Dijk, J. (2005). From digital divide to social opportunities. *Proc. 2nd Int'l Conf. for Bridging the Digital Divide.*

Van Hout, M. C., & Bingham, T. (2013). "Surfing the Silk Road": A Study of Users' Experiences. *The International Journal on Drug Policy, 24*(6), 524–529. doi:10.1016/j.drugpo.2013.08.011 PMID:24075939

Van Hout, M. C., & Bingham, T. (2014). Responsible Vendors, Intelligent Consumers: Silk Road, the Online Revolution in Drug Trading. *The International Journal on Drug Policy, 25*(2), 183–189. doi:10.1016/j.drugpo.2013.10.009 PMID:24268875

Van Vugt, M., Jepson, S. F., Hart, C. M., & De Cremer, D. (2004). Autocratic leadership in social dilemmas: A threat to group stability. *Journal of Experimental Social Psychology, 40*(1), 1–13. doi:10.1016/S0022-1031(03)00061-1

VanRoekel, S. (2011). *An Evening with Steven VanRoekel, Chief Information Officer of the United States. Remarks as prepared for delivery*. PARC. Retrieved from www.whitehouse.gov/sites/default/files/svr_parc_speech_final_0.pdf

Veenhoven, R. (2014) What we have learnt about happiness classic qualms in the light of recent research. In A Life Devoted to Quality of Life, Festschrift in Honor of Alex C. Michalos. Springer.

Verduyn, P., Ybarra, O., Résibois, M., Jonides, J., & Kross, E. (2017). Do social network sites enhance or undermine subjective well-being? A critical review. *Social Issues and Policy Review, 11*(1), 274–302. doi:10.1111ipr.12033

Wade, A., & Beran, T. (2011). Cyberbullying: The new era of bullying. *Canadian Journal of School Psychology, 26*(1), 44–61. doi:10.1177/0829573510396318

Walker, M. (2011). Disaster response increasingly linked to social media. *FierceGovernmentIT*. Retrieved from: http://www.fiercegovernmentit.com/story/disaster-response-increasinglylinked-social-media/2011-08-31#ixzz1eyTSaWhn

Wallace, E. (2016). *The Relationship Engine: Connecting with the People who Power Your Business*. AMACOM Div American Mgmt Assn.

Wang, G., & Seibert, S. E. (2015). The impact of leader emotion display frequency on follower performance: Leader surface acting and mean emotion display as boundary conditions. *The Leadership Quarterly, 26*(4), 577–593. doi:10.1016/j.leaqua.2015.05.007

Wehinger, F. (2011). The Dark Net: Self-Regulation Dynamics of Illegal Online Markets for Identities and Related Services. IEEE Computer Society.

Weick, K. E. (1995). *Sensemaking in organizations*. Thousand Oaks, CA: Sage.

Weigin, E. L., Campbell, M., Kimpton, M., Wozencroft, K., & Orel, A. (2016). Social capital on Facebook: The impact of personality and online communication behaviors. *Journal of Educational Computing Research, 54*(6), 747–748. doi:10.1177/0735633116631886

Wikipedia e-health. (2017). Retrieved 4 May 2017, from http://en.wikipedia.org/wiki/EHealth

Willson, M. A. (2006). *Technically together: rethinking community within techno-society*. New York: Peter Lang.

Wong, D. S., Chan, H. C. O., & Cheng, C. H. (2014). Cyberbullying perpetration and victimization among adolescents in Hong Kong. *Children and Youth Services Review, 36*, 133–140. doi:10.1016/j.childyouth.2013.11.006

Wood, R. E. (1969). *Martin Buber's ontology: An analysis of I and thou*. Evanston, IL: Northwestern University Press.

Woolf, N. (2015, March 18). Bitcoin 'Exit Scam": Deep-web Market Operators Disappear with $12m. *The Guardian*.

World Information Society Report 2007. (2007). Retrieved from http://www.itu.int/osg/spu/publications/worldinformationsociety/2007/WISR07

World Internet Users Statistics and 2017 World Population Stats. (n.d.). Retrieved March 23, 2017, from www.internetworldstats.com

Wright, M. F. (2013). The relationship between young adults' beliefs about anonymity and subsequent cyber aggression. *Cyberpsychology, Behavior, and Social Networking*, *16*(12), 858–862. doi:10.1089/cyber.2013.0009 PMID:23849002

Wright, M. F. (2014a). Cyber victimization and perceived stress: Linkages to late adolescents' cyber aggression and psychological functioning. *Youth & Society*.

Wright, M. F. (2014b). Predictors of anonymous cyber aggression: The role of adolescents' beliefs about anonymity, aggression, and the permanency of digital content. *Cyberpsychology, Behavior, and Social Networking*, *17*(7), 431–438. doi:10.1089/cyber.2013.0457 PMID:24724731

Wright, M. F. (2014c). Longitudinal investigation of the associations between adolescents' popularity and cyber social behaviors. *Journal of School Violence*, *13*(3), 291–314. doi:10.1080/15388220.2013.849201

Wright, M. F. (2015). Cyber victimization and adjustment difficulties: The mediation of Chinese and American adolescents' digital technology usage. *Cyberpsychology (Brno)*, *1*(1), 1. Retrieved from http://cyberpsychology.eu/view.php?cisloclanku=2015051102&article=1

Wright, M. F. (in press). Adolescents' cyber aggression perpetration and cyber victimization: The longitudinal associations with school functioning. *Social Psychology of Education*.

Wright, M. F., Kamble, S., Lei, K., Li, Z., Aoyama, I., & Shruti, S. (2015). Peer attachment and cyberbullying involvement among Chinese, Indian, and Japanese adolescents. *Societies (Basel, Switzerland)*, *5*(4), 339–353. doi:10.3390oc5020339

Wright, M. F., & Li, Y. (2012). Kicking the digital dog: A longitudinal investigation of young adults' victimization and cyber-displaced aggression. *Cyberpsychology, Behavior, and Social Networking*, *15*(9), 448–454. doi:10.1089/cyber.2012.0061 PMID:22974350

Wright, M. F., & Li, Y. (2013a). Normative beliefs about aggression and cyber aggression among young adults: A longitudinal investigation. *Aggressive Behavior*, *39*(3), 161–170. doi:10.1002/ab.21470 PMID:23440595

Wright, M. F., & Li, Y. (2013b). The association between cyber victimization and subsequent cyber aggression: The moderating effect of peer rejection. *Journal of Youth and Adolescence*, *42*(5), 662–674. doi:10.100710964-012-9903-3 PMID:23299177

Wyn, J., Cuervo, H., Woodman, D., & Stokes, H. (2005). *Young people, wellbeing and communication technologies*. Retrieved May 2, 2017, from www.vichealth. vic.gov.au

Yanosky, R., & McCredie, J. (2008). *Process and politics: IT governance in higher education* (Research Study 5). Boulder, CO: EDUCAUSE Center for Applied Research. Retrieved from http://www.educause.edu/ecar

Ybarra, M. L., Diener-West, M., & Leaf, P. (2007). Examining the overlap in internet harassment and school bullying: Implications for school intervention. *The Journal of Adolescent Health*, *1*(6), 42–50. doi:10.1016/j.jadohealth.2007.09.004 PMID:18047944

Ybarra, M. L., & Mitchell, K. J. (2004). Online aggressor/targets, aggressors, and targets: A comparison of associated youth characteristics. *Journal of Child Psychology and Psychiatry, and Allied Disciplines*, *45*(7), 1308–1316. doi:10.1111/j.1469-7610.2004.00328.x PMID:15335350

Yousef, W. S. M., & Bellamy, A. (2015). The impact of cyberbullying on the self-esteem and academic functioning of Arab American middle and high school students. *Electronic Journal of Research in Educational Psychology*, *23*(3), 463–482.

Zhou, Z., Tang, H., Tian, Y., Wei, H., Zhang, F., & Morrison, C. M. (2013). Cyberbullying and its risk factors among Chinese high school students. *School Psychology International*, *34*(6), 630–647. doi:10.1177/0143034313479692

Zimmerman, M. E. (1990). *Heidegger's confrontation with modernity: technology, politics, and art*. Bloomington, IN: Indiana University Press.

Zucker, L. G. (1986). Production of Trust: Institutional Sources of Economic Structure, 1840–1920. *Research in Organizational Behavior*, *8*, 53–111.

Zucker, L. G. (1986). *Production of trust: Institutional sources of economic structure. In Research in organisational behaviour* (p. 8). Greenwich, CT: JAI.

# Related References

To continue our tradition of advancing information science and technology research, we have compiled a list of recommended IGI Global readings. These references will provide additional information and guidance to further enrich your knowledge and assist you with your own research and future publications.

Adesina, K., Ganiu, O., & R., O. S. (2018). Television as Vehicle for Community Development: A Study of Lotunlotun Programme on (B.C.O.S.) Television, Nigeria. In A. Salawu, & T. Owolabi (Eds.), *Exploring Journalism Practice and Perception in Developing Countries* (pp. 60-84). Hershey, PA: IGI Global. doi:10.4018/978-1-5225-3376-4.ch004

Adigun, G. O., Odunola, O. A., & Sobalaje, A. J. (2016). Role of Social Networking for Information Seeking in a Digital Library Environment. In A. Tella (Ed.), *Information Seeking Behavior and Challenges in Digital Libraries* (pp. 272–290). Hershey, PA: IGI Global. doi:10.4018/978-1-5225-0296-8.ch013

Ahmad, M. B., Pride, C., & Corsy, A. K. (2016). Free Speech, Press Freedom, and Democracy in Ghana: A Conceptual and Historical Overview. In L. Mukhongo & J. Macharia (Eds.), *Political Influence of the Media in Developing Countries* (pp. 59–73). Hershey, PA: IGI Global. doi:10.4018/978-1-4666-9613-6.ch005

Ahmad, R. H., & Pathan, A. K. (2017). A Study on M2M (Machine to Machine) System and Communication: Its Security, Threats, and Intrusion Detection System. In M. Ferrag & A. Ahmim (Eds.), *Security Solutions and Applied Cryptography in Smart Grid Communications* (pp. 179–214). Hershey, PA: IGI Global. doi:10.4018/978-1-5225-1829-7.ch010

Akanni, T. M. (2018). In Search of Women-Supportive Media for Sustainable Development in Nigeria. In A. Salawu & T. Owolabi (Eds.), *Exploring Journalism Practice and Perception in Developing Countries* (pp. 126–149). Hershey, PA: IGI Global. doi:10.4018/978-1-5225-3376-4.ch007

Akçay, D. (2017). The Role of Social Media in Shaping Marketing Strategies in the Airline Industry. In V. Benson, R. Tuninga, & G. Saridakis (Eds.), *Analyzing the Strategic Role of Social Networking in Firm Growth and Productivity* (pp. 214–233). Hershey, PA: IGI Global. doi:10.4018/978-1-5225-0559-4.ch012

Al-Rabayah, W. A. (2017). Social Media as Social Customer Relationship Management Tool: Case of Jordan Medical Directory. In W. Al-Rabayah, R. Khasawneh, R. Abu-shamaa, & I. Alsmadi (Eds.), *Strategic Uses of Social Media for Improved Customer Retention* (pp. 108–123). Hershey, PA: IGI Global. doi:10.4018/978-1-5225-1686-6.ch006

Almjeld, J. (2017). Getting "Girly" Online: The Case for Gendering Online Spaces. In E. Monske & K. Blair (Eds.), *Handbook of Research on Writing and Composing in the Age of MOOCs* (pp. 87–105). Hershey, PA: IGI Global. doi:10.4018/978-1-5225-1718-4.ch006

Altaş, A. (2017). Space as a Character in Narrative Advertising: A Qualitative Research on Country Promotion Works. In R. Yılmaz (Ed.), *Narrative Advertising Models and Conceptualization in the Digital Age* (pp. 303–319). Hershey, PA: IGI Global. doi:10.4018/978-1-5225-2373-4.ch017

Altıparmak, B. (2017). The Structural Transformation of Space in Turkish Television Commercials as a Narrative Component. In R. Yılmaz (Ed.), *Narrative Advertising Models and Conceptualization in the Digital Age* (pp. 153–166). Hershey, PA: IGI Global. doi:10.4018/978-1-5225-2373-4.ch009

An, Y., & Harvey, K. E. (2016). Public Relations and Mobile: Becoming Dialogic. In X. Xu (Ed.), *Handbook of Research on Human Social Interaction in the Age of Mobile Devices* (pp. 284–311). Hershey, PA: IGI Global. doi:10.4018/978-1-5225-0469-6.ch013

Assay, B. E. (2018). Regulatory Compliance, Ethical Behaviour, and Sustainable Growth in Nigeria's Telecommunications Industry. In I. Oncioiu (Ed.), *Ethics and Decision-Making for Sustainable Business Practices* (pp. 90–108). Hershey, PA: IGI Global. doi:10.4018/978-1-5225-3773-1.ch006

Averweg, U. R., & Leaning, M. (2018). The Qualities and Potential of Social Media. In M. Khosrow-Pour, D.B.A. (Ed.), Encyclopedia of Information Science and Technology, Fourth Edition (pp. 7106-7115). Hershey, PA: IGI Global. doi:10.4018/978-1-5225-2255-3.ch617

Azemi, Y., & Ozuem, W. (2016). Online Service Failure and Recovery Strategy: The Mediating Role of Social Media. In W. Ozuem & G. Bowen (Eds.), *Competitive Social Media Marketing Strategies* (pp. 112–135). Hershey, PA: IGI Global. doi:10.4018/978-1-4666-9776-8.ch006

Baarda, R. (2017). Digital Democracy in Authoritarian Russia: Opportunity for Participation, or Site of Kremlin Control? In R. Luppicini & R. Baarda (Eds.), *Digital Media Integration for Participatory Democracy* (pp. 87–100). Hershey, PA: IGI Global. doi:10.4018/978-1-5225-2463-2.ch005

Bacallao-Pino, L. M. (2016). Radical Political Communication and Social Media: The Case of the Mexican #YoSoy132. In T. Deželan & I. Vobič (Eds.), *R)evolutionizing Political Communication through Social Media* (pp. 56–74). Hershey, PA: IGI Global. doi:10.4018/978-1-4666-9879-6.ch004

Baggio, B. G. (2016). Why We Would Rather Text than Talk: Personality, Identity, and Anonymity in Modern Virtual Environments. In B. Baggio (Ed.), *Analyzing Digital Discourse and Human Behavior in Modern Virtual Environments* (pp. 110–125). Hershey, PA: IGI Global. doi:10.4018/978-1-4666-9899-4.ch006

Başal, B. (2017). Actor Effect: A Study on Historical Figures Who Have Shaped the Advertising Narration. In R. Yılmaz (Ed.), *Narrative Advertising Models and Conceptualization in the Digital Age* (pp. 34–60). Hershey, PA: IGI Global. doi:10.4018/978-1-5225-2373-4.ch003

Behjati, M., & Cosmas, J. (2017). Self-Organizing Network Solutions: A Principal Step Towards Real 4G and Beyond. In D. Singh (Ed.), *Routing Protocols and Architectural Solutions for Optimal Wireless Networks and Security* (pp. 241–253). Hershey, PA: IGI Global. doi:10.4018/978-1-5225-2342-0.ch011

Bekafigo, M., & Pingley, A. C. (2017). Do Campaigns "Go Negative" on Twitter? In Y. Ibrahim (Ed.), *Politics, Protest, and Empowerment in Digital Spaces* (pp. 178–191). Hershey, PA: IGI Global. doi:10.4018/978-1-5225-1862-4.ch011

Bender, S., & Dickenson, P. (2016). Utilizing Social Media to Engage Students in Online Learning: Building Relationships Outside of the Learning Management System. In P. Dickenson & J. Jaurez (Eds.), *Increasing Productivity and Efficiency in Online Teaching* (pp. 84–105). Hershey, PA: IGI Global. doi:10.4018/978-1-5225-0347-7.ch005

Bermingham, N., & Prendergast, M. (2016). Bespoke Mobile Application Development: Facilitating Transition of Foundation Students to Higher Education. In L. Briz-Ponce, J. Juanes-Méndez, & F. García-Peñalvo (Eds.), *Handbook of Research on Mobile Devices and Applications in Higher Education Settings* (pp. 222–249). Hershey, PA: IGI Global. doi:10.4018/978-1-5225-0256-2.ch010

Bishop, J. (2017). Developing and Validating the "This Is Why We Can't Have Nice Things Scale": Optimising Political Online Communities for Internet Trolling. In Y. Ibrahim (Ed.), *Politics, Protest, and Empowerment in Digital Spaces* (pp. 153–177). Hershey, PA: IGI Global. doi:10.4018/978-1-5225-1862-4.ch010

Bolat, N. (2017). The Functions of the Narrator in Digital Advertising. In R. Yılmaz (Ed.), *Narrative Advertising Models and Conceptualization in the Digital Age* (pp. 184–201). Hershey, PA: IGI Global. doi:10.4018/978-1-5225-2373-4.ch011

Bowen, G., & Bowen, D. (2016). Social Media: Strategic Decision Making Tool. In W. Ozuem & G. Bowen (Eds.), *Competitive Social Media Marketing Strategies* (pp. 94–111). Hershey, PA: IGI Global. doi:10.4018/978-1-4666-9776-8.ch005

Brown, M. A. Sr. (2017). SNIP: High Touch Approach to Communication. In *Solutions for High-Touch Communications in a High-Tech World* (pp. 71–88). Hershey, PA: IGI Global. doi:10.4018/978-1-5225-1897-6.ch004

Brown, M. A. Sr. (2017). Comparing FTF and Online Communication Knowledge. In *Solutions for High-Touch Communications in a High-Tech World* (pp. 103–113). Hershey, PA: IGI Global. doi:10.4018/978-1-5225-1897-6.ch006

Brown, M. A. Sr. (2017). Where Do We Go from Here? In *Solutions for High-Touch Communications in a High-Tech World* (pp. 137–159). Hershey, PA: IGI Global. doi:10.4018/978-1-5225-1897-6.ch008

Brown, M. A. Sr. (2017). Bridging the Communication Gap. In *Solutions for High-Touch Communications in a High-Tech World* (pp. 1–22). Hershey, PA: IGI Global. doi:10.4018/978-1-5225-1897-6.ch001

Brown, M. A. Sr. (2017). Key Strategies for Communication. In *Solutions for High-Touch Communications in a High-Tech World* (pp. 179–202). Hershey, PA: IGI Global. doi:10.4018/978-1-5225-1897-6.ch010

Bryant, K. N. (2017). WordUp!: Student Responses to Social Media in the Technical Writing Classroom. In K. Bryant (Ed.), *Engaging 21st Century Writers with Social Media* (pp. 231–245). Hershey, PA: IGI Global. doi:10.4018/978-1-5225-0562-4.ch014

Buck, E. H. (2017). Slacktivism, Supervision, and #Selfies: Illuminating Social Media Composition through Reception Theory. In K. Bryant (Ed.), *Engaging 21st Century Writers with Social Media* (pp. 163–178). Hershey, PA: IGI Global. doi:10.4018/978-1-5225-0562-4.ch010

Bucur, B. (2016). Sociological School of Bucharest's Publications and the Romanian Political Propaganda in the Interwar Period. In A. Fox (Ed.), *Global Perspectives on Media Events in Contemporary Society* (pp. 106–120). Hershey, PA: IGI Global. doi:10.4018/978-1-4666-9967-0.ch008

Bull, R., & Pianosi, M. (2017). Social Media, Participation, and Citizenship: New Strategic Directions. In V. Benson, R. Tuninga, & G. Saridakis (Eds.), *Analyzing the Strategic Role of Social Networking in Firm Growth and Productivity* (pp. 76–94). Hershey, PA: IGI Global. doi:10.4018/978-1-5225-0559-4.ch005

Camillo, A. A., & Camillo, I. C. (2016). The Ethics of Strategic Managerial Communication in the Global Context. In A. Normore, L. Long, & M. Javidi (Eds.), *Handbook of Research on Effective Communication, Leadership, and Conflict Resolution* (pp. 566–590). Hershey, PA: IGI Global. doi:10.4018/978-1-4666-9970-0.ch030

Cassard, A., & Sloboda, B. W. (2016). Faculty Perception of Virtual 3-D Learning Environment to Assess Student Learning. In D. Choi, A. Dailey-Hebert, & J. Simmons Estes (Eds.), *Emerging Tools and Applications of Virtual Reality in Education* (pp. 48–74). Hershey, PA: IGI Global. doi:10.4018/978-1-4666-9837-6.ch003

Castellano, S., & Khelladi, I. (2017). Play It Like Beckham!: The Influence of Social Networks on E-Reputation – The Case of Sportspeople and Their Online Fan Base. In A. Mesquita (Ed.), *Research Paradigms and Contemporary Perspectives on Human-Technology Interaction* (pp. 43–61). Hershey, PA: IGI Global. doi:10.4018/978-1-5225-1868-6.ch003

Castellet, A. (2016). What If Devices Take Command: Content Innovation Perspectives for Smart Wearables in the Mobile Ecosystem. *International Journal of Handheld Computing Research*, *7*(2), 16–33. doi:10.4018/IJHCR.2016040102

Chugh, R., & Joshi, M. (2017). Challenges of Knowledge Management amidst Rapidly Evolving Tools of Social Media. In R. Chugh (Ed.), *Harnessing Social Media as a Knowledge Management Tool* (pp. 299–314). Hershey, PA: IGI Global. doi:10.4018/978-1-5225-0495-5.ch014

Cockburn, T., & Smith, P. A. (2016). Leadership in the Digital Age: Rhythms and the Beat of Change. In A. Normore, L. Long, & M. Javidi (Eds.), *Handbook of Research on Effective Communication, Leadership, and Conflict Resolution* (pp. 1–20). Hershey, PA: IGI Global. doi:10.4018/978-1-4666-9970-0.ch001

Cole, A. W., & Salek, T. A. (2017). Adopting a Parasocial Connection to Overcome Professional Kakoethos in Online Health Information. In M. Folk & S. Apostel (Eds.), *Establishing and Evaluating Digital Ethos and Online Credibility* (pp. 104–120). Hershey, PA: IGI Global. doi:10.4018/978-1-5225-1072-7.ch006

Cossiavelou, V. (2017). ACTA as Media Gatekeeping Factor: The EU Role as Global Negotiator. *International Journal of Interdisciplinary Telecommunications and Networking*, 9(1), 26–37. doi:10.4018/IJITN.2017010103

Costanza, F. (2017). Social Media Marketing and Value Co-Creation: A System Dynamics Approach. In S. Rozenes & Y. Cohen (Eds.), *Handbook of Research on Strategic Alliances and Value Co-Creation in the Service Industry* (pp. 205–230). Hershey, PA: IGI Global. doi:10.4018/978-1-5225-2084-9.ch011

Cross, D. E. (2016). Globalization and Media's Impact on Cross Cultural Communication: Managing Organizational Change. In A. Normore, L. Long, & M. Javidi (Eds.), *Handbook of Research on Effective Communication, Leadership, and Conflict Resolution* (pp. 21–41). Hershey, PA: IGI Global. doi:10.4018/978-1-4666-9970-0.ch002

Damásio, M. J., Henriques, S., Teixeira-Botelho, I., & Dias, P. (2016). Mobile Media and Social Interaction: Mobile Services and Content as Drivers of Social Interaction. In J. Aguado, C. Feijóo, & I. Martínez (Eds.), *Emerging Perspectives on the Mobile Content Evolution* (pp. 357–379). Hershey, PA: IGI Global. doi:10.4018/978-1-4666-8838-4.ch018

Davis, A., & Foley, L. (2016). Digital Storytelling. In B. Guzzetti & M. Lesley (Eds.), *Handbook of Research on the Societal Impact of Digital Media* (pp. 317–342). Hershey, PA: IGI Global. doi:10.4018/978-1-4666-8310-5.ch013

Davis, S., Palmer, L., & Etienne, J. (2016). The Geography of Digital Literacy: Mapping Communications Technology Training Programs in Austin, Texas. In B. Passarelli, J. Straubhaar, & A. Cuevas-Cerveró (Eds.), *Handbook of Research on Comparative Approaches to the Digital Age Revolution in Europe and the Americas* (pp. 371–384). Hershey, PA: IGI Global. doi:10.4018/978-1-4666-8740-0.ch022

Delello, J. A., & McWhorter, R. R. (2016). New Visual Literacies and Competencies for Education and the Workplace. In B. Guzzetti & M. Lesley (Eds.), *Handbook of Research on the Societal Impact of Digital Media* (pp. 127–162). Hershey, PA: IGI Global. doi:10.4018/978-1-4666-8310-5.ch006

Di Virgilio, F., & Antonelli, G. (2018). Consumer Behavior, Trust, and Electronic Word-of-Mouth Communication: Developing an Online Purchase Intention Model. In F. Di Virgilio (Ed.), *Social Media for Knowledge Management Applications in Modern Organizations* (pp. 58–80). Hershey, PA: IGI Global. doi:10.4018/978-1-5225-2897-5.ch003

Dixit, S. K. (2016). eWOM Marketing in Hospitality Industry. In A. Singh, & P. Duhan (Eds.), Managing Public Relations and Brand Image through Social Media (pp. 266-280). Hershey, PA: IGI Global. doi:10.4018/978-1-5225-0332-3.ch014

Duhan, P., & Singh, A. (2016). Facebook Experience Is Different: An Empirical Study in Indian Context. In S. Rathore & A. Panwar (Eds.), *Capturing, Analyzing, and Managing Word-of-Mouth in the Digital Marketplace* (pp. 188–212). Hershey, PA: IGI Global. doi:10.4018/978-1-4666-9449-1.ch011

Dunne, D. J. (2016). The Scholar's Ludo-Narrative Game and Multimodal Graphic Novel: A Comparison of Fringe Scholarship. In A. Connor & S. Marks (Eds.), *Creative Technologies for Multidisciplinary Applications* (pp. 182–207). Hershey, PA: IGI Global. doi:10.4018/978-1-5225-0016-2.ch008

DuQuette, J. L. (2017). Lessons from Cypris Chat: Revisiting Virtual Communities as Communities. In G. Panconesi & M. Guida (Eds.), *Handbook of Research on Collaborative Teaching Practice in Virtual Learning Environments* (pp. 299–316). Hershey, PA: IGI Global. doi:10.4018/978-1-5225-2426-7.ch016

Ekhlassi, A., Niknejhad Moghadam, M., & Adibi, A. (2018). The Concept of Social Media: The Functional Building Blocks. In *Building Brand Identity in the Age of Social Media: Emerging Research and Opportunities* (pp. 29–60). Hershey, PA: IGI Global. doi:10.4018/978-1-5225-5143-0.ch002

Ekhlassi, A., Niknejhad Moghadam, M., & Adibi, A. (2018). Social Media Branding Strategy: Social Media Marketing Approach. In *Building Brand Identity in the Age of Social Media: Emerging Research and Opportunities* (pp. 94–117). Hershey, PA: IGI Global. doi:10.4018/978-1-5225-5143-0.ch004

Ekhlassi, A., Niknejhad Moghadam, M., & Adibi, A. (2018). The Impact of Social Media on Brand Loyalty: Achieving "E-Trust" Through Engagement. In *Building Brand Identity in the Age of Social Media: Emerging Research and Opportunities* (pp. 155–168). Hershey, PA: IGI Global. doi:10.4018/978-1-5225-5143-0.ch007

Elegbe, O. (2017). An Assessment of Media Contribution to Behaviour Change and HIV Prevention in Nigeria. In O. Nelson, B. Ojebuyi, & A. Salawu (Eds.), *Impacts of the Media on African Socio-Economic Development* (pp. 261–280). Hershey, PA: IGI Global. doi:10.4018/978-1-5225-1859-4.ch017

Endong, F. P. (2018). Hashtag Activism and the Transnationalization of Nigerian-Born Movements Against Terrorism: A Critical Appraisal of the #BringBackOurGirls Campaign. In F. Endong (Ed.), *Exploring the Role of Social Media in Transnational Advocacy* (pp. 36–54). Hershey, PA: IGI Global. doi:10.4018/978-1-5225-2854-8.ch003

Erragcha, N. (2017). Using Social Media Tools in Marketing: Opportunities and Challenges. In M. Brown Sr., (Ed.), *Social Media Performance Evaluation and Success Measurements* (pp. 106–129). Hershey, PA: IGI Global. doi:10.4018/978-1-5225-1963-8.ch006

Ezeh, N. C. (2018). Media Campaign on Exclusive Breastfeeding: Awareness, Perception, and Acceptability Among Mothers in Anambra State, Nigeria. In A. Salawu & T. Owolabi (Eds.), *Exploring Journalism Practice and Perception in Developing Countries* (pp. 172–193). Hershey, PA: IGI Global. doi:10.4018/978-1-5225-3376-4.ch009

Fawole, O. A., & Osho, O. A. (2017). Influence of Social Media on Dating Relationships of Emerging Adults in Nigerian Universities: Social Media and Dating in Nigeria. In M. Wright (Ed.), *Identity, Sexuality, and Relationships among Emerging Adults in the Digital Age* (pp. 168–177). Hershey, PA: IGI Global. doi:10.4018/978-1-5225-1856-3.ch011

Fayoyin, A. (2017). Electoral Polling and Reporting in Africa: Professional and Policy Implications for Media Practice and Political Communication in a Digital Age. In N. Mhiripiri & T. Chari (Eds.), *Media Law, Ethics, and Policy in the Digital Age* (pp. 164–181). Hershey, PA: IGI Global. doi:10.4018/978-1-5225-2095-5.ch009

Fayoyin, A. (2018). Rethinking Media Engagement Strategies for Social Change in Africa: Context, Approaches, and Implications for Development Communication. In A. Salawu & T. Owolabi (Eds.), *Exploring Journalism Practice and Perception in Developing Countries* (pp. 257–280). Hershey, PA: IGI Global. doi:10.4018/978-1-5225-3376-4.ch013

Fechine, Y., & Rêgo, S. C. (2018). Transmedia Television Journalism in Brazil: Jornal da Record News as Reference. In R. Gambarato & G. Alzamora (Eds.), *Exploring Transmedia Journalism in the Digital Age* (pp. 253–265). Hershey, PA: IGI Global. doi:10.4018/978-1-5225-3781-6.ch015

Feng, J., & Lo, K. (2016). Video Broadcasting Protocol for Streaming Applications with Cooperative Clients. In D. Kanellopoulos (Ed.), *Emerging Research on Networked Multimedia Communication Systems* (pp. 205–229). Hershey, PA: IGI Global. doi:10.4018/978-1-4666-8850-6.ch006

Fiore, C. (2017). The Blogging Method: Improving Traditional Student Writing Practices. In K. Bryant (Ed.), *Engaging 21st Century Writers with Social Media* (pp. 179–198). Hershey, PA: IGI Global. doi:10.4018/978-1-5225-0562-4.ch011

Fleming, J., & Kajimoto, M. (2016). The Freedom of Critical Thinking: Examining Efforts to Teach American News Literacy Principles in Hong Kong, Vietnam, and Malaysia. In M. Yildiz & J. Keengwe (Eds.), *Handbook of Research on Media Literacy in the Digital Age* (pp. 208–235). Hershey, PA: IGI Global. doi:10.4018/978-1-4666-9667-9.ch010

Gambarato, R. R., Alzamora, G. C., & Tárcia, L. P. (2018). 2016 Rio Summer Olympics and the Transmedia Journalism of Planned Events. In R. Gambarato & G. Alzamora (Eds.), *Exploring Transmedia Journalism in the Digital Age* (pp. 126–146). Hershey, PA: IGI Global. doi:10.4018/978-1-5225-3781-6.ch008

Ganguin, S., Gemkow, J., & Haubold, R. (2017). Information Overload as a Challenge and Changing Point for Educational Media Literacies. In R. Marques & J. Batista (Eds.), *Information and Communication Overload in the Digital Age* (pp. 302–328). Hershey, PA: IGI Global. doi:10.4018/978-1-5225-2061-0.ch013

Gao, Y. (2016). Reviewing Gratification Effects in Mobile Gaming. In X. Xu (Ed.), *Handbook of Research on Human Social Interaction in the Age of Mobile Devices* (pp. 406–428). Hershey, PA: IGI Global. doi:10.4018/978-1-5225-0469-6.ch017

Gardner, G. C. (2017). The Lived Experience of Smartphone Use in a Unit of the United States Army. In F. Topor (Ed.), *Handbook of Research on Individualism and Identity in the Globalized Digital Age* (pp. 88–117). Hershey, PA: IGI Global. doi:10.4018/978-1-5225-0522-8.ch005

Giessen, H. W. (2016). The Medium, the Content, and the Performance: An Overview on Media-Based Learning. In B. Khan (Ed.), *Revolutionizing Modern Education through Meaningful E-Learning Implementation* (pp. 42–55). Hershey, PA: IGI Global. doi:10.4018/978-1-5225-0466-5.ch003

Giltenane, J. (2016). Investigating the Intention to Use Social Media Tools Within Virtual Project Teams. In G. Silvius (Ed.), *Strategic Integration of Social Media into Project Management Practice* (pp. 83–105). Hershey, PA: IGI Global. doi:10.4018/978-1-4666-9867-3.ch006

Golightly, D., & Houghton, R. J. (2018). Social Media as a Tool to Understand Behaviour on the Railways. In S. Kohli, A. Kumar, J. Easton, & C. Roberts (Eds.), *Innovative Applications of Big Data in the Railway Industry* (pp. 224–239). Hershey, PA: IGI Global. doi:10.4018/978-1-5225-3176-0.ch010

Goovaerts, M., Nieuwenhuysen, P., & Dhamdhere, S. N. (2016). VLIR-UOS Workshop 'E-Info Discovery and Management for Institutes in the South': Presentations and Conclusions, Antwerp, 8-19 December, 2014. In E. de Smet, & S. Dhamdhere (Eds.), E-Discovery Tools and Applications in Modern Libraries (pp. 1-40). Hershey, PA: IGI Global. doi:10.4018/978-1-5225-0474-0.ch001

Grützmann, A., Carvalho de Castro, C., Meireles, A. A., & Rodrigues, R. C. (2016). Organizational Architecture and Online Social Networks: Insights from Innovative Brazilian Companies. In G. Jamil, J. Poças Rascão, F. Ribeiro, & A. Malheiro da Silva (Eds.), *Handbook of Research on Information Architecture and Management in Modern Organizations* (pp. 508–524). Hershey, PA: IGI Global. doi:10.4018/978-1-4666-8637-3.ch023

Gundogan, M. B. (2017). In Search for a "Good Fit" Between Augmented Reality and Mobile Learning Ecosystem. In G. Kurubacak & H. Altinpulluk (Eds.), *Mobile Technologies and Augmented Reality in Open Education* (pp. 135–153). Hershey, PA: IGI Global. doi:10.4018/978-1-5225-2110-5.ch007

Gupta, H. (2018). Impact of Digital Communication on Consumer Behaviour Processes in Luxury Branding Segment: A Study of Apparel Industry. In S. Dasgupta, S. Biswal, & M. Ramesh (Eds.), *Holistic Approaches to Brand Culture and Communication Across Industries* (pp. 132–157). Hershey, PA: IGI Global. doi:10.4018/978-1-5225-3150-0.ch008

Hai-Jew, S. (2017). Creating "(Social) Network Art" with NodeXL. In S. Hai-Jew (Ed.), *Social Media Data Extraction and Content Analysis* (pp. 342–393). Hershey, PA: IGI Global. doi:10.4018/978-1-5225-0648-5.ch011

Hai-Jew, S. (2017). Employing the Sentiment Analysis Tool in NVivo 11 Plus on Social Media Data: Eight Initial Case Types. In N. Rao (Ed.), *Social Media Listening and Monitoring for Business Applications* (pp. 175–244). Hershey, PA: IGI Global. doi:10.4018/978-1-5225-0846-5.ch010

Hai-Jew, S. (2017). Conducting Sentiment Analysis and Post-Sentiment Data Exploration through Automated Means. In S. Hai-Jew (Ed.), *Social Media Data Extraction and Content Analysis* (pp. 202–240). Hershey, PA: IGI Global. doi:10.4018/978-1-5225-0648-5.ch008

Hai-Jew, S. (2017). Applied Analytical "Distant Reading" using NVivo 11 Plus. In S. Hai-Jew (Ed.), *Social Media Data Extraction and Content Analysis* (pp. 159–201). Hershey, PA: IGI Global. doi:10.4018/978-1-5225-0648-5.ch007

Hai-Jew, S. (2017). Flickering Emotions: Feeling-Based Associations from Related Tags Networks on Flickr. In S. Hai-Jew (Ed.), *Social Media Data Extraction and Content Analysis* (pp. 296–341). Hershey, PA: IGI Global. doi:10.4018/978-1-5225-0648-5.ch010

Hai-Jew, S. (2017). Manually Profiling Egos and Entities across Social Media Platforms: Evaluating Shared Messaging and Contents, User Networks, and Metadata. In V. Benson, R. Tuninga, & G. Saridakis (Eds.), *Analyzing the Strategic Role of Social Networking in Firm Growth and Productivity* (pp. 352–405). Hershey, PA: IGI Global. doi:10.4018/978-1-5225-0559-4.ch019

Hai-Jew, S. (2017). Exploring "User," "Video," and (Pseudo) Multi-Mode Networks on YouTube with NodeXL. In S. Hai-Jew (Ed.), *Social Media Data Extraction and Content Analysis* (pp. 242–295). Hershey, PA: IGI Global. doi:10.4018/978-1-5225-0648-5.ch009

Hai-Jew, S. (2018). Exploring "Mass Surveillance" Through Computational Linguistic Analysis of Five Text Corpora: Academic, Mainstream Journalism, Microblogging Hashtag Conversation, Wikipedia Articles, and Leaked Government Data. In *Techniques for Coding Imagery and Multimedia: Emerging Research and Opportunities* (pp. 212–286). Hershey, PA: IGI Global. doi:10.4018/978-1-5225-2679-7.ch004

Hai-Jew, S. (2018). Exploring Identity-Based Humor in a #Selfies #Humor Image Set From Instagram. In *Techniques for Coding Imagery and Multimedia: Emerging Research and Opportunities* (pp. 1–90). Hershey, PA: IGI Global. doi:10.4018/978-1-5225-2679-7.ch001

Hai-Jew, S. (2018). See Ya!: Exploring American Renunciation of Citizenship Through Targeted and Sparse Social Media Data Sets and a Custom Spatial-Based Linguistic Analysis Dictionary. In *Techniques for Coding Imagery and Multimedia: Emerging Research and Opportunities* (pp. 287–393). Hershey, PA: IGI Global. doi:10.4018/978-1-5225-2679-7.ch005

Han, H. S., Zhang, J., Peikazadi, N., Shi, G., Hung, A., Doan, C. P., & Filippelli, S. (2016). An Entertaining Game-Like Learning Environment in a Virtual World for Education. In S. D'Agustino (Ed.), *Creating Teacher Immediacy in Online Learning Environments* (pp. 290–306). Hershey, PA: IGI Global. doi:10.4018/978-1-4666-9995-3.ch015

Harrin, E. (2016). Barriers to Social Media Adoption on Projects. In G. Silvius (Ed.), *Strategic Integration of Social Media into Project Management Practice* (pp. 106–124). Hershey, PA: IGI Global. doi:10.4018/978-1-4666-9867-3.ch007

Harvey, K. E. (2016). Local News and Mobile: Major Tipping Points. In X. Xu (Ed.), *Handbook of Research on Human Social Interaction in the Age of Mobile Devices* (pp. 171–199). Hershey, PA: IGI Global. doi:10.4018/978-1-5225-0469-6.ch009

Harvey, K. E., & An, Y. (2016). Marketing and Mobile: Increasing Integration. In X. Xu (Ed.), *Handbook of Research on Human Social Interaction in the Age of Mobile Devices* (pp. 220–247). Hershey, PA: IGI Global. doi:10.4018/978-1-5225-0469-6.ch011

Harvey, K. E., Auter, P. J., & Stevens, S. (2016). Educators and Mobile: Challenges and Trends. In X. Xu (Ed.), *Handbook of Research on Human Social Interaction in the Age of Mobile Devices* (pp. 61–95). Hershey, PA: IGI Global. doi:10.4018/978-1-5225-0469-6.ch004

Hasan, H., & Linger, H. (2017). Connected Living for Positive Ageing. In S. Gordon (Ed.), *Online Communities as Agents of Change and Social Movements* (pp. 203–223). Hershey, PA: IGI Global. doi:10.4018/978-1-5225-2495-3.ch008

Hashim, K., Al-Sharqi, L., & Kutbi, I. (2016). Perceptions of Social Media Impact on Social Behavior of Students: A Comparison between Students and Faculty. *International Journal of Virtual Communities and Social Networking*, 8(2), 1–11. doi:10.4018/IJVCSN.2016040101

Henriques, S., & Damasio, M. J. (2016). The Value of Mobile Communication for Social Belonging: Mobile Apps and the Impact on Social Interaction. *International Journal of Handheld Computing Research*, 7(2), 44–58. doi:10.4018/IJHCR.2016040104

Hersey, L. N. (2017). CHOICES: Measuring Return on Investment in a Nonprofit Organization. In M. Brown Sr., (Ed.), *Social Media Performance Evaluation and Success Measurements* (pp. 157–179). Hershey, PA: IGI Global. doi:10.4018/978-1-5225-1963-8.ch008

Heuva, W. E. (2017). Deferring Citizens' "Right to Know" in an Information Age: The Information Deficit in Namibia. In N. Mhiripiri & T. Chari (Eds.), *Media Law, Ethics, and Policy in the Digital Age* (pp. 245–267). Hershey, PA: IGI Global. doi:10.4018/978-1-5225-2095-5.ch014

Hopwood, M., & McLean, H. (2017). Social Media in Crisis Communication: The Lance Armstrong Saga. In V. Benson, R. Tuninga, & G. Saridakis (Eds.), *Analyzing the Strategic Role of Social Networking in Firm Growth and Productivity* (pp. 45–58). Hershey, PA: IGI Global. doi:10.4018/978-1-5225-0559-4.ch003

Hotur, S. K. (2018). Indian Approaches to E-Diplomacy: An Overview. In S. Bute (Ed.), *Media Diplomacy and Its Evolving Role in the Current Geopolitical Climate* (pp. 27–35). Hershey, PA: IGI Global. doi:10.4018/978-1-5225-3859-2.ch002

Ibadildin, N., & Harvey, K. E. (2016). Business and Mobile: Rapid Restructure Required. In X. Xu (Ed.), *Handbook of Research on Human Social Interaction in the Age of Mobile Devices* (pp. 312–350). Hershey, PA: IGI Global. doi:10.4018/978-1-5225-0469-6.ch014

Iwasaki, Y. (2017). Youth Engagement in the Era of New Media. In M. Adria & Y. Mao (Eds.), *Handbook of Research on Citizen Engagement and Public Participation in the Era of New Media* (pp. 90–105). Hershey, PA: IGI Global. doi:10.4018/978-1-5225-1081-9.ch006

Jamieson, H. V. (2017). We have a Situation!: Cyberformance and Civic Engagement in Post-Democracy. In R. Shin (Ed.), *Convergence of Contemporary Art, Visual Culture, and Global Civic Engagement* (pp. 297–317). Hershey, PA: IGI Global. doi:10.4018/978-1-5225-1665-1.ch017

Jimoh, J., & Kayode, J. (2018). Imperative of Peace and Conflict-Sensitive Journalism in Development. In A. Salawu & T. Owolabi (Eds.), *Exploring Journalism Practice and Perception in Developing Countries* (pp. 150–171). Hershey, PA: IGI Global. doi:10.4018/978-1-5225-3376-4.ch008

Johns, R. (2016). Increasing Value of a Tangible Product through Intangible Attributes: Value Co-Creation and Brand Building within Online Communities – Virtual Communities and Value. In R. English & R. Johns (Eds.), *Gender Considerations in Online Consumption Behavior and Internet Use* (pp. 112–124). Hershey, PA: IGI Global. doi:10.4018/978-1-5225-0010-0.ch008

Kanellopoulos, D. N. (2018). Group Synchronization for Multimedia Systems. In M. Khosrow-Pour, D.B.A. (Ed.), Encyclopedia of Information Science and Technology, Fourth Edition (pp. 6435-6446). Hershey, PA: IGI Global. doi:10.4018/978-1-5225-2255-3.ch559

Kapepo, M. I., & Mayisela, T. (2017). Integrating Digital Literacies Into an Undergraduate Course: Inclusiveness Through Use of ICTs. In C. Ayo & V. Mbarika (Eds.), *Sustainable ICT Adoption and Integration for Socio-Economic Development* (pp. 152–173). Hershey, PA: IGI Global. doi:10.4018/978-1-5225-2565-3.ch007

Karahoca, A., & Yengin, İ. (2018). Understanding the Potentials of Social Media in Collaborative Learning. In M. Khosrow-Pour, D.B.A. (Ed.), Encyclopedia of Information Science and Technology, Fourth Edition (pp. 7168-7180). Hershey, PA: IGI Global. doi:10.4018/978-1-5225-2255-3.ch623

Karataş, S., Ceran, O., Ülker, Ü., Gün, E. T., Köse, N. Ö., Kılıç, M., ... Tok, Z. A. (2016). A Trend Analysis of Mobile Learning. In D. Parsons (Ed.), *Mobile and Blended Learning Innovations for Improved Learning Outcomes* (pp. 248–276). Hershey, PA: IGI Global. doi:10.4018/978-1-5225-0359-0.ch013

Kasemsap, K. (2016). Role of Social Media in Brand Promotion: An International Marketing Perspective. In A. Singh & P. Duhan (Eds.), *Managing Public Relations and Brand Image through Social Media* (pp. 62–88). Hershey, PA: IGI Global. doi:10.4018/978-1-5225-0332-3.ch005

Kasemsap, K. (2016). The Roles of Social Media Marketing and Brand Management in Global Marketing. In W. Ozuem & G. Bowen (Eds.), *Competitive Social Media Marketing Strategies* (pp. 173–200). Hershey, PA: IGI Global. doi:10.4018/978-1-4666-9776-8.ch009

Kasemsap, K. (2017). Professional and Business Applications of Social Media Platforms. In V. Benson, R. Tuninga, & G. Saridakis (Eds.), *Analyzing the Strategic Role of Social Networking in Firm Growth and Productivity* (pp. 427–450). Hershey, PA: IGI Global. doi:10.4018/978-1-5225-0559-4.ch021

Kasemsap, K. (2017). Mastering Social Media in the Modern Business World. In N. Rao (Ed.), *Social Media Listening and Monitoring for Business Applications* (pp. 18–44). Hershey, PA: IGI Global. doi:10.4018/978-1-5225-0846-5.ch002

Kato, Y., & Kato, S. (2016). Mobile Phone Use during Class at a Japanese Women's College. In M. Yildiz & J. Keengwe (Eds.), *Handbook of Research on Media Literacy in the Digital Age* (pp. 436–455). Hershey, PA: IGI Global. doi:10.4018/978-1-4666-9667-9.ch021

Kaufmann, H. R., & Manarioti, A. (2017). Consumer Engagement in Social Media Platforms. In *Encouraging Participative Consumerism Through Evolutionary Digital Marketing: Emerging Research and Opportunities* (pp. 95–123). Hershey, PA: IGI Global. doi:10.4018/978-1-68318-012-8.ch004

Kavoura, A., & Kefallonitis, E. (2018). The Effect of Social Media Networking in the Travel Industry. In M. Khosrow-Pour, D.B.A. (Ed.), Encyclopedia of Information Science and Technology, Fourth Edition (pp. 4052-4063). Hershey, PA: IGI Global. doi:10.4018/978-1-5225-2255-3.ch351

Kawamura, Y. (2018). Practice and Modeling of Advertising Communication Strategy: Sender-Driven and Receiver-Driven. In T. Ogata & S. Asakawa (Eds.), *Content Generation Through Narrative Communication and Simulation* (pp. 358–379). Hershey, PA: IGI Global. doi:10.4018/978-1-5225-4775-4.ch013

Kell, C., & Czerniewicz, L. (2017). Visibility of Scholarly Research and Changing Research Communication Practices: A Case Study from Namibia. In A. Esposito (Ed.), *Research 2.0 and the Impact of Digital Technologies on Scholarly Inquiry* (pp. 97–116). Hershey, PA: IGI Global. doi:10.4018/978-1-5225-0830-4.ch006

Khalil, G. E. (2016). Change through Experience: How Experiential Play and Emotional Engagement Drive Health Game Success. In D. Novák, B. Tulu, & H. Brendryen (Eds.), *Handbook of Research on Holistic Perspectives in Gamification for Clinical Practice* (pp. 10–34). Hershey, PA: IGI Global. doi:10.4018/978-1-4666-9522-1.ch002

Kılınç, U. (2017). Create It! Extend It!: Evolution of Comics Through Narrative Advertising. In R. Yılmaz (Ed.), *Narrative Advertising Models and Conceptualization in the Digital Age* (pp. 117–132). Hershey, PA: IGI Global. doi:10.4018/978-1-5225-2373-4.ch007

Kim, J. H. (2016). Pedagogical Approaches to Media Literacy Education in the United States. In M. Yildiz & J. Keengwe (Eds.), *Handbook of Research on Media Literacy in the Digital Age* (pp. 53–74). Hershey, PA: IGI Global. doi:10.4018/978-1-4666-9667-9.ch003

Kirigha, J. M., Mukhongo, L. L., & Masinde, R. (2016). Beyond Web 2.0. Social Media and Urban Educated Youths Participation in Kenyan Politics. In L. Mukhongo & J. Macharia (Eds.), *Political Influence of the Media in Developing Countries* (pp. 156–174). Hershey, PA: IGI Global. doi:10.4018/978-1-4666-9613-6.ch010

Krochmal, M. M. (2016). Training for Mobile Journalism. In D. Mentor (Ed.), *Handbook of Research on Mobile Learning in Contemporary Classrooms* (pp. 336–362). Hershey, PA: IGI Global. doi:10.4018/978-1-5225-0251-7.ch017

Kumar, P., & Sinha, A. (2018). Business-Oriented Analytics With Social Network of Things. In H. Bansal, G. Shrivastava, G. Nguyen, & L. Stanciu (Eds.), *Social Network Analytics for Contemporary Business Organizations* (pp. 166–187). Hershey, PA: IGI Global. doi:10.4018/978-1-5225-5097-6.ch009

Kunock, A. I. (2017). Boko Haram Insurgency in Cameroon: Role of Mass Media in Conflict Management. In N. Mhiripiri & T. Chari (Eds.), *Media Law, Ethics, and Policy in the Digital Age* (pp. 226–244). Hershey, PA: IGI Global. doi:10.4018/978-1-5225-2095-5.ch013

Labadie, J. A. (2018). Digitally Mediated Art Inspired by Technology Integration: A Personal Journey. In A. Ursyn (Ed.), *Visual Approaches to Cognitive Education With Technology Integration* (pp. 121–162). Hershey, PA: IGI Global. doi:10.4018/978-1-5225-5332-8.ch008

Lefkowith, S. (2017). Credibility and Crisis in Pseudonymous Communities. In M. Folk & S. Apostel (Eds.), *Establishing and Evaluating Digital Ethos and Online Credibility* (pp. 190–236). Hershey, PA: IGI Global. doi:10.4018/978-1-5225-1072-7.ch010

Lemoine, P. A., Hackett, P. T., & Richardson, M. D. (2016). The Impact of Social Media on Instruction in Higher Education. In L. Briz-Ponce, J. Juanes-Méndez, & F. García-Peñalvo (Eds.), *Handbook of Research on Mobile Devices and Applications in Higher Education Settings* (pp. 373–401). Hershey, PA: IGI Global. doi:10.4018/978-1-5225-0256-2.ch016

Liampotis, N., Papadopoulou, E., Kalatzis, N., Roussaki, I. G., Kosmides, P., Sykas, E. D., ... Taylor, N. K. (2016). Tailoring Privacy-Aware Trustworthy Cooperating Smart Spaces for University Environments. In A. Panagopoulos (Ed.), *Handbook of Research on Next Generation Mobile Communication Systems* (pp. 410–439). Hershey, PA: IGI Global. doi:10.4018/978-1-4666-8732-5.ch016

Luppicini, R. (2017). Technoethics and Digital Democracy for Future Citizens. In R. Luppicini & R. Baarda (Eds.), *Digital Media Integration for Participatory Democracy* (pp. 1–21). Hershey, PA: IGI Global. doi:10.4018/978-1-5225-2463-2.ch001

Mahajan, I. M., Rather, M., Shafiq, H., & Qadri, U. (2016). Media Literacy Organizations. In M. Yildiz & J. Keengwe (Eds.), *Handbook of Research on Media Literacy in the Digital Age* (pp. 236–248). Hershey, PA: IGI Global. doi:10.4018/978-1-4666-9667-9.ch011

Maher, D. (2018). Supporting Pre-Service Teachers' Understanding and Use of Mobile Devices. In J. Keengwe (Ed.), *Handbook of Research on Mobile Technology, Constructivism, and Meaningful Learning* (pp. 160–177). Hershey, PA: IGI Global. doi:10.4018/978-1-5225-3949-0.ch009

Makhwanya, A. (2018). Barriers to Social Media Advocacy: Lessons Learnt From the Project "Tell Them We Are From Here". In F. Endong (Ed.), *Exploring the Role of Social Media in Transnational Advocacy* (pp. 55–72). Hershey, PA: IGI Global. doi:10.4018/978-1-5225-2854-8.ch004

Manli, G., & Rezaei, S. (2017). Value and Risk: Dual Pillars of Apps Usefulness. In S. Rezaei (Ed.), *Apps Management and E-Commerce Transactions in Real-Time* (pp. 274–292). Hershey, PA: IGI Global. doi:10.4018/978-1-5225-2449-6.ch013

Manrique, C. G., & Manrique, G. G. (2017). Social Media's Role in Alleviating Political Corruption and Scandals: The Philippines during and after the Marcos Regime. In K. Demirhan & D. Çakır-Demirhan (Eds.), *Political Scandal, Corruption, and Legitimacy in the Age of Social Media* (pp. 205–222). Hershey, PA: IGI Global. doi:10.4018/978-1-5225-2019-1.ch009

Manzoor, A. (2016). Cultural Barriers to Organizational Social Media Adoption. In A. Goel & P. Singhal (Eds.), *Product Innovation through Knowledge Management and Social Media Strategies* (pp. 31–45). Hershey, PA: IGI Global. doi:10.4018/978-1-4666-9607-5.ch002

Manzoor, A. (2016). Social Media for Project Management. In G. Silvius (Ed.), *Strategic Integration of Social Media into Project Management Practice* (pp. 51–65). Hershey, PA: IGI Global. doi:10.4018/978-1-4666-9867-3.ch004

Marovitz, M. (2017). Social Networking Engagement and Crisis Communication Considerations. In M. Brown Sr., (Ed.), *Social Media Performance Evaluation and Success Measurements* (pp. 130–155). Hershey, PA: IGI Global. doi:10.4018/978-1-5225-1963-8.ch007

Mathur, D., & Mathur, D. (2016). Word of Mouth on Social Media: A Potent Tool for Brand Building. In S. Rathore & A. Panwar (Eds.), *Capturing, Analyzing, and Managing Word-of-Mouth in the Digital Marketplace* (pp. 45–60). Hershey, PA: IGI Global. doi:10.4018/978-1-4666-9449-1.ch003

Maulana, I. (2018). Spontaneous Taking and Posting Selfie: Reclaiming the Lost Trust. In S. Hai-Jew (Ed.), *Selfies as a Mode of Social Media and Work Space Research* (pp. 28–50). Hershey, PA: IGI Global. doi:10.4018/978-1-5225-3373-3.ch002

Mayo, S. (2018). A Collective Consciousness Model in a Post-Media Society. In M. Khosrow-Pour (Ed.), *Enhancing Art, Culture, and Design With Technological Integration* (pp. 25–49). Hershey, PA: IGI Global. doi:10.4018/978-1-5225-5023-5.ch002

Mazur, E., Signorella, M. L., & Hough, M. (2018). The Internet Behavior of Older Adults. In M. Khosrow-Pour, D.B.A. (Ed.), Encyclopedia of Information Science and Technology, Fourth Edition (pp. 7026-7035). Hershey, PA: IGI Global. doi:10.4018/978-1-5225-2255-3.ch609

McGuire, M. (2017). Reblogging as Writing: The Role of Tumblr in the Writing Classroom. In K. Bryant (Ed.), *Engaging 21st Century Writers with Social Media* (pp. 116–131). Hershey, PA: IGI Global. doi:10.4018/978-1-5225-0562-4.ch007

McKee, J. (2018). Architecture as a Tool to Solve Business Planning Problems. In M. Khosrow-Pour, D.B.A. (Ed.), Encyclopedia of Information Science and Technology, Fourth Edition (pp. 573-586). Hershey, PA: IGI Global. doi:10.4018/978-1-5225-2255-3.ch050

McMahon, D. (2017). With a Little Help from My Friends: The Irish Radio Industry's Strategic Appropriation of Facebook for Commercial Growth. In V. Benson, R. Tuninga, & G. Saridakis (Eds.), *Analyzing the Strategic Role of Social Networking in Firm Growth and Productivity* (pp. 157–171). Hershey, PA: IGI Global. doi:10.4018/978-1-5225-0559-4.ch009

McPherson, M. J., & Lemon, N. (2017). The Hook, Woo, and Spin: Academics Creating Relations on Social Media. In A. Esposito (Ed.), *Research 2.0 and the Impact of Digital Technologies on Scholarly Inquiry* (pp. 167–187). Hershey, PA: IGI Global. doi:10.4018/978-1-5225-0830-4.ch009

Melro, A., & Oliveira, L. (2018). Screen Culture. In M. Khosrow-Pour, D.B.A. (Ed.), Encyclopedia of Information Science and Technology, Fourth Edition (pp. 4255-4266). Hershey, PA: IGI Global. doi:10.4018/978-1-5225-2255-3.ch369

Merwin, G. A. Jr, McDonald, J. S., Bennett, J. R. Jr, & Merwin, K. A. (2016). Social Media Applications Promote Constituent Involvement in Government Management. In G. Silvius (Ed.), *Strategic Integration of Social Media into Project Management Practice* (pp. 272–291). Hershey, PA: IGI Global. doi:10.4018/978-1-4666-9867-3.ch016

Mhiripiri, N. A., & Chikakano, J. (2017). Criminal Defamation, the Criminalisation of Expression, Media and Information Dissemination in the Digital Age: A Legal and Ethical Perspective. In N. Mhiripiri & T. Chari (Eds.), *Media Law, Ethics, and Policy in the Digital Age* (pp. 1–24). Hershey, PA: IGI Global. doi:10.4018/978-1-5225-2095-5.ch001

Miliopoulou, G., & Cossiavelou, V. (2016). Brands and Media Gatekeeping in the Social Media: Current Trends and Practices – An Exploratory Research. *International Journal of Interdisciplinary Telecommunications and Networking*, 8(4), 51–64. doi:10.4018/IJITN.2016100105

Miron, E., Palmor, A., Ravid, G., Sharon, A., Tikotsky, A., & Zirkel, Y. (2017). Principles and Good Practices for Using Wikis within Organizations. In R. Chugh (Ed.), *Harnessing Social Media as a Knowledge Management Tool* (pp. 143–176). Hershey, PA: IGI Global. doi:10.4018/978-1-5225-0495-5.ch008

Mishra, K. E., Mishra, A. K., & Walker, K. (2016). Leadership Communication, Internal Marketing, and Employee Engagement: A Recipe to Create Brand Ambassadors. In A. Normore, L. Long, & M. Javidi (Eds.), *Handbook of Research on Effective Communication, Leadership, and Conflict Resolution* (pp. 311–329). Hershey, PA: IGI Global. doi:10.4018/978-1-4666-9970-0.ch017

Moeller, C. L. (2018). Sharing Your Personal Medical Experience Online: Is It an Irresponsible Act or Patient Empowerment? In S. Sekalala & B. Niezgoda (Eds.), *Global Perspectives on Health Communication in the Age of Social Media* (pp. 185–209). Hershey, PA: IGI Global. doi:10.4018/978-1-5225-3716-8.ch007

Mosanako, S. (2017). Broadcasting Policy in Botswana: The Case of Botswana Television. In O. Nelson, B. Ojebuyi, & A. Salawu (Eds.), *Impacts of the Media on African Socio-Economic Development* (pp. 217–230). Hershey, PA: IGI Global. doi:10.4018/978-1-5225-1859-4.ch014

Nazari, A. (2016). Developing a Social Media Communication Plan. In G. Silvius (Ed.), *Strategic Integration of Social Media into Project Management Practice* (pp. 194–217). Hershey, PA: IGI Global. doi:10.4018/978-1-4666-9867-3.ch012

Neto, B. M. (2016). From Information Society to Community Service: The Birth of E-Citizenship. In B. Passarelli, J. Straubhaar, & A. Cuevas-Cerveró (Eds.), *Handbook of Research on Comparative Approaches to the Digital Age Revolution in Europe and the Americas* (pp. 101–123). Hershey, PA: IGI Global. doi:10.4018/978-1-4666-8740-0.ch007

Noguti, V., Singh, S., & Waller, D. S. (2016). Gender Differences in Motivations to Use Social Networking Sites. In R. English & R. Johns (Eds.), *Gender Considerations in Online Consumption Behavior and Internet Use* (pp. 32–49). Hershey, PA: IGI Global. doi:10.4018/978-1-5225-0010-0.ch003

Noor, R. (2017). Citizen Journalism: News Gathering by Amateurs. In M. Adria & Y. Mao (Eds.), *Handbook of Research on Citizen Engagement and Public Participation in the Era of New Media* (pp. 194–229). Hershey, PA: IGI Global. doi:10.4018/978-1-5225-1081-9.ch012

Nwagbara, U., Oruh, E. S., & Brown, C. (2016). State Fragility and Stakeholder Engagement: New Media and Stakeholders' Voice Amplification in the Nigerian Petroleum Industry. In W. Ozuem & G. Bowen (Eds.), *Competitive Social Media Marketing Strategies* (pp. 136–154). Hershey, PA: IGI Global. doi:10.4018/978-1-4666-9776-8.ch007

Obermayer, N., Csepregi, A., & Kővári, E. (2017). Knowledge Sharing Relation to Competence, Emotional Intelligence, and Social Media Regarding Generations. In A. Bencsik (Ed.), *Knowledge Management Initiatives and Strategies in Small and Medium Enterprises* (pp. 269–290). Hershey, PA: IGI Global. doi:10.4018/978-1-5225-1642-2.ch013

Obermayer, N., Gaál, Z., Szabó, L., & Csepregi, A. (2017). Leveraging Knowledge Sharing over Social Media Tools. In R. Chugh (Ed.), *Harnessing Social Media as a Knowledge Management Tool* (pp. 1–24). Hershey, PA: IGI Global. doi:10.4018/978-1-5225-0495-5.ch001

Ogwezzy-Ndisika, A. O., & Faustino, B. A. (2016). Gender Responsive Election Coverage in Nigeria: A Score Card of 2011 General Elections. In L. Mukhongo & J. Macharia (Eds.), *Political Influence of the Media in Developing Countries* (pp. 234–249). Hershey, PA: IGI Global. doi:10.4018/978-1-4666-9613-6.ch015

Okoroafor, O. E. (2018). New Media Technology and Development Journalism in Nigeria. In A. Salawu & T. Owolabi (Eds.), *Exploring Journalism Practice and Perception in Developing Countries* (pp. 105–125). Hershey, PA: IGI Global. doi:10.4018/978-1-5225-3376-4.ch006

Olaleye, S. A., Sanusi, I. T., & Ukpabi, D. C. (2018). Assessment of Mobile Money Enablers in Nigeria. In F. Mtenzi, G. Oreku, D. Lupiana, & J. Yonazi (Eds.), *Mobile Technologies and Socio-Economic Development in Emerging Nations* (pp. 129–155). Hershey, PA: IGI Global. doi:10.4018/978-1-5225-4029-8.ch007

Ozuem, W., Pinho, C. A., & Azemi, Y. (2016). User-Generated Content and Perceived Customer Value. In W. Ozuem & G. Bowen (Eds.), *Competitive Social Media Marketing Strategies* (pp. 50–63). Hershey, PA: IGI Global. doi:10.4018/978-1-4666-9776-8.ch003

Pacchiega, C. (2017). An Informal Methodology for Teaching Through Virtual Worlds: Using Internet Tools and Virtual Worlds in a Coordinated Pattern to Teach Various Subjects. In G. Panconesi & M. Guida (Eds.), *Handbook of Research on Collaborative Teaching Practice in Virtual Learning Environments* (pp. 163–180). Hershey, PA: IGI Global. doi:10.4018/978-1-5225-2426-7.ch009

Pase, A. F., Goss, B. M., & Tietzmann, R. (2018). A Matter of Time: Transmedia Journalism Challenges. In R. Gambarato & G. Alzamora (Eds.), *Exploring Transmedia Journalism in the Digital Age* (pp. 49–66). Hershey, PA: IGI Global. doi:10.4018/978-1-5225-3781-6.ch004

Passarelli, B., & Paletta, F. C. (2016). Living inside the NET: The Primacy of Interactions and Processes. In B. Passarelli, J. Straubhaar, & A. Cuevas-Cerveró (Eds.), *Handbook of Research on Comparative Approaches to the Digital Age Revolution in Europe and the Americas* (pp. 1–15). Hershey, PA: IGI Global. doi:10.4018/978-1-4666-8740-0.ch001

Patkin, T. T. (2017). Social Media and Knowledge Management in a Crisis Context: Barriers and Opportunities. In R. Chugh (Ed.), *Harnessing Social Media as a Knowledge Management Tool* (pp. 125–142). Hershey, PA: IGI Global. doi:10.4018/978-1-5225-0495-5.ch007

Pavlíček, A. (2017). Social Media and Creativity: How to Engage Users and Tourists. In A. Kiráľová (Ed.), *Driving Tourism through Creative Destinations and Activities* (pp. 181–202). Hershey, PA: IGI Global. doi:10.4018/978-1-5225-2016-0.ch009

Pillay, K., & Maharaj, M. (2017). The Business of Advocacy: A Case Study of Greenpeace. In V. Benson, R. Tuninga, & G. Saridakis (Eds.), *Analyzing the Strategic Role of Social Networking in Firm Growth and Productivity* (pp. 59–75). Hershey, PA: IGI Global. doi:10.4018/978-1-5225-0559-4.ch004

Piven, I. P., & Breazeale, M. (2017). Desperately Seeking Customer Engagement: The Five-Sources Model of Brand Value on Social Media. In V. Benson, R. Tuninga, & G. Saridakis (Eds.), *Analyzing the Strategic Role of Social Networking in Firm Growth and Productivity* (pp. 283–313). Hershey, PA: IGI Global. doi:10.4018/978-1-5225-0559-4.ch016

Pokharel, R. (2017). New Media and Technology: How Do They Change the Notions of the Rhetorical Situations? In B. Gurung & M. Limbu (Eds.), *Integration of Cloud Technologies in Digitally Networked Classrooms and Learning Communities* (pp. 120–148). Hershey, PA: IGI Global. doi:10.4018/978-1-5225-1650-7.ch008

Popoola, I. S. (2016). The Press and the Emergent Political Class in Nigeria: Media, Elections, and Democracy. In L. Mukhongo & J. Macharia (Eds.), *Political Influence of the Media in Developing Countries* (pp. 45–58). Hershey, PA: IGI Global. doi:10.4018/978-1-4666-9613-6.ch004

Porlezza, C., Benecchi, E., & Colapinto, C. (2018). The Transmedia Revitalization of Investigative Journalism: Opportunities and Challenges of the Serial Podcast. In R. Gambarato & G. Alzamora (Eds.), *Exploring Transmedia Journalism in the Digital Age* (pp. 183–201). Hershey, PA: IGI Global. doi:10.4018/978-1-5225-3781-6.ch011

Ramluckan, T., Ally, S. E., & van Niekerk, B. (2017). Twitter Use in Student Protests: The Case of South Africa's #FeesMustFall Campaign. In M. Korstanje (Ed.), *Threat Mitigation and Detection of Cyber Warfare and Terrorism Activities* (pp. 220–253). Hershey, PA: IGI Global. doi:10.4018/978-1-5225-1938-6.ch010

Rao, N. R. (2017). Social Media: An Enabler for Governance. In N. Rao (Ed.), *Social Media Listening and Monitoring for Business Applications* (pp. 151–164). Hershey, PA: IGI Global. doi:10.4018/978-1-5225-0846-5.ch008

Rathore, A. K., Tuli, N., & Ilavarasan, P. V. (2016). Pro-Business or Common Citizen?: An Analysis of an Indian Woman CEO's Tweets. *International Journal of Virtual Communities and Social Networking*, *8*(1), 19–29. doi:10.4018/IJVCSN.2016010102

Redi, F. (2017). Enhancing Coopetition Among Small Tourism Destinations by Creativity. In A. Kiráľová (Ed.), *Driving Tourism through Creative Destinations and Activities* (pp. 223–244). Hershey, PA: IGI Global. doi:10.4018/978-1-5225-2016-0.ch011

Reeves, M. (2016). Social Media: It Can Play a Positive Role in Education. In R. English & R. Johns (Eds.), *Gender Considerations in Online Consumption Behavior and Internet Use* (pp. 82–95). Hershey, PA: IGI Global. doi:10.4018/978-1-5225-0010-0.ch006

Reis, Z. A. (2016). Bring the Media Literacy of Turkish Pre-Service Teachers to the Table. In M. Yildiz & J. Keengwe (Eds.), *Handbook of Research on Media Literacy in the Digital Age* (pp. 405–422). Hershey, PA: IGI Global. doi:10.4018/978-1-4666-9667-9.ch019

Resuloğlu, F., & Yılmaz, R. (2017). A Model for Interactive Advertising Narration. In R. Yılmaz (Ed.), *Narrative Advertising Models and Conceptualization in the Digital Age* (pp. 1–20). Hershey, PA: IGI Global. doi:10.4018/978-1-5225-2373-4.ch001

Ritzhaupt, A. D., Poling, N., Frey, C., Kang, Y., & Johnson, M. (2016). A Phenomenological Study of Games, Simulations, and Virtual Environments Courses: What Are We Teaching and How? *International Journal of Gaming and Computer-Mediated Simulations*, *8*(3), 59–73. doi:10.4018/IJGCMS.2016070104

Ross, D. B., Eleno-Orama, M., & Salah, E. V. (2018). The Aging and Technological Society: Learning Our Way Through the Decades. In V. Bryan, A. Musgrove, & J. Powers (Eds.), *Handbook of Research on Human Development in the Digital Age* (pp. 205–234). Hershey, PA: IGI Global. doi:10.4018/978-1-5225-2838-8.ch010

Rusko, R., & Merenheimo, P. (2017). Co-Creating the Christmas Story: Digitalizing as a Shared Resource for a Shared Brand. In I. Oncioiu (Ed.), *Driving Innovation and Business Success in the Digital Economy* (pp. 137–157). Hershey, PA: IGI Global. doi:10.4018/978-1-5225-1779-5.ch010

Sabao, C., & Chikara, T. O. (2018). Social Media as Alternative Public Sphere for Citizen Participation and Protest in National Politics in Zimbabwe: The Case of #thisflag. In F. Endong (Ed.), *Exploring the Role of Social Media in Transnational Advocacy* (pp. 17–35). Hershey, PA: IGI Global. doi:10.4018/978-1-5225-2854-8.ch002

Samarthya-Howard, A., & Rogers, D. (2018). Scaling Mobile Technologies to Maximize Reach and Impact: Partnering With Mobile Network Operators and Governments. In S. Takavarasha Jr & C. Adams (Eds.), *Affordability Issues Surrounding the Use of ICT for Development and Poverty Reduction* (pp. 193–211). Hershey, PA: IGI Global. doi:10.4018/978-1-5225-3179-1.ch009

Sandoval-Almazan, R. (2017). Political Messaging in Digital Spaces: The Case of Twitter in Mexico's Presidential Campaign. In Y. Ibrahim (Ed.), *Politics, Protest, and Empowerment in Digital Spaces* (pp. 72–90). Hershey, PA: IGI Global. doi:10.4018/978-1-5225-1862-4.ch005

Schultz, C. D., & Dellnitz, A. (2018). Attribution Modeling in Online Advertising. In K. Yang (Ed.), *Multi-Platform Advertising Strategies in the Global Marketplace* (pp. 226–249). Hershey, PA: IGI Global. doi:10.4018/978-1-5225-3114-2.ch009

Schultz, C. D., & Holsing, C. (2018). Differences Across Device Usage in Search Engine Advertising. In K. Yang (Ed.), *Multi-Platform Advertising Strategies in the Global Marketplace* (pp. 250–279). Hershey, PA: IGI Global. doi:10.4018/978-1-5225-3114-2.ch010

Senadheera, V., Warren, M., Leitch, S., & Pye, G. (2017). Facebook Content Analysis: A Study into Australian Banks' Social Media Community Engagement. In S. Hai-Jew (Ed.), *Social Media Data Extraction and Content Analysis* (pp. 412–432). Hershey, PA: IGI Global. doi:10.4018/978-1-5225-0648-5.ch013

Sharma, A. R. (2018). Promoting Global Competencies in India: Media and Information Literacy as Stepping Stone. In M. Yildiz, S. Funk, & B. De Abreu (Eds.), *Promoting Global Competencies Through Media Literacy* (pp. 160–174). Hershey, PA: IGI Global. doi:10.4018/978-1-5225-3082-4.ch010

Sillah, A. (2017). Nonprofit Organizations and Social Media Use: An Analysis of Nonprofit Organizations' Effective Use of Social Media Tools. In M. Brown Sr., (Ed.), *Social Media Performance Evaluation and Success Measurements* (pp. 180–195). Hershey, PA: IGI Global. doi:10.4018/978-1-5225-1963-8.ch009

Škorić, M. (2017). Adaptation of Winlink 2000 Emergency Amateur Radio Email Network to a VHF Packet Radio Infrastructure. In A. El Oualkadi & J. Zbitou (Eds.), *Handbook of Research on Advanced Trends in Microwave and Communication Engineering* (pp. 498–528). Hershey, PA: IGI Global. doi:10.4018/978-1-5225-0773-4.ch016

Skubida, D. (2016). Can Some Computer Games Be a Sport?: Issues with Legitimization of eSport as a Sporting Activity. *International Journal of Gaming and Computer-Mediated Simulations*, *8*(4), 38–52. doi:10.4018/IJGCMS.2016100103

Sonnenberg, C. (2016). Mobile Content Adaptation: An Analysis of Techniques and Frameworks. In J. Aguado, C. Feijóo, & I. Martínez (Eds.), *Emerging Perspectives on the Mobile Content Evolution* (pp. 177–199). Hershey, PA: IGI Global. doi:10.4018/978-1-4666-8838-4.ch010

Sonnevend, J. (2016). More Hope!: Ceremonial Media Events Are Still Powerful in the Twenty-First Century. In A. Fox (Ed.), *Global Perspectives on Media Events in Contemporary Society* (pp. 132–140). Hershey, PA: IGI Global. doi:10.4018/978-1-4666-9967-0.ch010

Sood, T. (2017). Services Marketing: A Sector of the Current Millennium. In T. Sood (Ed.), *Strategic Marketing Management and Tactics in the Service Industry* (pp. 15–42). Hershey, PA: IGI Global. doi:10.4018/978-1-5225-2475-5.ch002

Stairs, G. A. (2016). The Amplification of the Sunni-Shia Divide through Contemporary Communications Technology: Fear and Loathing in the Modern Middle East. In S. Gibson & A. Lando (Eds.), *Impact of Communication and the Media on Ethnic Conflict* (pp. 214–231). Hershey, PA: IGI Global. doi:10.4018/978-1-4666-9728-7.ch013

Stokinger, E., & Ozuem, W. (2016). The Intersection of Social Media and Customer Retention in the Luxury Beauty Industry. In W. Ozuem & G. Bowen (Eds.), *Competitive Social Media Marketing Strategies* (pp. 235–258). Hershey, PA: IGI Global. doi:10.4018/978-1-4666-9776-8.ch012

Sudarsanam, S. K. (2017). Social Media Metrics. In N. Rao (Ed.), *Social Media Listening and Monitoring for Business Applications* (pp. 131–149). Hershey, PA: IGI Global. doi:10.4018/978-1-5225-0846-5.ch007

Swiatek, L. (2017). Accessing the Finest Minds: Insights into Creativity from Esteemed Media Professionals. In N. Silton (Ed.), *Exploring the Benefits of Creativity in Education, Media, and the Arts* (pp. 240–263). Hershey, PA: IGI Global. doi:10.4018/978-1-5225-0504-4.ch012

Switzer, J. S., & Switzer, R. V. (2016). Virtual Teams: Profiles of Successful Leaders. In B. Baggio (Ed.), *Analyzing Digital Discourse and Human Behavior in Modern Virtual Environments* (pp. 1–24). Hershey, PA: IGI Global. doi:10.4018/978-1-4666-9899-4.ch001

Tabbane, R. S., & Debabi, M. (2016). Electronic Word of Mouth: Definitions and Concepts. In S. Rathore & A. Panwar (Eds.), *Capturing, Analyzing, and Managing Word-of-Mouth in the Digital Marketplace* (pp. 1–27). Hershey, PA: IGI Global. doi:10.4018/978-1-4666-9449-1.ch001

Tellería, A. S. (2016). The Role of the Profile and the Digital Identity on the Mobile Content. In J. Aguado, C. Feijóo, & I. Martínez (Eds.), *Emerging Perspectives on the Mobile Content Evolution* (pp. 263–282). Hershey, PA: IGI Global. doi:10.4018/978-1-4666-8838-4.ch014

Teurlings, J. (2017). What Critical Media Studies Should Not Take from Actor-Network Theory. In M. Spöhrer & B. Ochsner (Eds.), *Applying the Actor-Network Theory in Media Studies* (pp. 66–78). Hershey, PA: IGI Global. doi:10.4018/978-1-5225-0616-4.ch005

Tomé, V. (2018). Assessing Media Literacy in Teacher Education. In M. Yildiz, S. Funk, & B. De Abreu (Eds.), *Promoting Global Competencies Through Media Literacy* (pp. 1–19). Hershey, PA: IGI Global. doi:10.4018/978-1-5225-3082-4.ch001

Toscano, J. P. (2017). Social Media and Public Participation: Opportunities, Barriers, and a New Framework. In M. Adria & Y. Mao (Eds.), *Handbook of Research on Citizen Engagement and Public Participation in the Era of New Media* (pp. 73–89). Hershey, PA: IGI Global. doi:10.4018/978-1-5225-1081-9.ch005

Trauth, E. (2017). Creating Meaning for Millennials: Bakhtin, Rosenblatt, and the Use of Social Media in the Composition Classroom. In K. Bryant (Ed.), *Engaging 21st Century Writers with Social Media* (pp. 151–162). Hershey, PA: IGI Global. doi:10.4018/978-1-5225-0562-4.ch009

Ugangu, W. (2016). Kenya's Difficult Political Transitions Ethnicity and the Role of Media. In L. Mukhongo & J. Macharia (Eds.), *Political Influence of the Media in Developing Countries* (pp. 12–24). Hershey, PA: IGI Global. doi:10.4018/978-1-4666-9613-6.ch002

Uprety, S. (2018). Print Media's Role in Securitization: National Security and Diplomacy Discourses in Nepal. In S. Bute (Ed.), *Media Diplomacy and Its Evolving Role in the Current Geopolitical Climate* (pp. 56–82). Hershey, PA: IGI Global. doi:10.4018/978-1-5225-3859-2.ch004

Van der Merwe, L. (2016). Social Media Use within Project Teams: Practical Application of Social Media on Projects. In G. Silvius (Ed.), *Strategic Integration of Social Media into Project Management Practice* (pp. 139–159). Hershey, PA: IGI Global. doi:10.4018/978-1-4666-9867-3.ch009

van der Vyver, A. G. (2018). A Model for Economic Development With Telecentres and the Social Media: Overcoming Affordability Constraints. In S. Takavarasha Jr & C. Adams (Eds.), *Affordability Issues Surrounding the Use of ICT for Development and Poverty Reduction* (pp. 112–140). Hershey, PA: IGI Global. doi:10.4018/978-1-5225-3179-1.ch006

van Dokkum, E., & Ravesteijn, P. (2016). Managing Project Communication: Using Social Media for Communication in Projects. In G. Silvius (Ed.), *Strategic Integration of Social Media into Project Management Practice* (pp. 35–50). Hershey, PA: IGI Global. doi:10.4018/978-1-4666-9867-3.ch003

van Niekerk, B. (2018). Social Media Activism From an Information Warfare and Security Perspective. In F. Endong (Ed.), *Exploring the Role of Social Media in Transnational Advocacy* (pp. 1–16). Hershey, PA: IGI Global. doi:10.4018/978-1-5225-2854-8.ch001

Varnali, K., & Gorgulu, V. (2017). Determinants of Brand Recall in Social Networking Sites. In W. Al-Rabayah, R. Khasawneh, R. Abu-shamaa, & I. Alsmadi (Eds.), *Strategic Uses of Social Media for Improved Customer Retention* (pp. 124–153). Hershey, PA: IGI Global. doi:10.4018/978-1-5225-1686-6.ch007

Varty, C. T., O'Neill, T. A., & Hambley, L. A. (2017). Leading Anywhere Workers: A Scientific and Practical Framework. In Y. Blount & M. Gloet (Eds.), *Anywhere Working and the New Era of Telecommuting* (pp. 47–88). Hershey, PA: IGI Global. doi:10.4018/978-1-5225-2328-4.ch003

Vatikiotis, P. (2016). Social Media Activism: A Contested Field. In T. Deželan & I. Vobič (Eds.), *R)evolutionizing Political Communication through Social Media* (pp. 40–54). Hershey, PA: IGI Global. doi:10.4018/978-1-4666-9879-6.ch003

Velikovsky, J. T. (2018). The Holon/Parton Structure of the Meme, or The Unit of Culture. In M. Khosrow-Pour, D.B.A. (Ed.), Encyclopedia of Information Science and Technology, Fourth Edition (pp. 4666-4678). Hershey, PA: IGI Global. doi:10.4018/978-1-5225-2255-3.ch405

Venkatesh, R., & Jayasingh, S. (2017). Transformation of Business through Social Media. In N. Rao (Ed.), *Social Media Listening and Monitoring for Business Applications* (pp. 1–17). Hershey, PA: IGI Global. doi:10.4018/978-1-5225-0846-5.ch001

Vesnic-Alujevic, L. (2016). European Elections and Facebook: Political Advertising and Deliberation? In T. Deželan & I. Vobič (Eds.), *R)evolutionizing Political Communication through Social Media* (pp. 191–209). Hershey, PA: IGI Global. doi:10.4018/978-1-4666-9879-6.ch010

Virkar, S. (2017). Trolls Just Want to Have Fun: Electronic Aggression within the Context of E-Participation and Other Online Political Behaviour in the United Kingdom. In M. Korstanje (Ed.), *Threat Mitigation and Detection of Cyber Warfare and Terrorism Activities* (pp. 111–162). Hershey, PA: IGI Global. doi:10.4018/978-1-5225-1938-6.ch006

Wakabi, W. (2017). When Citizens in Authoritarian States Use Facebook for Social Ties but Not Political Participation. In Y. Ibrahim (Ed.), *Politics, Protest, and Empowerment in Digital Spaces* (pp. 192–214). Hershey, PA: IGI Global. doi:10.4018/978-1-5225-1862-4.ch012

Weisberg, D. J. (2016). Methods and Strategies in Using Digital Literacy in Media and the Arts. In M. Yildiz & J. Keengwe (Eds.), *Handbook of Research on Media Literacy in the Digital Age* (pp. 456–471). Hershey, PA: IGI Global. doi:10.4018/978-1-4666-9667-9.ch022

Weisgerber, C., & Butler, S. H. (2016). Debranding Digital Identity: Personal Branding and Identity Work in a Networked Age. *International Journal of Interactive Communication Systems and Technologies*, 6(1), 17–34. doi:10.4018/IJICST.2016010102

Wijngaard, P., Wensveen, I., Basten, A., & de Vries, T. (2016). Projects without Email, Is that Possible? In G. Silvius (Ed.), *Strategic Integration of Social Media into Project Management Practice* (pp. 218–235). Hershey, PA: IGI Global. doi:10.4018/978-1-4666-9867-3.ch013

Wright, K. (2018). "Show Me What You Are Saying": Visual Literacy in the Composition Classroom. In A. August (Ed.), *Visual Imagery, Metadata, and Multimodal Literacies Across the Curriculum* (pp. 24–49). Hershey, PA: IGI Global. doi:10.4018/978-1-5225-2808-1.ch002

Yang, K. C. (2018). Understanding How Mexican and U.S. Consumers Decide to Use Mobile Social Media: A Cross-National Qualitative Study. In K. Yang (Ed.), *Multi-Platform Advertising Strategies in the Global Marketplace* (pp. 168–198). Hershey, PA: IGI Global. doi:10.4018/978-1-5225-3114-2.ch007

Yang, K. C., & Kang, Y. (2016). Exploring Female Hispanic Consumers' Adoption of Mobile Social Media in the U.S. In R. English & R. Johns (Eds.), *Gender Considerations in Online Consumption Behavior and Internet Use* (pp. 185–207). Hershey, PA: IGI Global. doi:10.4018/978-1-5225-0010-0.ch012

Yao, Q., & Wu, M. (2016). Examining the Role of WeChat in Advertising. In X. Xu (Ed.), *Handbook of Research on Human Social Interaction in the Age of Mobile Devices* (pp. 386–405). Hershey, PA: IGI Global. doi:10.4018/978-1-5225-0469-6.ch016

Yarchi, M., Wolfsfeld, G., Samuel-Azran, T., & Segev, E. (2017). Invest, Engage, and Win: Online Campaigns and Their Outcomes in an Israeli Election. In M. Brown Sr., (Ed.), *Social Media Performance Evaluation and Success Measurements* (pp. 225–248). Hershey, PA: IGI Global. doi:10.4018/978-1-5225-1963-8.ch011

*Related References*

Yeboah-Banin, A. A., & Amoakohene, M. I. (2018). The Dark Side of Multi-Platform Advertising in an Emerging Economy Context. In K. Yang (Ed.), *Multi-Platform Advertising Strategies in the Global Marketplace* (pp. 30–53). Hershey, PA: IGI Global. doi:10.4018/978-1-5225-3114-2.ch002

Yılmaz, R., Çakır, A., & Resuloğlu, F. (2017). Historical Transformation of the Advertising Narration in Turkey: From Stereotype to Digital Media. In R. Yılmaz (Ed.), *Narrative Advertising Models and Conceptualization in the Digital Age* (pp. 133–152). Hershey, PA: IGI Global. doi:10.4018/978-1-5225-2373-4.ch008

Yusuf, S., Hassan, M. S., & Ibrahim, A. M. (2018). Cyberbullying Among Malaysian Children Based on Research Evidence. In M. Khosrow-Pour, D.B.A. (Ed.), Encyclopedia of Information Science and Technology, Fourth Edition (pp. 1704-1722). Hershey, PA: IGI Global. doi:10.4018/978-1-5225-2255-3.ch149

Zervas, P., & Alexandraki, C. (2016). Facilitating Open Source Software and Standards to Assembly a Platform for Networked Music Performance. In D. Kanellopoulos (Ed.), *Emerging Research on Networked Multimedia Communication Systems* (pp. 334–365). Hershey, PA: IGI Global. doi:10.4018/978-1-4666-8850-6.ch011

# About the Contributors

**Michael A. Brown Sr.** earned his PhD in Public Administration and Urban Policy, International Business, from Old Dominion University (ODU) in May 2011. He is teaching online social media, public relations and communication courses for Florida International University (FIU). Three of his online courses at FIU are recognized for excellence in education by Quality Matters (QM). QM is a nationally recognized faculty peer review organization for online and hybrid course design, signaling the best offerings in education. He is the author/editor of two new publications for 2017, Solutions for High-Touch Communications in a High-Tech World and Social Media Performance Evaluation and Success Measurements. He is an Air Force civil servant working as the deputy director of Public Affairs for a joint military organization. This PR professional has 40-plus years of military and civilian experience combined, and is an Air Force retiree who served 24 years in uniform.

**Leigh Nanney Hersey** is an assistant professor and MPA Coordinator at the University of Louisiana Monroe. She brings more than a dozen years of fundraising experience. She continues building on this experience through her research on philanthropy and volunteerism. Dr. Hersey earned her bachelor's degree in journalism from the University of Georgia and an M.Ed. in Athletic Administration from Temple University. Her Ph.D. in Public Administration is from Arizona State University with a graduate certificate in Nonprofit Leadership & Management.

\* \* \*

**Tihana Brkljačić** is psychologist, employed at Institute of Social Sciences Ivo Pilar in Zagreb as senior research associate. She earned her PhD in 2003 in social psychology from the Faculty of Philosophy at Zagreb University. She is also working as part-time professor at Zagreb University. Her main interests are in the field of communication and well-being. She published over 20 scientific papers, and presented her work at over 20 international scientific meetings.

**Jim Goodwin** is a career communications professional and a recent graduate of Georgetown University's School of Continuing Studies, where he earned a Master's in Professional Studies in Public Relations and Corporate Communication. Jim is a Public Affairs Specialist for the federal government and has more than 20 years' experience as a government communication professional. Jim is also a retired U.S. Marine, who spent his entire career in Public Affairs. He is currently pursuing an MBA with a focus on social media marketing from Southern New Hampshire University.

**Bridgette Harper** is an Associate Professor of Psychology at Auburn University at Montgomery where her research focuses on early adolescent peer relationships and emotional development.

**Zbigniew Hulicki** received the M.S. degree in electrical and electronic engineering from the Technical University of Moscow, Russia, in 1978 and the Ph.D. degree in telecommunications engineering from the AGH University of Science and Technology, Kraków, Poland, in 1983. In 1978, he joined Department of Telecommunications at the AGH University, where he is currently an assoc. Professor. From 1992-1994 he carried out research in Teletraffic Research Center at the University of Adelaide, Australia. He spent his sabbatical leaves at the universities in USA (Princeton), UK (Cambridge), Germany (Wuerzburg) and in Switzerland (ETH Zurich). He is an author of 6 books, over 80 research publications and actively participates in the IST projects of EU. He is Life Member of Clare Hall College, University of Cambridge, a member of the Poland IEEE Communications Society Chapter and a member of Polish Systems Society.

**Yulia Krylova** holds a PhD degree in Political Science from George Mason University and a PhD degree in Economics from Saint Petersburg State University. She works as a researcher at the Terrorism, Transnational Crime and Corruption Center (TraCCC) at George Mason University and as a consultant for the World Bank Group. Previously, she worked as Associate Professor of Economics at Saint Petersburg State University. In 2009-2010, she participated in the Fulbright Faculty Development Program at Duke University and Georgetown University Law Center. Her research interests lie at the intersection of the fields of anti-corruption policies, organized crime, and international development.

**Ljiljana Kaliterna Lipovčan** is research advisor and Assistant Director of the Ivo Pilar Institute of Social Sciences in Zagreb and Full professor of Organisational Psychology at University of Zagreb. She received her Ph.D. in psychology from the

University of Zagreb in 1989. Her research interests include subjective indicators of quality of life, psychophysiology of work and psychological consequences of ageing. She published two monographs and 88 research papers/book chapters; participated at 56 international and 31 national conferences. She leaded four international and 11 national projects and participated in several others projects. Currently she leads national project "CRO-WELL Croatian longitudinal survey of well-being" funded by Croatian Science Foundation.

**Azam Masoumi** is an MA student of TEFL. Azam Masoumi first studied physics at Islamic Azad University of Karaj, Karaj, Iran. After graduating in 2002, she has been working as a quality control manager for about 10 years. Following her interest in studying English language, she changed her major to English as a foreign language. Now, she is an MA student at the University of Zanjan, Iran. She is interested in sociology, philosophy, psychology, and anthropology, and her thesis is about the relationship between students' psychological characteristics and learning vocabulary via mobile phones.

**Elham Mohammadi** is an Assistant Professor of TEFL. A graduate of Tarbiat Modares University working as an assistant professor at the University of Zanjan (Iran). Teaches English and ELT courses at both B.A and M.A levels, with a field of interest revolving around new technologies and their capacity for creating new learning environments. Dr. Mohammadi has also conducted research on the evaluation of foreign language teacher education programs.

**Zvjezdana Prizmic-Larsen** received her Ph.D. in psychology in 2000 from the University of Zagreb in Croatia. She worked in Croatia as a Research Assistant at the Institute for Medical Research and Occupational Health, University of Zagreb, and later as a Research Associate at Institute of Social Science Ivo Pilar in Zagreb. She was awarded Fulbright Fellowship in 1996 and spent the year as a visiting researcher at the University of Michigan in Ann Arbor. Currently she works as a Research Scientist at the Washington University in St. Louis in Department of Psychological and Brain Sciences. Her main research interest is in well-being and area of positive psychology. Her earlier research and publications have been in the area of shiftwork and its effects on health, productivity, and worker satisfaction as well as in the area of affect, mood regulation and emotional ageing processes. She still keeps active collaborations with colleagues from Institute of Social Sciences Ivo Pilar, on several projects concerning subjective indicators of quality of life and well-being in Croatia.

**Gayla Schaefer**, MPA, is a communications professional with 20 years' experience providing public sector communications strategy and management. Her work has been published by IGI Global, Gannett Corp., Patriot Not Partisan, and multiple print and online publications. She lives in the Tampa Bay area with her husband and children.

**Michelle F. Wright** is a research associate at the Pennsylvania State University. Her research focus is on the contextual factors which influence children's, adolescents', and young adults' involvement in aggressive behaviors, with a special interest in social goals, peer status, and cultural values. She has published on these topics, with her most recent work focused on culture and anonymity, and their role in cyberbullying among adolescents.

**Ray Younis** was educated at the University of Sydney (BA Hons. MA Hons.) and the University of Oxford (DPhil). He has held teaching positions in philosophy at the University of Sydney, Oxford, UNSW, CQU and the University of Notre Dame (Sydney), among others, and senior managerial and leadership positions at Lincoln College (Oxford Univerity), University of Sydney, CQU, Notre Dame (Sydney) and Curtin University (Sydney), among others. He has received several awards and commendations for excellence at the University of Sydney, CQU and WEA, among others, including the Vice Chancellor's Award (on behalf of the Core Curriculum team) for excellence in teaching and learning at the University of Notre Dame (Sydney). He has contributed essays to many books, and over 20 academic journals and online collections. He was a film critic for many years (in Sydney) and a wine consultant (in Sydney and Oxford).

# Index

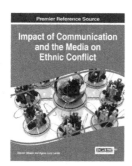

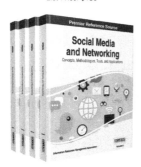
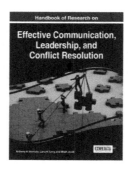

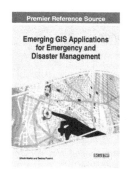
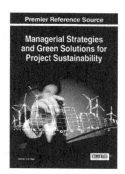

Printed in the United States
By Bookmasters